22 Ideas

to Fix the World

22 Ideas

to Fix the World

Conversations with
the World's Foremost Thinkers

EDITED BY Piotr Dutkiewicz AND Richard Sakwa

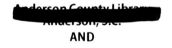

AND

*A joint publication of the Social Science Research Council
and New York University Press*

NEW YORK UNIVERSITY PRESS
New York and London
www.nyupress.org

References to Internet websites (URLs) were accurate at the time of writing.
Neither the author nor New York University Press is responsible for URLs that
may have expired or changed since the manuscript was prepared.

22 ideas to fix the world : conversations with the world's foremost thinkers /
edited by Piotr Dutkiewicz and Richard Sakwa.

    pages cm

    "A joint publication of the Social Science Research Council and New York
University Press."

    Includes bibliographical references and index.

    ISBN 978-1-4798-6098-2 (cl : alk. paper)

    1. Social problems. 2. Social change. 3. Economics. 4. Civilization, Modern—
21st century. I. Dutkiewicz, Piotr. II. Sakwa, Richard. III. Title: Twenty two
ideas to fix the world.

HN18.3.A13 2014

303.3'72—dc23

2013017722

New York University Press books are printed on acid-free paper,
and their binding materials are chosen for strength and durability.
We strive to use environmentally responsible suppliers and materials
to the greatest extent possible in publishing our books.

Manufactured in the United States of America

c 10 9 8 7 6 5 4 3 2 1

Contents

RETHINK THE NATURE OF HUMANITY

1

MUHAMMAD YUNUS with Piotr Dutkiewicz

2

WILL KYMLICKA with Raffaele Marchetti

TRANSFORM HOW THE GLOBAL ECONOMY WORKS

3

JOSEPH STIGLITZ with Shari Spiegel

4

HA-JOON CHANG with Manuel F. Montes

5

JOSÉ ANTONIO OCAMPO with Vladimir Popov

Acknowledgments

Many people and organizations contributed to this book. Above all we are grateful to World Public Forum (WPF) "Dialogue of Civilizations" and personally to Dr. V. I. Yakunin (founding president of the WPF) and Dr. V. I. Kulikov (WPF executive secretary and this book's project director) for their enthusiastic and very generous support for this project. Their financial and organizational support proved crucial to the realization of the very complex process of arranging conversations between many prominent thinkers in multiple locations worldwide. We feel that WPF is not just a sponsor but a true partner and full co-owner of this project. Our thanks go also to WPF staff for the vast logistical support they provided throughout the project.

The editors owe deep gratitude to many people around the world who gave their time and efforts—and reached out to their networks of contacts—for these interviews to happen. Thus a collective and heartfelt thank you goes to Jowshan A. Rahman, former chief of the Program Planning Section, UNICEF (Dhaka), and Lamiya Morshed from the Yunus Center (Dhaka); B. Biancalani from the Andrea Bocelli Foundation (Italy); M. Montes (Switzerland); V. Popov (New York); K. Kirişci (Istanbul); C. Calhoun (New York and London); and the many others without whose help this volume would not have been completed. We would also like to thank Ann Molon (Ottawa) for the translation of two chapters from Russian. We are also grateful to RIM (Research in Motion) for making two interviews possible, as well as to Magna Fund and Kinross Fund for their support in editing and publication.

This book's format owes much to Jan Dutkiewicz, who suggested the idea that most of the interviews be conducted not exclusively by the editors but by multiple interviewers, themselves renowned specialists in fields similar to the interviewees'. This approach definitely added depth to all the conversations presented in this volume.

We are most grateful to all the contributors, both interviewers and interviewees, for quickly grasping the dynamics of the project and for the effective and remarkably problem-free way in which the conversations were conducted. These are—as you will soon see—genuine conversations rather than classic interviews: both interlocutors in the discussions are deeply knowledgeable about the issues at hand, and thus ideas are not simply drawn out of a single source but amplified, shared, and developed.

Our families—whether they like it or not—are involved in what we do, in particular when our activities bring some inevitable tensions to our minds and schedules. This was indeed the case with this book, which has accompanied and occupied us for more than a year. As such, Piotr Dutkiewicz is truly grateful to Ewa Hebda-Dutkiewicz for her continuing support and motivation, and Richard Sakwa is most grateful for all the work of Roza Sakwa, for her sharp eye and careful editing of the chapters.

It is a pleasure to acknowledge the support and encouragement received from Ilene Kalish and her team at New York University Press. Ilene immediately grasped the point of the book, and we were much cheered by the way she has exercised her calm and professional expertise in the production of this work.

There are, of course, far more than twenty-two ways of fixing the world, but if the conversations presented here can advance the process of finding remedies to the challenges facing the collective life of humanity, then our endeavor will have succeeded.

CANTERBURY AND OTTAWA, 4 JANUARY 2013

Introduction

Piotr Dutkiewicz

It is trivial at this point to state that the world is in crisis. The after-effects of the most recent global financial crisis continue to have major implications for the lives of tens of millions of people around the world, just as they continue to influence the fate of policymakers, political systems, and corporate behavior. Myriad other global crises—of democracy, governance, ecology, and inequality, among others—all contribute to a precarious present. Quite simply, we live in uncertain times—in a sort of 'inter-regnum' between old and new ruling paradigms.

This book is about ideas on how to cope with these global uncertainties. This is not a manifesto that presents a single, unified plan of action for moving forward. Rather, this book seeks to draw the contours of the near future, be it political, social, economic, or environmental. Its many eminent contributors propose innovative approaches to better understanding what is needed, to borrow Albert Einstein's words, to "survive and move to higher levels." Finally, this book is about ideas that can help to shape policies within and beyond national borders on a global scale.

What unites the contributors of this volume is that we believe that we live in a very fragile world. We need to have new ideas coming from different cultures and intellectual traditions to understand better both the threats that we face and potential solutions to the problems confronting us. We believe that by comparing the experience and ideas of some of the foremost thinkers in the world we can start devising practical advice on what can be done to allow us to achieve some degree of peace and prosperity in the years to come.

This means addressing multiple interconnected economic issues, but also the more broadly interconnected problems of limits to development, poverty alleviation, inequality, ecological crises, regional disparities, new modes of power shaping new structures of global dominations, the future of urbanization, strained multicultural coexistence, and the growing role of religion amid a wave of global postsecularism.

The idea for this book came to me in 2010, after the main blows of the financial turmoil of 2007–9 had already struck. As we lived through shock and deep crisis for almost two years, I was expecting a deep rethinking of the fundamental approaches to development and our expectations of the market and the institutions supporting it. Nothing like that happened. The crisis did not trigger an intellectual renaissance or even a set of more or less comprehensive ideas that could have been innovative enough to prevent similar tragedies in the future. In fact quite the opposite happened. Policymakers either seemed to ignore the substantive aspects of the problem or simply dusted off old cookbooks full of recipes from the 1930s, as if the current crisis were a carbon copy of the Great Depression. We have simply not been able to transcend the barriers of our past knowledge and our accepted paradigms, as if our collective imagination were permanently stunted.

As this project began, it became apparent I was not alone in my concerns. As one of our contributors, Jonathan Nitzan, remarks, "The Great Depression of the 1930s triggered such a revival. That crisis transformed the way we understand and critique society: it gave birth to liberal 'macro' economics and anticyclical government policy; it rejuvenated Marxist and other streams of radical thinking in areas ranging from political economy to philosophy to literature; and, by shattering many of the prevailing dogmas, it allowed the mutual insemination of ideologically opposing approaches. One would have expected a revival similar to that which followed the Great Depression in the current crisis, but so far the signs of such a revival are nowhere to be seen." Ha-Joon Chang laments that for the majority who control capital or wield intellectual influence, "everything is fine. Even if it doesn't look fine, it's actually fine because we are all rational and markets are efficient.

So even if it looks chaotic and stupid, it really is the best of all possible worlds."

My next, obvious question, then, was whether such an evaluation of our collective intellectual quandary was justified. Intuitively my preliminary answer was that there is neither a lack of ideas nor a lack of practical solutions but that most of these were simply not part of the dominant discourse that shaped the public mind. An intervening variable, I believe, is a lack of imagination among the global political class coupled with a very real fear of attempting new (and unproven) solutions. The only way to verify these ideas was to ask prominent thinkers how they saw the prospects of global human well-being and whether those ideas are implementable enough to serve as a guide to policies. In other words, we consulted those willing to speak truth to power. I was very pleasantly surprised and heartened that so many people and organizations were enthusiastic about the central idea and were keen to join me, including the coeditor of this volume, Richard Sakwa, and the project director of this venture, Vladimir Kulikov.

The choice of interlocutors was in a sense quite arbitrary and was based in large part on the perceived novelty of their contributions to our deeper understanding of policy-relevant ideas in key global issue areas. This is, of course, not an exhaustive set of leading thinkers on our uncertain world, and we hope that these conversations spark many more discussions and projects among academics, policymakers, and activists. The result of the fascinating process of digging deep into many great minds follows this introduction and will be subject to your own interpretations and evaluation. But before you delve into the book, I owe you a comment about the initial thesis that served as the take-off point of this volume: it proved to be correct. There are in fact many innovative ideas about how to look at our world and address its many problems. Equally important, there are people who can turn these into viable policy solutions.

We must recognize, however, that there is a multiplicity of reasons that such ideas are not in demand; they are rejected, marginalized, suppressed, or ridiculed. There are groups of people who have built their career, identity, and wealth on a particular kind of economics and a particular kind of expert advice. They are used by the dominant power structures and by those elites who benefit so much from this economic status quo and indeed from the ongoing crisis.

Thus this book is a challenge to the intellectual status quo by proposing what we state in its title: *22 Ideas to Fix the World*. This volume is neither left nor right; it adopts a mostly evolutionary approach to change by proposing concrete solutions to strategic areas of our life that we all treasure.

RETHINK THE NATURE OF HUMANITY

1

"All human beings have unlimited potential, unlimited capacity, unlimited creative energy"

Photo by Spencer Platt/
iStockPhoto.

MUHAMMAD YUNUS

in conversation with Piotr Dutkiewicz

Muhammad Yunus is a Nobel Prize winner (2006) for combating poverty via the micro-credit system that he developed in Bangladesh and spread to other countries in Asia. He previously was a professor of economics, where he developed the concepts of micro-credit and microfinance. These loans are given to entrepreneurs too poor to qualify for traditional bank loans. Presently he is chancellor of Glasgow Caledonian University.

Muhammad Yunus is famous as an economist and a philanthropist, but he takes issue with both labels and with the way that mainstream economics and philanthropy are practiced.* He sees poverty, an issue he has sought to tackle in his writing and through his business endeavors, as a systemic problem that robs individuals of their capacity for self-realization. He argues that only in a system that values money above all else and sees humans as atomized, selfish actors can ills like poverty and unemployment be seen as natural or even desirable. He argues that most economics excludes the possibility of humans

* All headnotes written by Piotr Dutkiewicz.

being selfless and seeking nonfinancial gain from business and, conversely, that charitable work, by ignoring financial gain, can lack sustainability or create dependency among its recipients. He proposes instead a model of social business that uses the market system to deliver solutions to social ills. His is a political perspective that sees potential in the poor, the disenfranchised, and migrants and an economic approach that focuses on human selflessness. Yunus's field-tested theories suggest a new way to think about emerging from our current crises.

PD: What is poverty?

MY: We can approach poverty in many different ways. It can mean lack of opportunities, lack of income, lack of a future, lack of a dream for a future. This is one way to look at it. Another way poverty can be considered is as a denial of all human rights, in that a poor person lacks access to what we see as human rights: right to food, shelter, and so on. Poverty can be looked at as a situation where you leave creative human beings in a total waste, in the sense that they are not being useful to society or themselves. Poverty can be looked at as a blockage of the energy that all these people have to contribute to society. This is related to a belief that I have that all human beings have unlimited potential, unlimited capacity, unlimited creative energy. Simply, some have the opportunity to unleash that potential, be it a fraction or all of it, and others are denied the chance to even explore these capacities that exist within them. The other thing I should mention is that poverty is not created by poor people. Poverty is not in a person; it is something that is imposed on the person.

PD: It's an externality?

MY: Yes, in the sense that it is not in the person, but is imposed by external forces, which I see as the system as it prevails. The system creates poverty.

PD: Poverty is universal?

MY: As long as the system is universal, poverty is also universal.

PD: Is poverty in Bangladesh the same as poverty in the United States or elsewhere?

MY: Yes, everywhere. It is caused by the same process and the same system and the same faults in institutions, and the same faults in the basic conceptual framework in the economy. Think of poor people as a bonsai tree. You can take the best seed of the tallest, best tree, but you put it in a small flower pot and it will only grow so big. It cannot hope to grow as big as it would in the forest. And you ask the question "What is wrong with this tree?" And you think that maybe the seed is at fault. But it's not, as we picked the best seed. So what is it? The real reason is that we didn't give it the soil in which to grow, so it can only grow in a limited way. So we have the tree we see in the forest, but only in a miniature version. So I see poor people as bonsai people. There is nothing wrong with the seed; simply, society never gives them the space to grow.

PD: Can we change part of the system through reform strategies, or do we need more radical changes or even a new system?

MY: All of the above. It depends on what you want to achieve. For example, you can retain the system and reform it a little here and there so that some slight improvement takes place. So you have a little bonsai; you make its pot a bit bigger, and it will grow bigger, but it will still not grow to the potential of the seed. So I think you have to correct the whole platform, the whole pot, so that everyone has the same soil conditions.

PD: Is this environment mainly rooted in economics, politics, or the relationship between economics and politics?

MY: I am looking at the list of people you will be interviewing for this book, who focus on the environment, food security, capital markets, and other questions. And each one is a problem. But my point is that these are not separate issues. These are manifestations of the basic problem in the structure we have built. And these manifestations branch out in many directions. The environment is deteriorating, global warming is occurring, the planet is becoming threatened, health care is missing, people don't have the health they deserve, unnecessary deaths are caused, food security is in danger and we probably will run out of food for the billions of people who live on this planet. These are not separate issues. Only we are looking through our own glasses, and each one of us sees only what their glasses allow them to see. So they see only food, or only the environment. And this is the fundamental flaw in the way we have conceptualized the world itself. Moreover the basic flaw I see in the whole structure is misinterpretation of the human being. We now have only one kind of human being: a human being who is dedicated to making money. So we create a structure where money is central. We are all chasing money because in this world business means making money, maximizing profit, accumulating value. So the central focus of everything we do in the world is about chasing money. When money plays a facilitating role, it is fine, but instead money itself has become central.

PD: So money-cum-capital has become a pillar.

MY: Not just a pillar: the key. Everything we do is decided by it. Money has become a habit, an obsession, an addiction. So once we do that, every human being is interpreted as a money-maker. And we are desperately trying to make money because that's how our success is measured. The more money you make, the more successful you are. So we train our students, we train our young people to go out and make more money. If you were to look at the world from outside, it would look as if human beings were nothing more than money-making robots. Everybody is so busy because all they are thinking, all their commitment, all their initiatives are about making money. I see this as a fundamental flaw in interpreting the human being. Human beings are not single-dimensional; they are multidimensional. But the economists who theorize this system interpret human beings in a very narrow way. And because they conceptualized this and because we believed them, we become such animals—single-minded robots making money, pushing each other to make money—and in the process we create all these problems.

Because we have no time to look at the environment, we have no time to look at the poor, we have no time to do anything else. And that is the fundamental flaw in the whole system. We have to rediscover human being and interpret it in the real sense of *human being*. We have a system now where money is a means and an end. I understand a system where money is a means, but I don't understand why money-making should be an end. Money-making as an end is unacceptable. The real question of ends, of "Why am I here on this planet?," is not raised in our textbooks or our theories. What is the purpose of our lives on this planet? The system should be consistent with our purpose. I'm not saying the purpose is defined by somebody else. You define your own purpose. But when you leave, what is it that you want to see that you have achieved? Money cannot be the purpose. It cannot be the only thing we achieve.

PD: Why should we care? Some people will say, "If we make people a bit less impoverished, they will demand more, and we simply cannot afford more, financially or as a planet."

MY: Right, and this goes back to a single-dimensional interpretation of human beings. The single dimension that economists focus on, and focus on exhaustively, is the selfishness of human beings. So out of selfishness we have developed all these theories. And it looks very nice. Selfishness works out, the economy works out.

PD: This is the principle of the market.

MY: Precisely. I think human beings are selfish. There is no doubt about it. And this came out of self-protection. This was the origin of selfishness. I want to protect myself, my family, and so on. But it has been overblown in economic interpretation. There is a fundamental difference between selfishness, in the sense of not caring if you damage others, and selfishness as self-protection. Moreover all human beings are equally endowed with something called *selflessness*. And that was completely forgotten. When I raise this question about selflessness, economists answer, "Well, why don't you step outside of the economic world? Be a philanthropist. Work in charity. Give away your money." And I say that I'm not talking about giving away my money, but about selflessness in the economic world. How can we create a business on the basis of selflessness? What would that look like? How might I create a business to solve certain problems rather than simply to create financial benefit for myself?

PD: Solve different problems at different scales?

MY: Right. Like the problems in this book. How might we try to solve them in a "business way"? So what's the difference between the business way and the charity way? In the charity way, when I give money away, it goes out and never comes back. If you want to multiply it, you need fresh money for every action, so charity is a wonderful concept, but it has very limited application because you can do it only once with your own money. But what if, somehow, I can transform this project into a business, and so keep the charity objective but do it in a business way? So I send the money, it does its work, and then it comes back. And then I can achieve much more with that money. I can make changes, make it more efficient, bring in technology. I have created many such companies. I don't make money out of them. That was not the intention. The intention was solving problems. And I call these *social businesses*. They are non-dividend companies created to solve the problems we see around us. The human mind is so creative that it can come up with business ideas, self-sustaining ideas to solve these problems. So you create an engine that works and never stops. It's a self-fueling engine.

PD: Are you drawing on any philosophical foundations here? Is there a relation between social business and Muslim interest-free banking, for instance?

MY: Not at all. This is a very secular idea. The principle is that you can create a business, for instance, to find decent jobs for five unemployed people. That is my business. I have created this business not to make money for myself but to employ five people, give them a decent income, and cover its own costs. It goes on running, but this is a social business because it is cause-driven. So this is not banking.

PD: On what scale can this be done? Is it possible to eradicate poverty this way through individual action? Or could this be institutionalized into state action?

MY: If I can create five jobs in a business way, I have shown the way. Then maybe you can create five jobs too. If I have shown you can have a social business that costs you nothing to run and eventually will give the initial investment back, I have sown the seed, which now can be planted to solve the problem of unemployment. I also raise the question of why there should be unemployment. What's wrong? Is there something wrong with human beings that make them unemployed? Young people who have done everything possible, are energetic, creative, educated, but are not employed—Is it their fault or the fault of the system? I say it's the fault of the system. If the system cannot take care of the able-bodied human beings that belong to it, throw out the system because it doesn't work. We have to design a new system where the word *unemployment* will be totally unknown. So you need to redesign. First, you need to reinterpret the human being as both a selfish and a selfless being. Second, recognize that selflessness can also be expressed through business. Problems are caused by selfishness, but we have no methodology to solve them other than giving charity. I don't want to leave this to the government. Governments don't have the power to do all this because the way we create problems—the speed and the energy with which we create them—governments cannot match that energy and those resources to solve the problems. So problems accumulate. Problems become massive.

PD: If we are talking about the eradication of poverty, there is the social business approach you presented. But there is also the so-called Chinese way, government-led programs that have lifted 500 million people out of poverty in the past fifteen years.

MY: My question is whether the government approached this in a charitable way in the sense of giving people food, housing, and so on, or if it created jobs. And if it is the former, then I say there is a better way.

PD: But if governments stimulate job creation or undertake social business, you accept that?

MY: Absolutely.

PD: So the distinction is not between these initiatives being government-led or private, but rather it's a question about the concept.

MY: Exactly. So governments can have social businesses and governments can learn from the private sector to do social business (and the private sector could learn from the government). So instead of segmenting things and saying problems need to be taken care of by the government, and we citizens only create problems, I am saying we citizens are as good at creating problems as we are at solving problems. Similarly, government should also continue to solve problems. They are not excluded from that. But I do not feel comfortable when I see governments giving charity only as welfare. Welfare for a temporary period is fine, especially when people are in distress. But to say I should take care of people forever is unacceptable. When you do that you have destroyed that human being. I have seen people who are in third-generation unemployment, fourth-generation unemployment. This is a gross failure of the system. How can human beings be kept in a sort of zoo where you feed them, house them, but don't allow them to perform basic human activity, in the sense of not allowing them to perform activities and take pleasure in what they have done?

PD: Your ideas have recently started being taken on board not only by emerging economies but also by developed countries that were hit by the crisis.

MY: My approach does not discriminate between developing and developed countries. You can have your social business in Brooklyn or Dhaka or Rome. If you have a problem, you can try to design a business to solve that problem.

PD: Let me switch angles a little bit here. Can we say that poverty is dangerous? And by this I mean, does it threaten stability?

MY: First of all, let me say that poverty is unacceptable. It doesn't make sense. Why should anybody be poor? If that person has the same capacity as anybody else, who gave anyone the capacity to destroy that person? You have to believe that poverty is not caused by that person, as I have said. So the idea is to create a system that allows people to take care of themselves.

PD: You sound like a revolutionary when you say we need to create the antisystem. Are you a revolutionary?

MY: I don't play around with words. If I say I am doing something antisystem, that's what I'll do. And that's what I did with microcredit.

PD: But that was in a sense done within the existing market system.

MY: But ask yourself: What is microcredit? What is Grameen Bank? Everything the conventional banking system does, I do the opposite. The conventional banking system goes to the rich; I go to the poor. They go to men; I go to women. They go to the city center; I go to the village. They say people have to come to their office; I say no, the bank should go to the people. This is a system that works and solves problems that the conventional system doesn't. Similarly for employment, I think you can create a reverse system where every-body's employed.

PD: What is interesting about your approach is not only the alternative model itself but an alternative reason for why we should create it.

MY: Look, I am not saying poverty is a threat because "they" are approach-ing "us," taking over our countries, jobs, and so on. I am saying these are creative people and it's an enormous capacity they are bringing to you. Celebrate it. That's what the USA historically did. They took people in. And that's the basis for their economy. A guy who was totally poor in his own country could go to the USA, start at the bottom, and work to create a business. The environment in their home country was not conducive to that, but in a new environment they flourished. I often give the example of a child born in the streets and another born in a palace. By some magic you switch these two children. Wait twenty years. The child who was born in the streets but grew up in the palace becomes a prince, behaves like a prince, and nobody suspects anything. The child who grew up in the streets is a criminal. So is what you become in the person or in the environment? Poverty to me is that simple. With migration, for example, you are afraid because "they" are bringing poverty to you. But you have contributed to making those people be the way they are. So you have to correct the system. You can't look at whether the person is from inside or outside. You have to look at their capabilities.

PD: You have become a worldwide symbol of success for many people. But can you tell me about some of the challenges you have faced?

MY: When you do something new, there is always some opposition. But that is part of the game and nothing to be upset about. You challenge some people and they challenge you. It takes time. All I am trying to do now is address the young people. Their minds are not set. If I can explain to them about the two kinds of businesses and ask them which kind of business they'd like to work in—would they like to create a social business or a for-profit business? And you can do both. This is not either/or. You can be selfish and selfless. Money-making is a means, and you can use money to fulfill your ends. Money-making can lead to happiness, but economists never let us explore the possibility that making others happy can also bring us happiness. This is not something I do for nothing. I make myself very happy when I see that I have solved someone else's problem.

PD: Why, then, is there persistent criticism of microcredit?

MY: Because microcredit the way we designed it was created as a social business. But there are others who want to make money out of it. We thought all the benefits should go to poor people. But others picked up the idea, saw it worked and could make money, so they started microcredit banks to make money off the poor people. I spoke out against this, telling them they were taking the very route we opposed, doing loan-sharking and misusing our objective. And of course people complained about this. With Grameen, our purpose was not to bring people additional misery. If we are increasing their misery, they don't need us. We wanted simply to reduce people's misery. But those who are in it to make money couldn't care less, as long as they made money. So they used microcredit in a conventional sense, and that's where things went wrong. Many people have been critical of this. I have been very vocal about this, saying those approaches are not microcredit.

PD: It could be argued that by taking only some people out of poverty, you can create or exacerbate inequalities between those who are now out of poverty and those who are still in poverty. Do you see these tensions?

MY: If microcredit is done in a business way, everybody's welcome and the sky is the limit. If you do things in a charity way, there are limits and there may be problems of inequality. There can be transitional problems. You cannot help everybody at once. So it depends on your perspective. But this is not a permanent thing, where some will always be left out. Our system is designed to help anyone it can. We do not discriminate, expecting you to bring your own capital, your credit score. If you are a human being, that is good enough for us.

PD: What is it about you as a person that draws you to these issues and drives you to create these projects?

MY: That is for others on the outside to study. But I will tell you this: I feel that things can be done. And whenever I see a problem, my mind starts working. I ask myself, "Why don't I design a business to address this problem?" As a result I have created more than fifty companies. And each time it's been all about addressing a problem. At first I was not conscious of this. I simply saw a problem and designed a business to solve the problem. I never had any intention of making money out of it. People started asking me why I created companies if I don't want to make money. I said that the idea of making money never entered my mind. I was always looking at the problems, solving them, and I felt happy with that. Even owning a share of these companies never entered my mind. I still do not own any shares. So this was not something at the time that I designed and then did.

Now I am reflecting on it and realizing why I did it. And I'm realizing that this is a space on which most people are missing out. Because economists have denied that this window of opportunity exists. I am now addressing big companies, and I tell them, "You are doing fine making money, but would you like to create a social business?" So now I have joint ventures—for instance, with the Danone milk products company—and they are excited, and I tell them that the more they do it, the more they will get excited, the more excited their employees will get, because this is an opportunity you never knew you had. Moreover these companies have access to so much technology, and I tell them there is no reason why this planet should have any of the problems it has, and that's because of the power of technology. But all the technology we have in the world belongs to the business world. And what do they do with the technology? They want to make more money. But if we could use this technology to approach problems, the problems would disappear. Human creativity is far superior to our problems. But we never connected human creativity to problem solving in a business way.

PD: I believe your ideas are even more important today than previously because poverty has now visibly hit—or at least become more visible— in those countries that are perceived as rich.

MY: Exactly. The crisis has come to a point now that we see the inadequacies of the present structure. There is not only poverty but also unemployment, which hits people politically. Look at the situation in Europe right now. There is no way they can figure out how to address this problem. They can work on it so that maybe next year it might be 10 percent less or 1 percent less. But why should there be unemployment?

PD: In your view the market exists so that people can be employed rather than generate money?

MY: The market should do both. When I sell my yoghurt, it is sold in the market, but its purpose is to solve malnutrition. I am not denying the market, but I am saying that today's market is a restrictive market. The only players in the market are the money-makers. What I'm saying is that the problem-solvers can also join the market and solve problems. And the same people who want to make money often also want to solve problems. For instance, why not create an alternative stock market? Rather than seeing what shares you can buy and sell to make a dollar, why not invest in companies that are solving problems, not to make dividends but to help?

PD: But, you know, sometimes politics interferes in the economy.

MY: But with investment it is my individual decision. In that sense politics cannot interfere with me. I want to create a company to solve a

problem. And politics cannot tell me creating a company to solve problems is illegal. Not taking profit out of my company is a personal decision. I am not asking that new laws be created for me. I am also not
suggesting the creation of special privileges for social businesses, like
tax benefits. The reason I say that is because if you give them privileges,
then fake social businesses will be created. So I say there should be a
level playing field for everybody. And that's your choice. But you still
run it like a business. And you still love doing it. When people ask you
what you do, you say you run a social business and you love it.

2

"Minority rights are a part of human rights"

Photo courtesy of Will Kymlicka.

WILL KYMLICKA

in conversation with Raffaele Marchetti

Will Kymlicka is the Canada Research Chair in Political Philosophy at Queen's University in Kingston, Canada, and a visiting professor in the Nationalism Studies Program at the Central European University.

A world-renowned expert on minority politics, Will Kymlicka delves into a number of aspects of his field in this revealing and ultimately hopeful conversation with Raffaele Marchetti. The political theorist sees inequality, both social and economic, as one of the main problems facing the modern world. He briefly traces the history of modern multiculturalism and argues that progress, albeit fragile, has been made globally through the proliferation of various iterations of the idea of human rights. Now, he argues, the challenge is to convince majority groups that social relations with minorities are not a zero-sum game and that society as a whole can benefit from rights and privileges being granted to minorities. His vision, however, is a pragmatic one. While recognizing the role of global forces in the world, Kymlicka argues that we must still think and work within the constraints of the model of the nation-state wherein cultural and social recognition for minorities is often necessary for the amelioration of their material conditions. Kymlicka argues that we must recognize that all identities are shaped through social and political projects, which is not an excuse for defending the status quo of dominant identities or for overlooking flaws among minorities. Rather, this is a call for a more universal politics of mutual understanding.

RM: Tell us how you read the world we live in.

WK: It's a world of staggering inequalities. Some people are born into very fortunate circumstances, into a world that gives them enormous opportunities for flourishing. Other people are born into circumstances that condemn them to a much harsher life. The world almost seems designed to make life comfortable for people like me—white, English-speaking, male, professional—while putting up all sorts of barriers and burdens for others. That has always seemed like an extraordinary injustice to me.

RM: How did we end up in this situation? Was it the result of intentional actions or unintended processes? Are there special interests behind this?

WK: Of course, the rich and powerful fight hard to defend their interests and resist efforts to take away their rights or resources; that's a universal constant of human history. But what is more contingent, and more puzzling, is why dominant groups so often assume that helping the disadvantaged will necessarily come at their expense. It's not a universal constant that social relationships are perceived in such zero-sum terms. I see this all the time in my own field of ethnic relations. Dominant ethnic groups assume that any rights or powers extended to ethnic minorities will inevitably come at their own expense, and so they systematically and almost automatically resist every proposal for minority rights. But why should extending language rights or self-government to minorities, for example, necessarily make life worse off for majorities? Why can't both majorities and minorities flourish, and each benefit from the others' flourishing? I think this knee-jerk majority resistance to minority rights is often unthinking, and ultimately irrational, even from a self-interested point of view. Where these zero-sum assumptions are made, societies get caught in a vicious circle of distrust and insecurity that makes everyone worse off. It undermines the possibilities for democratic freedoms, for social learning and cooperation, and even for peace. In an ideal world, dominant groups would have a much stronger sense of justice and would be more willing to share their good fortune with others out of a sense of solidarity, even if it did involve some sacrifice on their part. But even in the absence of a sudden improvement in people's sense of morality, I think we can make progress by challenging these unreflective beliefs that social relationships are zero-sum, and that "we" can flourish only by oppressing "them."

RM: In terms of trends, where are we going? Do you think things are getting better or worse?

WK: That depends on which side of the bed I get up on. You can look at the past couple of centuries and say there has been clear progress: we have basically abolished slavery, delegitimized colonialism, and made remarkable strides in the rights of women and children. In many ways, the world is less cruel and less violent than it used to be. We have developed a world culture of human rights. It's fragile, and it's sometimes more rhetoric than reality, but it's meaningful. I have no doubt that the world is a much better place as a result of the human rights revolution than it was before. There really have been profound changes in the way that we think about human dignity and the value of human life. These are big macro-level changes in the world. That's the good side. On most days I think that it's a better world out there and that the normative logic of human rights is still at work, extending into gay rights, rights for people with disabilities, animal rights, and minority rights.

ON the other hand, these changes are very unevenly spread across the world, and moreover are vulnerable to retreat. Most obviously, they are hostage to geopolitical factors. Think of 9/11. We were making progress on a range of issues relating to immigration, multiculturalism, and citizenship, and then 9/11 just completely shifted the direction. It didn't reverse all of the progress of the human rights revolution, of course, but anxieties about security and about the alleged conflict between the "West" and the "Muslim world" have cast a very large shadow over many of these issues. And even if we somehow overcome that setback, I can imagine other setbacks down the road. Think of environmental issues. Knowledgeable people speculate about new waves of conflicts arising out of water shortages, oil shortages, global warming. You can easily imagine circumstances that could exert pressure against the progressive trends.

RM: The overall context for this is the phenomenon of globalization, the process of progressive integration at the supranational level in different dimensions: political, economic, legal, social. Is global integration something we should welcome?

WK: Integration into international structures has often been helpful for minorities. Yet states and minorities can get trapped into very negative dynamics, each side viewing the other in zero-sum terms. When this happens, being able to take advantage of international norms and international organizations can be beneficial. Minorities around the world have suffered intensely at the hands of their own states in recent history, and there is a lot of hope that the presence of international actors can improve state-minority relations. Globalization, in this sense, is potentially a positive development for minorities.

ON the other hand, the form of globalization that we've had over the past thirty years has been tied to a particular economic agenda, usually called *neoliberalism*, which has often been harmful. It's helped some groups within some countries, including some minority groups, who have benefited from access to global markets. But it has degraded the quality of democratic life and public institutions and increased the vulnerability of many groups. In fact it has often deprived minorities of various forms of protection and support that were built into the old modes of governance. The radical restructuring of the economy and the welfare state, often pushed by international organizations, has put a lot of stress on individuals and groups and state-minority relations. In my field there is a lot of debate these days about *neoliberal multiculturalism* and the way it has been promoted by international organizations. Globalization has pushed states to be more accommodating of minorities (that's the *multicultural* part), but it has also restructured the economy in neoliberal ways. And the relationship between the multicultural part and the neoliberal part is very hard to disentangle in many countries.

THIS is a particularly intense debate in relation to indigenous peoples. The UN has promoted an ambitious Declaration on the Rights of Indigenous Peoples, including rights to self-government and to land, which are intended to protect their ability to maintain their culture and identity. At the same time, the World Bank seems to be promoting models of "development" that presuppose that indigenous peoples must adapt themselves to the requirements of the global marketplace, and hence adopt the logic of capitalist rationality. Critics argue that the World Bank's neoliberal imperative to adapt to the global market has essentially gutted the UN's Declaration of any real meaning: in short, that the logic of neoliberalism has essentially trumped any meaningful multiculturalism. My own view is that there is a lot more contingency and contestation in these relationships than many people recognize and that globalization has not (yet) imposed a single simple uncompromising logic of neoliberalism on everyone. Many minorities and indigenous peoples are finding creative ways to take advantage of new international norms and institutions, to offset their vulnerability at the hands of states, while still contesting many of the demands and expectations of neoliberalism.

RM: Now, to tackle a core topic of your work: multiculturalism in contemporary society. To begin with, society has throughout history been "plural," but how did this plurality become an issue to be addressed?

WK: I would argue that pluralism became an issue with the rise of the nation-state. The politicization of minority groups needs to be understood as a reaction to the way dominant groups use the state to protect and promote their national identity. For the past two centuries, we have operated with the assumption that a normal state should be a "nation-state"; that is, it should have a clear national identity, a national language, and some sort of shared national culture. And in order to become such a nation-state, various nation-building projects must be adopted. It is the task of public institutions to inculcate the national identity: in schools, in public space, in museums, in the media, and so on. This model emerged first in the West, and with the end of colonialism it has been embraced throughout most of the world. So for the past two hundred years we've lived in a world of nation-building states, and it's important to get a balanced assessment of both what this sort of nation building has achieved as well as the problems it has created.

On the one hand, nation building has in many ways been a success, not just from the perspective of dominant groups trying to promote their identity but also from the perspective of building functional democracies. The fact is that there are functional benefits to nation building from a liberal democratic point of view. Democratic self-government is simpler if people speak the same national language, and a welfare state is easier to build if people have a sense of solidarity that can often accompany a shared national identity. A shared national identity can also help to develop trust and social capital. There has been a lot of work in the social sciences about how national identities can serve as a kind of "social glue" in contemporary societies and how nationhood gives dignity to the broad masses, not just to elites. Nationhood valorizes "the people," unlike earlier models of the state that emphasized the superiority of elites. So even if you don't care about promoting the interests or identity of the dominant group and instead care only about promoting a well-functioning liberal democracy, you might conclude that a certain amount of nation building was beneficial. Nation-building projects in many countries have helped to stabilize political communities and to develop vibrant national cultures that include both elites and the masses.

HOWEVER—AND it's a big however—these projects have come at a huge price for many minorities. At its very worst, nation building has led to the killing or expelling of minorities. We have many examples of that in the past century. Even when it has not led to violence, it has often involved coercive assimilation, and stigmatization of anyone who resisted assimilation. In many countries, if anyone tried to express their minority identity, they were seen as somehow disloyal, "un-American," alien, a threat, a fifth column, culturally deficient, backward, primitive, and so on. And this often led to cycles of distrust and polarization, in which the majority comes to believe that it can flourish only by suppressing the minority. So nation building has had unjust and destabilizing effects, alongside its more benign effects in promoting democratic consolidation. And these negative effects have become harder to ignore, not least because minorities themselves have become so much more vocal in challenging and resisting projects of assimilation and stigmatization.

TO put it in a nutshell, the goal of my work has been to think about how we can preserve the real benefits that come from nation building but reduce or eliminate the injustices it imposes on minorities. I don't believe that there is any alternative to nation-states in the near future—we are far from living in a postnational world—and so political life will continue to be structured around national identities. But nor can we hope to return to the day when minorities passively and quietly accepted their fate to be either assimilated or excluded. We need to build more multicultural and pro-minority conceptions of nation-states.

RM: Is there any specific turning point we can identify after which minorities became an issue?

WK: There are different turning points for different parts of the world. In the West, there was a clear turning point in the 1960s. A range of different minorities started to mobilize politically, including indigenous peoples (like American Indians), substate national groups (like the

Scots or Quebecois), as well as immigrant groups (like the Jamaicans in Britain). These groups started to mobilize not because they were all of a sudden treated worse as compared to ten or twenty years earlier but rather because the legitimacy of their treatment was now put into question. Old models of ethnic and racial hierarchies—many of which had been quite stable for centuries—were all of a sudden being challenged, and minorities felt justified in demanding a new deal.

Of course, this change didn't come out of nowhere. The story really begins with the Second World War and the way the horrors of Nazism revealed the dangers of racism and racial ideologies. That had two consequences. First, it delegitimized colonialism, leading in the rest of the world to national liberation movements. Second, partly inspired by these national liberation struggles, it led within the United States to the civil rights movement. It's impossible to overstate the global significance of the political mobilization of African Americans that started in the 1950s. This was arguably the first time that a historically subordinated minority had successfully used the tools of liberal democracy to challenge their exclusion. They didn't take up arms but rather used Gandhian nonviolent protest and disobedience, political mobilization, and legal advocacy to challenge the way that they were discriminated against, subordinated, and stigmatized. This then inspired other minorities to challenge their historical subordination.

I'm very interested in this chain of influences, from Third World anticolonialism to African American civil rights to global minority rights. It's clear if you read the autobiographies and histories of these minority struggles, they all talk about how important the African American example was for them. They learned from it, they studied it, and they adopted many of its strategies. But minorities around the world, while inspired by African Americans, often faced quite different challenges. African Americans were saying to whites, "We're no different from you. Our skin color is not significant. A difference has been artificially imposed on us and used to discriminate against us." The main goal of the civil rights struggle was the nondiscriminatory enforcement of basic human rights. Many minorities were in the opposite position, in the sense that they had a strong sense of separate identity and cultural difference, which the dominant group refused to acknowledge. They had been subject to assimilation and forced to act as if they were no different from any other citizen, even though they often wished to maintain and express a different identity and culture. So while they too campaigned for an end to discrimination, they also demanded positive recognition of difference in the form of multiculturalism or minority rights.

RM: Why should we care about cultural recognition?

WK: Issues of recognition are intrinsically important for many people. Being stigmatized can be a real harm, a real cruelty. Imagine you're the parent of a gay child, and you have the choice of two schools. One is a prestigious school whose graduates are more or less guaranteed good economic prospects, but it's also a school known for being homophobic, so your child is going to be bullied and insulted. The other is a school that might not be as good academically but is known to provide a safe and comfortable environment for gays. What is more important: economic prospects or social acceptance? Parents might make different choices when confronted with that question, but I hope everyone can agree that it's an unfair choice to have to make: no one should have to forgo economic opportunities in order to avoid stigmatization. It can be terrible to be stigmatized because of your difference or your otherness. In this respect I think many issues of ethnic minority rights are like gay rights. Feeling you have constantly to deny or hide who you are because otherwise you're going to be stigmatized can be a profound burden to carry around. Part of what multiculturalism does is to provide public acknowledgment of the worth and respect owed to minorities. And we should not trivialize this.

Having said that, we should not reduce multiculturalism to being just about the symbolic affirmation of identity. In most contexts, groups subject to stigmatization are also subject to very real forms of discrimination as well. And even if we think that fighting discrimination is more important than according cultural recognition, the reality is that the former often requires the latter. The stigmatization of a group's identity makes it harder for that group to mobilize for its real economic and political interests.

RM: Critics would say that these kinds of identities are just constructed and consequently that these claims are based on something that is not genuine.

WK: It's true that ethnic and national identities are constructed, in part through the work of "ethnic entrepreneurs" who try to consolidate their preferred conception of these identities. These identities are not innate, and they have not existed since time immemorial. They are the result of conscious political projects to (re)create identities. All of that is true. But I think we need to be even-handed in the way we apply that observation. After all, we can say the same about dominant national identities. There's no reason to think that "Spanish" is somehow a more authentic or natural identity than "Catalan." As I noted earlier, these dominant national identities are also the product of conscious political projects of nation building. Yet dominant groups clearly care a great deal about having their (constructed) identity upheld and rendered visible in public space. They want their language used in public institutions, their culture and history taught in public schools, and so on. So if there's something puzzling about people caring about constructed identities, then it is equally a puzzle for majority groups as for minority groups. And however we respond to that puzzle, we need to do so in an even-handed way. It would be perverse and unfair to give the majority free rein to imprint its national identity on public institutions, while denying the minority the right to do so.

There's a more general point here. We shouldn't focus only on minorities and ask why minorities are concerned about identity, culture, language, religion, and so on. We can answer that question only if we first recognize that dominant groups are equally interested in their identity, culture, language, and religion and in using public institutions to reproduce them. And it is precisely in response to the majority's identity-building projects that minorities have mobilized behind their own identity. The issue is not whether we are for or against politicized identity projects but rather how we can fairly respond to the existence of conflicting identity projects and how we can ameliorate the injustices caused by the majority's identity projects.

RM: Very often in the public debate there is a tension between cultural differences and human rights. How is it possible to respect cultural difference and yet comply with human rights?

WK: This is one of the questions that requires stepping back and remembering the larger social and historical context. Struggles for minority rights and multiculturalism emerged as part of the human rights revolution and took the form of challenging older ideas and practices of racial supremacy and ethnocentrism. In that context, minorities were saying to majority groups, "You claim to believe in human rights, you claim to believe in the equality of races and peoples, and you claim to disavow ideologies of racial supremacy, yet we can still find manifestations of these ideologies in how we as a society evaluate job candidates or how we select immigrants, or in our public symbols, school books, media representation." If you go back to the 1960s and 1970s and look at the first claims that emerged under the rubric of multiculturalism and minority rights, they were targeting what we would now all agree are historical residues of earlier official commitments to racism. Here in Canada, for example, we still had public symbols (flags, anthems) that portrayed indigenous people as savages. The practices of Western states were for a long time explicitly grounded in notions of racial supremacy. After the Second World War we committed ourselves to norms of non-discrimination, and the state dropped most of its explicitly discriminatory laws, but it's been a continuing struggle to identify and challenge the many ways in which these earlier practices continue to shape social and political life. And the most powerful weapon in the toolkit of minority groups was human rights principles. It was precisely in the name of human rights that minorities first mobilized for their rights and multiculturalism.

BUT, of course, if human rights are the basis on which minorities make their claims, then human rights also constrain what kinds of claims minorities can make. After all, it is not just majorities who have long-standing practices that are inconsistent with human rights principles. Many minority groups have their own historical forms of racism, sexism, homophobia, or caste prejudice, all of which are equally delegitimated by human rights norms. And so if you frame minority claims in a human rights framework, you need to be consistent. An upper-caste immigrant from India cannot say to Canadians, "I have a human right that you whites respect me as a full and equal person and not discriminate against me, but I refuse to have any interaction with this lower-caste Indian." That's blatantly self-contradictory. So having situated multiculturalism within this framework of human dignity and human rights, it means that in order for minorities to effectively make their claims for respect and inclusion against a dominant group, they have to challenge their own forms of sexism, homophobia, racism, and anti-Semitism.

Obviously this is not a smooth or painless process. Both majorities and minorities continually try to find ways to conceal these hypocrisies and double standards and to selectively pick and choose which human rights they intend to respect. But I believe there is a clear trend by which both states and minorities have come to recognize the logic of human rights claims. We can see this clearly in the emergence of jurisprudence around minority and indigenous rights, both within national courts and at the UN. There is now a well-developed body of principles and case law that clarifies how minority rights fit into a larger human rights framework, and how human rights both inspire and constrain minority rights. The idea that there's a kind of radical discontinuity between human rights claims and multicultural claims is not tenable. There are hard cases and gray areas, as in every area of the law, but the core principle that minority rights are a part of human rights is now well-established.

RM: That's clear enough in relation to the Western context, but does this help us explain and reinterpret political reality worldwide?

WK: I've been invited to discuss these issues in many parts of the world, and in most cases I've been struck by how quickly and widely this liberal, human rights–based conception of multiculturalism has taken hold, at least at the level of discourse. Whether it is in Latin America or Eastern Europe, both minorities and government officials have learned to talk the talk of liberal multiculturalism. This discourse emerged in the West only in the 1970s, but by the 1990s it was already effectively a global discourse.

But not everywhere. When I went to China, for example, it was clear that this discourse has not been embraced by the Communist Party, which continues quite explicitly to assert what are essentially supremacist ideologies. According to the government, the Han Chinese are the elder brothers, the competent, civilized people who have the responsibility to look after their younger brothers, the minorities, who are undeveloped, backward, and not ready to govern themselves. So it's the right and responsibility of the Han Chinese to bring civilization to the margins. This idea is not found just in China; a recent book called *Civilizing the Margins* showed that this idea is quite widespread in Southeast Asia.[1] This assumption that dominant groups in China and Southeast Asia have the right and duty to bring civilization to minorities on the margins is rooted in old ideologies of racial supremacy and paternalism, and of course is exactly the same discourse that whites used in Canada vis-à-vis indigenous peoples up until the 1960s. It wasn't so long ago that European settler-states used the same discourse. But one effect of the human rights revolution in the West has been to discredit these old supremacist and paternalist mind-sets. No one today could talk that way in Canada about indigenous peoples.

I don't have a full explanation for why liberal multiculturalism has taken root more in some regions than in others. I suspect an important role is played by NGOs (nongovernmental organizations). Wherever there's real freedom of association and a vibrant civil society, we find a proliferation of civil society groups whose mandate reflects ideas of liberal multiculturalism, partly because there is foreign funding for such associations but also because it speaks to the aspirations of many locals. You not only find NGOs using liberal multiculturalist discourse, but also that they are training local media to use this discourse, pushing for school curricula to use this discourse, teaching local bureaucrats to do so. All of this is a manifestation of globalization. Wherever a free civil society exists, we can quickly find local organizations being integrated into global networks that work to diffuse the discourse of liberal multiculturalism.

RM: The obvious accusation here would be that this is Western imperialism deploying "soft" means.

WK: On one level that's right. It is Western funding and Western endorsement that gives recognition and resources to local actors who are promoting liberal multiculturalism. But these issues arise wherever the state seeks to turn itself into a *nation*-state, which is, of course, another Western import. Postcolonial states have imported this model of the nation-state and in the process have embarked on the same sorts of nation-building projects as in the West. And the result in postcolonial states has been the same as in the West: namely, injustice to minorities.

RM: Taking a long-term perspective, do you see a convergence toward this policy of multiculturalism or increasing resistance? Is this a logic that's going to be applied worldwide?

WK: I don't want to say that the move to multiculturalism is irreversible, since there will be—and have been—moments of resistance, retreat, and backlash. But I do think that one change is more or less irreversible: namely, minorities around the world are today more likely to be politically mobilized rather than passive in the face of injustice and exclusion.

The real issue is under what conditions dominant groups or the state will actually listen to what minorities are saying and come to some reasonable settlement. And here things are much more contingent and variable over time and across the globe. I think the answer largely depends on what dominant groups and the state view as the cost—social, economic, and (geo)political—of these accommodations. If there has been a meaningful trend toward minority rights in the West, it is not primarily because members of majority groups have suddenly become generous and warmhearted toward minorities. Rather, it's because majorities have come to believe that these accommodations are not high-risk. Extending minority rights does not threaten the basic security of individuals or of the state. Within Western democracies, issues about the treatment of minorities today are basically just questions of domestic social policy. People may disagree about how best to address these issues, but they aren't seen as matters of life and death, for either individuals or the state. In many parts of the world, however, it remains the case that relations between the state and minorities are viewed as posing an existential threat. This goes back to my comment earlier, about how often majorities view minority rights in zero-sum terms: our flourishing depends on their suppression.

RM: Despite the overall process of convergence you have just drawn, there is also resistance to these ideas in the heart of the West. For instance, the British prime minister David Cameron and the German chancellor Angela Merkel both stated that the old days of multiculturalism have gone and that we should think about something else.

WK: I have two responses to the high-profile statements about the death of multiculturalism by people like Merkel, Cameron, and the French president Nicolas Sarkozy. First, those claims are exclusively in relation to multiculturalism for immigrant groups. That's an important form of multiculturalism, but we mustn't lose sight of the fact that there are other types of minorities, and in relation to them progress toward multiculturalism continues.

RM: I would like now to move to the final part of the interview and talk about the future challenges within the agenda of multiculturalism.

What kinds of policy challenges do you think need to be addressed? By whom?

WK: In the West we have made real strides in relation to historical national minorities and indigenous peoples. I would go so far as to say that in some countries we have more or less achieved true justice between dominant groups and historical minorities, which is an extraordinary achievement. Think about the German-speaking minority in South Tyrol in Italy. Although a minority within Italy, and although they have historically been the victim of Italian nation-building projects, today they have gained the sorts of minority rights that ensure real justice. Italy has allowed German speakers to have full use of their language, fair representation in public institutions, and cultural respect. It's hard to think on what basis the German speakers in South Tyrol could claim to be treated unjustly. And I would say the same about the Quebecois here in Canada. After many years of being subordinated, today they have something very close to real equality. This is the clear trend for historical national minorities across the West, and I see no real danger that this trend will be reversed. With respect to indigenous peoples, the progress is less evident, in part because the level of injustice from which we started was so much greater. But if we think about the changes since the 1960s in the treatment of indigenous peoples, they are in fact hugely important and meaningful. There remain dramatic inequalities in life chances, in life expectancy, in health status, and in educational outcomes, and so we have unfinished business in relation to indigenous peoples here in the Americas and in Scandinavia. But the gaps have been diminishing, and I think we're moving in the right direction.

The bigger challenge is in relation to immigrant groups. This is where we see strong resistance to liberal multiculturalism, and in some cases (like the Netherlands) real backlash. In some cases, this is tied to very specific local events and personalities, but one general theme seems to be the role of Islam and doubts about whether Muslims are able or willing to play by the rules of liberal democracy. The resistance and backlash seems to be stronger in those countries where the category of "immigrant" is equated or conflated in people's minds with "Muslim." Obviously this tendency has been greatly exacerbated by 9/11 and subsequent bomb terrorism in Madrid and London, but it arguably dates back to Salman Rushdie and the *Satanic Verses* affair in 1988. There have been vast amounts of ink spilled on this issue, and I'm sure everyone knows the arguments and counterarguments.

All I'll say here is that this is not a problem that we're going to resolve quickly. In my view, with this question, as with most issues in immigration, we are talking about long-term processes. It's not something one can decide or predict based on a single event or point in time. The success of immigration is an intergenerational process. There are always going to be conflicts and misunderstandings and misperceptions with the first generation. I think the evidence will show that multiculturalism can indeed help.

TRANSFORM HOW THE
GLOBAL ECONOMY WORKS

3

"We can have faster economic growth if we reduce inequality"

JOSEPH STIGLITZ

in conversation with Shari Spiegel

Joseph Stiglitz is a recipient of the Nobel Memorial Prize in Economic Sciences (2001) and the John Bates Clark Medal (1979). He is a university professor at Columbia University and also chairs the University of Manchester's Brooks World Poverty Institute.

Photo courtesy of Columbia University and Joseph Stiglitz.

The Nobel laureate and renowned economist Joseph Stiglitz has long been a critic of many aspects of mainstream economic theory and policy. Here he delves into the history and failures of modern macroeconomics, which, most recently, failed to either foresee or address effectively the global economic crisis. He argues that other areas of economics have developed theories, such as behavioral economics and new paradigms of monetary economics, which can serve as building blocks for a new framework. Two areas that were not well-addressed in the standard paradigm and need to be addressed in new economic thinking are sustainability and inequality. Professor Stiglitz focuses on the issue of inequality and argues that it impinges both on individuals' capacity and society's ability to use best its human resources. In the context of the recent economic slowdown, he argues that policymakers need to focus on both the near term and the medium term simultaneously, since near-term policies have medium-term effects. Policy should focus on stimulating employment and consumption, including investment in small and medium-size enterprises that typically cannot access capital markets and have to rely on banks. Banks, in this view, should be harnessed to serve society's economic needs rather than simply their own profit motive. Finally, he looks at national policies within a globalized world and calls for greater global governance and coordination of policies, while still allowing for differentiation, especially for developing countries.

ss: Let's start by talking a little bit about the failure of the economic model and how you see economics going forward. What do you think are the problems with existing economic models? Can we still use existing models, or do we need a completely new economic model, or something else altogether?

js: The most obvious problems with economics were in macroeconomics. The standard paradigm didn't predict the crisis. According to the paradigm, crises, such as the recent crisis, couldn't even occur. After the bubble broke, it said the problems were contained. It didn't give a very good set of prescriptions about how to respond when in fact it turned out that they were not contained. It was almost a perfect record of malperformance.

Then you have to ask the question: Was it just bad luck, or were there fundamental flaws with the theory? I think the answer is that the theory has fundamental flaws, many of which were raised over a long period of time but to which very little attention had been given.

Perhaps one can go back thirty or forty years. Keynesian economics grew out of the Great Depression and was successful in part because it provided an interpretation of that cataclysmic event. In the 1970s the key problem in macroeconomics was inflation, for which the focus of traditional Keynesian economics was not so relevant. There were two fields in economics: micro and macro. Micro was based on assumptions about well-functioning markets, while macro was based on seemingly simple descriptions of how markets worked. Market failures were pervasive—indeed macroeconomics focused on the market failure of persistent unemployment. The poor economics students had to learn two different disciplines in different courses with totally different perspectives.

The economics profession wanted a kind of intellectual coherence between the two fields. There were two ways of brining the two together: to make macro like micro or to make micro like macro (which would imply acknowledging that there were market failures and unemployment). The main strand of economics took the view that micro theory was right and tried to make macro like micro, with the underlying assumptions of well-functioning markets and no such thing as unemployment. To simplify the analysis, many macroeconomists went even further and used a representative agent model.[1] In a representative agent model everybody's the same person, which means you can have no information asymmetries and no financial markets. Over the years, the economics profession realized that the representative agent model was overly simplistic—to put it mildly. They began a polemic exercise to make it better. The modifications were, however, just tinkering around a flawed foundation. And that's the model that failed. Meanwhile the irony was that there were significant advances in microeconomics over this time, which attacked the old microeconomics that had provided the basis of the new macroeconomics. Information asymmetries, incomplete markets, incomplete contracts, bargaining, and game theory all undermined the traditional microeconomics on which modern macroeconomics had been based.

In the ensuing decades there has developed in various parts of economics a much better understanding of how people and markets actually behave (e.g., behavioral economics). There have been particularly significant advances in financial markets (e.g., the theory of banking in Bruce Greenwald and my book *Towards a New Paradigm of Monetary Economics*).[2] All the elements that provided the critique of the existing macroeconomic theory had been worked out well before the crisis. The problems posed by bankruptcy cascades and interlinking markets were well understood by microeconomists but, unfortunately, not by macroeconomists and central banks. The insights of these advances in microeconomics were not included in the standard macroeconomics. In a way, this is good news for the economics profession today because what it says is that we have the building blocks for creating a new macroeconomics. We know a lot about how to go forward in that field.

ss: In addition to not predicting the crisis, the standard economic models didn't say much about some of the big challenges confronting us, such as how to ensure sustainable development in a world of limited resources. To think about sustainability, we need to think about pricing public goods and externalities, as well as incorporating intergenerational issues. Do you think the existing models can incorporate sustainability, or do we need a completely new framework for sustainable development?

js: There are many elements of sustainability: economic, social, political, environmental. What in some sense was remarkable was that the standard paradigm ignored *all* of these. The central assumptions of the model (such as perfect rationality) implied that there were no bubbles. The way the models were structured ensured stability. The models didn't address economic sustainability because markets were sustainable by definition and/or as a direct consequence of the unrealistic assumptions embedded in the models.

The models also excluded public goods like the global environment. Any good measure of how well we are doing must also take account of sustainability. Just as a firm needs to measure the depreciation of its capital, so too our national accounts need to reflect the depletion of natural resources and the degradation of our environment. Yet the empirical work didn't even recognize that GDP was a flawed (and for some purposes, biased) measure of output. When many macroeconomists did empirical testing of the model, they were insensitive to problems that we had spent a lot of time talking about when I was a graduate student and in the early years of my own research, such as problems of aggregation, problems of measurement, and problems of mismeasurement. In a sense even the measures of performance that became common were wrong. That was the point of the Commission on the Measurement of Economic Performance and Social Progress, which I chaired.[3]

ss: So how would you think about incorporating sustainability into economic models of the new economic thinking?

js: Well, one aspect that you raised is intergenerational equity, which is really a very important issue in debates all over the world. Again, this is an example of something that the standard macroeconomic model excluded. The representative agent model was based on one individual (singular) with an infinite lifetime. It ignored distribution within a population (which has been one of my main critiques of these models) and also distribution across generations.

One of the justifications of the extreme simplification employed by the standard macroeconomic models was that it enabled the construction of models that would be of use to policymakers. But what's so striking about the models is that they are bad for policy purposes, in the sense that they don't incorporate a lot of things we care about, such as distribution of income across or within generations. We know that intergenerational effects are first-order, not only from the point of view of social equity (which they never talk about) but also from a descriptive point of view of where the economy is going. There are, however, alternative models that can be used to incorporate intergenerational equity and sustainability into our analysis. (The overlapping generations model is one approach that was extensively studied in an earlier literature.)[4]

ss: So would you say that the tools are there to move forward, that it's not that we need to get rid of the existing "model" of economics and come up with something completely new but that we need to start using the tools we have to reformulate the existing model? Or, rather, a series of models?

JS: Right. A series of models. Maybe, in a hundred years, we might have one big model, but as you know, every model is a simplification. The criticism of the standard macroeconomic paradigm is not that there were simplifications; it is that they were the wrong simplifications. These models were very precise, but they were precisely wrong.

SS: You said that one of your main critiques of the standard model is that it ignores distribution within a population. Perhaps we can talk more about inequality. Your book, *The Price of Inequality*, is focused on inequality in the United States, but maybe we can broaden the discussion and begin talking about global inequality.[5]

JS: When you start talking internationally, there are a few key observations. The first is, you might say, an element of success—that if you erased the names of countries and just looked at the people of the world, there is a sense in which there has been a reduction in global inequality. This is largely a result of the fact that China has moved four or five hundred million people out of poverty. That's important globally. But we live within our own countries, and we're much more sensitive to inequalities within countries than to global inequality. In most countries around the world, with the exception of a few, such as Brazil in Latin America, inequality is growing.

The second point I want to make is that there are many dimensions to inequality—not just income but also wealth and health and opportunity. And the United States does particularly badly in several of these dimensions. Most other advanced industrial countries recognize the right of access to health. We don't. We're unique in that respect among the advanced countries. The evidence also shows that the United States has one of the worst, if not the worst, inequality of opportunity within the advanced industrial countries.

SS: Which is somewhat ironic, since the United States has historically seen itself as the "land of opportunity." When would you say that the

United States became one of the worst countries in terms of equality of opportunity?

js: There have been marked increases in inequality and inequality of opportunity over the past thirty years. It's affected greatly by education, and education in turn has been affected by a weakening of public education and greater economic segregation. There's an interaction, I think, between the level of inequality and inequality of opportunity. If you have more economic inequality, it's not a surprise that you get more economic segregation, and that means you get more inequality of opportunity.

There's one aspect that I think also needs to be emphasized in terms of both inequality and inequality of opportunity that is reflected at birth. Recent work has shown that there are large differences in birth weight, and that poor mothers have low–birth weight children.[6] Low birth weight is correlated with lifetime performance. One of the reasons that has been identified for why poor women have smaller babies is that they are exposed to more environmental hazards. Poor women are more likely to live near health hazards, and that shows up in the low birth weight of their children, which is transmitted across generations, so that low–birth weight children will have low–birth weight children, which is part of the intergenerational transmission mechanism of inequalities. It's very depressing.

ss: Perhaps you could talk about the links between globalization and the growing inequality that we're seeing.

js: Right, so on the positive side, I think globalization has helped China and that China has managed globalization well. While according to the Gini coefficient inequality in China has grown, but it has grown in such a way that everybody has moved up.[7] Some have moved up more than others, but a substantial number of people have moved out of poverty. But globalization has also had an adverse effect on inequality within most countries, and some countries overall have been adversely affected by globalization.

There are several different facets of globalization. Financial market globalization has been associated with instability, and instability is bad for growth, and particularly bad for the poor. Financial and capital market liberalization has been associated with lower flow of funds to smaller businesses, has weakened the bargaining power of workers, and has been associated with a weakening of the progressivity of taxes.

Globalization of trade has also led to greater inequality, though of a quite different character. There are three issues here. First, Samuelson's factor price equalization theorem says that low-wage workers in the advanced industrial countries are in effect competing with low-wage workers in developing countries, which drives down the wages of low-income workers and increases inequality in industrialized countries. Even people like Paul Krugman, who at first thought that globalization was less important in increasing inequality, have changed their minds and now agree that this is indeed an important factor contributing to inequality in developed countries. In developing countries, the effects are somewhat different because the factor price equalization goes the other way; that is, it should be pulling up wages of unskilled workers. Globalization pulls up the income of those who participate in the traded sector. It still increases the gap between these individuals and, say, subsistence farmers, but it's less invidious, in that it's not directly hurting any group. Second, the way globalization has been managed has led to workers' bargaining power being undermined, which has also led to lower wages. The third point here is that unfair trade agreements can hurt everybody in the developing countries. For example, there are a number of provisions of trade agreements that reduce access to drugs and especially generic medicines. Restrictions on industrial policies in trade agreements can hurt growth. More broadly, the way we've framed trade policy serves the interests of the developed relative to the developing countries.

ss: So globalization has been one reason behind rising inequalities. On the other side, what would you say the impact of inequality has on been on global development, and particularly on sustainable development?

js: I think you want to focus on how different aspects of inequality and inequality of opportunity affect development. Inequality of opportunity leads to underutilization of the capacities of the bottom, which is a waste of human capital and human resources. Any economy requires investments in infrastructure, education, and other public investments. There is econometric work that shows, as one would expect, that more divided societies have a harder time generating political support for public investments. There are two reasons for this. One is that the rich don't need a lot of public support and social protections. The other is that the rich worry that a stronger state will use its power to redistribute or impose fairer taxation, so they prefer a small state.

ss: Which we've definitely seen in the United States.

js: Exactly. And if you don't make public investments, you grow more slowly. Third, when you have more inequality, economic inequality gets translated into political inequality, and the two together lead more broadly to rent-seeking activities. I use the term *rent-seeking* in a very broad sense, not only to include the old-fashioned rent-seeking like monopolies and corporate welfare, but also more subtle rent-seeking associated with financial sector deregulation, corporate governance laws that allow CEOs to walk off with a lot of money, and so on. As a result, more resources go into rent-seeking and less go into productive activities. There is also an association between inequality and instability, and it's a two-way relationship, where instability leads to inequality, as we've talked about before, but inequality also leads to instability. In my book I talk about the mechanisms through which this happens.

ss: Have you thought about the idea of vertical versus horizontal inequality? Some economists and other social scientists say that horizontal inequalities across groups (such as racial groups) are more likely to lead to social conflict or violence than vertical (or more purely class) inequalities, which cut across a society.

js: There are a couple of aspects of the question you raise. Part of it has to do with this issue of identity. The question is who you compare yourself with, which is why global inequality is less salient for most people than national inequality. There's some evidence, which I cite in my book, that inequality within your neighborhood, within a small area, has more adverse effects on behavior. That is to say, what they have discovered is that if you are poor and you live in a neighborhood where everybody is rich, you will spend more and you will wind up more in debt, and that indebtedness has consequences. In my book I discuss some of the adverse effects of what happens when someone is confronted constantly with this kind of inequality. You know, people in the workplace are more sensitive to somebody in their own firm getting paid more than they do for comparable work than somebody in some other firm. And that will adversely affect their effort. Now this other dimension of what kinds of inequality give rise to social conflict is actually a very interesting one.

ss: I've wondered whether there are implications of this for conflicts, as well as the possibility of agreement, in Europe, where you have one union with different countries where inequalities between countries have been rising.

js: One question I get asked all the time is if I think the European crisis will break out into conflict. I also get asked frequently whether I think that the growing inequality in the United States is likely to lead to conflict there. In the case of the United States, I don't see that happening. I could see problems of alienation, moves toward the right, and other adverse effects on our society, but not necessarily open conflict.

so too in Western Europe: I am less worried about "violent" conflict than about political conflict. In the case of Spain, it is clear that the country is at risk of falling apart. Cataluña has a strong separatist movement, and there are strong separatist movements elsewhere. You can understand why this is. Cataluña is being criticized for not meeting its budget deficits, but Cataluña says that the only reason this is the case is because they're subsidizing the rest of the country and that they'd be fine if they didn't have to do so. Meanwhile they have 20 percent unemployment. So they're asking the question: Is it worth it to us to subsidize the rest of the country? These types of economic divisions within and across different population groups could potentially risk undermining social cohesion.

ss: One more general question on inequality—and maybe it's a bad question: What would you say to people who argue that there is a trade-off between growth and inequality, and that inequality is necessary for growth?

js: That's so old-fashioned. The textbooks in the 1950s said there's a trade-off between democracy and growth, and we have to give up democracy if we want to grow. The whole point of my book and its title (*The Price of Inequality*) is to say that's wrong, that we can have faster economic growth if we reduce inequality. Now obviously if you got rid of all inequality, there would be no incentives and there would be a problem. If you tax people at 100 percent they won't work, but we're not close to that. So there are many ways we can reduce inequality and grow more strong.

ss: Let's talk about some of those ways and about potential policy responses.

js: I begin with what I find most disturbing, which is inequality of opportunity, which is clearly related to things like education, environmental justice, making sure your labor market is working to make sure jobs are being created for everybody who wants a job. Going beyond that, each part of the inequality we talked about—the increasing share at the top, the hollowing out of the middle, the increase in poverty at the bottom—has its own remedies.

ss: You mention policies to ensure that everybody has a job. In debates about how to stimulate employment in the current recession, some economists argue that policies need to focus on stimulating aggregate demand, while others argue that we need to focus on structural issues. I think that your position is more nuanced and suggests these two are interlinked.

js: But in a very complicated way in the following sense: right now the problem is a shortage of demand, and that ought to be the focus of our attention. When the economy is growing, it's easier to make structural changes because there are opportunities to move people from one industry to another, and Keynesian policies to stimulate demand are important elements of this. It's not just a question of timing—policies are interdependent, and most affect both the short term and the medium term. My concern with Europe, for example, with some of the so-called structural policies, is that I am not sure they're right, but even if they were right in the medium term, the short-term effects on demand could be negative. The obvious example is that if right now you weaken bargaining rights of workers, wages are going to go down even further, and that will weaken aggregate demand, and unemployment will increase. Rules that affect job protection can be important in affecting firms' decisions to hire, but if they're not hiring because there is no demand for their goods, that doesn't help very much. To be fair, labor markets even in economies in recession still have hiring going on; it's just that the pace of hiring and job loss are out of kilter.

ss: How do you think the structural changes you see going on in the economy affect inequalities, and what are potential policy responses?

js: The structural change in moving from a manufacturing economy to a service-sector economy requires people getting retrained and often moving their location. And one of the reasons markets do not handle that kind of restructuring is that the wealth of workers who are in the "dying industries" (which may be industries that are actually very successful in terms of productivity increases, but because they are so successful in productivity increases, employment is going down) is often decreasing, particularly if the workers are in a manufacturing area like Detroit. As a result, they don't have the wealth to move to another area or to retrain, so that you need government to help move them from the industries of the past to the shops of the future.

ss: Which implies "smart" fiscal policies. One of the main responses to the recent crisis has, however, been monetary policy. What are your views on the role of monetary policy and the recent rounds of quantitative easing in stimulating demand? And what would you say is the impact of these on inequality?

js: I think, in terms of employment, which I think is really the most important thing for affecting inequality, particularly in the middle, fiscal policy is really the major instrument. For the United States and for many other countries that have really low or even negative real interest rates, spending more and investing more is desirable. Even for countries that can't borrow more, the balanced budget multiplier is what's relevant.[8] So I think fiscal is the way to go.

One of my main criticisms of quantitative easing, the increase in money supply by central banks through the purchase of government and other securities, flooding financial institutions with capital, is that they draw attention away from fiscal policy because people always have the hope that monetary policy is going to work. But it hasn't worked, and it's not likely to work. We began our discussion talking about the failures of traditional macroeconomics. Nowhere were those greater than in analyses of monetary policy. And one of the reasons they failed so badly is that they focused excessively on inflation and on the interest rate as *the* transmission mechanism—as opposed to either credit availability or the banking system, which takes rates on government treasury bills (T-bills) and converts them into lending rates. The spread between rates on government paper and lending rates is taken as an endogenous variable, which is never explained. Now let's come back to QE2 and QE3. One of the striking things is that QE3 was supposed to help the mortgage market by lowering long-term interest rates and mortgage rates. While the effect on long-term interest rates is debatable, the effect on mortgage interest rates is not very debatable: it's almost unobservable. You can debate why that is the case, but it should be fairly obvious that there would not be a perfect transmission mechanism from T-bill rates to lending rates, especially in the context of a very imperfectly competitive mortgage industry.

It seems to me that the fundamental flaw of QE2 and QE3 is that monetary policy exists today in a global context. Money can go anywhere. And then the question is only why you would expect the money to flow back to the United States when our economy is moribund while other economies are growing rapidly.

One of the reasons that it's flowing out is that the channels for flowing in are blocked. Namely, we put all our efforts into resuscitating the big banks, which are more interested in credit default swaps (CDS) and gambling than they are in lending to small and medium-size businesses. You know, in terms of priorities, banks make a lot of money out of credit default swaps and a lot of money out of abusive credit card practices.

ss: JPMorgan Chase's unexpected multibillion-dollar recent loss, which was from a group that was meant to be hedging the bank's positions but instead was engaged in risk-taking through CDS and other instruments, is the perfect example of this.[9] Why lend when you can make so much money from positions in derivatives that are categorized as "hedging"(even though they're ultimately being used for speculation and risk-taking)?

js: Right. And SME (small and medium enterprise) lending is not very interesting. So you need to focus on the banks that actually have SME lending as part of their business model. And we didn't. This is one of the criticisms of the Obama administration: they paid too little attention to regional community banks that focus on SME lending. I told them that! Now they say, "We're worried about it," but that transmission channel is blocked.

There are also complementarities between fiscal policy and other domestic policies and monetary policy. Let me give you an example that goes back to the theme of sustainable development. If we had created a price for carbon, we would have created demand for retrofitting the economy, which would, in turn, have created a demand for investment all down the line from big companies through small companies. You have to get the banks back to lending. If we had created demand for investment and fixed the intermediaries (or the banking system), then monetary policy would have enabled us to supply the money and create the conditions in which the money would have been invested back into the United States.

ss: Another question, then, would be the impact of all this on inequality.

js: One of the concerns is that there may be negative effects on demand—as well as on equality—through two channels. The first is the wealth effect. Elderly people who are dependent on T-bills saw their interest income go down. What is interesting is that the Federal Reserve (the Fed) does talk about the wealth effect, but in a very peculiar way. They believe that lower interest rates will stimulate consumption because the stock market will go up. So they focus on the wealthy, whereas we know their marginal propensity to consume is very low. Furthermore these interventions by the Fed are described as temporary, but you have to ask why temporary interventions that might blip the price up a little bit temporarily would lead to spending now. This might be premised on a life-cycle effect for the rich. In a life-cycle model, if your paper wealth goes up, you consume more. But meanwhile the Fed doesn't talk about the consumption effect on the poor. Clearly they're doing a salesmanship job and not a serious job, although it'll be interesting to know the magnitude of these effects.

The second concern, where there is some controversy, is the effect of unleashing this money on commodity prices. An increase in commodity prices is equivalent to a real income decline for typical Americans because it means a redistribution from consumers in Europe and America to commodity producers. Again, since the marginal propensity to consume of consumers and producers is different, this results in a lowering of global demand.

There is another way in which Fed policy over the longer period of time has contributed to inequality. This is the single-minded focus on inflation, without taking into account historical patterns in a ratchet effect that decreases labor's share of income. When you have a recession, with downward pressure on wages (as we saw in 2001), which then start to recover, the Fed says, "Oh my God, there's going to be inflation! The cost of labor is going up!" So they start raising interest rates.

ss: There is one more element. With interest rates so low, the Fed is, in essence, giving away free money to the banks, which affects inequality.

js: Right. In the 2008–9 recovery, it was clearly just a case of giving money to the banks. And it's going on even now in the third tranche of quantitative easing (QE3). As I mentioned before, mortgage rates have not come down by very much. Lowering interest rates, without its being passed on to borrowers, is a gift to the banks. So it's been a consistent policy of the Fed, whether it's intentional or not, it has had that effect.

ss: And whether it's intentional or not, without restricting bonuses, the implications are . . .

js: That's right. "I'm going to give money to the banks so they lend more, but by the way, they can take that money and do anything with it that they want, even though it was supposed to be for capitalization" is a statement that just means "I'm giving money to the bankers."

ss: You said earlier that monetary policy exists today in a global context. More broadly, we ultimately need to think about national policies in a globalized world. I'd like to end with a discussion of how we should reconcile the nation-state with globalization.

js: What is clear is that as we become more interdependent there is greater need for collective action and rules of the game that ensure mutual gains. Interdependencies create externalities, and externalities create market failures that need to be dealt with by some kind of regulatory mechanism. The problem is that global governance defined as the ways we make rules and regulations is inadequate and undemocratic. There's a democratic deficit. The consequence of this is that often we have rules where we don't need to have them and don't have rules where we need them. Where we do have rules, they are there to the advantage of certain groups rather than others and are not so much efficiency-enhancing as they are redistributive. An example is intellectual property, where there is a broad consensus that it is a restraint on trade and that the American-style intellectual property regime was not good for the United States, let alone for developing countries. It was basically a special interest legislation favoring the pharmaceutical and entertainment industries, and not the set of rules that the real innovators or academics would have advocated. And yet they have now become part of our global regime of intellectual property. Financial sector liberalization is another example where it was a set of rules foisted by the financial industry and not by those who would ask, "What kinds of real capital flows will contribute to stable long-term investment?" Such policymakers would say, "Let's restrict some of these flows because they are destabilizing." But that's not what policymakers were focusing on. They were not focusing on standards to deal with externalities. They were focusing on sheer market power.

ss: Some experts opine that there is a need for uniform banking regulations across countries. I wonder if you agree with that.

JS: No. There seems to me to be no reason to have universal regulations. First, you have to begin with the obvious observation that different countries are in different positions. It's the same thing as intellectual property rights. The intellectual property regime that's optimal for one country is not optimal for another. One country is trying to catch up, while another is trying to maximize its rents. In the area of banking, the most important concern is the supply of funds to domestic SMEs. Capital markets might work for the large enterprises, but small firms are dependent on banking. Banking regulations are there to focus on how to get a financial system that provides credit to those who can't participate in the capital market. So what would be the appropriate set of regulations for a small economy might be very different from what is appropriate for the United States, or what is appropriate for a developing economy would be different from what is appropriate for a developed one. Countries should be able to regulate who enters and the terms on which other countries' banks can enter their country. This idea of uniformity is predicated on the view that we have adopted the European single-market principle and that any countries' banks could operate in any other country without further regulation. And if you adopt that principle, which even Europe now is beginning to understand was flawed, you have a problem because you can say, "Well, that bank is operating under different rules than my bank, and that foreign bank has an advantage over me because of this different set of rules." There is a certain truth in that, but it's a foolish position because the foreign banks may be at an advantage because of the fact that they are subsidized by their taxpayers when they go bankrupt. And that was why the UN Commission that I chaired came out with the view that every country ought to have a position that when entrants come in they should be organized as subsidiaries and not as branches and then be regulated like local banks. Who owns the local banks is not important, but we do care about how they behave.

SS: And a similar question is the issue of regularization of controls on capital flows. There is an argument that capital controls should be coordinated and that countries should do so because otherwise there could be beggar-thy-neighbor policies put into place.

JS: Let me say that the issue for small countries is different from that for big countries. If Barbados decides to do capital controls, it's not going to have a global effect.

SS: But what if Brazil does it?

JS: Right, if Brazil does it, it will have effects on some other countries. So potentially it has externalities. Even Brazil may not be big enough to have serious externalities. . . .

SS: Then let's say China.

JS: China does have externalities. So the first best solution would be a coordinated agreement on the kinds of controls—that doesn't mean the same controls, but at least a discussion and awareness of the spillover effects. Even this is hard to get. But there are externalities, and this goes back to the reason we have global agreements. There is a need for collective action for controlling externalities. So that, I think, is an intellectually coherent view. The problem is that many people in the financial community argue that you shouldn't have any controls until you reach a global agreement. And they have been using the inability to reach a global agreement as an excuse for doing nothing.

SS: Which is the same argument with uniform financial market regulations.

JS: Exactly. And that's a mistake. What I have said repeatedly is that the first priority of every country is protecting its citizens in terms of protecting its economy, and therefore one shouldn't wait until there is a global agreement. Go ahead and protect your economy, and then let's negotiate to get an improvement over that.

ss: You've written about capital account management in developing countries. (In fact we've written about it together in *Stability with Growth* and *Capital Market Liberalization and Development*).[10] But I'm wondering if you see any policy responses in developed countries, such as the United States, which are the source of the flows.

js: Right. I'm writing about this now in a new paper. QE2 and QE3 were a competitive devaluation, which has effects on other countries. Developing countries have had to respond to the increased liquidity by imposing capital controls and offsetting capital market interventions, some of which are costly. Developed countries didn't try to coordinate with the rest of the world on this. What I say in my paper is that it would be better if we coordinated monetary policy. Why is monetary policy any different from capital controls?

4

"If you make consistent, gradual changes, they can add up to something enormous"

Photo courtesy of Ha-Joon Chang.

HA-JOON CHANG

in conversation with Manuel F. Montes

Ha-Joon Chang is a development economics expert and one of the most influential anti-neoliberal economists of his generation. He teaches at the Faculty of Economics and the Centre of Development Studies at the University of Cambridge.

Always one to give frank opinions about all matters economic, Ha-Joon Chang offers a no-holds-barred assessment of the current state of economic practice and theory. The diagnosis: neither is in good shape. While the recession, contrary to popular belief, is over in many countries, the crisis is not. Chang argues that if any theory had failed as badly in practice as free market economics, it would have been discredited and even banned, and yet, even in the face of the crisis, this idea persists. Taking issue with the field of economics and the elites who benefit from free markets, he argues that change will be difficult but that it is necessary, especially in economic theory and in the real-world regulation of financial markets and practices. However, unlike those who call for a massive overhaul of the entire global economic system, Chang argues for a pragmatic, gradualist approach that need be neither sweeping nor global. Revolutions, he suggests with his typical candor, are neither guaranteed to happen nor to have the desired effects if they do happen; slow changes, on the other hand, though less appealing, may allow us to begin to build a more sustainable economic system for the future.

MM: What do you see as the current economic situation?

H-JC: Technically speaking, the 2008 global recession has ended, as the definition of a recession is a fall in output for two or more consecutive quarters. But, of course, no one thinks it has actually ended because many countries in the North haven't recovered their precrisis level of income. In many countries, unemployment is still very high, not to mention countries like Spain and Greece, where unemployment is over 20 percent. Even in the USA the official unemployment rate is 9 percent, but there are huge numbers of people who actually want to do full-time work but cannot find it and thus are engaged in part-time employment. Others have given up on finding employment. All these people are technically not unemployed, but they actually are. If you include them in the statistics, some observers claim U.S. unemployment could be 15 percent. And there are countries like the United Kingdom, which have gone back into recession. So, even though technically the United States and many other countries have started growing again, I don't think we're even halfway through the crisis.

MM: Do you think it's just a matter of ratcheting down to a lower level of economic activity in the rich countries? Or will there be pressure to try to recover to at least the previous levels?

H-JC: If we don't make serious changes to our policies, it will basically be like Japan in the 1990s (the "lost decade"). Technically you may not be in a permanent recession, but you grow a little bit and then go down again, and then some external event happens and everyone panics, then you might recover, but something might happen again, and so on. I think basically we are looking at a repeat of what happened in Japan in the 1990s.

MM: In the case of Japan, there was no rethinking of economic theory or economic policies. Do you think this current situation will allow some opening for rethinking policies?

H-JC: Well, you know, even in Japan there was some rethinking of policy in the sense that the Japanese never had been Keynesian, but throughout the 1990s and 2000s they increased government spending enormously, so they became a lot more Keynesian than before. They also started what today is called quantitative easing. The Japanese have been doing that since the late 1990s. So there were some policy changes, but you are right that in terms of economic thinking they were completely lost. The problem with the Japanese economics profession is that until the fall of the Soviet Union, their university faculties were completely dominated by these scholastic Marxists who had very little interest in the real world. So when those people lost their hegemony, you either had neoclassical economists or nothing. And when these neoclassical economists gained influence, the neoliberal (or free market) agenda was pushed by people like Junichiro Koizumi (prime minister of Japan from 2001 to 2006), who kept saying, "We need to make ourselves more and more like America. That's the way to recover." We all know what happened as a result.

MM: I would like to give you the opportunity to move this discussion to where you want to go. I wanted to start this discussion, but I don't want us to walk into a corner from which we can't get out. So the other question is: In the end, what do you think is the most important problem? But one thing I wanted to put on the table first is the question of what you think of economic thinking and economic policymaking. So we can start with the Japanese and move from there.

H-JC: Well, with Japan, as I said, there were some important policy changes, but in terms of economic thinking, I think they got even more confused than before. Now with the 2008 crisis, in the beginning there was the anticipation that this would change economics. Frankly, if any other theory had failed in the way that free market economics failed in 2008, that theory would probably have been banned. In the beginning, there was some *mea culpa* even from free market economists, like the conservative American judge Richard Posner, who admitted that even Keynes made a lot of sense.[1] So there was a bit of that, but I don't think economics is really changing. Unfortunately, there is an insufficient admission of flaws. For instance, I used the following example in the last chapter of my latest book, *23 Things They Don't Tell You about Capitalism*.[2] When the queen visited the London School of Economics, she asked, "How come nobody predicted this?," and the best answer the Royal Economic Society could come up with was "Oh, ma'am, each economist was doing his or her job quite well, but we failed in our collective imagination. We failed to see the forest for the trees." But come on, what imagination? Concepts like imagination have no place in free market economics, which justifies laissez-faire policies on the assumption that everyone is rational and therefore "knows what he or she is doing." So basically, they didn't have any decent argument to provide. And frankly, that allows a bit more of an opening for different ideas. Outside academia there is a great demand for different kinds of economics, although there is little change inside the economics profession itself.

MM: Where do you think things are going? On what will politicians be able to base their policies?

H-JC: That's the thing. I think there are two problems here. One is the fact that academia is the part of the world that changes the slowest. Politicians can be voted out, business leaders can lose their jobs, but university professors have tenure. You know, the famous German physicist Max Planck once said something to the effect that "science progresses one funeral at a time." Change in academic economics is like that too. And frankly, it's quite a difficult problem. This whole group of people who built their career and identity on a particular kind of economics, they are not going to give up that easily.

But the more important point is the underlying power structure. The people at the top with power and money, they benefit so much from this economic status quo and this idea that "everything is fine. Even if it doesn't look fine, it's actually fine because we are all rational and markets are efficient. So even if it looks chaotic and stupid, it really is the best of all possible worlds." They benefit so much from people believing in that kind of economics that they're not going to let things change that easily.

MM: This is a bleak picture.

H-JC: I think so, yes. But you know, you need to look at the long run. Two hundred years ago people thought that demanding the emancipation of slaves was crazy. A hundred years ago, a lot of "respectable" people thought women didn't deserve votes. Fifty or sixty years ago, those who demanded decolonization were hunted down as terrorists by the British and the French. But these "outrageous" demands have been met over time. So in the long run I remain an optimist, but in the short run it is quite bleak. On the other hand, over the past two centuries, what is right in economic theory has always been decided by power struggles. If enough citizens rise against free market economic theory that has failed them so comprehensively, the economics profession will have to change. Paradoxically, to help these citizens take the initiative, bankers have behaved so outrageously that now even normally patient Americans and Britons are beginning to rise up against these people. So who knows? I mean, who would have thought that Hosni Mubarak, president of Egypt since 1981 until toppled by the February Revolution of 2011, would end up in jail? If someone had predicted this two years earlier, a lot of people would have laughed. So I'm not saying that these changes are not going to happen, but I don't think they're going to happen in the way that some people imagined at the beginning of the crisis. It is not as if all of these guys who advocated free market policies on the basis of the so-called efficient market hypothesis that have completely failed us are suddenly going to be kicked out of their university jobs. No, it's not like that.

MM: If you were to think about where to change, keeping in mind that all these things are connected to each other, where would you start?

H-JC: I think the key is the financial sector. We have to regulate the financial sector. I don't mean doing more of the same regulation, but regulating in a completely different way. My friend Joe Stiglitz loves the directed credit program that was used in Japan and other East Asian countries up till the 1980s. Why can't we use this idea in order to address the current complaint that they are releasing all this liquidity through quantitative easing but banks are not lending to business? Well, let's make lending to business a condition of liquidity access. This sort of conditionality (and many more stringent and unreasonable conditions) has long been imposed on World Bank and IMF (International Monetary Fund) loans. Why do you refuse to impose conditionalities on loans to commercial and investment banks? Another thing we have to do is ban most of these complex financial products whose safety cannot be guaranteed. And we have to, in one way or another, separate investment banking from retail banking.

MM: In the general banking system in Germany, there is one regulator for one part of the sector, and another for the other part.

H-JC: Investment banking, when it was first started in Germany, was rather different from what it has become in the Anglo-Saxon countries today. In the beginning, the investment bank in Germany was like venture capital. So the investment banks lent some money to promising businesses and made a lot of money by selling their shares when the successful ones launched their initial public offering (IPO). That's why it's called *investment* banking. Now they rarely do that kind of thing. So it has worked in Germany. But, you know, the Germans also have different arrangements in other parts of the financial system. For example, hostile takeovers are virtually impossible. So in the Anglo-American countries you might also have to change the rule about hostile takeover, about who can actually buy what kinds of companies. One problem is that so many companies have been bought up by private equity funds, and these guys are not into long-term business; they basically want to restructure the firm, sell what they can, make it more profitable by squeezing the workers and the suppliers, and then, three or five years later, sell it to someone else. Perhaps some businesses can be easily restructured in that way, as in the retail sector, but if you're talking about industries that require long-term investment, maybe you need to put in rules regarding what private equity funds can or cannot do to acquire these companies. For instance, they might have to agree to keep the company for ten years.

MM: So that way they would only buy companies that will actually make money, not just ones that they can make money from, because they would be forced to make long-term investments.

H-JC: Right, exactly. Because without solving this problem, there will be no fundamental changes, as this short-term–oriented deregulated financial system is exactly what was (and is) wrong with the countries where this current financial crisis started—the United States, the United Kingdom, Iceland, Ireland. Basically you had a purely short-term–profit-driven financial system that discouraged investment, reduced worker morale, and reduced long-term productivity. So unless you fix that, we are going to keep having the same problem. And, on top of that, as the financiers were making money, they used it to lobby for more deregulation, which made it even easier for them to make money. They were basically winning a license to print money. If someone says you can borrow thirty or forty or fifty times your worth, that's a license to print money. They did that, and that gave them even more power, and that then led to their capture of the political system. Political leaders became dependent on their donations; they also control the media, so politicians have to be nice to them. In the United States they basically occupy the government. How many of the former secretaries of the Treasury, before the 1980s, were Wall Street men? But after the 1980s the majority of them were. So unless you break that hold, you're not going to change the political balance of power. So everything points toward financial regulation.

The good thing about this is that they have done so many things wrong and they keep doing bad things even after this mess, so I think there is, insofar as some politicians have guts, enough political capital to do some radical things. Actually, I was quite shocked to read an article written by an American banker in the *Guardian* newspaper, who said basically that these days bankers are whining about how cumbersome these new regulations are going to be, but when Franklin Roosevelt implemented the Glass-Steagall Act, which contained many things that were more radical than what is being proposed today (especially the legal separation of retail and investment banks), the banks were given one year to implement all the changes. Meanwhile today's banks are receiving kid glove treatment; for example, they were given nine years to meet the 2010–11 Basel III standards of capital adequacy, stress testing, and market liquidity risks.

MM: Do you think this can be done individually in each country?

H-JC: Why not? The typical argument is that "Oh, but we will lose our business to other countries that do not implement the same regulations." I say "Let them go." Look, there is no evidence at all that these banks have actually been benefiting the American or British economy, so if they want to go and ruin the Dutch economy or the German economy, let them go and try. That should be the national attitude everywhere. If every national policymaker were to take that attitude, the banks and their capital couldn't go anywhere. Even Switzerland is tightening hedge fund regulations, so much so that these guys are threatening to leave, but where would they go? Maybe they can go to Monaco, but where else?

MM: One way of thinking about the depression of the 1930s is that they followed their principles to the end and they let all the banks go bankrupt. Is that a piece of history that's holding people back from going after the banks?

H-JC: Yes, but that's the wrong approach. Just think about it. I think it's silly, unless you have lots of little banks like America did in the nineteenth century, to let banks go bankrupt because this creates a huge confidence problem. And, in a way, the only reason we are not in the kind of mess that we could have been is because the governments basically nationalized all these banks that were going to go bankrupt. But the way they did was so outrageous. I mean, the British government controls nearly 80 percent of the Royal Bank of Scotland, and yet it refuses to tell this bank to lend to small and medium enterprises (SMEs), while at the same time worrying that banks are not lending to SMEs. They are not even applying basic capitalist logic, which states that if you control more than half the shares of a company, you can do whatever you want. In the United States they were even more worried about offending the financial industry, so when they gave the bailout money, they took stocks but only in the form of so-called preferred stocks, which have priority in dividends but no voting rights. So they actually refused to take control! This is the extent to which the financial sector has captured the politicians.

MM: Our discussion so far has concerned the rich, developed countries. But much of your expertise is on developing countries. Where do the developing countries stand in this universe? Do they play along? Do they just manage to survive? Are they waiting for the revolution in the rich countries?

H-JC: I think the trouble is that developing countries have become so open in the past thirty years that they find it difficult to push things toward genuine reform. I mean, China may control the capital account, but in terms of international trade, for an economy of its size, it has huge trade dependence. The dependence of any continental-size economy—be it the EU or the United States or Japan—on international trade is basically between 10 and 15 percent of GDP. China's is around 35 percent. And most of these markets are in the North, so if things go wrong in the North, what is that going to do? Brazil, South Africa, Chile all suffer hugely from inflows of speculative capital, which puts enormous pressure on their exchange rates. Companies in those countries are going crazy because they cannot export because the exchange rates are just not viable. So I think it's not as if these countries are saying, "Those developed guys are in decline, so now we will rise and take over the world." Many of them are doing better than the rich countries, but they are also suffering and may suffer more in the future. Also, what we have to realize is that despite all the talk of the rise of the South, the South is still quite insignificant. The Chinese economy is not even 10 percent of the world economy. Countries in the North like to inflate that number by using purchasing power parity income figures because that makes developing country incomes look larger, which makes it easier for them to say China (or India, Brazil, or whatever country they want) is not a developing country anymore, and therefore that it should not expect any special treatment, and so on.[3]

IT's a devious game. But if you look at market exchange GDP, China's income is not even 10 percent of world income. India and Brazil are at two-point-something percent each. South Africa is at 0.5 percent. So put all these BRICS (Brazil, Russia, India, China, and South Africa) together and we're basically talking about 15 to 20 percent of the world economy. And if you think the 15 percent can take over the 70 percent, you are seriously mistaken. So while I don't want to sound too negative about the relative rise of developing countries like China and India, we have to put this into perspective. These countries definitely are becoming more important and they are beginning to flex their muscles. But there is a long way to go before we can say that these countries are truly influential—just think about what happened to the G20 when they needed money. They said, "This is going to be the new global governing body." But since 2010 nothing has happened.

MM: What do you think are the most interesting things going on in your field these days? What are the most interesting new developments in development theory, in economic theory?

H-JC: Unfortunately there are not that many interesting developments. Given the scale of the crisis of the economic system and the crisis of economic theory that backed it up, you would think people would be thinking about economics in a completely different way, but in theoretical terms there is very little that is new. It's the same old song again and again. Maybe there's a bit more acceptance of the fact that history and institutions matter, but even that is done in a very peculiar, neoclassical way, where even these things are ultimately seen as products of selfish rational choice. I think that there is one positive development, not at a deep theoretical level but at the applied policy level, which is much greater acceptance of industrial policy, which used to be a taboo subject in polite circles. I cannot remember how many invitations I've received to conferences on industrial policy in the past few years. This is mainly from the developing countries, but also from the OECD (Organization for Economic Cooperation and Development) and even some sections of the U.K. government. And even though there is still a huge amount of debate on exactly how you do it, whether you should target, whether you should use subsidies or tariffs or whatever, as well as about political conditions, such as conducting an industrial policy in very corrupt countries, at least now there is a debate, whereas five years ago most economists refused to talk about this. The revival of the debate on industrial policy, as far as I can see, is the only bright spot.

MM: Can industrial policy be introduced without changing political arrangements in countries?

H-JC: Well, you know, there is also a debate about that because even some pro–industrial policy people are skeptical about introducing industrial policy into countries without the right political conditions, but my view is that it depends on how much you want to do it. So if you suddenly want to do what South Korea did in the 1960s and 1970s, you might need radical change, but, for example, Ethiopia is now trying to capture some of the market for very labor-intensive manufacturing in sectors like garments, and for that you do not need major political rearrangements. You first have to start using some industrial policy and show that it may work before you expand it. Once you succeed in some areas, you gain more political support and it becomes easier to expand. I think it is wrong to say that we shouldn't even try because it's unlikely to succeed. You also have to start in a small way to build capacity. These policies, after all, require government officials who know how to do these things. I mean, yes, if you are in the Democratic Republic of Congo, probably thinking about industrial policy is a waste of time, but I think there are many countries where some small-scale support can be arranged without too much corruption and inefficiency and that those things can make a difference.

MM: I agree that we cannot predict where changes will start. What everybody reading this book will ask is how change will happen. And you have made the argument that we shouldn't accept certain arguments, right?

H-JC: Right. I'm talking about arguments like "If you want to regulate finance, you have to regulate it everywhere." I think that argument was basically invented by people who don't want changes. It is based on the premise that what is going on in the financial sector is universally good and you cannot afford to lose even one bit of it. But we are not arguing for closing all the banks or abolishing the stock market. We are proposing that we have to restrict certain types of unproductive or even counterproductive activities in the financial sector, and if those activities migrate somewhere else, that's actually good for you. So there are a lot of British people wringing their hands about losing business to Frankfurt or Paris. But your attitude should be: if the Germans want to take over toxic activities, let them do it. And, as I said, if every nation takes that attitude, these activities will die. We don't have to think about changes in a way that is—how can I put it—all-or-nothing. Very often people think that unless you completely change everything, nothing will happen. But it doesn't work like that.

With financial regulation, you might have a bigger goal, but you start with something more immediate and more realistic and then slowly expand. Like with industrial policy in developing countries, you cannot be overly ambitious, but you have to start somewhere. Through that, you build policy capabilities and credibility, build linkages with the private sector, all of which will allow you to take the next step, to do something more difficult and more ambitious. I think we need to avoid this all-or-nothing view of change. Even if everything needs changing, you cannot change everything all at the same time. This is why revolutions fail so frequently.

But on the other hand, you do not want to say that since you cannot change everything, you should do nothing. Because then you are walking into the trap of people who do not want change. I think basically we need to take a gradualist view of change. If you make consistent, gradual changes, they can add up to something enormous. That's how China changed. I'm not saying I'm completely positive about what's going on there, but the point is that you start with some little experiments and slowly build them up. It looks like a very bad way of reforming the socialist system, and people like Jeffrey Sachs say "No! You need a big bang!" The Swedish "transition" expert Anders Aslund says, "You need to do it now or it will never happen because conservative interests will regroup and thwart reform." But that way you end up with much inferior results. Continuous, small changes—admittedly, if you do it for one or two years, it will amount to nothing—done for thirty years can change quite a lot. I'm not saying that radical changes never work but that they are much more risky. Gradual changes are more powerful than one big change that may or may not come, and even if it comes, it may not work as you had planned.

5

"The new order is being born, but the old order is still strong"

Photo courtesy of José Antonio
Ocampo.

JOSÉ ANTONIO OCAMPO

in conversation with Vladimir Popov

José Antonio Ocampo is a former United
Nations undersecretary general for economic
and social affairs and former finance minister
of Colombia. He is professor and director of
the Economic and Political Development program in the School of International and Public
Affairs at Columbia University.

In a discussion that spans regions, economic systems, and modes
of analysis, José Antonio Ocampo analyzes a changing global economic order. In clear terms, but without resorting to simplification,
he outlines the primary challenges facing the global community in
the wake of the current crisis and makes a number of suggestions
for regulatory and systemic changes that might bring some degree
of stability and predictability to an out-of-control system without
taking the wind out of the sails of the market. Some of these, like
increased oversight of cross-border finance and an increased social
role for global institutions, may find many supporters; others, like
the call for the creation of a global, nonnational reserve currency, are
sure to provoke lively debate. Ocampo also tackles the question of
what effects continuing crises and changes have on different actors in

the world economy, with a focus on what it means to be a developing country in the modern economy. Rejecting one-size-fits-all models of development, he contextualizes the plight of industrializing countries and paints a picture of a complicated road ahead for the majority of the world's states as they chart an uncertain path toward a state of development which, as recent history has shown, is neither linear nor stable

VP: The first question is about global economic restructuring. Over the past sixty years, restructuring has been most remarkable. In 1950 the United States and Western Europe accounted for half of the world output, but today only for 35 percent because of the growth of Asia. So the question is: Do you think this poses a problem, and will the West accept this rise of the South, or at least the rise of East Asia?

JAO: I think there are economic and political implications of what has happened. In economic terms, the essential question is whether the world is really moving away from the center-periphery system. This is a system in which developing countries essentially export to industrial countries whatever is required by the North. In the past, these were commodities and raw materials. Now there is a large share of manufactured goods. The rise of East Asia (including China) as an important exporter to the developed countries is part of that system. And a large part of intraregional trade in East Asia is the production of parts and components of goods that are at the end assembled and sold to the developed countries. That trade is also part of the center-periphery system.

Whether there is something else going on and we're starting to see a truly South-South trade is a good question. Growing trade between China and India and intraregional trade in Latin America (which is limited) are some examples. I think this is important because developing countries are catching up with industrial countries (which has been spectacular in East Asia) but, in my view, there is not really yet a new global economic system.

THIS is even clearer in the case of finance, which is truly a center-periphery system in which world finance is still concentrated in a few financial centers located in the industrial world: New York, London, Zurich, and, much less so, Tokyo. Now you can say Hong Kong, but Hong Kong has become more the international financial center of China than a true global financial center. And then there is Singapore.

I think this is important because a true South-South system is starting to emerge, but the old center-periphery system is still dominant. In my view, therefore, South-South economic relations are still subordinate in trade and even more in finance or, for that matter, in technology, where the center-periphery system is even stronger. I feel this is important because unless the "global South" (to use that terminology) becomes truly autonomous from the center, its political autonomy is also going to be limited. I think this is even true of China. China knows that, although it's investing amazing resources to become a technology center, it is still a technology-dependent country. They don't have the technological autonomy or the capacity to be outside the system.

I actually sense that there has been much less change in this regard than is generally emphasized. Now, in political terms, of course there is a continuing debate about the need to have adequate representation of countries in economic decision making. That was the central issue of the 2002 UN Monterrey Conference on Financing for Development, where developed countries committed themselves to increasing the voice of developing countries in international economic decision making.[1] Again, there have been some steps in that direction, but this process is slow. Indeed the reforms of the IMF (International Monetary Fund) and the World Bank have still a long way to go. And there is the additional problem of the growing heterogeneity of the developing world. Paradoxically, in the old North-South negotiations, the South was less powerful but more influential because it was more united in the objective of reforming the global economic system.

VP: When was this?

JAO: I'm talking about the 1970s.

VP: At that time the Soviet Union was still there and, together with the South, was pushing to restructure the world economic order under the slogan of a New International Economic Order.

JAO: And as I have pointed out, there was a sense of unity in the South. I don't sense that today. So, despite lots of talk about the rise of the BRICS (Brazil, Russia, India, China, and South Africa), there is basically not the same sense of solidarity. Just think about the two major powers in the developing world: India and China. It's not that frequently that you see them taking the same position on international issues. The United States has one essential advantage as a world leader: it is capable of leading a stable "Western coalition," which includes Western Europe and Japan. We don't see yet something like that arising in the global South. This is just to make the point that while there are huge changes going on, the structure is very much the same. In a sense, the new order is being born, but the old order is still strong.

VP: So you are pretty skeptical about this issue?

JAO: I hoped we would be experiencing faster change. And what my analysis implies is that the leaders of the South have to become more self-conscious of the need to work together to change the current order. And in particular areas they do so, for instance, in the fight for voting power in the IMF and the World Bank. But in others they don't. Just take the selection of the World Bank president in 2012, in which I was a candidate, or the selection of the IMF managing director in 2011. In the former, developing countries jointly proposed two candidates, but many of them ended up supporting the American candidate.

VP: In the recent (May 2012) elections of the director general of the International Labor Organization, developing countries were also divided, right?

JAO: There was much more unity in the past. And, as you said, there was the Soviet Union, which was really an alternative bloc. There is nothing like that today. The global South lacks unity, and the Soviet Union failed in the end because it was technologically weak.

VP: Previously Japan, Korea, Taiwan, Singapore, and Hong Kong caught up with developed countries. In fact these five are the only examples in the history of developing countries that managed to join the rich countries' club. Are you skeptical that this trend is going to continue?

JAO: No, it might happen. I said catching up or convergence, as it is now called in the economic literature, may occur for several countries. And there is actually a fairly broad-based convergence in income levels that has been going on since the beginning of the twenty-first century. It could actually accelerate now also because of the contraction in the industrial world during the 2008–9 Great Recession and sluggish growth afterward. So there is a convergence of income, which is quite the opposite of the trends in the nineteenth and twentieth centuries. That may continue, but my point is that this doesn't necessarily change the system.

VP: Because of the weakness of the South and because the South is not united?

JAO: Many of the new powers of East Asia became part of the U.S. coalition, starting with Japan and Korea, and then Taiwan. You may say that others, like Singapore, are also part of it. So the success of these countries has not created an alternative system. Convergence in income may happen, and a general convergence is taking place, but that doesn't mean we have a new world economic system.

VP: The recent economic crisis is usually called the Great Recession, with the implication that it is similar to the Great Depression, although, of course, in quantitative terms it cannot be compared to it. In the Great

Depression, the reduction of output was something like 30 percent in the United States (annual GDP from 1929 to 1932) and it was also deep in some major European countries. Recently we saw an overall reduction of the output of industrial countries of 2 to 4 percent in 2009. So it's nothing like the Great Depression. But most economists consider this recession unique. Is it really unique? Does it mean this is a crisis of the system as we know it, or is it just another "cyclical recession," maybe deeper than previous recessions, but just a cyclical recession nevertheless?

JAO: First of all, this is the worst financial crisis of the era of financial globalization that started in the mid-1960s with the reconstruction of world finance around the euro-dollar market. In that sense, it is by far the biggest crisis. In terms of intensity, the two previous ones, the emerging economies' crisis that started in East Asia in 1997 and the Latin American crisis of the early 1980s, were much weaker as world crises as they were largely concentrated in emerging and developing countries. I think the major implication is that there will be a change in the trajectory of growth patterns, as crises usually generate huge structural changes. This will happen mainly in developed countries, because developing countries have not suffered as much this time. These industrial countries, and European countries in particular, may experience changes that go well beyond typical cyclical change.

Now, in relation to the link between this and the previous question, I think it is legitimate to ask whether this recession in fact is accelerating the movement away from the U.S.—or let's say North Atlantic—hegemony in the world economy. That's certainly what is going on. But the periphery is finding it increasingly hard to avoid the full effects of the recession and slow growth in the industrial world. And you can see that after the post-recession recovery (2010-11), during which the South seemed more autonomous, the weight of the slow-growth industrial world is having strong effects in developing countries. In fact the cycles of the developed and the developing world are quite impressively synchronized. So de-linking, the story that was emphasized a couple of years ago, is not happening yet.

VP: In 2009 the reduction of gross world product (GWP) totaled 3.4 percent—the deepest recession since 1944–45, when output fell in major countries that fought in the Second World War due to conversion of the defense industry. Actually, for sixty years after the Second World War we haven't had any recession deeper than this one. (Annual GWP fell only three times in this period: in 1974 by 0.4 percent, in 1975 by 0.8 percent, and in 1982 by 1.4 percent.) Why, then, was the recent recession the worst one?

JAO: I think what makes the recent recession special is the deep financial crisis of the center. The center has not had a financial crisis like this one since 1929. The United States has, of course, a good record of financial crises. In recent decades we had the Latin American debt crisis of 1982, which was also a U.S. banking crisis, but was excellently managed from the point of view of the United States, so much so that Latin America effectively paid for that U.S. banking crisis.

Then there was the 1987 savings and loan crisis in the United States, which had domestic effects, and then the information and communications technology, the so-called dot-com, crisis of 2001. So the United States and its financial sector have a good record of crises, but none of the previous crises was as deep as this one. Europe also has a good record of crises. The Scandinavian countries had banking crises in the early 1990s, and Spain also had a ruinous financial crisis in the late 1970s and early 1980s. So crises are not unusual. But in recent times there had never been a synchronized financial crisis happening at the same time in the two major financial centers of the world, New York and London, and on top of that in other Western European countries. I think that's what makes this crisis so deep and unique.

This is clearly associated with the overextension of credit and lack of regulation of finance. But there are aggravating factors. For example, the report of the Stiglitz Commission on global finance presented to the president of the UN General Assembly in 2009, Joe Stiglitz himself in a recent book, and the former chief economist of the IMF, Raghuram Rajan, share the view that some of the distributive problems that have been building up in the industrial economies have contributed to making this crisis worse.[2] In particular, stagnant incomes forced middle-income U.S. households to go into debt in order to maintain their standard of living in the midst of the rising costs of housing. The major point they make is that over-indebtedness of households is associated with the worsening of income distribution.

vp: Let us go to the international monetary and financial system. Most people probably would say it is out of order. After the collapse of the Bretton Woods system in 1971, neither nation-states nor the international financial system have the capacity to cope with the increased flow of capital over national borders. This leaves us with at least two questions. First, if nothing is done, then where do we end up? What would be the implications of leaving the international monetary and financial system as it is (in particular, capital flows pretty unregulated as they are now)? And the second question: What do you think should be done, and of course what are the chances that political economy would allow the necessary reforms to happen?

jao: I think there are three separate issues here. Or let me say there are two separate issues, but the first has two dimensions that are usually not put together. The first is the regulation of finance. In this regard, the crisis has generated a response in the form of more regulation of domestic finance. And some people even think it is desirable to shrink the size of the financial system in industrial countries. There are, however, still significant gaps in regulation. And there is an irony that, by saving the financial system, the rescue packages and bailouts recreated a powerful political voice that is now weakening the efforts toward financial regulation. But in general, I think, in Europe and in the United States there has been a strengthening of regulation and that it may be permanent. It probably will not be as strong as I and some other people would like it to be, but, in any case, it is going on.

The second issue, which as I said is a sub-issue of the former but is often not recognized as such, is the regulation of cross-border finance. One of the greatest ironies of the whole regulatory process is that this form of finance has been entirely left aside from regulatory efforts. In the dominant view, countries are supposed to strongly regulate domestic finance but to leave cross-border finance without any regulation, as if it was not finance. Even countries that are strongly in favor of financial regulation, like the United States, when it comes to cross-border finance are against any regulation. The situation in Europe is even more ironic, because they are strengthening their own regional regulation, but at the same time they have the least regulated system of cross-border finance in the world. This is despite the fact that part of the European problems was clearly generated by cross-border financial flows. Furthermore this has implications for Central and Eastern Europe: if they want to be part of the European system, they cannot regulate cross-border finance. The third issue is the international monetary system. We may want to return to that.

VP: You mean there should be regulation of cross-border finance between European countries, within the European Union, and the eurozone itself?

JAO: Yes, so long as they don't have a truly integrated financial market, there should be some regulation of cross-border finance within the eurozone.

VP: But the founding principle of the EU is to have the free movement of goods, services, capital, and labor. And if you have one currency, as in the United States, for instance, how can you regulate flows between states?

JAO: But if you look at the European crisis, a large part of the problem was market failures in financial markets: they made possible cross-border flows that in the long term led to unsustainable external debt ratios.

VP: Like Greece borrowing from German banks, which were willing to lend quite a bit?

JAO: Right. When the European Union was launched, the risk premiums of the European periphery came down to very close to the risk premium of Germany. And that generated a massive flow of resources to the periphery, which generated the typical problems we know in developing countries: current account deficits and accumulation of debts. There was a fiction that this was not a problem. Of course, you can regulate debt levels in other ways, but the eurozone has not evolved into an integrated financial area, and it is now going backward in terms of financial integration. If you don't have an integrated financial area, you cannot avoid regulating cross-border finance within Europe. Now this idea generates strong allergies in the European discussions. I even said to one of the members of the European Systemic Risk Board, "You have to think seriously about limiting at least some forms of cross-border finance. You may want to have high levels of financial liberalization within Europe, but you don't want another Iceland, where a small country was providing unsustainable levels of cross-border banking services to citizens of other countries." In order to have fully effective regional financial regulation, Europe may need to at least regulate what forms of cross-border finance are allowed within the eurozone.

TAKE also agreed Basel-III principles. One of them is the need for countercyclical macroprudential regulation, and there is agreement that it has to be implemented at the national level because boom-bust cycles are not the same in different countries, and indeed they were not in Europe. For example, there were boom-bust cycles in real estate in a few European countries but not in all countries. At the international level, macroprudential regulation may require some regulation of cross-border finance, However, the G20 efforts to re-regulate finance left entirely aside the issue of cross-border finance. So this question ended up being discussed in the IMF, with lots of debates still going on, with major countries being totally opposed to any regulation of cross-border capital flows.

VP: How about the international monetary system?

JAO: It is a good question whether the flaws of the international monetary system also contributed to the crisis. I think there is mixed evidence in that regard. The major problem is the role of the U.S. dollar. We created by default a fiduciary dollar standard in the early 1970s, that is, an international monetary system based on paper dollars. It has shown significant resilience but certainly contributed to the generation of the global payments imbalances. However, I'm not totally sure that the problems of the dollar system or global imbalances were really among the causes of the recent crisis.

IN any case, the international monetary system that we have is inconsistent with the current globalization process, and we thus have to move into a different system. There are, in particular, instabilities related to the fact that the system uses a national currency as the major international currency. To start with, the monetary policy of one country largely becomes the monetary policy of the world, but the decision-making process in that country does not necessarily take those global repercussions into account. Another problem is the long-term increase in the net debt of the United States, which is a bomb waiting to go off. One more problem: cyclical swings associated with the nature of this system. Every major adjustment of the dollar has entailed a world crisis. I mean all those recessions that you have in your graph.[3] There are also major swings in the real exchange rate of the dollar and the current account of the United States that have major global implications. But again, even if it's not the most appropriate system, it is unclear whether it was really one of the sources of the current global economic crisis.

VP: But do you expect that the future international monetary system will be based on national currencies? You are also envisaging a global currency?

JAO: There are two alternatives, which I think can be partly complementary. One is the evolution of the current arrangement into a multicurrency system. In fact we partly have a multicurrency system now because we have the dollar, the euro, and, to a lesser extent, other currencies like the British pound, the Swiss franc, and the yen, and now we are moving into a system where the Chinese yuan will be part of that "basket." However, I am one of those who consider that this multicurrency system may be even more unstable than the system that we currently have. The other alternative, which can be partially adopted, and I think may be forced by the circumstances, is to move into a true international currency. That is my own proposal, on which I have written extensively.[4]

VP: If it will not be politically feasible to move to greater use of a single international currency, do you think that countries could agree on adopting some limits on the level of reserves and exchange rate movements? Many economists and politicians argue that the current system, without a limit on the amount of reserves, is creating global imbalances. So in order to regulate these imbalances there should be some rules about how many reserves you can accumulate and to what extent you can underprice your currency (of which many are accusing China).

JAO: It's actually a good question whether China is actually manipulating its currency. My view is that it certainly did it in the past but does not necessarily do so now, as reflected in the massive adjustments in its trade balance. But, anyway, I think a system of multiple global reserve currencies is a system that needs rules about exchange rate movements of some sort. Of course, this cannot be going back to fixed exchange rates. I don't think that's feasible.

VP: Do you consider Europe to be an optimal currency area? And do you think that, with hindsight, maybe the introduction of the euro was premature, or was premature without the appropriate financial arrangements or without regulation of cross-border capital movement?

JAO: Let me tell you my reading of those European events. Europe in the past was much more interested in regional trade integration than in anything else. Thus the European project was basically about trade integration. Of course, that would never have happened without the strong political motivations generated by the Second World War. So, economic integration was also seen as a step to build up peace. Now, the movement toward deep economic integration implied, in their view, the need to restrict exchange rate movements. The reason is simple: if you are deeply integrated, exchange rate movements have a major impact on trade, which may erode the commitment to free trade. Because of that, after the Bretton Woods arrangement collapsed, in effect they built up a sort of new Bretton Woods among themselves to try to keep exchange movements relatively limited (the "snake" in which European currencies floated together vis-à-vis the dollar, then the European Monetary System, etc.). So they were obsessed with exchange rate stability. And I think they were correct.

I teach my students that, even if I disagree with the gold standard, the globalization of the late nineteenth and early twentieth centuries was at least consistent in the sense that if you want a more integrated international trading system, you may also want to limit exchange rate variations. Now we almost take for granted that we can have deep integration and flexible exchange rates. But this is probably an inconsistent system because you can have more effects on trade through exchange rate movements than through trade agreements. But let's leave the reflections on the global system aside. For the Europeans, deep integration of their markets was seen as inconsistent with flexible exchange rates. So for a long time their priority was to limit exchange rate movements among themselves, which included for decades controls on cross-border capital flows.

They agreed on the dismantling of capital controls in 1990. And what happened after they dismantled capital controls? Two years later they had the European monetary crisis. They then decided that the only way to have exchange rate stability is to have a monetary union, and so they speeded up the transition toward the euro area. I don't think the theory of optimal currency areas has anything to do with this. In a sense, by reinforcing trade, they may have created an optimum currency area, but that was never the motivation. The motivation was always deep trade integration and the corollary of limiting exchange rate movements. In the end, they thought that a monetary union was the only possible solution, given the elimination of capital controls as part of their trade integration efforts, in this case of financial services.

So, you may say (and this is in fact what I believe) that the mistake may have been the total elimination of cross-border capital account regulations. It was premature to launch a monetary union without many of the preconditions. Indeed one of the major problems of the European economy today is that there was never true financial unification, which is really remarkable. Most banks continue to be essentially national and are also the major holders of the debt of the specific country. These problems have worsened after the crisis, according to the European Central Bank. So, instead of deep integration of financial services, you have greater segmentation of finance. The elimination of that segmentation was very slow and has been reversed. Even regulation and deposit insurance continued to be national. You may say that monetary union would help create financial integration, but it didn't happen. A corollary of this is that the discussion about a banking union is much more important than the discussion about the fiscal union.

VP: So, by capital controls—by controlling the funds that move between countries—you basically mean rules that would not allow, for example, either Greek banks or the Greek government to borrow either internationally or nationally (which doesn't matter since they borrow in euros) more than they can afford?

JAO: Right.

VP: The next question is about the world economic order and governance. You were recently one of the candidates for the post of the president of the World Bank. The question is: How can the World Bank be reformed, and what are the shortcomings of the system of world governance that we have?

JAO: We don't have world government. We have a system of world governance, but quite a weak one. Since the system is based on intergovernmental decisions, you explicitly deny the existence of a global government. National governments continue to be the basic building block. In the case of Europe, it's a more complicated story, because they have given some powers to the European Commission and to the European Parliament. You could say that they are in a transition to a regional government, but there are many policy areas that remain national or even local. Reinforcing the European government through a fiscal union and a banking union is what they are discussing now.

I have argued for some time, with many others, that the basic problem of the current globalization process is an asymmetry between the integration of markets and the lack of political integration. As for your question about what to do, it goes certainly beyond the World Bank. What I have written, again with many others, is that we need to create a system of intergovernmental decisions at a high level to coordinate the global economy.[5] This power cannot be given to one institution, such as the World Bank or the IMF, because they would only cover one part—a small part— of the system. That's why the 2009 Stiglitz Commission convened by the president of the UN General Assembly, to which I belonged, proposed the creation of a Global Economic Coordination Council.[6] This would be a UN body (it has to be a UN body, because the UN is at the helm of the system) in which the IMF and World Bank would participate as specialized agents of the UN system, and the World Trade Organization would be brought formally into this system. That body would have the capacity to coordinate these specialized agencies of the system. Similar proposals have been made in the past to create what has been called an Economic Security Council or a Sustainable Development Council. This is, therefore, the reincarnation of an old idea, and I think a feasible one.

VP: In this council every country would have one vote?

JAO: No. We extensively discussed this issue. You cannot have a relevant world economic council based on a one country–one vote system. You have to have a weighted vote of some sort because otherwise the council would be irrelevant.

VP: And then you'd need a qualified majority for some major decisions?

JAO: Yes, or even better, double majorities.

VP: And what reforms for the World Bank do you envisage?

JAO: The IMF is probably the institution that has been most reformed in recent years. But there is much more that can be done, particularly again as part of the efforts to reform the international monetary system. In the case of the World Bank, during my campaign, I proposed that it has to deal with three issues. The first is its historical mandate, which is fighting poverty in the world and, more broadly, helping the convergence in living standards around the world. The second issue is participation in the provision of global public goods. In this area, the major task of the Bank has to be helping to restructure the energy systems, basically because most of the expansion in energy consumption will take place in developing countries, and this is an area that requires lots of financing, as opposed to other global public goods, where the finance issue is not the central one. And the third is to serve as a forum for the long-term restructuring of the global economy. There is no institution that conducts a dialogue between developed and developing countries. You can say that the IMF deals with global imbalances, which are the short-term dimension, but the long-term dimension is the restructuring of global manufacturing, its relation to global trade, the rise in the trade of services, and how to benefit from the linkages that all of those processes generate. So the World Bank should serve as a forum for discussion and perhaps for the generation of some norms for how global economic restructuring takes place.

VP: Let us talk about development models and development theories. You were saying that every developing country today faces this or the other problems, growth constraints, and there is no magic recipe for growth. And you have talked more than once about the growth diagnostics, saying that growth requires twenty-five preconditions and the role of the development economist is to figure out which particular ingredient is missing.[7] The question is: What is the most promising model today? The East Asian model is being praised, of course, but also there are dire forecasts. Paul Krugman predicted long ago that East Asian growth is going to end pretty much as Soviet growth ended at one point because it is all about overaccumulation of capital, and marginal capital productivity tends to decline. So the question is about the appropriate models of economic growth, catch-up development, and the new ideas in development economics.

JAO: Let me say that there are some common elements of successful development, but the first lesson that we have learned from experience is that one size does not fit all. That, in a sense, is the overriding principle. Let me start with that statement, because I don't think that the stories of success in developing countries have been necessarily the same. They have different trajectories. One thing that is common, however, is technological upgrading. What you cannot do is a process of development that does not include technological upgrading. How you do it is, of course, complex and it does not necessarily follow the same path everywhere. For example, people who have discussed industrial policy have always come to the conclusion that industrial policy is done differently in different places. There is no universal model.

VP: Something works in one place, but when you try to apply it in a different place, it doesn't work.

JAO: This is actually the same reflection as that of Dani Rodrik on institutions. As he puts it, the function may be the same, but how you exercise those functions in different institutional contexts is different. This is so for two essential reasons. The first one, which is the one that Rodrik and historical institutionalism has emphasized, is that countries are locked into their own histories. There is a path dependency, so what you have done in the past will affect your future. Countries have different paths, and they will have different futures. The second is an old reflection of Latin American structuralism (sometimes called dependency theory), which was presented as the difference between development and under-development at the time. The essential idea is that the world economy is a hierarchical system, in which the developed countries are at the center, or perhaps for this story, at the top. The trajectory of the developing coun-tries would be necessarily different from that of the developed countries, as they need to rise within a hierarchy that has many mechanisms to keep them in their subordinate place. This is the same as with income distribution within countries: the trajectory of a person who is born in a poor household is necessarily different from that of a person born in a rich household. We don't live in an equal opportunity word, neither at the national nor at the international level. So Walt Rostow's view that there are uniform "stages of economic growth" is essentially wrong.

VP: Marx's schema was very similar to Rostow's in this sense.

JAO: Yes, Marx's schema was basically the same. But what the depen-dency theory school said was that development and underdevelopment are actually different manifestations of one unique system. So, in this view, and going back to the center-periphery model, underdevelopment (the term used at the time), which is the characteristic of the periphery, is as much the product of the development of the world economy as the high income levels of the center. In other words, the evolution of the world economy creates inequalities. And for that reason, it is not the same to develop at different times because the periphery is trapped in the inequalities that characterize the global economy at a given point in time, and you have to solve the problem of how to move up within the international hierarchy. The task will be tougher the lower you are in the hierarchy or the later you try to rise.

THE problem of the industrialization of Japan was different from that process in Korea, which in turn is different from China, which will be different from the late-late-late industrializers in Africa, say, Kenya. It is very different to industrialize when you have one or two leaders in the world than when you have many more leaders that have preceded you in the industrialization process. That was the basic reflection of Latin American structuralism. Development depends at any point in time on where in the structure you are located. There are no uniform stages of growth.

VP: Maybe I can ask you a few questions about Latin America, as this is one of the major areas of your expertise. Why, over the past thirty years, has Latin America not been as economically successful as East Asia?

JAO: There is a huge discussion on that issue. Going back to my statement that what is common in success in development is the accumulation of technological capacities, let me analyze what Latin America achieved during the different phases in its development process. In our book with Luis Bértola on Latin American economic history, we talk about four stages.[8] The first is state building after independence in a nonglobalized world economy. Then you had the first globalization around 1870–1929, which was the stage of export-led growth. It was followed by a period of state-led industrialization, and then you have the era of market reforms (usually called neoliberalism, but again I hesitate to use this term because it is more complex than that).

NOW, in terms of building technological capacities, there is no question that the most successful stage in the development of Latin America was state-led industrialization. That's when Latin America really built capacities, in technological terms and in the diversification of production structures, as well as in terms of state building, infrastructure development, and social services. And it was also the most successful in terms of economic growth, with a few exceptions. And moving away from this model actually led to slower growth. In contrast to that, if you look at East Asia, they still in effect have state-led industrialization, though certainly an export-oriented one. It is export-oriented state-led industrialization, which has kept at the center of the strategy the need to develop production and technological capacities. That's what is now missing in Latin America. Another way I have expressed this point is by framing it in terms of static efficiency versus dynamic efficiency, if we understand the latter as the process of production diversification and the accumulation of technological capacities. State-led industrialization may have been bad in terms of static efficiency, but it was very good for dynamic efficiency. The current model has the opposite features.

VP: Let's move to the broader question of income inequality, a question that really puzzles me. There was some progress in Latin American countries recently in the reduction of income inequality. Brazil and its Bolsa Familia program is very much praised. To reduce income inequality without confiscation, without redistribution of property, is the sort of trick that not many countries manage to pull off. What is the magic touch?

JAO: Let me say it's still a very weak magic touch. Because what you have in several Latin American countries is a worsening of income inequality in the 1980s and 1990s that was reversed in the 2000s. But the average level of inequality today is not all that different from 1980. It's not yet a long-term improvement but a reversal of an adverse trend, and Latin America continues to have, with sub-Saharan Africa, the worst income distribution in the world. There is also a continuing discussion about the reasons for the recent improvement. The consensus seems to be that the major reason has been the reduction of skill premiums among wage earners. The worsening of inequality was caused by an increase in skill premiums as people with university education tended to earn increasingly more relative to the unskilled. And now there was a reversal of that process.

VP: And why was that?

JAO: My interpretation is that it was a result of three things. The first was the improvement in the levels of education. This is the area where policy has been most important, and not necessarily short-term but rather long-term policy. The second was a demographic transition, as the labor force ceased to grow as fast as it once did. Together with rising education levels, this means that the supply of unskilled labor actually started to shrink in several countries. An increase in the skilled labor force together with a reduction of unskilled labor implied that Latin America, broadly speaking, ceased to be a region of abundant low-skilled labor. The third factor is good economic growth since 2004 in several countries. You can add more specific policies: the effect (generally modest) of conditional cash transfers, that have spread through Latin America, and the effect of minimum wages or stronger bargaining power of labor in some countries (Argentina, Brazil, and Uruguay, for example).

VP: The last question is about the environment and global warming. If developing countries are going to have the same energy consumption as developed countries (which is today on average about six times greater than in developing countries), total emissions will increase dramatically. So today, more and more often, developing countries are telling developed countries, "You have polluted the whole globe while you developed and are now trying to tell us not to use the same means to develop as you did." Nonetheless the mainstream view is that developing countries should contribute to the reduction of global emissions. Is this a fair demand to make of them?

JAO: This situation is even more complicated than that, because global warming is caused by accumulating greenhouse gas emissions. So the argument is correct. But the major issue is that this problem cannot be solved today without the developing countries. It is unfair, but developing countries have to be on board. And to allow developing countries to enjoy rising energy consumption, the world needs a veritable technological revolution. In other words, the world needs a system that will allow developing countries to grow without generating the same environmental mess that the developed countries generated. A subordinate problem is raised by the climate justice movement, which basically argues that this is not a problem of developing countries versus developed countries, but it is a problem of rich versus poor. According to a country's level of development, emission reduction should target certain social groups rather than countries. I think they have a point.

RECOGNIZE EVERYONE IS RESPONSIBLE FOR THE ENVIRONMENT

6

"This is not Planet Earth; it's Planet Ocean"

PAUL WATSON

in conversation with Jan Dutkiewicz

Paul Watson founded and is president of the Sea Shepherd Conservation Society, a direct action group devoted to marine conservation. The group is the subject of a reality television show, *Whale Wars*.

Photo by Mike Muller.

Veteran environmental activist Paul Watson offers a provocative, counterintuitive, and iconoclastic view of the state of an environment in crisis. Basing his analysis on a long-term conception of ecological history as well as recent examples of environmental crises, his central premise is that the environmental movement is not about saving the planet itself but saving the planet as it is for future human generations. From this perspective, the planet will survive environmental degradation and eventually evolve new life, but it is the human race that may not adapt fast enough. This view clashes with our dominant approaches to protecting the environment and offers up new priorities: we should focus on protecting oceans rather than land, prevent biodiversity depletion rather than talk about climate change, and battle individual inaction rather than institutional intransigence. Bucking the trend of most mainstream environmental approaches, Watson dismisses the notion of sustainability as being unfeasible on an overpopulated planet and criticizes corporate "green-washing" of consumerism. He does not, however, single out modern capitalism as the sole cause of ecological destruction. Instead he suggests that humanity has lost touch with its ties to nature and that, regardless of the political or economic system, it constitutes a threat to the planet. He calls for a biocentric approach to nature whereby humanity views itself as part of its ecosystem. This candid interview is a sobering suggestion that the environmental crisis is, in the long run, more of a threat than the economic crisis.

JD: To think about the state of the environment today is, for most people, to think about a litany of well-known recent disasters: Fukushima, the Gulf of Mexico oil spill, the Canadian tar sands, but also continuing deforestation, species extinction, pollution of waterways. The list seems to go on, and it seems to be grim. How would you describe the current state of the environment? And is there space for hope within that picture?

PW: I think that the most pressing concern right now is the diminution of biodiversity, especially in our oceans. We're literally eating our oceans alive. I'm talking here about overfishing, pollution, acidification, the destruction of coral reefs. These are extremely serious things happening. And I don't think people really grasp just how intimate our relationship is with the oceans. Not only do they provide 8 percent of our oxygen, but they regulate weather, have an effect on the climate, and have a considerable effect on our lives. If the oceans die, we die. But I think that for the most part they are out of sight and out of mind. They are just not linked to any sense of reality we have as humans, and there really is no awareness about how serious the situation is.

JD: Is that simply due to the fact that humans live on land? Does that explain the difference in the efforts made at conservation of terrestrial biotic environments and the relative neglect of the oceans?

PW: I think that we have to understand that this is not Planet Earth; it's Planet Ocean. And therefore the oceans are more important in many ways than the land. We can absorb a lot of damage on land, but the oceans can absorb only so much before they begin to collapse, which is already happening. The Polynesians used to be able to get by quite well with their ecosystem because of the system they had based on the notion of taboo. An area would be declared taboo, which meant that it was off-limits to exploitation, like fishing, for a number of years to let the area regenerate. This was serious business. If you got caught fishing in such an area, you could face the death penalty. And that meant that they never really wiped out their fisheries or drastically altered their environment. But there is no taboo in the world today. I think the Mediterranean, for instance, should be taboo for the next fifty years to let it try to regenerate. But that's not how we operate. Fisheries and companies that produce fish-finders work on the premise that fish can run, but they can't hide.

That's the problem. They can't hide. And we're overfishing everything. Every single fishery in the world is depleted and facing collapse. Most of this damage has been done since 1950. The problem is something I call *the economics of extinction*. It works like this: When people go to the supermarket they think, "Well, there's plenty of fish here, so there must be plenty of fish in the ocean." But what they're not seeing is that it takes more and more sophisticated technology to extract fewer and fewer fish. And that technology costs more and more money every year, which means that the fisheries industry needs to take out considerable loans from banks in order to buy the technology to catch these fish, which means they are in debt, which means they need to try to catch ever more fish to pay off the loans. It's a vicious circle. Then you have a situation where the industry is directly investing in extinction, which is the case with the bluefin tuna. Now this is a fish that costs about $75,000 per fish, and some can be sold for as much as $300,000. With that kind of price on its head, people are going to hunt for it, even if stocks have been reduced to only about 5 percent of what we think were its original numbers. They don't really care if they go extinct because the tuna can be frozen and stuck in warehouses, and as the numbers go down in the oceans, the value in the warehouses goes up. So if the fish becomes extinct, and the only bluefin left are frozen in warehouses, you're looking at million-dollar fish. The only concern here is profit. The industry is not concerned about the long-term survival of the species.

And that's the problem in general. Our entire economic and political system looks at things in terms of very short time periods. To be an environmentalist or conservationist, you have to be able to look ahead and ask, "What is the impact of all of this on the next hundred years, the next thousand, the next million?" But we don't look ahead that far.

JD: You're linking extinction to market processes. But in the past you have also, unlike a lot of people working in the field of political ecology, de-linked your critique of extinction from a strict critique of capitalism. You have critiqued all kinds of economic systems and political systems throughout history as being detrimental to the environment. Can you speak about this relationship you see between the environment and humanity beyond modern market capitalist society?

PW: In many ways, I don't see any difference between communism, socialism, or capitalism when it comes to the economics of how we engage with the environment. It's all exploitation. And whether you're exploiting in the name of socialism or the name of capitalism, it doesn't make any difference to the earth. There are no politics when it comes to conservation. I mean, I get accused of being a right-winger as much as I get accused of being a left-winger. I'm not either of those. In fact you don't get much more conservative than conservationists. That is the meaning of the term. The people who are destroying the planet are the radicals. For instance, the "conservative" Republican Party in the United States, to me, has a very radical political philosophy.

The problem really gets down to this: there are three basic laws of ecology, and no species can survive on the planet without abiding by those laws. The first is the law of diversity: that the strength of an ecosystem is dependent upon diversity within it. The second is the law of interdependence: that species are dependent on each other. The third is the law of finite resources: that there is a limit to growth, a limit to carrying capacity. As our numbers grow, from three billion to four billion, to seven billion, and so on, we are stealing the carrying capacity of other species. So they have to be removed from the planet in order to accommodate our increasing numbers. Now that comes into conflict with the law of interdependence, because we're now removing species that are essential for our long-term survival. As the famous conservationist John Muir once said, "When we try to pick out anything by itself, we find it hitched to everything else in the Universe." When you remove one species, it causes this domino effect right down the line.

Now the other problem is that as we cause these problems, we, as a species, look around for scapegoats. We ask who is responsible. And it's never us. In Canada, for example, when the cod were disappearing, they blamed the seals. So they got a seal hunt, but the point was to find a scapegoat because the government could not explain to the public and to fishermen that the Department of Fisheries and the fishing lobby had caused the cod fishery to collapse through greed. Scientists and activists had been warning them since the early 1980s that this was going to happen, but they claimed they had the best science, the most reliable population models, so there was no way a collapse could happen. That is, until 1992, when it happened, and then they blamed the seals. But from a conservationist point of view—or maybe biocentric is more correct—if you want more fish, you want more seals. The biggest predators of cod, other than humans, are mackerel, herring, and other fish that feed upon the baby cod: the very same species that are targeted by seals. Normally seals don't go for cod, but when you reduce seal populations, you increase populations of fish that prey on cod. I always look to history as a guide on this. In the sixteenth century, when Jacques Cartier first came to the New World, there was no shortage of fish. You could throw a wicker basket into the Gulf of Saint Lawrence and pull it out full of fish. And at the time there were 45 million seals, so obviously seals were not responsible for eating all the fish. There is only one reason for the collapse of the cod: overfishing caused by human greed.

JD: You've written previously that humans tend to think of themselves as being outside the ecosystem and that we need to think of ourselves as living within the ecosystem. How can such a change in mind-set be achieved, and how would it change our approach toward nonhuman nature?

PW: For most of our history, humans have been biocentric, meaning that we look upon ourselves as a part of the ecosystem. Only in the past ten thousand years have we become anthropocentric, meaning we see reality as revolving around us independent of nature. So we've become alienated from natural processes. This ties in, of course, with the development of agriculture. We became dependent on our own creations. This ongoing process and way of thinking just is not sustainable in the long run. Nature is resilient, but not that resilient. And it's about numbers, really. But of course that's something that nobody wants to talk about. But the planet is just not capable of supporting seven billion people. And as numbers increase, you see much more of a burden being placed on the ecosystem overall. Indigenous cultures in many places still retain at least some sort of biocentric outlook. One of the reasons Sea Shepherd flies the flag of the Five Nations on our ships is that they understand this. Traditionally the Iroquois, for instance, believed that major decisions should not be made unless the consequences of that decision on future generations were taken into account.

The other problem we have is the incredible talent of humans to adapt to diminishment. We forget how things were and we accept how things are. Now that was probably a pretty good survival trait when you were in a hunter-gatherer or early nomadic society, but now it's very dangerous. I'll give you a simple example. Back in 1965 the very idea that one day we'd be buying water in plastic bottles and paying as much for that water as for the equivalent amount of gasoline, and then throwing out that plastic into landfills, would have been completely ridiculous. We've been sold into paying for things we don't need to pay for. Let me give you another example: You go a fish market these days and you'll see fish like the turbot. This is a fish that twenty years ago we threw away. It was even referred to as a "trash fish." But now we've adapted because we don't have the cod and these other species. So we're replacing depleted species with new ones, and consumers forget about the old ones. We just move on. And that kind of arrogance and adaptation without paying attention to what's disappearing or what we've destroyed will certainly be our undoing.

JD: On that note: everyone is saying that we're living in a time of crisis. But most of this dialogue revolves around social upheaval, economic policy (or lack thereof), and so on. Much of the dialogue, explicitly or implicitly, says that the environment can wait, has to wait. You take the opposite stance. Why is it especially important to speak about ecology and environmental protection in a time of crisis?

PW: The only real crisis is an ecological crisis. Consider how many extinctions we are facing, the permanent destruction of coral reefs, and much more. The economic crisis, first and foremost, is not real. These crises are fabricated. If we had allowed the economic system, such as it is, to evolve naturally, if you will, we would have had a depression; the money we're dealing with doesn't exist. There is no "wealth." It's all just a myth. Real wealth to me cannot be measured in economic terms. To me, a living tree has more value than a tree you cut down to turn into paper because it contributes more to our well-being in the long run because it provides oxygen, provides habitat for other species, and so on. The Kayapo people of the Amazon have a word for our civilization. They call us the Termite People because we eat everything up. We are constantly gobbling up resources without any really intelligent understanding of what we're doing.

JD: You've infamously likened humanity to a virus, leading some people to label you a misanthrope.

PW: Oh, I am a misanthrope! There's no argument about that. I don't mind being called a misanthrope because I think it's a realistic thing to be. We are a virus that attacks the immune system of the planet, eroding its ability to sustain itself. But people of course don't want to hear all these things. I have also been criticized for saying worms are more important than people, which people thought was very outrageous. But it's true. Worms can live on the earth without people, but people cannot live on the earth without worms. Any species that is essential for our survival has to be more important than we are. And after all, bacteria rule everything, they make our lives possible. In fact we're not individuals but symbionts. Each and every person is a collection—a community—of trillions of bacteria, which again brings us back to the law of interdependence. These bacteria manufacture vitamins in the body, help us digest our food, even groom our eyelashes. But for the most part people don't know that, people don't care, people don't want to hear about it, people are repulsed by the idea. Personally I find it fascinating that we are so inextricably connected with all these other species.

JD: That very idea challenges the notion that we are atomized, autonomous units.

PW: Exactly. We could not live independently of other species. The best way to explain it is how I explain it to kids when I speak at schools. The earth is a spaceship. It's doing exactly what a spaceship does: traveling around the galaxy at five hundred miles a second, and like any spaceship it has a life-support system. And our life-support system is the biosphere. And that life-support system is maintained by the ship's crew. We humans are not crew. We're passengers. We're having a great time amusing ourselves, but meanwhile the crew is running the ship. And what are we doing? We're killing the crew. And there are only so many crew members you can get rid of before the life-support system starts to crumble and the ship becomes inoperable. Those crew members are the bacteria, the worms, the insects, the fish, the trees, the plants. To kill off the crew members that run Spaceship Earth just does not make any sense at all.

JD: Let's move on from the problems to the potential solutions. You are known for advocating a diversity of tactics in environmental activism, meaning everything from letter writing to legal and educational campaigns through bearing witness and direct action. People seem to focus almost exclusively on the latter. They equate your name, Sea Shepherd, and your work in your days with Greenpeace with direct action. This is also where most criticism of you and your work comes from. Can you speak about the various tactics you advocate and the use of direct action?

PW: I have always felt that the strength of any movement lies in diversity in the same way that the strength of any ecosystem lies in diversity. The diversity of strategies and tactics within the environmental movement is extremely important. I was a director of the Sierra Club for three years, for instance, which has a completely different approach to the other initiatives in which I have been involved. I support education, litigation, legislation, all of these things, which contribute to the same end. What I don't support are megalithic ecocorporations. These big organizations basically suck the energy out of people through money and effort and really do nothing but perpetuate themselves. And they really don't do anything because they're afraid they'll offend their supporters or sponsors or something like that. The strength of the environmental movement lies in individuals: the passion and commitment of individuals and small groups of individuals and small organizations. I don't want to see five or six mega-organizations. I want to see a million different ones addressing a million different issues with a million different ideas.

I am not a pessimist because I believe that the answer to impossible problems lies in ideas that might seem impossible. We just have to imagine the impossible being possible. I mean, think beyond the environment. Let's say in 1972, the very idea that Nelson Mandela would be president of South Africa was unimaginable, unthinkable, impossible. But it happened. And I think the same type of things can happen with environmental activism. And I have faith that, among young people especially, people will come up with new ideas. It's a combination of three things that are needed: courage, passion, and imagination. And that's what I try to encourage among my crew members in Sea Shepherd. I look for passion in crew members. When people say, "Oh, your crew are inexperienced, your crew are not competent, your crew are this and that," I tell them I don't want professionals. I want passionate individuals. It's like Ernest Shackleton, when he went to the South Pole. He was criticized for not having a professional crew, and he responded that he wanted passionate men who would get him where he wanted to go. I couldn't do what I do out on the high seas without those volunteers. You don't buy that kind of passion. You don't buy that kind of courage. They constantly amaze me.

And there's a growing base to draw upon because more and more people are seeing that you can accomplish things this way. One of the things I do in Sea Shepherd is constantly encourage people to use their own initiative and use their own direction. For instance, back in 1979 I had a nineteen-year-old crew member named Alex Pacheco, who asked, "What are we going to do about the way they treat chimpanzees in laboratories?" I said, "Well, Alex, this is the Sea Shepherd Conservation Society, and we're not going into laboratories. But why don't you do something about it?" So he went back to Maryland and exposed what was going on in laboratory testing on chimpanzees. He then went on to found People for the Ethical Treatment of Animals (PETA). It was one nineteen-year-old guy. It was his idea. He carried it forward, and that just shows you the power of the individual. That's the main thing I try to encourage. Each and every one of us has the ability to change the world.

JD: What do you see when you look at environmental policy globally, in terms of both shortcomings and progress?

PW: Well, the only positive things I see are being done by people and small organizations worldwide. Whether it's women planting trees in

Kenya or Chico Mendes and what he did (until his recent death) in Brazil in fighting deforestation, or people like Jane Goodall raising awareness about other species or Steve Irwin and his approach to educating children. It's all really individuals. Take David Wingate, a biologist in Bermuda. If it wasn't for him, the Bermuda petrel (*cahow*) would be extinct now. That one man saved that one species. So if you had one million people saving a million species, then you could see how things could actually get accomplished. Again, that's what I try to encourage. If people come on my ship and say "You know, I'm really interested in this one particular thing," I tell them, "Go out and pursue it." Then they say, "But doing it seems awfully difficult." To which I reply, "If it was easy, everyone would be doing it." Look, you have to just go out there and do it. The only causes worth actually fighting for are lost causes, really.

JD: So as far as policymakers and governments, what can they do? What should they do?

PW: First of all, I don't expect anything from governments. The whole nature of government is such that they cause problems. They don't solve problems. I have yet to see any real progress come out of government-led initiatives. I'll give you an example. In 1972 I attended the United Nations Conference on the Environment in Stockholm. The number one issue on the agenda at that conference was out-of-control human population growth. We listened to our world leaders tell us that we had to do something, we had to stand up, we had to make a difference, this was all-important. Twenty years later I attended the UN Conference on the Environment in Rio de Janeiro and population wasn't on the agenda. It just disappeared because it was too controversial. And meanwhile the very people who were telling us in 1972 that we had to take a stand were now calling those who wanted to talk about population growth "radicals." Why? Because we listened to them in Stockholm. I think one of the things with me is that I've never really changed, while many of my colleagues from back in the day have gone on to become part of the system.

JD: You've quoted David Forman in writing that "we need to rewild the planet" and follow a tradition in conservation thinking that advocates the creation of human-free wild space. But in modern scholarship there is also a broad contingent that casts doubt on the notion of wildness and of "nature" untouched by humans. William Cronon famously has written, "We mistake ourselves when we suppose that wilderness can be dissociated from our culture's problematic relationships with the nonhuman world." Cronon and others call the notion that we have of wilderness "a cultural myth." They call for humanity making a home in nature rather than nonhuman nature being rewilded.

PW: What does he mean by that?

JD: I suppose he means that humans have historically been an integral part of various ecosystems and that we cannot think of a historically human-free nature in our imaginary of what it might mean to rewild.

PW: A few hundred thousand humans might have been a part of nature (which is not to say they were not destructive), but seven billion people certainly are not part of a healthy ecosystem. I don't think what he's suggesting is possible with these numbers. But I've long advocated—and I get criticized for this—that we should not have communities over twenty thousand people. We should not have big cities. We should live simpler lives. And I think this will happen anyway as we run out of resources. I think once we pass peak oil and peak minerals, we won't have the resources required to carry on with the current overkill. But we do have to adapt to nature. Nature is not going to adapt to us. At least not in a way that lets us keep living the way we've been living.

JD: That's a grim prediction. Let's shift back to speaking about the environmental movement. There are now a lot more people aware of the problems that humans are causing. You can speak to many people about notions like biodiversity, the need for marine protected areas, the importance of top predators in ecosystems. But simultaneously there seems to be this move toward greening of business as usual and green-washing of marketing messages. How do you view both this greater social awareness about environmental issues and the potential that it may lead to mission creep or subversion?

PW: Well certainly, there are massive attempts to co-opt environmental concerns through green-washing. But look, there is no such thing as "sustainable." The term *sustainability* in the sense of *sustainable development* was coined by the Brundtland Commission of the United Nations in 1987, but to me it really means business as usual under another name. There is no such thing as "sustainable fisheries" or "sustainable agriculture." In the end, industrial processes are going to be destructive, and, again, it all links back into numbers. There are too many people, too many consumers. So the main question facing environmentalism concerns getting these numbers down. But as soon as you bring this up today, you're dismissed as a radical, a misanthrope, a Nazi, or whatever else. But that's a very easy way of dismissing the argument. Look, I'm not advocating death camps. That's absurd. I'm talking about establishing voluntary programs to lower the population growth rate. You know, when I was on the board of the Sierra Club and we tried to push it to return to its original stance on immigration, population growth, and other issues, we were treated as if we'd just pulled out *Mein Kampf* or something. All of a sudden we were called anti-Mexican, because that was the political context. I got a call from the *Oakland Tribune* and they asked, "What do you have against Mexicans?" I told the guy, "Did I ever mention anything about Mexicans? I have nothing against Mexicans. I don't give a damn if 100 percent of the population of California happened to be Mexican. Let's just talk about policies and education to ensure we have fewer people." But they didn't seem to get that message. Talking about population always gets into the politics of race, totalitarianism, but that's not what it's about.

JD: Do you see this reaction within the environmental movement itself?

PW: Yes. And it's due to fear. People are afraid of being labeled this or that, or being seen as being politically incorrect. For instance, when we first got involved in trying to end the whale hunt by the Makah Nation on the West Coast, nobody wanted to touch that. That was "racism." But it's not. It would be racism if we didn't touch it just because of the color of the hunters' skin. We'd be saying it's not okay for us, but for you over there, who are different and backward, it's okay. But again, people hate that argument. No other environmental group would touch it. Now you even have environmental groups who support indigenous hunting of endangered species, even when it's done with modern methods or for profit—such as, for instance, the annual slaughter of pilot whales in the Faroe Islands—because it's part of "culture" or "tradition." This is non-sense because it doesn't make the killing go away or make species any less endangered. But these groups get bogged down in public opinion. And especially with the biggest organization, they're afraid that they're going to lose donations. For example, with our organization, and with many other smaller organizations, if someone calls and says "Look, I am opposed to what you're doing and I'm withdrawing my donations," I will reply, "Thank you, sir, but you chose to join and support us. We did not join you or your program. So we're not going to conform to you or your agenda. We will take your input on board, but if you don't like what we do, please take your money to another cause you do support." We're not here to give people what they want or tell people what they want to hear or do things just because people want to see them done. We act in the interests of our clients, and our clients are not people.

JD: Speaking of addressing a wider audience, your own group has recently gone more mainstream with a reality TV show called *Whale Wars* and numerous celebrity endorsements. Do you feel that being seen in the mainstream media and in a sense joining the system is necessary for the environmental movement?

PW: We're only part of the mainstream in the media because we live in a media culture. It's a way to get your message across. But for us it doesn't affect what we do in the field. Marshall McLuhan famously said that the media define our reality, and we need to adhere to the rules that exist and that the media makes up. There are ways to get your message across to a wider audience. We need to sell our message, if you will. But that hasn't affected our view on biocentrism; it hasn't affected our tactics on the ocean. I've been doing this for thirty-five years, and strategies change. If we start doing things that are ineffective or that lead to people getting hurt, we're not going to last long.

JD: "What is the future of environmentalism?" is a question that is often tossed around. Is that a question that can even be asked? Can the environmental movement be encapsulated by one label and therefore one future? And, if it can, then what is the future of environmentalism?

PW: The future of environmentalism is that as long as there is an environment, there is going to be an environmental movement. In the broadest sense, environmentalism is how we live in our environment and how we try to protect it. I don't believe for a moment that we can destroy the planet. The planet is not going to be killed by human beings. But we can and do cause so much damage to other species and we are in the midst of a major event that has since been dubbed the Anthropocene or Holocene extinction. We know, from the five previous extinction events, that it takes the planet about 10 to 20 million years to recover from each one. If you're Planet Earth, what's a few million years? The planet will eventually recover from anything we can throw at it. So really, what anyone's talking about when they talk about environmentalism or conservation—whether they know it or not—is the survival of our own species. If we want to be here and continue to be here, we have to learn to live within the laws of ecology. It's really about our own survival. So when people ask me "What are you doing for people?," I tell them, "I'm protecting the oceans" or "I'm protecting the forests." In the long run, those are far more important than organ-donor programs or trying to cure cancer. Because these major issues ultimately affect us all.

EVERYONE, regardless of where they stand politically or socially or culturally, all have an equal stake in having clean air, clean water, biodiversity. But even here environmentalism runs into problems. A lot of the major organizations, for instance, are really focusing on global warming. I'm not saying it's not a major problem, but there is no solution to it, really, nor do we really understand it. So a lot of organizations are making a lot of money from it, scaring the hell out of everybody, but I wonder if they're really accomplishing anything. The only way we'll deal with global warming is if we all stop driving cars, flying in airplanes, producing consumer goods, but that's not going to happen. So rather than fruitlessly trying to solve a problem that's too big to actually solve, we should be focusing on protecting biodiversity and wild spaces to minimize the impact of global warming on nonhumans and allow nature to try to stabilize the climate, or at least minimize its impact on us. Look, nature is going to adapt. The planet will adapt one way or another. Humans may well adapt, but that does not mean we'll be able to carry on with business as usual.

7

"We need to become a planet of gardeners . . . to make our cities function as integral parts of nature"

Photo courtesy of Mike Davis.

MIKE DAVIS

in conversation with Joe Day

Mike Davis is a distinguished professor in the Department of Creative Writing at the University of California, Riverside, and an editor of the *New Left Review*. He received a MacArthur Fellowship Award in 1998.

A stalwart of the American left, Mike Davis is not known for pulling punches, and he does not hold back in a wide-ranging discussion that covers population growth, urban decay, the end of U.S. hegemony, and the need for utopian thinking. In connecting the proverbial dots between many of the existential problems facing the world, he argues that they create synergies among themselves. Throughout, Davis's contention is that many of the ideas, models, and even technologies needed to address our various crises already exist but have often been forgotten, marginalized, or co-opted in the interests of profit and power. Davis suggests that the world's population problem, for instance, is not about population numbers in and of themselves but rather about the spatial, political, and economic constraints placed on people and the means of feeding and employing them. An expert on cities and urban spaces, Davis discusses issues as diverse as transnational migrant communities, the failures and opportunities of city renewal, and the (often racial) dynamics of crisis and American suburbia. Finally, he turns his attention to the role of the United States in the world and paints a picture of an aging empire, one increasingly illiberal domestically and decreasingly influential globally, and clinging to global dominance more due to the inertia of globalization than to sound policymaking. This interview aims to call the reader to think of and work toward a better tomorrow.

JD: How would you rank the major threats facing humanity at present?

MD: Threats obviously cannot be weighed in isolation; rather we must focus on their convergence. The future, to say the least, will be overdetermined by some very vicious circles. Let me start with probable synergies between population growth, climate change, and food security, then briefly explore their connection to cities and unemployment.

Our children, it is almost certain, will participate in the biological climacteric of our species, sometime between 2060 and 2090, when global population peaks around 10 billion. To feed this future humanity, food production must almost double. But for the first time in history it is doubtful whether global arable area can be significantly increased in the face of rampant urbanization and conversion of high-quality agricultural land. The technological and scientific intensification of agriculture, meanwhile, must contend with chaotic changes in crop geography and soil productivity as a result both of global warming and groundwater depletion.

Climate models consistently predict that a vast belt of the northern subtropics from Mexico to the Indus Valley will face epic drought as a new weather normal, while the great megadelta regions of Asia simultaneously fight life-and-death battles against rising sea levels and supercyclones. In addition, the continued mining of groundwater in South and East Asia (made possible by the millions of tube wells drilled since the 1960s) portends agricultural decline or even collapse in some of the most productive irrigated food belts. In several recent white papers,

Columbia University water researchers have pointed to the cases of the Punjab and Gujarat, where the abandonment of farmland due to groundwater depletion is already happening on an alarming scale.

Present-day water storage, irrigation, and flood-control infrastructures are therefore unlikely to sustain current levels of agriculture output to midcentury, much less support a dramatic expansion of production. Hydrological chaos and desertification, moreover, will require that people or water (or both) be moved hundreds, even thousands of miles. It's difficult to imagine how these transfers can be accomplished without catastrophe as long as national frontiers and rivalries prevent the planning of water resources and population resettlement on semicontinental scales.

JD: Are there factors that might stem this tide?

MD: Some pundits, of course, will argue that such bleak predictions underestimate the revolution in plant genomics (the creation of super-drought-resistant crop varieties, for instance) as well as allied advances in precision irrigation. But the successful application of the new sciences presupposes an unprecedented global agricultural adjustment program, prioritizing grains over meat and carried out in the interests of smallholders and farm laborers as well as the urban poor. Otherwise a genomic revolution in the countryside implemented by Big Ag and oriented to the production of animal proteins or biofuel will simply lead to the displacement of hundreds of millions of rural people, who will be dumped into cities and their squalid fringes without any guarantee of subsistence. An example close at hand has been the exodus of rural people from northern Mexico to the U.S. Southwest over the past fifteen years. The longest modern drought has interacted with NAFTA policies (especially the import of "industrial" corn from the United States) and neoliberal water policies to destroy an entire class of subsistence farmers and small ranchers.

Meanwhile the machinery of urban job creation has broken down almost everywhere except for East Asia. Currently an estimated 40 percent of the global labor force is unemployed or scratches for survival in the so-called informal sector. In a deep structural sense they have become redundant to a world economy controlled by one thousand or so colossal corporations and banks. The earth's three billion inhabitants under the age of twenty-five face especially grim employment futures. And the banks, as many of us now know firsthand, manage the creation and destruction of wealth with one goal in mind: to allow the 1 percent to consume all the good things of the world in this lifetime. Too much of the economic surplus desperately needed for agricultural moderniza-tion and urban sanitation has been siphoned off into insane, Versailles-like fantasies. Kilometer-high skyscrapers may tower above deserts, but a majority of humanity still lives in shacks and dreams about potable water and a minimum wage.

Indeed, as we stand on the precipice of a synchronized global reces-sion that may yet dwarf the 1930s, can anyone—including the good ole boys in Chicago—convincingly argue that capitalism (in whatever flavor, including red) will actually guarantee food security, adapt our habitat to a more extreme environment, and provide meaningful voca-tions to 10 billion people?

The last item, jobs, is the most important, since the solutions to all the other global threats and negative synergies—climate change, species extinction, food shortages, possible rollback of the antibi-otic revolution, nuclear proliferation—depend directly or indirectly upon exploiting the windfall wealth of peak human population. What the grim theologians of Malthusian persuasion dread as three bil-lion more mouths might be better celebrated as three billion more minds coming to our rescue. The "threat of threats" is leaving that human potential undeveloped rather than mobilized in a vast public works program to repair our damaged civilization. No environmen-tal demand should be raised without making some quotient of youth employment part of the proposed remedy. It is clear that we need to become a planet of gardeners, in Patrick Geddes's sense of constant communal tinkering to make our cities function as integral parts of nature. But we need to build this new Ark quickly. And since rob-ber barons aren't likely to put the future to work or transform peak demography into a planet-saving productive force, we need alternative carpentry skills. That's why I'm still a socialist.

JD: How much do our problems hinge on the growth of populations, consumption, and waste?

MD: Two simple distinctions are critically important. First, the demographic challenge is not population growth per se but its geographical distribution and age skew. Second, a "rich" standard of living does not necessarily entail unsustainable resource consumption. Let me deal with population and consumption one at a time.

As for population, already committed demographic change, according to the UN's latest *Population Prospects*, will produce a strange Goldilocks world by midcentury. Europe (only Iceland has high fertility), Korea, and Japan will have too many old, dependent people relative to their active workforces; indeed in a number of cases, above all in Russia, absolute populations will shrink far below twentieth-century levels. China, our usual stereotype of an infinite labor supply, is the surprise arrival in this geriatric category, but thanks to its single-child policy that encourages the abortion of daughters, it is a low-fertility country that will experience a rapid rise of the dependency ratio to European levels after 2020. Indeed, from a peak population in 2025, the Chinese population could fall by an incredible 450 million during the rest of the century. On the other hand, Africa will have too many young people relative to even the most optimistic model of accelerated development and employment growth. Right now fertility decline in Africa has been paused by poverty and lack of social security. Nigeria is a fantastic case, with a projected 2100 population of 730 million, equivalent to all of Europe's today. But even "planet Nigeria," if it should come to pass, won't be a problem of too many Nigerians but just of where they're located. Africa's youth bulge is the obvious solution to Europe's senility and another reason why "human citizenship" (protected but flagless rights to work, migrate, and vote) must become the central democratic demand of this century.

WHEN it comes to consumption, the widespread belief that the Kardashian family (drawn from an American reality television program) is single-handedly destroying the planet is untrue. On the other hand, it is obvious that several Earths would be required to support all of their neighbors and would-be imitators. Too many environmentalists, in my opinion, embrace the argument that begins by identifying a decent standard of living with American levels of household consumption, posits (correctly) that the renewable resource base doesn't exist to provide 10 billion people with so much stuff, then deduces that economic equality at a high level would require the death of wild nature. Ergo, growth must stop; poor people should stay poor or (preferably) die. The selfishness of this neo-Malthusian syllogism should be apparent, but its real mistake is the assertion that there is a linear relationship between the size of the environmental footprint and quality of life. It's rather like equating obesity with happiness and health.

JD: As in the nineteenth century, when one aspired to be "prosperous," both in land and in girth?

MD: I personally believe that the only possible way to save the environment is to make everyone rich, to make everyone wealthy through their equal citizenship in public affluence. The genius of the city—as both utopian project and unending experiment—is the substitution of public space and communal consumption for private wealth. Household space need only be a decent minimum if community centers, campuses, Internet nodes, and public recreation are free and accessible.

Conversely, the disaster of the suburb is to replace the environmental economies of plazas, parks, and public baths with the leaden footprint of auto ownership, lawns, and privatized consumption. Gentrified cities, for their part, celebrate public space but only after the removal of unsightly and "dangerous" popular strata. The working classes of New York, Paris, and San Francisco, for example, have been exiled to peripheries devoid of the traditional cultural apparatus of urban life; the historical cores, meanwhile, have barricaded themselves with high admission fees and tolls that deter nonaffluent families from visiting museums on the weekend or taking in an occasional play. The same perverse principle reigns everywhere: those who have the greatest need of public culture and open space usually have the least access.

But the city (the source of 80 percent of our total carbon footprint according to UN-Habitat), paradoxically, is the only possible solution to its own environmental problem—at least to the extent that we are willing to share and enjoy wealth in common. That's why I like the New Urbanist slogan of "re-urbanizing the city." Indeed Peter Calthorpe and William Fulton and their colleagues have reintroduced some classical planning ideas about pedestrian scale, mixed-income housing, and in situ waste and water treatment.[1] These are invaluable guidelines, and the movement's critics should be careful that they don't throw out the baby when they recycle the bathwater.

But the New Urbanism at best promises "smart sprawl," not a planet-saving revolution in urban life that embraces public affluence to mitigate the damage caused by private wealth. To find more radical templates we must go back to that astonishing era, roughly from William Morris and Patrick Geddes to the Bauhaus and Vkhutemas (the Russian state art and technical school established in 1920), when the radical modernist imagination was passionately engaged in experiments to create alternative urban commonwealths. Those of us in wealthier cities or campus communities are surrounded by bits and pieces of these dreams: bungalows and garden housing, district heating and solar power, great libraries and parks, "neighborhood unit" planning, case-study houses, and so on. We have to imagine how they might be reintegrated into their original holistic visions as democratic habitats now centered on low-carbon social consumption. In any event, only utopias are now realistic.

JD: Future demographic problems aside, isn't China's warp-speed modernization one version of utopia? Hundreds of millions of people have been lifted out of extreme poverty, while China's demand for raw materials simultaneously stimulates prosperity in the rest of Asia, even Latin America and Africa. I suspect that your eco-Marxist pessimism may underestimate the dynamism of globalization. In any event, what do you think will happen in China and the other BRICS (Brazil, Russia, India, China, and South Africa) in the next period? Are they the alternative future, as many pundits and futurists claim?

MD: As usual, let me begin obliquely. The Ukrainian economist Mikhail Tugan-Baranovsky scandalized the small world of Marxist economics with his thesis that capitalist business crises were not inevitable, as Marx maintained, but could be avoided to the extent that profit was recycled in capital goods. Make steel to build railroads to transport steel to shipyards to build dreadnaughts, and when the economy begins to slow down, produce more steel and build more railroads and dreadnaughts. Keep repeating. In a Tugan-Baranovsky world, in other words, consumption—whether wage or luxury goods—was a by-product, not the ultimate goal, of industrialization. This was a perverse challenge to the conventional idea that investment booms could drive economies only in spurts before markets had to face the test of households' ability and willingness to consume (Keynes's "effective demand"). His model was viewed as an impossible limit case in the curiosity cabinet of economic theory.

Thanks to Deng Xiaoping and his successors, Tugan-Baranovsky has been hugely vindicated in modern state-capitalist China. He undoubtedly deserves a generously monumental statue, ideally in one of the half-empty shopping malls or unsold luxury estates that symbolize the wild building boom unleashed by President Hu Jintao's 2008–9 stimulus plan. As every economic historian will acknowledge, no large, dynamic peacetime economy in world history has ever devoted such a large percentage of its GDP to investment or such a small proportion to household consumption. Indeed China and the USA have become mirror opposites: we consume more than 70 percent of our national income and invest only 15 percent; in China, by contrast, the share of fixed investment has risen to 46 percent of GDP, while private consumption has fallen to a bare 34 percent. Building construction alone constitutes one-seventh of China's GDP—triple the corresponding share in the U.S. economy at the height of the real estate bubble in 2005–7.

The boom has not necessarily been a boon for ordinary Chinese. If the Beijing Olympics advertised the government's ability to create instant world-signature skylines, it also demonstrated a chilling authoritarian will to displace overnight hundreds of thousands of residents, destroying their traditional alley neighborhoods (*hutong*) and celebrated courtyard housing (*siheyuan*). Even the ghost of Robert Moses, the master builder of New York's bridges and highways, would find it difficult to comprehend the speed or scale of urban renewal in China or the ruthlessness with which municipalities (in China, usually a regional unit) finance themselves by confiscating and developing peasants' land.

Understandably, much of the world doesn't want to know about the human casualties of China's ascent or the fragility of its real estate bubble as long as the Chinese continue to buy their iron ore, aluminum, oil, and machine tools. Although most of us still think of China first and above all in terms of its global export offensive, its imports are what have kept countries like Brazil, Australia, and the ASEAN (Association of Southeast Asian Nations) bloc—as well as Russia, Saudi Arabia, and even Germany—in the growth lane for the past four years despite the U.S. and now eurozone débâcles.

JD: So, in critical respects, both the rise of the BRICS as well as the pre-2008 surge of many advanced economies were largely side effects of China's audacious but ill-planned growth?

MD: Until recently this BRICS-led boom within the bust was celebrated with futurist hyperbole and declarations of belief in perpetual economic motion. But the Chinese leadership has often been stunningly frank in acknowledging the explosive inequality, poor planning, financial sleights of hand, official corruption, and overinvestment that have produced this miracle growth. Now the voices of the Bloomberg and Murdoch press, as well as the *Economist*, are singing a dirge in unison.

THE business pundits and financial prophets ask the same questions: How would China deal with a universal slowdown, especially a protracted crisis that augured secular de-globalization? Is a second mega-stimulus from Beijing possible, and would it immunize Asia and the BRICS from the euro pox? And, most important, what would happen to globalization without a Chinese deus ex machina? China's capacity to build a Great Wall against the economic chaos in the West is doubtful and, even if theoretically possible, would require the incoming fourth-generation leadership to tackle quickly unresolved structural contradictions as well as the immediate challenge of stimulating without inflating the economy. Three structural issues strike me as both urgent and intractable.

First, rational public investment in China is undermined by the quasi-independent political machines that govern the major metropolitan areas and have been responsible for tremendously wasteful investment on prestige and field-of-dreams projects. In crucial respects, the Chinese state is far less centralized than, say, Russia and gives even more scope to corrupt deals between state-owned banks and provincial elites. The extraordinary Bo Xilai scandal in Chongqing in 2012, in which his wife was allegedly involved in the murder of a British businessman, Neil Heywood, leading to the populist's dismissal as Communist Party leader and removal from the Politburo, may be as much about the need to rein in these local warlords as any threat posed by neo-Maoism.

Second, China's ability to act as a global superpower is constrained by its continuing dependence on U.S. markets and thus the renminbi's peripheral status as a reserve currency. Here's where we should be especially cautious about declaring the onset of a third cold war. Beijing, for sure, has taken advantage of Washington's irrational distractions in the Middle East to build its own dynamic spheres of influence in Africa and South America to secure supply chains and markets. This has been widely interpreted as China's drive to become the new hegemon, even at the risk of a new cold war and possible military confrontations with the United States and its Asian allies. Although such speculations find other, minor confirmations, such as Barack Obama's provocative dispatch of Marines to Australia, it is hard to believe that they constitute much more than political theater. In truth the economic relationship between the two powers is already a decisive deterrent. Beijing and Washington remain joined at the hip by the dollar in the financial equivalent of MAD (mutually assured destruction).

This is one of the oddest relationships in history: the USA overconsumes, China overproduces; the USA grows a huge trade deficit, but then China lends back the debt to allow Americans to continue their unbalanced spree, while both countries strike bellicose poses toward one another. Some still worry about the doomsday when China sells of all its U.S. Treasury bonds, but the euro crisis has only strengthened the case for the dollar as the ultimate safe haven while the renminbi remains in diapers. The dollar thus remains the principal shackle on China's desire for recognized global equality with the USA.

But it is a third structural challenge that is the most decisive: whether the new leadership has the will and capacity to reduce radical socioeconomic inequality by raising wages and providing what this "communist" country so sorely lacks: universal social security and decent public education. Economic justice, indeed, is a more explosive issue in China than in other countries.

If globalization has abetted the transformation of so many former industrial powers into service-sector economies, it has conversely catalyzed in China the emergence of an ultra-urban-industrial society with at least 200 million manufacturing workers, miners, and construction laborers. This is the biggest and most "classical" proletariat in world history, and assumedly the Politburo in Beijing remembers enough of Marx to know that it rules over angry pages from *Das Kapital*. As a direct corollary, democracy is not just a "liberal" issue in China; it automatically raises the question of independent trade unions and the rights of migrant workers.

JD: The United States is a deeply compromised actor on the world stage, but the Obama administration has made inroads in terms of improving our profile overseas. Pew polls show U.S. favorability ratings up 12 to 58 percent across Asia since 2008, for example. In spite of coercive tactics and elective targeting of foreigners and Americans as terrorists (and perhaps, in some quarters, because of those ethical derogations), the United States remains the central arbiter of world affairs, even as that centrality diminishes. How can we better direct our remaining legitimacy and reach to address some of your concerns above?

MD: In this context *we* is not a pronoun that I've used since I burned my draft card in 1965. Moreover, like most people on earth, I want the United States to close its bases and bring its legions home. Obama may remain rock-star popular, but the signature of his foreign policy has been drones, not development aid. But how long can such imperial overreach continue? The uber-debate that burns through the pages of every foreign affairs and international relations journal is the future of American power in what clearly looks like the Chinese or East Asian century. It is a debate often framed by the concept of *hegemony*. Although it began its career in an obscure corner of Marxist theory, the hypothesis that world economic order depends upon a hegemon is now thoroughly domesticated in foreign policy and international relations discourse.

The idea is simple and seductive: since the seventeenth century an open world market has required a liberal power willing to provide such crucial "externalities" as an ample supply of reliable money, a powerful navy to keep sea lanes clear of piracy, strong demand for diverse imports, a financial surplus for overseas investments, and an encompassing ideology of free trade. In the absence of a committed hegemon, international capitalism relapses into neomercantilism and wars for the control of strategic resources.

The Netherlands, so the story goes, was the first modern nation-state to provide these public goods—albeit in a quasi-mercantilist mode—to trading communities across the entire world ocean. After the unification of England and Scotland in 1707, the British displaced the Dutch and eventually automated global balances of payment with the gold standard—the real ruler of the world in the long nineteenth century.

Then, of course, Britain was bankrupted by the First World War, and the United States, which had loaned billions of dollars to the Allies to purchase American munitions and war materials, became Europe's creditor and Britain's reluctant successor. Ideology in this case lagged somewhat behind economic reality, but by 1945, with old-fashioned American isolationism and pacifism suddenly as extinct as temperance, we began our long revel in a fusion of economic, military, and cultural supremacy unseen since imperial Rome.

JD: How do these dynamics carry over into the new millennium?

MD: The old American Century has now ended amid seemingly epochal but at times enigmatic shifts in the foundations of international power. The hegemony paradigm sensu stricto provides a short menu of possible scenarios. The first is to anoint China as the rising hegemon that will gradually wrest or inherit the chief military and economic responsibilities of world superpower from the USA. The deepening of the Chinese home market as well as the opening of its financial system are often proposed as prerequisites for this job description. From a second standpoint, the Pacific circuits of the global economy are seen as inherently unstable as long as Americans overconsume and East Asians overproduce. Europe alone has the solid economic and technocratic foundations for sustaining globalization in the difficult decades of the early twentieth century. Third, there is the Obama vision of remodernized American world leadership based on "smart power," green tech, and a semiglobal NAFTA. The conditions for such a renaissance include a vast program of infrastructure and education investment, renewal of the manufacturing sector, and, implicitly, the de-linking of U.S. policy in the Middle East from right-wing agendas in Tel Aviv.

For the reasons that I discussed earlier, none of these alternative futures seems very plausible: China is not a big enough engine to pull the world economy; German neomercantilism is destroying the fiction of European community; and Washington has the lowest IQ since the 1920s. Thanks to German and American conservatives, the Keynesian

card has been removed from the deck of policy options. A true apoca-
lyptician might proclaim the eventual return of a Mad Max world like
the 1930s, when the international economy fractured into regional monetary and trading blocs. Indeed, as I discovered a few years ago when I
declined an invitation to be part of a brainstorming session at the Naval
War College (they read my book on slums), some Pentagon strategists
are now seriously contemplating the scenario of de-globalization.

It is not yet around the corner. I think a more realistic extrapolation
of current economic turbulence, given the eurozone's implosion and
China's ominous real estate bubble, would be another decade of mold-
ering U.S. hegemony over a fundamentally stagnant world economy.
You might call this the "posthegemonic" scenario since it preserves
but hollows out the dominating roles of the dollar and the Pentagon.
The dollar, for instance, has shown that it has no real competitor as
a storage unit of pillaged wealth, yet it increasingly has little relationship with actual U.S. economic performance. Similarly U.S. supremacy
in advanced weapons technology and conventional war-making power
may be close to its historical zenith, but that preponderance is little
deterrence to car bombers or computer hackers.

Washington's powers of internal repression and surveillance likewise
increase exponentially, but its capacities for rational decision making
and geopolitical planning wither. It's easy to blame the Koch brothers,
television demagogues, and crazed Obama haters for structural deadlock in government, but the deeper problem (at least from a historian's
standpoint) is that the political system is owned by elites who no longer have a fundamental commitment to growing the national GDP. The
overriding goal in both the domestic and global arenas has become the
protection of existing wealth and inequality rather than the creation of
new, more widely shared prosperity.

JD: I'd like to return to a comment you made earlier, regarding the
utility of utopias and utopian speculation. My suspicion is that what
avenues remain open for transformational change depend on both the
development of newly viable utopian conjecture and the melding and

scaling of some of the more modest, partial, alternative life-ways you describe for collegiate America. Do you see a viable future in incremental experimentation or an increasingly stark divide between crisis and praxis, wholesale in either case?

MD: *Utopia* in the most profound sense is not the dream of paradise but the defense of the necessary against the realistic. It's the refusal to accept the triage of humanity implied by the vicious circle of inequality and environmental degradation. It's a politics that clings stubbornly to the Enlightenment project of universal human progress, refusing to accept any compromise of fundamental human welfare and rights. And it's clarity about the principal roadblock to that progress. The practical means of producing a decent human future already exist but are everywhere opposed by the power of wealth. *Utopia* in a second sense, of course, is the practical architecture of that alternative future, envisioned less as a grand design than as a huge toolbox from which communities can forge solutions on a participative scale. But even incremental utopias still require some historical agency to sum the brilliant bits and pieces into a strategy for social and environmental transformation. This once existed.

In the period that seems to me most heroic, from the 1880s until the 1930s, avant-garde architects and industrial designers could realistically hope that the victory of working-class movements would lead to the reconstruction of the Victorian urban world. Indeed serious beginnings were made, under the aegis of Social Democrats in Amsterdam, Vienna, Frankfurt, and Berlin, and under far more austere circumstances with the Constructivists and their allies in the Soviet Union. In a similar "real-utopian" spirit, we can also count the New Deal's planned communities, first-generation kibbutzim in Palestine, social housing in Popular Front France, and public art in Mexico. The end of the age began in 1934 during the Austrian Civil War, when the great Karl Marx-Hof was bombarded. (And the act of forgetting continues today with the dereliction and destruction of the superb Constructivist architecture of the 1920s in Russia.)

AFTER the end of the Second World War and the rise to power of parliamentary Labor and Socialist parties, the building of social housing resumed on an unprecedented scale but *without* any of the larger
designs for alternative urbanism centered around magnificent public
spaces that were the soul of the 1920s experiments. Building residential estates quickly and without heavier taxation meant industrialized
construction on cheap land on the urban outskirts. The integration of
affordable housing into the historical cultural fabric was abandoned.
Thus the left, ironically, expelled much of the traditional social base
from the central cities; when suburban factories closed down in the
1980s and 1990s, the result, of course, was the stigmatized violent housing estate, the very image of postmodern dystopia.

I've spent much of my life looking for dreams buried in the rubble of
bad or abandoned public urbanism. We are told, of course, that utopia
can't be recycled, but if the communal and green experiments of today
are to grow into relevant alternatives for large numbers of unprivileged
urban dwellers, then we must recover some of the radical, synthesizing
political imagination of the early twentieth century. As I argued earlier,
environmental survival and social justice must come together in the
design of urban space and collective consumption.

JD: Can we imagine a democratic synthesis of advanced technology and
ennobled public life that was the core of the original socialist-modernist
vision?

MD: I don't know. But I do believe that if anything can give a second life
to alternative urbanism, it's the global riot breaking out in physical and
virtual public space. I'm thinking not only of the insurgent squares in
Egypt and Spain and the Occupy movement in the USA but also of the
magnificently subversive logic of the open-source and peer-production
movement. Cooperation, not competition; free knowledge, not intellectual property; the right to play, not to profit—are all slogans that aspire
to a new world. At the very least, a lot of barbed wire has been torn

down to let millions of us graze freely on the informational commons without permission from Google or Bill Gates.

I recognize, of course, that subversion can in turn be subverted and that bagging your own groceries or giving away free blogs can be tantamount to firing a retail clerk or a struggling young journalist; there are numerous contradictions in the open-source vision, just as there are in the simplistic populism of the Occupy counterculture. And the great digital landowners surely will welcome docile hippy-geek sharecroppers while sending their gunmen to slaughter the more defiant squatters.

But, as in the days of the original Greenwich Village and Montparnasse, of Red Barcelona or Red Vienna, some culturally fertile, autonomous space again exists outside the corporate fence. Yochai Benkler at Yale Law School has become the Fourier of this New World. His *The Wealth of Networks: How Social Production Transforms Markets and Freedom* is a brilliant exposition of the emancipatory potential of networked information environments as well as the most acute analysis since Marx of fundamental contradictions "between the forces of production and the relations of production."[2] It's a book that will inspire you to pick up your musket and rush down to defend the digital commons from the Redcoats.

Benkler, however, is primarily and understandably focused on defending the electronic public sphere and pays little attention to the parallel growth of the Orwellian surveillance state. As is obvious in my earlier remarks, I'm terrified by the invisible eyes behind my computer screen, as well as by the overwhelming noise (meaningless information) level of my children's digital worlds. Critical social theory urgently needs to explore this dialectic of the utopian and dystopian, anarchism versus totalitarianism, in the wired urban environment. As Régis Debray has long complained, the left traditionally has almost nothing to say about media or the production of information. But I'm sure if Marx were alive today he'd be eagerly following Benkler into the labyrinth of connectivity, with all of its monsters and angels.

JD: Speaking of past futurisms, what do you make of Fredric Jameson's decision a few years ago to embark on a textual reassessment of Thomas More's *Utopia*? Or, from (shallow) right field, have you read any of Francis Fukuyama's recent political anthropology in *The Origins of Political Order*? Why these turns from popular dialecticians of either ideological pole toward remote, premodern timeframes and texts?

MD: Well, St. Thomas is a more encouraging topic than Nietzsche or the Nazi Carl Schmitt, other recent obsessions of left intellectuals. Similarly I have no complaint about Fukuyama's enthusiasm for Montesquieu or his interest in the politics of chimpanzees. And if Slavoj Žižek wants to chase Hegel's shadow over hill and dale for one thousand pages, mazel tov.

But theory, even as it has become performance art, has never seemed more gray or irrelevant or, for that matter, more disconnected from concrete politico-economic analysis. Especially in France and the United States, philosophy and haute cultural critique seem to disdain the cuisine offered by serious social-scientific research. Some academic fields, to be sure, have willingly committed suicide in the quest for elegantly quantified trivia (economics and political science are the principal examples), but universities and research institutes still produce bumper crops of important area studies, histories, geographies, and paradigmatic debates.

The monographic foundation, in other words, has already been built for rethinking and updating social theory; to an unprecedented degree we know the world part by part but are lacking in comparison and synthesis. It's time to move from the spinning wheel to the loom. But an aversion to manual labor seems to infect the lecture circuit. If Hardt and Negri, for instance, had spent a few months in a good social science library, I doubt that they would have come up with anything as silly as *Multitude*.[3] (On the other hand, a better grounded, less hypnotic argument probably would have been a flop at the university bookstore.)

I fear you are prescient in detecting an intellectual retreat from the battlefields of modernism. Yet, like the bad bourgeoisie in Buñuel's *The Exterminating Angel*, left intellectuals, at least of my generation, are locked in a room called the twentieth century, and escape for us is impossible. However weary or overpublished we've now become, we must still act as a rescue party, retrieving dreams and ideas from the rubble created by the twin *defeats* (not failures) of modernism and socialism. (To rescue nineteenth-century liberalism, Fukuyama will have to find his own place to dig.) Being a *passeist* in this sense, I contend, is an active way of living in the future.

JD: What about the cosmopolitanism of your children's generation? Could the transnational character of their lives offer unforeseen options for better futures, or do you see those migrations as more closely bound to the undertow of globalization?

MD: Imagine globalization as a central utility—dollars moving as electrons—that powers the corporate world economy via transformers called banks and circuit-breakers called states. Then picture a nearby slum that has jerry-rigged some wiring to one of the trunk lines, allowing residents to siphon a little power for themselves. At the end of the day our chief political goal must be public ownership and democratic management of the central utility, but how that might work will be partly defined by how people are already using their bootleg connections to create novel transnational networks.

A striking example is the hypergeographic character of the contemporary immigrant neighborhood in North American cities and towns. Today's transmigration is very different from the great wrenching European emigrations of the nineteenth and early twentieth centuries. Although important circular labor flows existed and many a village in Galicia or Galway depended upon remittances from America, the dominant pattern was an irreparable break with home.

Transmigration has a different logic. It is essentially a monogamous if often undocumented marriage between two places: an original town or neighborhood in a poorer country and a new town or neighborhood, often panethnic, in a richer country. As a result, the locations coevolve as people cycle through both, bringing home money and cultural novelties, sending back traditional customs and unemployed cousins. One Mexican community, for example, now identifies itself humorously but accurately as "San Juanico, Illinois, and Chicago, Michoacan." There is no longer an "ould sod" and "new country" but a transnational division of labor between two locations to optimize the cultural and economic survival of a single community.

Immigrants have organized thousands of hometown societies to facilitate these links, often coordinating investment and saving, as well as overseeing the survival of local customs. These capillary systems, even if difficult to sustain over generations, offer the smartest and most efficient channels for development aid, as well as a grassroots alternative to a fascist walled border or an exploitative neo–Bracero Program. But their vital role is usually unrecognized in immigration debates north of the border, while in Mexico there is ferocious competition to manipulate hometown networks as mini political machines.

In any event, communal transhumance, supported by grassroots networks, is redefining our concept of the city (which now must include "transnational suburbs") as well as the politics of identity. Emigration traditionally has destroyed or impoverished local identities, but now it has become a last-ditch strategy for their survival. (In contrast to tourism, that other form of modern transhumance, which, locust-like, consumes landscapes and transforms local culture into self-caricature.)

As I emphasized earlier, the true global problem (given perverse future demographics) is actually *undermigration,* which is why it is important to enfranchise the networks that make transnational civic life possible. Otherwise nativists and erstwhile immigration reformers (especially those who argue for legalized exploitation) will continue to throw people and their dreams into a Darwinian pit.

JD: In *Ecology of Fear: Los Angeles and the Imagination of Disaster,* you included a rather infamous update of Ebenezer Howard's 1902 ringed diagram for the Garden City of Tomorrow.[4] Yours is more of a target, including bandwidths for contagious diseases and bio-threats as well as outer orbits for our correctional and militarized perimeters. In *Planet of Slums*, by contrast, you catalogue insurgent urban formations that develop first interstitially, then sometimes boundlessly.[5] Whatever their extent, slums self-replicate with rhizome-like vigor and often without, or in spite of, much formal infrastructural or political hierarchy.

With over half of humanity urbanized, do you see fundamental changes in the geometry of cities—in their patterns of growth, their scales and navigability, their basic identity as discrete formations?

MD: First of all, we must acknowledge that urban studies lives in a self-generated epistemological fog, with almost all research and debate focused on megacities like Shanghai and Los Angeles or futuristic mirages like Dubai and Las Vegas. According to UN-Habitat projections, the populations of the largest metropolitan regions with more than 10 million inhabitants (there will be fourteen of them in China alone by 2020) will constitute at maximum about 10 percent of the earth's population. But the actual majority of urban dwellers, today and tomorrow, will reside in smaller cities with fewer than 200,000 inhabitants—that is to say, in locales that have been of little interest to urbanologists or social scientists.

By the same token, the current fascination with the human ecology of the slum has disproportionately focused on "celebrity slums" like Kibera in Nairobi, Dharavi in Mumbai, or Cité-Soleil in Port-au-Prince (Haiti) where the poor live hive-like in staggering densities close to urban centers. By contrast, most of the global slum population and informal working class counted by the UN in fact live on urban peripheries, in slum suburbs beyond the field of vision of anyone except perhaps for the police and army. Residents of the historical core in rich cities as well as poor are notorious for their cluelessness and lack of curiosity about life on the outskirts of town.

Yet it is precisely the smaller cities, slum peripheries, and periurban countrysides (*desakotas*, as they are called in Asia) that provide the fabric out of which the great urban power centers weave the metropolitan areas that in some cases (China, West Africa) will eventually merge into polycentered megalopolises like Tokyo-Yokohama or Bos-Wash

(Boston-Washington). In the classic spirit of the Regional Plan Association, which pioneered a metropolitan-scale perspective of New York from 1922 onward, we desperately need true cross-sections and comprehensive geographies of emergent urban systems in Africa and Asia that include these modal but usually invisible elements. Without a clearer view of ordinary urban situations, urban theory risks turning all swans black, as would be the case if we extrapolated the future of the city as Dubai or, conversely, as one of Asia's garbage mountains.

I don't discount the possibility that the arrival of new technologies may produce some startling metamorphoses in the organization of high-density human habitats. (Remember that the framework technology of the "modern" city—the telephone, steel-frame buildings, underground trains, and the like—dates back to the reign of Queen Victoria.) It has become especially commonplace to celebrate a future of networks with the implicit assumption that both physical and informational space will become less hierarchical and more flexible.

This is a consoling dream, but the "Internet of things"—that is to say, the universal incorporation of information-processing into built environments—could equally become the architecture of totalitarianism. Will hovel walls become magic windows through which all of world culture and learning can be experienced, or will sentient dwellings become the ultimate Benthamite Panopticon prisons—or both? It seems increasingly likely that the relationship between freedom and technology will ultimately be decided by the politics of urban design as embedded microprocessing and nanomachines confer "intelligence" on physical surfaces and structures (as well as garments and toys).

But my mind is too obsolete to even begin to imagine how this urban singularity might work out in the 2020s and 2030s. In the meantime, new urban geometries are being defined by four major vectors. The first is the global movement of capital in an age when so many large cities are forced to compete with one another for fixed investment, with little or no support from their national governments. (American cities tragically are the paradigm.) Even in good times and in relatively wealthy countries, the economic foundations of urban growth are unstable as industries become nomadic and competing urban governments undermine each other's bargaining power vis-à-vis corporate decision makers. The short-term profit perspectives of the private equity and derivative dealers, moreover, are directly opposed to the long-term stability of municipal bond markets and the fiscal flows that service public debt.

This links directly with the current patterns of infrastructural investment. Without massive support from national governments, cities have little confidence that they can actually amortize public investments in local infrastructure and education. And even where the national commitment to modernization remains fervent, as in China, the state is deliberately investing in the past, not the future. China had a unique opportunity to reinvent the modern city in the 1990s, when the success of its export industries gave it both the wherewithal and the imperative to build on a gigantic scale. It quickly established the largest-scale regional planning agencies in the world and at the highest levels began discussing how to ensure a more equitable urban hierarchy by shifting investment from the booming coast toward poorer inland cities.

Some of this was very impressive (can you imagine the White House discussing how to move surplus capital from Seattle to Detroit?), but its fatal flaw (as Richard Rogers pointed out long ago) was the decision to open cities to traffic and make the private automobile and the suburban home the icons of Red capitalism, thus squandering most of the advantages of late modernization and the ability of learning from others' mistakes. The bicycle is being murdered to achieve the internal economies of scale that make a world-class auto industry possible. The Chinese car market is already the world's largest, and Beijing aspires to dominate sales in the so-called developing world. Car ownership has grown at astronomical rates in countries like Egypt and Indonesia over the past generation, and by 2020 it is estimated that half of the world's 1.3 billion cars, trucks, and buses, along with hundreds of millions of scooters and motorbikes, will gridlock the streets of poorer countries.

The third vector of contemporary urbanization has been the rampant destruction or pollution of the natural matrix. The great Scottish naturalist and pioneer urbanist (he invented the term) Patrick Geddes was the first to demonstrate, in the 1890s, that cities were ecologies whose health depended upon the conservation of watersheds, the reuse of waste as fertilizer, and the preservation of agricultural greenbelts. He demonstrated that in principle the metabolic exchanges between dense human settlements and their countrysides could be sustainably regulated through landscape architecture, regional planning, and a gardening ethos. A century before "green cities" were on anyone's agenda, Geddes was planting their seeds in Dublin, Palestine, India (whose recycling practices he particularly admired), and, of course, his own beloved Edinburgh.

What is happening today in much of the developing world, even in China, is a Geddesian nightmare. As I mentioned earlier, cities' profligate and unnecessary consumption of farm land is undermining agricultural self-sufficiency, while at the same time regional aquifers are being depleted or poisoned by sewage and watersheds so overrun and deforested that flood dangers increase in direct proportion to the decline in water storage. The issue here is not just abstract sustainability. It is urban survivability in the next few decades. We should never forget that accelerating urbanization of our species is an experiment without precedent, a runaway train headed down tracks that have yet to be built.

Finally, there is the ghost that goes unmentioned in most discussions of urban trends and futures: the countryside. Too many experts and pundits, in my opinion, uncritically accept current rates of urbanization as inevitable, when in fact they are accelerated by the massive neglect and oppression of the rural poor. Any discussion about the fate of cities must also be a debate about the future of the countryside. One of the great enemies of a decent life is the unnecessary sprawl that disorganizes rural society without incorporating villagers into any authentic urban culture. As Jan Bremen reminds us in landmark studies of landless Indian laborers, there are hundreds of millions of poor people in Asia struggling for survival in migratory cycles between the village and the city without a secure foothold in either. Perhaps once upon a time, even just twenty years ago, migration to the city gave significant life advantages to a majority of newcomers, but this advantage has been considerably eroded by overurbanization and structural unemployment.

Earlier I argued that the environmental movement must be centrally concerned with creating jobs and revalorizing collective consumption. By the same token, the fight for urban justice must simultaneously encompass the fight for rural justice and a sustainable, modern village life.

8

"We are all interdependent on this earth"

OLZHAS SULEIMENOV

in conversation with Rustem Zhangozha

Olzhas Suleimenov is a Kazakh poet, writer, politician, and diplomat. He serves as a Kazakhstan representative to UNESCO (Paris).

Photo courtesy of Olzhas Suleimenov.

In this interview with one of Kazakhstan's most renowned poets and public figures, Olzhas Suleimenov, Professor Rustem Zhangozha seeks insight from inside the Central Asian region into its recent social and political history. This conversation paints a dynamic picture of political and cultural contestation under Soviet rule and after the collapse of the Soviet Union. Spanning a wide range of topics, including perestroika, the European Union, antinuclear activism, and the potential for Central Asian unification, this conversation not only provides insight into this dynamic region but provides us with ideas on how lessons learned from its politics might be applied at a global level.

RZH: What is your perception of the overall position of the Central Asian region on the geopolitical map of the world? This is a region rich in mineral resources and agricultural lands. It is located in an exceedingly important zone where the geostrategic interests of the world's leaders and major transnational corporations come together. At the same time, this is a transit zone for the world economy's major sectoral centers: the countries of the Asia-Pacific region, the Russian Federation, and the European Union.

os: The peoples of the region are worthy of their rich cultural heritage. This is equally true of the considerable portion of the civilian population that has lived in the region for a relatively short period of time, spanning several generations, after having resettled from the central regions of Russia, Ukraine, and the Caucasus and having become full-fledged citizens of Central Asia. This factor has significantly affected the ethnosocial and demographic makeup of the Central Asian population, forging what is today a strong, multicultural unit, a homogeneous political nation. This is thanks to universal cultural values, whose integration into the region's social and demographic body of citizens was implemented through many centuries of tolerant coexistence. This is why Central Asia represents a futuristic model of the social order to come, a social order made up of people of different religious faiths.

rzh: It's hard not to agree that the shared way of life of ethnic groups—largely the common traditions of their nations, linguistic affinity, a common religious faith, the nature of dryland farming, transboundary water resources, and other factors—creates a favorable resource for intraregional integration. Nonetheless the reality is that there are intensifying centrifugal forces at play in the relationship between the newly established countries of the region. Are there objective arguments and mechanisms for reorienting the developmental vectors from the direction of centrifugal force to that of centripetal force?

Os: Definitely. What I said earlier is not to be taken as a given today in the region. For this very reason, robust, comprehensive measures must be taken to implement a model of regional unity. The community of historians and cultural experts and, last but not least, the political elites must work to harmonize interethnic and interfaith relations. I see this as a task for a new generation capable of employing the entire arsenal of tools developed by contemporary humanities and honed through their application in practice.

In this situation, it is critical to resolve relational issues between the Central Asian countries. Either they become a guarantee of the internal economic and political stability of each of the countries, as they are "communicating vessels" with respect to one another, or they become a negative, deconstructive practice, the primary cause of intraregional tension, which could then escalate into harsh confrontation. For the time being, as one political expert puts it, "The peoples of Central Asia sleep in one bed, but dream different dreams." However, reality has its own rational logic, unlike dreams.

RZH: What do you consider to be the unique cultural and social values that have evolved throughout the history of the peoples of the Central Asian region? Might these values become integrated into the axiological system of human civilization as it evolves in the third millennium? What do you consider essential for the harmony of both intraregional relations among the states of the region and the successful integration of Kazakhstan and the other countries of the Central Asian region into the international community?

OS: As one Sufi aphorism goes, "When you don't know what will happen in the future, rewrite your past." In contrast, in the words of Jorge Luis Borges, "To alter the past does not mean altering only one event; it means striking out its consequences, which would have had an infinite continuation. In other words, it means creating two universal histories." For every Sufi, there is a Borges. The way that I understand it is that changing the past means removing the knots and the notches etched on the trunk of universal history—even more so, on the history of peoples who have lost their statehood. For this reason, many historical facts have been removed and edited by interpreters of the historical past, for whom history is divided between "ours" and "theirs." And that means that "their" history could be censored according to "our" interpretation. An erroneous tradition emerged in the official history books of describing wars and ignoring the reality that the peoples had for centuries lived side by side and worked together in different aspects of their lives, including the cultural domain. It is for this reason that a review of the past should not consist of a rewrite of history but a revision of our understanding of our own history, as one of constructive intercultural cooperation.

I must admit that my generation was somewhat of a target for Soviet ideology, with clichéd perceptions of our past imposed upon us within rigidly drawn ideological boundaries. This was a set of rules for the permitted interpretation of the past, historical memory and its symbols, known as the class approach. Any allusions to a more adequate reading of history and contemporary reality, opened up between the lines in the works of historian-scholars and in works of fiction, were recognized by us through metaphors and allegory.

Generally speaking, this ideology was Eurocentric, with universal human values expunged from the culturological model and replaced with ideologically biased theories of class struggle and the building of a communist future, while the cultural and historical traditions of the peoples that made up the Soviet Union were ignored.

RZH: It seems that no one has ever asked you about your interest in protohistory, logically stemming from your background as a geologist.

OS: You are right. I will try to tie in that particular point here. Having been born and raised in the Russian-speaking environment of Alma-Ata back in the day, I couldn't help but be influenced by the powerful tide of Russian literature and the genius behind it. I completely agree that my interest in the domain of protohistory is certainly the result of my being drawn subconsciously to deep cultural strata, not as a historian, with the historians' professional methods and tools for interpreting source materials and artifacts, but as a human being, trying to see what lies beneath, in layers of history and culture hidden from human eyes. I can't exclude the possibility that it was that very thing, that youthful fascination with geology, that explains my motivation to study cultural strata that lie much deeper but which gradually influence the very nature of contemporary processes.

The monumental work *The Tale of Igor's Campaign* is known as the Hippocrene of Russian literature. This is where I began my "excavations of the tectonic plates" that determine the substantive features of Russian literature. However, the deeper I delved into the world described in this epic work, the more keenly I sensed that many episodes and idiomatic figures that had gone undeciphered by specialists, as well as concepts and terms, reveal the full analogy with real history and the poetics of the Kazakh (and broader yet, Turkish) poetic legacy. This led me to surmise that this historical monument was an irrefutable testament to the lost cultural and historical unity of the nomadic and settled civilizations of Eurasia and its contact zone: the forest steppe. The work is a testament to their genetic connection and their mutual completion of each other.

But this is one level of my understanding of Eurasia, as a historical and cultural discourse. Another aspect of this guesswork was that I had acquired the right to have my own independent voice. This occurred thanks to the expansion of the area of historical and cultural cohesiveness, in which my ancestors lived and where I too resided. Before that, I had been permitted only to listen diligently and repeat after my teacher, "big brother," what my past had been and who I was.

RZH: This message would serve well as an epigraph to your book AZ i YA, which made such waves in the research community at the time and attracted a large reader following, particularly among those whom you called "small-numbered peoples." The book AZ i YA was perceived by them to be a manifesto that freed their desecrated sense of self-worth as nations to discover in their own past, in their traditional culture a power propelling them toward the rebirth of their all but lost cultural values. And it was this that made it possible to restore their sense of historical and cultural identity.

os: I must admit that I myself was surprised at first by the intense public response to my research. There were no underlying political motives
in my study of *The Tale of Igor's Campaign*. It was solely a historical-lin-
guistic analysis of the text, from which ensued a simple conclusion: the
ancient Russian literary work undeniably testifies to the closest of links
between the settled and nomadic civilizations in the forest steppe zone
of the Eurasian continent. At that time, the last thing on my mind was
that I was breaking down the country's hierarchy of peoples' national
cultures, a structure established in the Russian Empire and inherited by
the ideologists of the Soviet Union.

Acceptance of my understanding of the relationship between these
cultures within the country meant rejection of the idea of a "big
brother" bestowing culture upon his "little brothers." This was likely
the Rubicon, past which I became convinced that the search for truth
always leads to freedom—to the freedom to create, the freedom to
choose your own life journey, the freedom to create relationships with
the people around you.

RZH: You were the initiator and leader of the Nevada-Semipalatinsk
Movement, the first-ever Soviet antinuclear movement, which put a
stop to testing of nuclear weapons on both testing sites in the Soviet
Union—Semipalatinsk and Novozemelsk—in October 1989. In August
1991 the Kazakh authorities closed the Semipalatinsk site for good,
which launched an international moratorium on nuclear testing. And
so the Nevada sites fell silent. Could you elaborate in some detail on
how the movement came to be, and on the goals and principles underpinning the ideas of the movement?

oc: As long as humankind has nuclear weapons, the threat of their use
in conflicts between states will remain one of the leading problems of
our times. After Semipalatinsk and Nevada, all the official test sites on
earth—on the Moruroa Atoll, in the Lob Nor Desert—ceased testing.
But unofficial testing occurs now and again. Israel, Pakistan, India,
and North Korea now have nuclear weapons. And no appeals from the

UN have had any effect. Secretly several "threshold" states have been preparing to join the nuclear pool. How do we stop the spread of this scourge?

You ask what nongovernmental, civil society organizations like Nevada-Semipalatinsk can do. We were successful because we were able to take advantage of the historical moment when the USSR first began positioning itself in its foreign policy as a democratic state. The first democratic elections to the Supreme Soviet of the USSR (the parliament) were held at that time. We were able to coordinate people's diplomacy with parliamentary diplomacy. We appealed to the voters to vote only for those who called for the cessation of nuclear weapons testing as part of their electoral campaign. We explained that if the cold war was over (something that Mikhail Gorbachev and Ronald Reagan were saying for all the world to hear), then why were we continuing to sharpen our nuclear sword? We also convened an international conference in Alma-Ata, called Electors against Nuclear War. Approximately three hundred participants came from the USA to support our demands. Our movement actively supported representatives of all the antiwar nongovernmental organizations. A parliamentary association, For a World Free of Nuclear Weapons, was established in the Supreme Soviet of the USSR. More than a third of the members of the Supreme Soviet joined the association. And these active parliamentarians were able to get the Supreme Soviet to vote for a resolution banning the testing of nuclear weapons on the ground, under the ground, and in the air. And so, for the first time ever, a union between people's diplomacy and parliamentary diplomacy led to decisions being made that were fought for by the overwhelming majority of the electorate.

In New York in January 1991 our movement's initiative came to fruition with the establishment of the Global Anti-Nuclear Alliance, which united all the antiwar and environmental movements of the world. The inaugural conference took place at the UN building. Through active outreach with the electorate, we proposed that the parliaments of the world become engaged in the fight against nuclear weapons and, above all, the parliaments of the nuclear club states. The proposal for the first campaign was to work on preparing an interparliamentary referendum on the question "Do we need nuclear weapons?" This was how a robust platform was put in place for the continuation of the referendum and its expansion beyond the parliaments.

That was the plan. Other events in the early 1990s got in the way of its full-fledged implementation. However, the theme Electors of the World against Nuclear Weapons retained its relevance. And now the union of people's and parliamentary diplomacy is capable of doing so much. Now, what is the leading reason for obtaining deterrent weapons? Aggressive neighbors? The virtual ability to use nuclear weapons remains in the hands of both the traditional nuclear weapons states— USA, Russia, United Kingdom, France, and China—and more recent nuclear weapons possessors: India, Pakistan, North Korea, and Israel.

It could be said that nuclear weapons took on the function of "deterrent weapons" due to the extreme threat they pose. Who in the twentieth century posed a potential threat to peace: the USA in its confrontation with the former Soviet Union? An irreconcilable pair of communist powers, China and the USSR; which forgot about their mutual grievances after the departure of their leaders at the time, Mao Zedong and Nikita Khrushchev? But now, after a complete victory in the cold war, the collapse of the USSR and the Eastern bloc, who is a threat to the United States and the European Union? International terrorism? Yes. But nuclear weapons are ineffective in combating terrorism. In the current situation, the assertion that the impossible is possible is made in order to justify the probability of nuclear weapons use.

The logic of certain politicians, who insist on the legal preservation and improvement of the existing arsenal of deterrent weapons while arguing that an aggressor might appear in the future, is already a threat to all of humankind, in and of itself. Understanding this threat predetermines the very next goal of the global anti–nuclear weapons movement. The policy of countries that either consider themselves to be members of the "nuclear pool" or aspire to join it will lead to nuclear arsenals being built and topped up. Meanwhile nuclear weapons will be accorded the status of means of national defense. All of which goes to say that these weapons with their national qualifiers—American, Russian, Chinese, and so on—are there in their capacity as status symbols to acknowledge that these countries are great powers.

And this is why all peace-building movements, including the anti-nuclear weapons movement, see as their priority to explain to the public what total cataclysm awaits if nuclear weapons are used. But an even more important job, as I see it, is to fight the demonization of any social and political group that is said to represent a threat to peace.

RZH: What are the next steps toward a total ban on nuclear weapons?

OS: The universal understanding of the fact that nuclear weapons in their present state are the most effective means for humanity's self-destruction, for the reason that the very first act of nuclear self-defense of any individual state will set in motion the chain reaction of all-out nuclear war. This can be avoided in only one way, and that is if international legislation is passed stripping nuclear weapons, and any other weapon of mass destruction, for that matter, off their status as means of national defense and recognizing them as means of ensuring the planet's safety.

They will become a universal asset, belonging not to the states but to all of humanity. That is, states possessing nuclear weapons will agree to put their arsenals under the jurisdiction of the UN Security Council, and the common arsenal will be cut back to an agreed minimum of several dozen warheads, which will be maintained as police clubs to threaten those regimes that get it into their heads to acquire these forbidden weapons. But it will never come down to the use of the warheads, because the Council of the powers, having given up their nuclear arsenals, would react to such activities much more promptly and consistently. Not the way it is now.

RZH: How do you feel about the peaceful atom, nuclear energy? You are known to be in opposition to the construction of a nuclear power station in Kazakhstan, although the republic ranks among the leading three uranium-rich countries in the world.

Os: Yes, as long as there is no such thing as a waste-free thermonuclear reactor, I am against the development of nuclear energy. The earth is already overloaded with waste from existing nuclear power plants, and that waste will soon show humanity and the biosphere exactly what it is capable of.

I speak out against the construction of a nuclear power plant in Kazakhstan, but what might an alternative be? Seventy-four percent of the energy consumed in our country is produced by thermoelectric power plants fueled by coal and oil. Construction of yet another thermoelectric station has just begun in Balkhash. It will burn 12 million tons of Ekibastuz coal with an ash content of 42 percent. In Europe they are moving away from nuclear power and gradually decommissioning coal-fired and even gas-fired electrical power plants. For example, Germany has shut down several nuclear plants and increased the contribution of wind energy to 20 percent. Denmark is promising to produce 85 percent of its electrical energy with wind turbines by 2020. For the present, the majority is skeptical about so-called alternative energy sources: solar panels and wind turbines. But just look at Europe today, where wind is used to produce 100,000 megawatts of power. It would take thirty-six nuclear reactors or 72 million tons of hydrocarbons or 780,000 railcar loads of coal to produce this much electrical energy. The ways in which power is currently produced are what define the degree of civilization of the world's states. Improved wind turbines will soon be able to produce many times more energy than is currently produced in the world today by nuclear, thermal, and hydroelectric power stations.

RZH: In one interview, you said that the sudden and unexpected mass manifestation of genuine democracy in the Soviet Union was what caused it to collapse. The society proved to be unprepared for such exposure to the truth about itself. In another interview, you clarified that one of the main reasons for the failure of Gorbachev's perestroika was that it was improvised. Political, social, and economic programs under perestroika were not well thought-out. And so things didn't go the way they were expected to, which led to the collapse of the country and a simulated transition from quasi-socialism to just as quasi-capitalism. You were a people's deputy of the USSR at the time, and in that capacity you were a member of the Constitutional Commission of the USSR Supreme Soviet.

os: Gorbachev understood that Marxism's main mistake lay in renouncing private ownership of the means of production and allowing only state and collective ownership. And he wanted to add private cooperatives and farms onto existing kolkhozes (collective farms) and the giants of state-owned industry, as had been done in the People's Republic of China for five years at that point. But the Chinese had done this under the rigid control of the ruling party. That is why they were able to create a combination of three forms of ownership—state, collective, and individual—which led to the explosive development of the country. By his ill-considered actions, Gorbachev allowed the premature dismantling of the ruling Communist Party, thus losing hold of power. And without the power, it was no longer feasible to carry out such reforms. In the end, the country fell apart, and the combination of the three forms of ownership never materialized in the majority of the newly founded states. In a world of lawlessness, aggressive privatization swallowed up both state and collective property, which, objectively speaking, reduced the whole management and economic infrastructure to ruins.

If Gorbachev had not been in such a hurry to get down to perestroika when he came to power in the spring of 1985, and instead had commissioned the design of a draft program integrating the existing Chinese reform experience, then the country would have met with a less dramatic fate. But these are all could-haves and should-haves, and they have nothing to do with the real events.

rzh: What other geopolitical designs could you name that suffered from the gaps in the perestroika design process?

Os: A goodly number have accumulated in the past few decades. I will name the biggest: the European Union is design. Although it was in the works for decades, it nonetheless also saw hurried developmental decision making with unplanned-for consequences from the very first years of its existence. In the early 1990s the European Union was made up of fifteen Western European countries. If this number had remained in effect, I am sure that the union would not be experiencing the kind of problems it is having now. But politics got ahead of economics. They hurried to bring the countries of Eastern Europe into NATO, and the leap from fifteen to twenty-seven was something the European coffers couldn't withstand. The European Union is disintegrating, and not even the Nobel Peace Prize can save it.

The idea of a united Europe is wonderful in and of itself. It was ripening for centuries. It arose and took shape under the influence of the North American integration process. Victor Hugo dreamed of seeing the United States of Europe in his time. And it is regrettable that a design with the potential to launch the unification of the nations of the whole Eurasian supercontinent, from the Atlantic to the Pacific in the East and to the Indian Ocean in the South may never be fully realized.

It's worth noting that there are a number of similarities between the EU and the USSR. The Soviet Union broke up into fifteen new states. And, almost simultaneously, the European Union emerged as fifteen states came together. The processes of integration and disintegration in geopolitics sometimes occur simultaneously. One union is replaced by another. I wonder whether the creation of the Eurasian Union (Russia, Kazakhstan, and Belarus) by 2015 will affect the integrity of the EU and in general find an equal response in the West.

RZH: In your words, the problem of Eurasian Union integration seemed to surface inadvertently. Kazakhstan is a multiethnic country and has a demographic structure that took shape in your childhood and youth. How do you personally experience life in a multicultural society? Will you continue to live there?

OS: As for the future of the Central Asian region and my country, Kazakhstan, I find it more comfortable living in an ethnically diverse environment. My perception of the idea of multiculturalism is a positive one. I believe that nations made up of many ethnic groups are models for human communities of the future. In the course of their development, the great nations are transformed into mini-humankinds, and they minimize the danger of potential global confrontations in this very way. Naturally, this process is not as smooth as we would like it to be. But the undeniable fact is that it is happening and gaining momentum, gradually neutralizing interethnic and interreligious relations.

RZH: Allow me to recall your statement of thirty years ago, to the effect that independence should not be the ultimate goal for the national liberation movements. Your formula—"from centuries of dependence through a period of independence to an era of conscious interdependence"—is universal in nature. It could function as a basis for the domestic and foreign policy of any decolonized people in Asia or Africa.

os: Not only the decolonized. Is there really a people, a social stratum, even an individual that hasn't experienced the state of dependency? Let's take the family as the primary cell of the social order. All of the social developmental stages can be traced from it. The child is dependent on the parents. He grows, strives to become independent, and, having matured, becomes cognizant of the interdependence that exists between him and his family. It isn't right for a gray-haired former child to feel dependent on his parents or absolutely independent of his parents, for that matter. This is true of the relationships between the peoples of the former Soviet Union. The tragic misconception held by the Bolsheviks when they ignored the inherent interdependence of all the social groups and estates in the society made it possible to pit the classes against each other to the point of total destruction of their "enemies." In multiethnic societies, the realization of the interdependence of the nations and cultures happens more rapidly. The political and cultural elites simply need to facilitate this process, to help people understand that we are all interdependent on this earth. We are all that is animate and inanimate in nature. This new century should be called the century of interdependence, because only the realization of our universal interdependence will help humankind to survive. And not just to survive physically but to live with a sense of freedom, which means constructively, without fear of tomorrow.

9

"Think communally"

VLADIMIR YAKUNIN

in conversation with Vladimir Kulikov

Photo courtesy of Vladimir
Yakunin.

Vladimir Yakunin is head of the Department of State Politics of the Faculty of Political Science at Lomonosov Moscow State University, doctor of political sciences, founding president of the World Public Forum "Dialogue of Civilizations," and president of Russian Railways Joint Stock Company.

In a rare interview, the Russian businessman and philanthropist Vladimir Yakunin shares his unique worldview with Vladimir Kulikov. Yakunin argues that the current global paradigm of human relations (interpersonal, international, and relating to the world's environment and resources) is a predatory one. Eschewing mainstream critiques of capitalism, he argues that such predation occurs in both the East and the West. He suggests that predominant ideologies based on rampant individual consumption and the satisfaction of self-interest not only undermines social stability but can be harmful to capitalism itself. In opposition to what he terms "wild capitalism," Yakunin proposes a focus on collective interests and advocates a higher level of state regulation to temper predation while allowing the market to play an important role in society. He also argues that collective thinking actually represents the interests of the majority of the world's population—crossing class and civilizational lines—and has the potential to lead to more courageous and constructive politics, both internationally and at the national level. For Yakunin, the way forward lies in evolutionary (rather than revolutionary) movement rooted in engagement with new and productive ideas, which, in turn, will shape the tangible world of economics, politics, and society.

vk: You are a person with very different interests and achievements: you are one of the leading businessmen in Russia and Europe, while at the same time you are the founder of the World Public Forum "Dialogue of Civilizations." Looking at the world through the prism of these two preoccupations, what concerns you, what problems do you think we need to address, what issues need resolving?

vy: The first thing that needs to be said is that human beings are an organic component of earth's ecological system. They are a part of that vast and living world that is the natural environment of our planet. He who shows no restraint in the utilization of the resources that have been given to him by the earth, and I am referring not only to minerals here, but to the natural environment on the earth as a whole, is like the politician who thinks only "from election to election." Every thinker, every leader, and generally every conscious human being has the obligation to rise to a level of awareness that encompasses more than current problems, to reflect on his place in the eternal flow of life and his responsibility to future generations.

Sadly, predation is one of the drivers of the existence and development of the modern paradigm of the global world and globalization. I want to emphasize that it is not even greed, but predatory use of one's own kind by using the best new techniques out there for manipulating others. There is much in these processes that resembles neocolonialism. They manifest themselves, for example, in such things as the European Union signing agreements with the developing countries wherein the latter supply it with natural resources without the right to regulate their own tariffs or customs fees. This is robbery, pure and simple. It deprives the economies of the developing countries of all capacity to acquire the resources essential to their further development. Predation also manifests itself in the fact that from the moment personal material prosperity became a measure of success to be attained by any and all means without moral limits, man has ceased to see himself as part of a social order [*sotsium* in Russian; henceforth *socium*]. He perceives himself to be an individuum, a state of being promoted in Western society, whereby only personal interests represent the fundamental value. That is—de facto—the end of the social state (or welfare state) approach and, with it, the end of key concepts for communal survival such as reciprocal dependence, commitment, loyalty to the nation and state, and trust.

VK: A situation where we use people and resources predatorily, as you put it, prompts the question: Reform something or change the system?

VY: Happily, I don't suffer from bifurcation of the self. To answer your direct question, naturally I stand for evolutionary change in the existing paradigm, because any revolution is akin to a major war. It is those who would make predatory resource consumption and the paradigm of domination the cornerstone of development who incite us to engage in a major war. However, in order to ensure a positive outcome to this evolutionary process, a new approach must be developed for transitioning to a new paradigm. This idea must be accepted by consensus by the majority of civilizations, by the majority of countries in existence today. I want to stress that the immense number of meetings that I have been involved in, and ten years of WPF (World Public Forum) "Dialogue of Civilizations" activities have brought me to the belief that the overwhelming majority of people from very many social backgrounds, different nations, and different civilizations support exactly this developmental path. In the end, it is the human, moral component that is more inherent in humanity than the predatory, wolf-like image. It is also in everyone's interest to "think communally," as the system that is

leaving everyone to fend for themselves (that is shifting socially generated problems to the individual to solve them) is setting individuals into
fierce competition, thus destabilizing the whole system and, paradoxically, jeopardizing the gains even of those few in charge who are the
main beneficiaries of this system.

vk: Which means you believe that social support for this new
thinking originates in different social strata and groups that are
cross-civilizational?

vy: Yes.

vk: And even those who today are involved in business and up to their
ears in the market system are also seeing the emergence of signs of serious limitations on their own development?

vy: Yes. That's one thing. And another thing is that they are also people.
They have families. They live in the real world. And in that real world,
the desire to make the world a better place for their children begins
to conflict with the predatory tendencies. They get involved in charity.
They begin to help those in need. This far from corresponds to the existing model of predatory capitalism, or the predatorily oriented global
economic system.

vk: You speak of collectivity. This collectivity in a different form or
a different language might be called communality? Could the current
Western design be called or tentatively characterized as "noncollective
communality"?

vy: Perhaps, since the Russian language is very rich. I'm not sure that
this can be adequately expressed in English. That would then require
clarification as to what a *collective* means. A collective is a kind of social
communality, where communality equates to unity. And if today the
principle of the Western socium consists in the primacy of personal

freedom, the self, and personal interests, that is to say, complete "individualism," then that is not communality; rather it is just a collectivity. To my mind, that is the difference between *communality* and *collectivity*, terminologically speaking. I think that these clarifications provide a significantly improved description of what I was just talking about than the version you offered. Let me try another explanation. What we can see is a divorce between political rights and social rights. Legally speaking, many Western societies guarantee many rights to all citizens, but the ability to exercise those rights is becoming narrower and narrower since many people cannot exercise them in full. Thus a "citizen de jure" is not the same as a "citizen de facto," thus making the notion of collectivity or communality irrelevant, and this is to the detriment of the well-being of society at large.

VK: But the logic of capital is such that it cannot help but be predatory, as capital's main rule is accumulation, not charity and social compassion.

VY: Yes, the logic of capitalism, wild capitalism, lies in the predatory acquisition of the labor of many. But humankind is developing and culture is advancing, embodying questions of a philosophical nature: What is morality? What differentiates humanity from other living creatures? What is the correlation between fairness and necessity? The theory of the state is also evolving from the rule-of-law state to a *social state* and should end up as an *ethical state*. This last concept cannot be translated into English by the word *moral*. In a very general fashion, translating the thought of Fyodor Dostoyevsky, the ethical is that which neither infringes upon nor demeans another human being. However, we currently seem to be moving in a destructive direction of diminishing the role of the "social" in state activities and further emancipating business from any ethically (community-) based supervision, thus making business generally immune from all values other than the maximization of profit.

vk: Let me continue along these lines. You are a large-scale business-man. In that respect, I would like to ask what profit range you would consider to be indicative of nonpredatory capitalism or other noncapitalist system that can offer people a decent life and a good salary.

vy: When I was talking about predation in the existing model, I was not only and not so much referring to value added, which is what actually generates profit, at least according to Marx. It seems to me that all of the serious economists espouse this position. Therefore this is not what I'm talking about, nor am I referring to labeling a specific political system with some negative moniker. When I was referring to predation, I mostly had in mind consumption without regard to the impact on the environment, the impact on the social milieu, the ramifications for perfectly specific individuals, be they the youth, children, the elderly, or the sick. From this point of view, existing Western society has truly come a long way in the domain of *social benefits*, with the creation of a whole system of social security. But if one were indeed to look at this from a practical standpoint and not only a theoretical one, one would see that these *benefits* appeared on the line of fire between two social systems, two social ideologies: capitalism and socialism. If this battle had never happened, they would never have seen the light of day in the Western world, plain and simple. It was this struggle that led to the convergence of the nascent capitalism with its present form, which, strictly speaking, cannot be called "classic capitalism." This confrontation between these two ideologies is a major achievement. It led not only to negative results under the Soviet experiment but also to positive changes in people's lives in the West, people who had sold the only thing they possessed: their labor. For some reason virtually no one ever talks about this. As far as I can recall, you are the only scholar so far to have put the question this way.

vk: What do you think is the most important idea, the key to making it possible to change the system through evolution?

vy: First and foremost, two key points are absolutely essential to the future paradigm. The first deals with the animal in the human, and that is the drive for self-preservation. The way that the natural environment is being intensively and irresponsibly exploited today means that if we don't protect the environment, then we won't be able to survive and we will perish. Self-preservation, instinctive to any living creature, is a manifestation of the animal in the rational human being. However—now, this is the fundamental consideration—only the human spirit is capable of filling human life with ethical content and an appropriate attitude to self, other people, and the world at large.

vk: The newborn paradigm will likely be a child of intense social and political struggle? That means the principle of competition, the principle of struggle, as I have mentioned, is an absolutely essential element of any alternative. If there is an alternative, there is going to be struggle. It could be a battle of ideas, it could be a physical struggle, but struggle is always present in the world. And it's impossible to imagine a world without it—well, at least without a battle of ideas.

vy: To change the paradigm one must include change in social responsibility, on the part both of the state and the everyman. The individuum.

vk: The individuum. How do you understand this?

vy: Absolute individualism and what is purportedly absolute freedom of the individual are cornerstones of the contemporary model of Western society. I hold that absolute freedom of the unit cannot exist in the socium, because if it is a collection of absolutely independent, non-interconnected, mutually unaccountable units, then the socium does not exist. Then society simply cannot exist and, consequently, neither can governance. Also, an individual cannot respond meaningfully to global challenges, cannot cope with increased burdens put on him or her by the withdrawal of the state.

vκ: Why you are so anti-individualistic in your approach?

vy: Consider this: The social situation in the Western world shows that the nurturance of this extreme individualism has in fact affected the basis for the consolidation of society in the most destructive way. If I am, or what is mine is, the most important thing, then why should I have to look after anyone else? Let's go back to Dostoyevsky. He wrote that all the treasures of the world are not worth a child's tear. That is the notion of ethics in the Russian interpretation; in the English version, as I already mentioned, this interpretation of the word does not exist. It might be translated as *morality*, but these are different things, different concepts. From my standpoint, the contemporary development of human society is on an upward curve. Remember Hegel's spiral? We are once again approaching a stage where sociologists and social psychologists are starting to talk about the value of collectivism.

vκ: Only in the new circumstances of the twenty-first century?

vy: Arguably, yes. What political goals are set on this basis is one thing; what the *substance* of this definition consists of is quite another, and it is extremely important. I am certain that if humanity's survival is in question and we want to resolve the problems of the demographic degradation of human society, in general—and you and I know that the current symptoms of a demographic tragedy are not specific to European countries or only to Russia, but are common to virtually all countries—so, if we seriously ponder the subject of human development, humanity's survival, demographic survival, then we must of necessity conclude that these things will be possible only in the event that what is stratifying is not an atomized society of individuums but a society wherein the principles of moral responsibility for what human beings do to other people and how it affects others becomes the primary principle. And that is where the answer lies.

vk: How can you explain why the West and East are looking so very similar in that aspect for which you criticize the West?

vy: Well, first off, because a shift occurred that eliminated alternatives. And the last known "theoretical" description of the stages of development of Western society, Western economy, and the Western state—the theory of neoliberalism—having unexpectedly attained dominance in the 1980s, became the sole option for more than twenty years from a scholarly point of view. For all intents and purposes, an alternative model has remained somewhat intact in China but it is still far from being an established counter-hegmonic system. It's absolutely appropriate, therefore, to refer to the emergence of that essentially dominant ideology. It's absolutely correct. It is not an ideology espoused by one party. It is the embodiment in idea of that level of self-awareness that society has achieved.

vk: Of course, you can imagine, it's really self-evident, that such ideas meet with adamant opposition and run counter to liberal individualism. What is the source of this resistance? Where will support for new ideas originate?

vy: It's an illusion that the majority of humankind buys into the currently dominant paradigm. First, we are talking about the political and economic elite, and it always makes up at the most only 10 percent of the whole population in all societies. Consequently, when the elite says "We are the most important, we are the voice of all humanity," they are simply taking credit for that which does not belong to them. For the majority of humanity, such principles as preservation of the human race, happy children, a just world, and a world without war are the highest priorities and reasons for living.

we must articulate the wishes of the majority. We get told a lot of tales about political correctness. It is politically incorrect for a European to cast doubt on the absolute righteousness and the absolute truth that emanates from across the ocean, whether it's in the domain of economics, finance, or social relations. It was politically incorrect when President Chirac of France, Prime Minister Berlusconi of Italy, and Chancellor Schroeder of Germany announced to President Bush of the United States that interference in the affairs of and occupation of Iraq was a mistake. And they paid for this political incorrectness with their political futures. But these were courageous people, who convinced others, including President Putin of Russia, to come round to their way of thinking as to whether the attack on Iraq was just or not.

WHAT are we left with in the final analysis? In the end, we have both the British and the Americans admitting that fictitious data were used to justify the invasion of Iraq. This means that public opinion was manipulated on a global scale, and no one was held accountable. How could that be? A guy off the street steals a $1.50 hotdog and he gets dragged off to jail. People essentially committed high treason against society, and no one even talks about it. Where are those ethics and morals that we are being urged to practice?

VK: Let's move from global to regional issues. How can we evaluate a community of regions, or a community of a new order, where there will be no more hegemons? What kind of world will that be? More stable or less so? After all, that kind of transformation will require a regional mind-set.

VY: You know, I believe that any transformation is destined to result in general instability. Any transformation, say, the transition from one socioeconomic-technological system to the next, has always been accompanied by serious instability in the world, sometimes even triggering armed clashes. It seems to me when we speak of a contemporary human community of people living on earth, we assume that it consists of a whole collection of groupings, which we call civilizations. There is a Chinese civilization, a Russian Orthodox civilization, an Anglo-Saxon or European civilization, a Latin American civilization, and so on. If we

say that the spiritual foundations of the civilizations are the basic components for the future regional nurturance of a new paradigm, then it's
clear what the place of the World Public Forum "Dialogue of Civilizations" will be in the whole elemental design system of this paradigm. If
we switch to the level of a specific country and talk about the regions of
this country, then, at that point, that is an internal relationship within
one sovereign state. For example, within one civilization, Ukrainians
are different from Belarusians, who in turn are different from Russians,
who in turn are different from Kazakhs, and so on. But sometimes they
are all joined together in one territory, one history, and one culture. It
is a unified civilization, because it shows the attributes of unification:
unified territories, historical unification of cultures, and a single developmental history. At the same time, if we are talking about regional
communities, then it must be understood that the endless fragmentation of the world into smaller and smaller spaces, where each is his own
master and where each produces his own currency, is an idea that is
counterproductive and downright dangerous.

THE world today has been globalized through constant and widespread
exchange of technologies, communications systems, means for shipping
cargo, means of passenger transportation—all of which are positive
aspects of globalization. However, when globalization is discussed as
a means of unification, when the universality of one specific civilization's values is imposed, then this must be expected to inevitably cause
regional tensions and conflicts, potentially resulting in an escalation of
global conflicts.

VK: If the dominant logic of the market system did not correspond with
Russian socioeconomic reality, why did Russia go for what was pretty
much a carbon copy of that model?

VY: Because they apparently bought the Western "success" propaganda.
Having rejected the communist ideology and the principles and values
that had evolved in our society, we had to fill the void with something

else. And what we went for was basically typical and dominant in the Western world.

vk: Could you please elaborate a bit on your idea as to why the political establishment is no longer up to the challenges of the twenty-first century?

vy: We have already touched on this today. Now, this question has, for me, taken on the contour of two pyramids. According to modern history, humankind developed from man's animal state to the homo sapiens state, which is the rational human being that has passed through successive stages of societal development. This has been reflected in various theories: primitive man, primordial man, medieval man, Homo economicus, and so on. This process can be visualized as a pyramid with the material component—the economy and economic relations—at the base and with man and his spiritual values at the apex. Then, historically what happens is the gradual changing of the pyramid, based on the opposition of the two paradigms: the paradigm of the society of free competition (capitalist society) and the social paradigm of the world of universal fraternity. That was how the destruction occurred, and with it a change of pyramid. To break the opponent, in order to take the upper hand and then victory, it had to reeducate and reformat man accordingly. And what was the result? There emerged a pyramid in which spirituality began to be trumped by economic goals. When the pyramid turns upside down, then the existing elite's political goals become the base and the scenario for further societal development, where everything is subordinated to the political agendas of the elite that perpetrated the takeover. It is understood that the process includes education, economy, culture, everything.

THE unstable state of the pyramid, as well as the imbalance between all the elements of the "new" paradigm, is quite evident today. Then, an essential task for the next stage of world development is to restore the pyramid to a stable state at a new level of awareness of what man really is. Man is, first and foremost, a social creature; therefore the problems of the socium and social and spiritual issues can be resolved only on the basis of normal values historically developed by humanity.

VK: Let's go back to the previous question. You know, every idea always has a very complex drive mechanism. Now, you are effectively talking about a kind of survival culture. Well, we received a letter from Mohammad Khatami, the former president of Iran (1997–2005), whose letter on "Dialogue of Civilizations" was issued as a response to Samuel P. Huntington's assertions in his essay "The Clash of Civilizations." He writes, "I started the dialogue of civilizations in order for peoples to get to know one another, but they replaced it with an alliance of civilizations, which I do not support, so that peoples who don't know each other would suddenly start fighting side by side or against terrorism or against something else. I tried to expand the dialogue of civilizations to encompass culture, but UNESCO said that they would only use those models of tolerance that are acceptable within European culture." When we talk about this survival culture, are you not afraid that, just like Khatami, if you are successful in developing a new paradigm and new approaches, they will again be transformed into something else, in the final analysis, something quite the opposite content-wise?

VY: As we know, Khatami was the first to come up with the idea of creating a dialogue of civilizations, and it is important to me that he so clearly differentiates between the "Alliance of Civilizations" and the "Dialogue of Civilizations." However, with the deepest of respect that I have for Khatami, it's also important to emphasize that he was nevertheless unable to avoid the practical error of counting on being able to implement the principles of dialogue within the framework of the UN, an organization of states. After all, diplomats negotiate, and they do it as per the instructions they receive from the state, that is, from the ruling elite. So the initial idea of having the civilizations get to know each other and start to freely collaborate is alive and well in the World Public Forum "Dialogue of Civilizations." It's working because, rather than being a gathering of representatives of a specific country, it is representatives of one civilization or another who come together, wanting to get to know each other and develop an integrated agenda that they can all sign off on. Maybe this is just a pipedream, but perhaps down the road, the ruling elite itself might come to understand that the principle of survival dictates the need to bolster the civilizational component of civil society, in particular. That said, I would like to refer to a paradigm that could emerge in the foreseeable future as a paradigm of consistent, stable human development, rather than one of survival.

VK: Let's ask about something very dear to you: Russia. What can Russia contribute to the ideas that we have been discussing? Russia is to be feared; Russia is misunderstood; Russia is deciphered with myths; Russophobia is a reality. In that case, what positive elements can Russia offer the world community today?

VY: Speaking in the vocabulary of the poet Nikolai Gumilev, in Russia there still exists a vital impulse of internal movement, internal energy, internal passion for changing the world, although it is considerably scaled down and plainly disregarded, and that is something that the world needs so badly. With all the shortcomings we have and the poverty in Russia, that historic spirit that exists in Russia struggles with the spirit of unbridled predatory mercantilism.

IT is precisely this energy that Russia, her science, her philosophy, her religion, if you like, can give generously to the world, not because everybody else should be like us—we know our weaknesses only too well—but because the world needs our passion[1] with its not insubstantial track record of successfully confronting terrorism's negative passion and the horrors of unrighteous wars and absolutely unjustified domination, neocolonial domination, to mention just one.

VK: Do you think that many Western countries show a certain cynicism, a certain duality with respect to Russia?

vy: I believe that what is of prime importance here are clear-cut pragmatic goals and pragmatic indicators that make it possible to measure
the impact on our society of any given decision, and only then to evaluate whom any given decision could benefit politically or economically.
I, for one, am absolutely convinced that from the standpoint of the
increased competitiveness of the West and its ability to gain renewed
momentum today, it would be completely natural not to seek to isolate
Russia, for example, but rather to strive for rapprochement with Russia. The reason is that rapprochement creates multiple synergies of an
economic, resource, human, educational, typological nature, in fact,
synergy of every description.

vk: I see a certain set of contradictions in you. For one thing, it's clear
from our interview that there is an immense dose of idealism in your
way of thinking, but then, in contrast, you are deeply pragmatic. You
cite Marx and at the same time you quote the Bible. What are we to
make of this? And I have a second question. On the one hand you
defend all things Slavic, all things Russian; on the other hand, you just
said that the East also needs the West.

vy: Well, you're actually the one coming to conclusions about roman-
ticism, idealism, pragmatism, the Bible, Marx, and so on. I do think
the comment is justified. First and foremost, man has to live in peace
with himself. That is, with respect to one's personal life, man must live
in peace with himself. He shouldn't act in ways he thinks are amoral
because that destroys the human spirit and human life. He should
assess his own strengths as realistically and objectively as he can, so
as not to do himself harm trying to come across as something other
than he really is. I don't have those internal contradictions you refer
to. They are not part of my makeup. In that respect, I could call myself
rather well-balanced, in harmony with myself even. All of this brings
me back to the philosophical question of what came first: the idea or the
action. You know, the more I live on this earth, the more I start to grav-
itate away from a materialistic concept toward an idealistic concept,

not from the point of view of idealism but from that of a philosophical school of thought, a philosophical teaching. It seems to me that the idea is not only a driver of progress, but the idea is also capable of reconciling the material contradictions of life.

so, for me, what you call idealism is in fact not an abstraction of reality but the creation of an image of the future or the present that makes it possible to overcome the difficulties of day-to-day life, the current state of being, where I must compromise and do things that perhaps I would rather not do. But that is in my private life. However, when we talk about an attempt to serve, which is also an inherent part of the Russian nature, then you are absolutely right. I defend my worldview, my civilizational identity, because something is definitely telling me that there is quite an aggressive offensive brewing, or should I say attack in the making—I can't find the right word here—and it's going to be aimed at that identity. Why is that? This is where I want to defend that identity because the concept of collectivism, synergy, responsibility, service—this is what I think makes up part of our civilizational code, if you like. Could this be called idealism? Yes, it could, but we saw how this idealism manifested itself during the Second World War. We saw how it manifested itself when people sacrificed everything for an idea during the first five-year plans. This is the truth, not pure invention, and I am not sitting in judgment upon the validity or invalidity of the ideas that drove them, but these were ideas that people followed nonetheless.

UNDERSTAND THE GLOBAL BALANCE OF POWER

10

"Recognize the structural crisis of the world-system"

Photo courtesy of Immanuel
Wallerstein.

IMMANUEL WALLERSTEIN
in conversation with Kevan Harris

Immanuel Wallerstein served as distinguished
professor of sociology at Binghamton University until his retirement in 1999 and as head of
the Fernand Braudel Center for the Study of
Economies, Historical Systems, and Civilization
at Binghamton University until 2005.

In a conversation that revisits and expands upon ideas that he has worked on throughout his career, Immanuel Wallerstein reflects on a world-system in crisis. He explains the origins and current applications of his seminal notion of a world-systems analysis and applies it to the current geopolitical landscape. He argues that U.S. hegemony is indeed in decline, and much more visibly so today than in past decades, but that this decline should not be thought of as precipitous, nor should the United States be thought of as no longer a leading world power. On the other hand, the fate of the United States is directly tied to the continuing financial crisis, and Wallerstein cautions that we cannot simply return to the status quo, as politicians in the United States and elsewhere continue to suggest. He also highlights the importance of movements from Occupy to the Arab Spring in speaking to cogent problems and placing social issues on the public agenda, but he cautions that all such spontaneous movements face the threat of burning out without having lasting effects or of being co-opted. In a world-system facing a structural crisis, he argues that what is needed are new tactics and strategies to face up to an unpredictable and unprecedented situation. But he also argues for pragmatism in action, whereby people's immediate needs are met and suffering alleviated, without losing sight of medium- and long-term goals for social, political, and economic transformation.

KH: For over three decades you have been on record as predicting the relative decline of the hegemonic power of the United States. This prediction followed from the theoretical conclusions you drew out of world-systems analysis, which reframes international relations over the long-term historical development of the capitalist world-economy. The reception of your prediction, in the media as well as by other scholars, has gone through its own rise and decline since the 1970s. But ever since the 2008 world financial crisis, talk of U.S. decline has gone mainstream. Can I ask, therefore, how one knows decline and crisis when one sees them?

IW: Hegemony is a concept that has to be followed historically. I define it this way: you get your way 95 percent of the time on 95 percent of the issues. That's being hegemonic. Whatever the language, whatever the official version of this, the reality is that you can do that. The United States, in this sense, was hegemonic more or less from 1945 to the end of the 1960s. It got its way all the time. I define hegemony as a kind of quasi-monopoly on geopolitical power, and like all quasi-monopolies, it exhausts itself for various reasons. And when it begins to decline, it doesn't go from all to nothing. The hegemonic power fights back and tries to maintain itself, so you go through a period where there's a relative decline; that is to say, it's no longer true that it gets its way 95 percent of the time on 95 percent of the issues, but it gets its way on a lot of issues by making various kinds of compromises, by operating in various ways to slow down the decline.

I see this having largely occurred in the case of the United States more or less between the early 1970s and the year 2000. It was a decline, but it wasn't a disastrous decline. And then along came George W. Bush, who tried to reverse the decline, but what he did was counterproductive and led to what I call a *precipitate decline*, so that by 2010, let's say, it's no longer true that the United States can get its way most of the time.

How do we know that? Well, we know that because other countries are beginning to act directly counter to the way the United States wishes them to act, and the United States is simply unable to do anything significant about it. They begin to ignore the American point of view, even if they do it at first gingerly because the United States remains a very powerful actor and could slap back in ways that are rational or irrational, so countries are a little bit careful, but basically they can begin to ignore it. And you can go to a further stage where they ignore the United States entirely. For example, today in the Middle East I think the United States is simply ignored. It's not only Russia and China that ignore the United States; it is Saudi Arabia and Iran and Egypt and Qatar and even Turkey. All these countries are doing what they think is the appropriate thing to do, whether or not the United States actually approves of this.

Now, is the current wave of unrest a sign of hegemonic decline? Well, I don't think that proves the United States isn't hegemonic, yet it is made in some ways more possible by the fact that the United States can't sit on this unrest in any significant way. But there was a big wave of unrest when the United States was still hegemonic, and I have tried to argue that this earlier wave was almost facilitated by the fact that the United States was hegemonic, so I think those have to be analyzed separately.[1] The growth of U.S. debt: is that a sign of hegemonic decline? Yes it is, in the sense that if you don't have the money to do things by yourself, you're weaker. Take the first Gulf War. The United States moves in with its army and defeats Saddam Hussein and pushes him back, but it was unable to pay for it. That is quite remarkable. If you look at the actual figures, 90 percent of the bill was paid by four countries, namely Germany, Japan, Kuwait, and Saudi Arabia.[2] It is one thing for them to cough up the money, but that very fact gives them a certain independence vis-à-vis the United States. Not having the money is definitely a sign of increasing weakness because the United States now has to play games with China and other countries because they are big buyers of U.S. bonds—that is, of course, a weakness.

KH: You argue that, unlike the earlier rise and fall of hegemonic powers such as the Dutch and the British, the hegemonic crisis of the United States is bound up with a structural crisis of capitalism as a world-system. Yet terms such as the *Great Recession* and the *Great Stagnation* imply that capitalism will endure, just as occurred in previous global economic crises. What are the particular structures of the capitalist world-economy that are now in crisis, and why is this crisis different?

IW: Capital accumulation occurs via production, in which the entrepreneur receives as profit the difference between the sales prices and the costs of production. The producer tries to minimize the three generic costs of production: personnel costs, the costs of inputs, and taxation. There are three kinds of personnel costs. In the case of unskilled and semiskilled workers, rising costs due to their syndical action have been contained primarily by the operation of the runaway factory, that is, by the relocation of production processes to areas with "historically" lower wages. Sooner or later the costs again become too high because of syndical action and lead to a further move. Over five hundred years, this "runaway" technique has exhausted its possibilities because of the de-ruralization of the world-system, which has been quite dramatic in the past fifty years.

Meanwhile the cost of cadres has also risen, for two reasons. The ever-larger scale of productive units requires more intermediate personnel. And more cadres are needed to counter the syndical organization of the low-skilled personnel. The rise in overall payments to the top managers has also been spectacular, particularly recently. The basic reason is the separation of ownership and control, which has made it possible for the top managers to appropriate rent from the firm's receipts.

The costs of inputs have also been going up. Capitalists externalize as many costs as they can, in particular, disposal of toxic waste, renewal of raw materials, and construction or reconstruction of infrastructure. The origin of the debate about toxic disposal is due to the fact that the world has exhausted most vacant public domains for the waste, such that the impact on public health has become much more obvious. In addition, the large increase in global population has led to a worry about the exhaustion or shortage of natural resources.

Further, products produced for sale on the world market require both transport and communications; however, the costs have risen considerably, leading to a discussion about who should pay the bill: the producers, who use the infrastructure, or the general public. Finally, there is the rising level of taxation, the result of the expansion of government size and functions. There is equally an expansion of private taxation, that is, corruption of officials and the demands of organized mafias. There are more people to bribe and ever more room for mafiosi protection rackets. The biggest source of increased taxation, however, has been the result of the democratization of world politics. Popular social movements have fought to get the governments to provide education, health services, and life-long revenue flows, the combination of which we call the "welfare state." Over time, the demands for each have steadily expanded in two ways: the levels of services demanded and the increased geographical locales in which the demands have been made. In short, the three basic costs of production—personnel, inputs, and taxation—have all risen constantly and have moved so close to the asymptotes that the system cannot be brought back to equilibrium via all the standard mechanisms used for five hundred years.

KH: Yet it seems that political and economic elites in the United States and Europe are approaching the continuing fallout of the 2008 financial crisis with the assumption that the world can go back to the way it was in the 1990s with some minor adjustments and belt-tightening. At the same time, the solutions they are applying—fiscal austerity, loose monetary policy, a few bankers harangued before the cameras—is clearly not returning the world to anything resembling the state of affairs before the financial crisis. Instead they are exacerbating social tensions and undermining the livelihoods of millions of people. Was this inevitable? Is this approach eroding Western states' sources of power? Or can they stave off the worst aspects of the crisis just by pushing it onto other countries and regions? And do these other countries and regions have the power to push back?

IW: If you look at the 2008 presidential campaign between Barack Obama and John McCain, both of them were arguing that U.S. power had declined but could be restored, at least to the strength it had in the 1990s. They had different formulas about how to do this. McCain's was more like the first term of George W. Bush: be more macho, assert your power. And Obama was saying, "No, we have to work it out diplomatically with our allies, pull them along, and that will restore our power." I think they both believed this was possible. And in fact I think that's a widespread assumption of the North American public and of large parts of the European public, that the United States can restore its "leadership."

Is that inevitable? No, I don't think so; I think this is a misperception. Partly, of course, leaders can't get out too far ahead of their voters or they won't get reelected, or elected in the first place; on the other hand, voters don't change if leaders keep saying they don't need to change in their perception of the world. So this is the kind of situation in which it makes a difference what line the leader takes and how much he's willing to invest in making people understand that you can't go back to the 1990s, and you certainly can't go back to the 1950s or 1960s. But there are ways of adjusting to reality. The decline of a hegemonic power doesn't mean that from one day to the next the United States becomes Paraguay. It's not only a very powerful country but also a very wealthy country, and, as I sometimes say, there's a lot of fat on which you can live for a long time. But you have to be realistic about it. It took quite a while before the British were realistic about their relative decline, and sometimes one suspects they are still not entirely realistic about it. But nonetheless you can adjust to it.

There's nothing inevitable about it, but it's true that the current situation is one in which neither the American people as a whole nor the political leadership is ready to accept the fact that the United States is no longer the leader. This is a big shock. It took people a long time to get used to being the hegemonic power and invest their psyche in it, and now you're asking them to realize that the United States is not number one; it's just one of a group of powerful countries in the world. That isn't easy, but it can be done.

So, yes, U.S. political leaders definitely believe they can go back to the 1990s, quite explicitly in many ways. When Obama points to the merits of what Bill Clinton did, that's what he's implying. I don't think it's terribly useful, but I understand his need as a politician to be sure that he can get reelected. Once reelected, will he still say that? I don't know. They change lines slowly. To take a different kind of example, you know the old story about Franklin Roosevelt—he had a bunch of labor leaders come to see him and they persuaded him that he had to change his line. And he said, "Go out and make enough fuss so that you can force me to do it." In a sense, what has to happen is that people force the leader to do it, and the leader wants to be forced. I think that's what Angela Merkel is doing in Europe right now. She wants to be forced to do the kind of things that the German public doesn't want her to do.

KH: You have written that world-systems analysis is not a theory, yet most of the time when I encounter your work in other places, it is still labeled as "world-system theory" or in many cases, "world system theory" without a hyphen between the two nouns. This is far from an academic trifle, since your usage of the term connotes a view of global social change quite different from that in orthodox social science. What is the significance of your terminology, hyphen and all?

IW: The problem of the hyphen in the term *world-system* has to do with a linguistic problem. The concept of a *world-economy* was taken as a direct translation from the historian Fernand Braudel, who invented the term *économie-monde* with a hyphen, that is, distinguished in his mind and my mind from *économie* (no hyphen) *mondiale, mondiale* being the adjective for world, while *monde* is a noun. *Économie-monde* is two nouns tied with a hyphen. Where did that come from? Well, Braudel got it from Fritz Rörig, a geographer who wrote in the 1920s about *Weltwirtschaft*. But in German there is no hyphen and no two separate words, because that's the way the German language works. Braudel decided from the context that Rörig was not talking about *économie mondiale* but *économie-monde*, and that's because it is *a* world, not *the* world.

That is, a world is a social entity that has a reality, but it is not necessarily planetary, so only *the* world would be planetary. This turns out to be very important because Braudel and I are both arguing that when neoclassical economists or others talk about world economy or international economy, they have the idea that there exist national economies that enter into some kind of trade relations with each other, and then that becomes the international economy. First you have the national, then the international. But for Braudel, and then for me, it's the opposite. First you have the *économie-monde*, and then within that states try to do various things within their political frontiers. But then we face the English language. English is a problem because *world* (no hyphen) *economy* is exactly the phrase that all the classical economists were using to refer to the *économie mondiale*. So I said the only way I can do this in English is to distinguish between *world economy* and *world-economy*.

I had to insist on the hyphen so I could get a translation of *économie-monde*, but then the same thing would work with *world-system* and *world-empire*. So we end up with *world-systems analysis* because there are multiple kinds of world-systems in the history of the world, but there is only one capitalist world-economy that survived. Well, it's taken me twenty or thirty years to get people to understand how important the hyphen really is. When I read people who write about me, I often notice that they use really outdated formulations. It's not that I've changed my view fundamentally, but I've become increasingly careful about the terminology, so I say that you have to look at my latest writings to really understand what my point of view is about core-periphery, about multiple world-systems, about class struggle. In one sense, my book *World-Systems Analysis: An Introduction* was an attempt to be very careful, but I've since seen there are some things in there that are not so careful.[3]

Now, why don't I like calling it a theory? Because a theory is a closure, and I thought it was far too premature to close anything. I believe this is the case for the explanation of historical systems, which are large-scale and long-term, so I have resisted the appellation *world-systems theory* for the kind of work I do, instead insisting that I was engaged in world-systems analysis.

KH: You have written four volumes thus far of *The Modern World-System*, and particular arguments therein, while controversial at the time of publication, are perhaps more accepted today. After all, "globalization" and an interconnected global economy are now taken for granted in contemporary social science. To what extent has world-systems analysis gone mainstream?

IW: Well, globalization as a concept has been around since the 1980s and is now mainstream. It is often said this is something the view of world-systems analysts fathered. Or it is said that "they" are now accepting "our" views and it's become mainstream ideology. I don't think they really are. I think they're faced with the reality of the interconnectedness of the world-system today. What they are saying is "Yes, that's so, but it's very recent and it's the result of x, y, and z." I've written a long critique of globalization theory, which says, in effect, "Look, what we said is that what they call globalization started in the sixteenth century; they're saying it started in 1945 or 1970, that it's something brand new."[4] I don't consider that an acceptance of the theses advanced in my writings.

But, having said that, it's perfectly true that if you look at world scholarly reaction as of 1970 compared to 2010 or so, we have made some headway. I mean, I see us still as a minority point of view within world social science, but it's not as weak as it was when we were being

dismissed, basically, as crazy. Some of our early arguments are no longer made with the same urgency as they used to be because our targets have been refuted so many times, but modernization theory hasn't
died. It's weaker, but it's there. Nomothetic social science hasn't died;
neither has idiographic social science. So, in summary, we have made
some progress, and I've even written about what happens if we become
mainstream and disappear, to which I say, "Problems never stop."[5] But
we're not mainstream yet. We're not mainstream by any means.

KH: The most recent and fourth volume of the *Modern World-System*
covers a wide range of nineteenth-century intellectual and social history, revolving around what you term *centrist liberalism*. A striking
argument you make is that the main political ideologies of the past two
centuries that viewed themselves as being in competition with each
other—that is, conservatism, liberalism, and radicalism—eventually
ended up as three variants of centrist liberalism. Yet centrist liberalism
also entered a period when social demands from below for egalitarianism along with categories of class, gender, ethnicity, and citizenship
formed one of the main bases of social movements from the nineteenth
century onward. How did this taming of competing ideologies develop?
And could we therefore say that the most dangerous foe of liberalism
were those individuals and movements who took this ideology the most
seriously and tried to apply it?

IW: I label these three main ideologies conservatism, liberalism, and
radicalism. I call the last radicalism because radicalism took a whole
variety of ideological versions, of which socialism is one. Anarchists
were radicals; Fourierists were for a while radicals too, and so forth.
The three main ideologies started as out as three different things. It isn't
until 1848 that I see the triumph of centrist liberalism and the other
two becoming variants (or "avatars"). Conservatism accepted the necessity of reform to prevent revolutions, and they did very well at that.
Radicalism didn't accept the tactic of reform because of the difficulty of
fomenting revolution; instead I would say that they realized after 1848

that the tactic which was the favored one prior to 1848—spontaneous uprising—didn't work because it was too easy to put down. So they then said that the solution to that was to organize and to build a structure toward the revolution.

It's a contradiction in terms: the organization is necessary in order to be a powerful fighter; but the organization means you develop a bureaucracy, which then begins to have interests that are different from the actual end product of revolution that is envisaged. So through this process they come to what is sometimes called reformism. Of course, there's the big split between the Second and Third International which predates that and goes back to the Bolsheviks. The idea that you could vote yourself into power, which was the basic Bernsteinian assumption—that if you could get universal suffrage, you would have a majority of workers, and the workers would vote themselves into socialism—missed the whole point of why all workers would not necessarily vote for a socialist party. But it was at least something you could conceive of as possible if you had elections and you had a parliamentary system. If you don't have elections and a parliamentary system, as in Russia, then how are you going to vote yourself into power? So you come up with an ideology that we have to have an insurrection, organized, and at a certain point they seized power—they stormed the Winter Palace. Well, okay, but that missed the point that they then became a state, and due to the pressures of the interstate system they had to modify their policies. So neither form of strategy worked, which has been the main problem for movements under the umbrella of the term *radicalism*.

Now, centrist liberalism did generate the space for social demands from below, in the sense that centrist liberalism defined citizenship. But citizenship became such a threatening idea that they had to figure out how to limit citizenship. They did this by creating a whole concept of active and passive citizens; that's the language of Abbé Siéyès, who proposed such a distinction immediately after the 1789 French Revolution. Active citizens were allowed to vote, while passive citizens were just equal before the law but didn't have the right to vote. That immediately raises the question of how do we, who are passive citizens, become active citizens? And that's what generates all these movements, which are attempts to become active citizens: the vote for women, or the vote for workers, or the vote for minority groups.

All those social movements gradually became successful, but they are always generating new forms of exclusion. Citizenship is supposed to be an inclusionary concept, but it is simultaneously an exclusionary concept. So the taming worked because of the pressures of the system on everybody to act in ways that were contradictory to other things that they wanted. So they had to organize, but the organization was kind of a self-defeating process. Was the most dangerous foe of liberalism those individuals and movements who took the ideology most seriously and tried to apply it? Yes, but it is a recent phenomenon. What people have discovered is that the official line of centrist liberalism is in contradiction with their actual policies. So some people have said, "Well, let's take the official line seriously and insist that they follow the official line." And that as a tactic has had some impact over the past thirty years. Let's force them to take it seriously and fully integrate and deliver rights. Well, I don't know how widespread this kind of tactic is, but it has had a certain degree of promise.

But given the fact that we are moving into the structural crisis of the world-system, tactics that worked within the continuing capitalist world-economy, as long as it was a normally functioning system, is one set of things, but tactics and strategies that work when you're in a structural crisis may be quite different.

KH: Let's turn to that. The era of social movements associated with 1968, you have written, was a rebellion against both the holders of political and economic power as well as against the old left movements themselves. And ever since that period we have seen the rise of a multitude of movements and demands, sometimes at odds with each other. Now, four decades later, there is a new upsurge of unrest which, in a way, recalls the breadth and reach of 1968. To what extent are the various movements of this decade, such as the Arab Spring, the Occupy movement and its European varieties, or middle-class protests in Russia, China, and India a continuation of 1968?

IW: Well, on the one hand they are a continuation of the spirit of 1968 in the sense that I see the spirit of 1968 as the revolt against authority structures—world authority structures, national authority structures, all kinds of institutional authority structures—and people saying to authorities, "You are oppressing us in numerous ways and we don't believe anything that you say." Is that happening? I think that element was very strong in what happened in the communist world in 1989, and I wrote an article with Giovanni Arrighi and Terence Hopkins about 1989 being the continuation of 1968.[6] The same thing is true of Occupy and the Arab Spring.

But these uprisings have all the limitations of spontaneity. That is to say, they exhaust themselves; they get repressed. Do they leave a legacy? Yes, they leave legacies, they really do. So 1968 left a legacy on the old left movements, which are still around but radically different than they were before 1968. The Occupy movement is leaving a legacy—I don't know if the movement itself is even going to survive, we'll have to see—but it's already left a legacy in the sense that the whole issue of social polarization and inequality has become a mainstream issue, whereas three years ago it wasn't even there.

But immediately, of course, there is an attempt to co-opt these movements or limit them. There are two ways of reacting to these kinds of spontaneous uprisings. One is to hit them hard over the head, and that's done all the time. And the other is to co-opt them, in the very simple sense of taking over the movement, defining it narrowly, declaring triumph when a leader is changed or a particular thing is changed that doesn't really change anything else very much. Let's take one example. It's clear that the initial strength of the movement in Egypt in Tahrir Square was along the lines of the spirit of 1968. The army says, "We're on your side, boys. We'll throw out Mubarak, and we'll arrange new elections, and so forth, but we'll now be in power." Well, they didn't want to change the system; they just wanted to change the leader. For a time they succeeded, but whether it could last is another kind of question.

But that kind of thing, where a spontaneous uprising that is very strong, that shakes up everything and is then suppressed or co-opted rather rapidly, leaves a legacy, and then you go on to the next one. We may be beyond that for Egypt or Greece or the United States, but it's all part of a constant process of uncertainties, of instabilities of the existing system, which is part of the crisis in the world-system.

Now one of the things I said about 1968 was that the period of 1945–68 was the height of U.S. hegemony and the strongest period of economic growth in the history of the world-system. So why in this very period do antisystemic movements come to power more or less everywhere? Communist parties in one third of the world, social democrats in one third, national liberation movements in the last third? Isn't that a contradiction? I would say no, it's not. Actually, it makes every bit of sense because it's the same thing as what industries that have quasi-monopolies do: one of the reasons why an industry with a quasi-monopoly exhausts itself is that stoppages of work cost more to a quasi-monopoly in terms of revenue than further concessions to the workers who are demanding a pay raise. So they give it, and times are good for the workers. Except that if you keep doing this, it becomes too expensive and you'll have undermined your system. What is good for a few years is not good for twenty years.

It's the same thing for a quasi-monopoly on geopolitical power. If the United States was a quasi-monopoly, disruptions of various kinds— revolutions in Third World countries, for example—interfered with the processes that were advantageous to the hegemonic power, so they made concessions in terms of autonomy or whatever else because it's cheaper for retaining the quasi-monopoly than hitting over the head. But bit by bit that adds up, and you've undermined your quasi-monopoly. So it's not a contradiction that antisystemic movements came to power everywhere after 1945, and 1968 was the explosion that results from having made these concessions. The spirit of 1968 was directed both against the world power and its collusive ally, the Soviet Union, as well as the antisystemic movements that had previously come to power but hadn't changed the world. So it's a double effect. And that leaves a lasting legacy. The United States had a collusive power and it lost that in 1989, which is not a plus but a minus for the United States, and it undermines the ability of the antisystemic movements to argue their old case of being the exclusive holder of revolutionary validity, with everybody else being subordinate to that.

KH: Today a key debate within social movements is over the question of organization, tactics, and strategy. On the one hand, there is a hesitation to create hierarchical organizations and to assign leaders to run them, but on the other hand, organizational power is a tried and true method of putting pressure on political and economic elites. This was, of course, the debate in the mid-nineteenth century between anarchists and socialists. So are we simply replaying this debate today? Or, given the structural crisis in capitalism and the potential for a new world-system, is the current debate fundamentally new? Are there the same dangers in organizational power today as in the nineteenth and twentieth century?

IW: Well, we are replaying that debate today, but we are not simply replaying it, since my argument is that we are in a structural crisis for all the reasons that I mentioned before. Out of this crisis, we get a systemic bifurcation of possible outcomes, and we now have what I call the spirit of Davos versus the spirit of Porto Alegre (the meeting place of the alter-globalization World Social Forum). The spirit of Davos wants to create a system that's different from capitalism but shares its worst features, such as hierarchy, exploitation, and polarization. The spirit of Porto Alegre wants to create a relatively democratic, relatively egalitarian world. And those are the two options, so to speak, so now the question is the strategy. But each side is also split.

So if I talk about the spirit of Porto Alegre, there is this strong movement that is still continuing the spirit of 1968, saying, "No, we don't want verticalism; we want horizontalism, and we want multiple organizations talking to each other. We don't want priority to x or y or z; they all have to be done. We have to learn from each other; we can't denounce each other." And lo and behold, there are others who say, "That sounds like anarchism to us, and it won't work because you have to organize, and to organize you have to have a new International." (Sometimes they even use that language.) So you have this big argument that's replaying, if you will, the argument of the nineteenth century. Is it simply that? No. Because everybody is aware that there was this argument, and they are all aware of what happened in 1968. So there's a kind of third group who are saying, "Maybe we can somehow combine the horizontalist approach and the verticalist approach by having multiple organized things but not one single organized thing." And that debate is continuing.

Now I say there is a similar debate on the other side, on the side of Davos, and that's the debate about "How do we get to this good world that we want?" One group says, "Hit them over the head and hit them over the head hard." And the other says, "No, we have to sound progressive. Everything must change so that nothing will change. We'll be green capitalists, we'll be this, we'll be that. We'll negotiate with the people in Porto Alegre." So we've got four sides with two possible outcomes. It is very confusing intellectually and politically, which is one of the many reasons why you can't predict the outcome. We're in the middle of that now, and we've been in the middle of that for thirty or forty years already, and we're going to be in the middle of that for another twenty to forty years. But at some point it tilts definitively. We can't predict at what point or which way we'll tilt. We are in the middle of a complicated, murky, difficult struggle.

And then the whole question becomes what kind of tactics you use to move toward the change that you want. I argue for the idea of combining short-run *and* middle-run tactics. I say that people are suffering. There is real suffering out there. There are people who have lost their jobs, who have nothing to eat. To tell such people that if they just stick with it, in thirty years everything will be wonderful, that's irrelevant. They are suffering today. And a movement that can't respond to today's suffering is not going to get anywhere. So I say you have to do things that will minimize the pain, without arguing that minimizing the pain changes the system. What is minimizing the pain? It might be to pass a particular piece of legislation, elect a particular person at a particular point who is the lesser evil. But this doesn't change the system. You have to say that time and time again. So minimizing the pain is not reformism; it is responding to immediate needs of people, without which you get nowhere.

But then you have to have the middle run, which is transforming the system, in which there's no compromise. Now, are there things you can do that move in that direction at various points? We ought to be having an intellectual debate about the middle-run strategy to transform the world, to tilt it in a direction so that we come out of the bifurcation with our side having won and created a new world order.

Is that certain? Absolutely not. There's no way of knowing, but then I always end up by saying, "Look, for several thousand years Western philosophy has debated determinism versus free will and everybody has always argued for one or the other. I say let's historicize it: it's the one in some points of time and the other in other points. When the system is operating normally, it's determinist." What does that mean? That means, and let's come back to the French Revolution, for example, you put a lot of social effort into transforming the world, and in the end you got pulled back to some kind of moving equilibrium. So it didn't transform the world. That's a determinist situation. But when everything is up for grabs because you're in a structural crisis, you can't get back to equilibrium, so every little input pushes something in some wild direction.

I often end my talks by saying we are like butterflies in the world climate. We can affect our situation, but we don't know whether there are enough other butterflies operating in the same way at every instant because there are an infinite number of possibilities. We are in a free will situation in which we can affect the outcome, without knowing if we will succeed.

11

"Re-create the social state"

Photo courtesy of Zygmunt
Bauman.

ZYGMUNT BAUMAN

in conversation with Vincent Della Sala

Zygmunt Bauman is emeritus professor of
sociology at the University of Leeds. He was
awarded the European Amalfi Prize for Sociology and Social Sciences in 1992 and the Theodor W. Adorno Award of the city of Frankfurt in 1998.

In this challenging discussion with Vincent Della Sala, the sociologist
Zygmunt Bauman focuses on the state of flux—the interregnum—in
which the world finds itself. He suggests that we are seeing an increasing separation between politics and power, between the means available to enact change and the vastness of the problems that need to be
addressed. In this new world, we are living through what he terms a
liquid modernity, where change is the only constant and uncertainty
the only certainty. This is a world with no teleology but also one far
from an end of history. In this context, he sees Europe as still being a
battlefield, this time in the struggle between the Westphalian sovereign
state model and new forms of supranational politics and governance.
Paradoxically Europe is seeking to address this issue, including the

re-creation of a new social state and space, through the technocratic means of an unelected bureaucratic mechanism. As such, Bauman poses what he sees as a key question for today's politics: how to re-create the social state in a globalizing planet.

VDS: There is a sense of foreboding in much of the commentary on the current state of affairs in the world. Many have drawn parallels with the 1930s: a shifting balance of power, the social and political consequences of sticking slavishly to orthodox economic ideology, and the "double bind" that you have talked about concerning the inadequacy of the Westphalian state to deal with problems that do not originate within its borders. Do you share in this sense that we are on the edge of major social, political, and economic upheavals whose political outcome is, at best, uncertain?

ZB: It all depends on the choice of perspective. Comparisons, time-bound by nature, throw a different light on developments and suggest different meanings each time a short-term perspective is replaced by a long-term one. The crises of the 1930s can be viewed now as premortem agonies of the solid-modern, nation- and state-building era, with its absolutist ambitions and thus also an inherent totalitarian tendency. Such agonies are now by and large behind us; it is rather the dearth of normative regulation, unending deregulation, and the overall decline of the public (all in all, the opposite of that past era's ambitions and practices) that underpin our current troubles. They marked, after all, the time of unprecedentedly brash—indeed impertinent—ambitions and self-confident intentions to build a thousand-year Reich or, as Stalin put it, of certainty to prove that no fortress exists that the Bolsheviks could not conquer.

A proper timescale to compare with the present one is the early—initial, inceptive—period of modernity, the time of the collapse of the ancien régime ever more evidently losing its hold over human undertakings and plight, with only a vague idea of the emergent forms of life destined to replace the old regime. (The British press of the early nineteenth century showed no inkling of awareness of being in the midst of what, only by the end of that century, after the fact, was to be dubbed the Industrial Revolution.)

Today's states, the highest-level political instruments in our possession, are not in a position to entertain any certainty as to the impermeability of the ramparts meant to defend their own local fortresses, let alone the intention, or at least a dream of conquering the new ones, placed explicitly outside the realm of their rule—"outside" in both the spatial and the temporal spaces. I believe that the incommensurability of the time dimension of the developments and processes that shape our present and delineate our future options and the time perspective of the state administrations—the sole available instruments of collective purposeful actions—create the most crucial "double bind" in which political actors are embroiled. Governments lend their ear to the demands of their electors with an eye on elections no further than five years ahead. The developments and processes in question, however, started well before they have been called into office and disclose the full awesomeness of their outcomes long after they leave office.

VDS: If we go back two decades to the early 1990s, it seemed that the future belonged to amorphous, ambiguous political structures, such as the European Union, which allowed for fluidity in the construction of identity and belonging as well as the organization of political power. The end of the cold war contributed to a sense of optimism, but it was not the only factor. There are a list of developments—the wars in the former Yugoslavia, China's entry into the World Trade Organization, the emergence of the security state, and so on—since the heady days of German unification and the Maastricht Treaty in Europe that suggest that maybe the world is not ready for Europe and that Europe may not be ready for the world. If I can borrow the title from a chapter in one of your earlier books, I would ask: Are we closer to a world that is hospitable to Europe today than two decades ago?

ZB: In a nutshell, in the early 1990s the world seemed to stand at the threshold of a new world order, preparing for a final leap forward. The bipolarity of the communist versus capitalist (in another idiom, totalitarian versus democratic) planet for half a century effectively masked the subterranean processes of the globalization of interdependence that put paid to the three or so centuries of the long march toward full and indivisible territorial sovereignty of the nation-state perched on the tripod of economic, military, and cultural autarky. With the bipolarity removed, many people began to treat seriously Francis Fukuyama–style inane proclamations of the impending "end of history": that having swept out of its way, one by one, successive (and temporary) irritants blocking its way and delaying its progress, history has reached, or almost, its predestined destination.

In practice, the fall of the Berlin Wall ushered in an era of "interregnum," that is, an updated version of Antonio Gramsci's notion, a state of affairs in which the inherited means of getting things done no longer work, yet the new and more adequate ways have not been invented, let alone deployed. This particular interregnum has been caused by the progressive separation and divorce of power (the ability to have things done) and politics (the ability to decide which things are to be done) and the resulting disparity between the tasks and the tools serving them: on one side, power increasingly free from political control, and, on the other side, politics increasingly suffering a deficit of power. Increasingly global and extraterritorial power was confronted with a politics as territorial and local as before.

I believe that the plight of Europe as, simultaneously, a disposal bin for globally produced challenges and a leading laboratory in which the ways and means of confronting, tackling, and hopefully resolving them are designed and tested, becomes over the years all too clear. It is here, inside the European Union and in its immediate vicinity, that the potentially most seminal battles between the relics of post-Westphalian order and the emergent, birth-pangs-ridden supranational politics are waged and fought. The fate of each successive battle is as a rule in the balance, whereas the victory in the continuing war is anything but predetermined. But contrary to the repeated alarms, the tipping point preventing a return to the old-style Westphalian settlement has been by now reached and perhaps passed.

vds: Following from and related to the previous question: Are we simply in a period of transition in which we have become painfully aware that the old (namely, the Westphalian state and the attendant notions of sovereignty) means are inadequate to meet contemporary challenges, but we have yet to imagine, let alone begin to construct, what will take its place?

zb: When, more than ten years ago, I tried to unpack the meaning of the metaphor of "liquidity" in its application to the currently practiced form of life, one of the mysteries persistently haunting me and staunchly resisting resolution was the status of the liquid-modern human condition. Was it an intimation, an early version, an augury, or a portent of things to come? Or was it, rather, a temporary and transient—as well as an unfinished, incomplete, and inconsistent—interim settlement, an interval between two distinct yet viable and durable, complete, and consistent answers to the challenges of human togetherness?

I have not thus far come anywhere near to a resolution of that quandary, but I am increasingly inclined to surmise that we presently find ourselves in a time of interregnum—when the old ways of doing things no longer work, the old learned or inherited modes of life are no longer suitable for the current *conditio humana*, but when the new ways of tackling the challenges and new modes of life better suited to the new conditions have not as yet been invented, put in place, and set in operation. We don't yet know which of the extant forms and settings will need to be "liquidized" and replaced, though none seems to be immune to criticism, and all or almost all of them have at one time or another been earmarked for replacement.

Most important, unlike our ancestors, we don't have a clear image of a "destination" toward which we seem to be moving—which needs to be a model of *global* society, a global economy, global politics, a global jurisdiction. Instead we react to the latest trouble, experimenting, groping in the dark. We try to diminish carbon dioxide pollution by dismantling coal-fed power plants and replacing them with nuclear power plants, only to conjure up the specters of Chernobyl and Fukushima. We feel rather than know (and many of us refuse to acknowledge) that power (that is, the ability to do things) has been separated from politics (that is, the ability to decide which things need to be done and given priority), and so in addition to our confusion about "what to do" we are now in the dark about "who is going to do it." The sole agencies of collective purposive action bequeathed to us by our parents and grandparents, confined as they are to the boundaries of nation-states, are clearly inadequate, considering the global reach of our problems and of their sources and consequences.

We remain, of course, as modern as we were before, but these *we* who are modern have considerably grown in numbers in recent years. We may well say that by now all or almost all of us, in every or almost every part of the planet, have become modern. And that means that today, unlike a decade or two ago, every land on the planet, with only a few exceptions, is subject to the obsessive, compulsive, unstoppable change that is nowadays called *modernization*, and to everything that goes with it, including the continuous production of human redundancy and the social tensions it is bound to cause.

Forms of modern life may differ in quite a few respects, but what unites them all is precisely their fragility, temporariness, vulnerability, and susceptibility to constant change. To "be modern" means to modernize—compulsively, obsessively—not so much just "to be," let alone to keep accustomed identities intact, but forever "becoming," avoiding completion, staying underdefined. Each new structure that replaces the previous one as soon as it is declared old-fashioned and past its use-by date is only another momentary settlement—acknowledged as temporary and "until further notice." Being always, at any stage and at all times, "post-something" is also an inalienable feature of modernity. As time flows, "modernity" changes its forms in the manner of the legendary Proteus. What was earlier dubbed (erroneously) *postmodernity*, and what I've chosen to call, more to the point, *liquid modernity*, is the growing conviction that change is *the only* permanence, and uncertainty *the only* certainty. A hundred years ago *to be modern* meant to pursue "the final state of perfection." Now it means an infinity of improvement, with no "final state" in sight and none desired.

VDS: As you rightly mentioned, events at the end of the past century were mistakenly interpreted as the end of history. More specific to Europe, the process of European integration was also seen as contributing to the end of history, doing away with the scourges of nationalism as well as class conflict. The Westphalian order, which, as you point out, is dissolving with its replacement not yet apparent, was just as much about managing class relations in the modern industrial world as it was about expressing national interests. Would it be fair to say that the current economic crisis in Europe is worrying precisely because the clash of economic interests, which had always been easily placed within broader historical narratives, does not find a way to define itself in an age of "liquidity"?

ZB: You may indeed put it that way. The apparently resilient and stable backbone holding the flesh of historical meanders is now in tatters, with no agency in sight as much as contemplating the reassembly of bits and pieces. Once more the "economic interests," just as in times of the separation of business from households (defined retrospectively by Max Weber as the birth point of the Industrial Revolution and modern capitalism), are set afloat, with fewer and fewer reference points—either material or conceptual—to hold them in place or confine the choice of trajectories. In time, they stumble from one crisis to another, each signaling another round of redistribution of global wealth and rearrangement of global forces. In space, they shift the local foci of globally generated crises: capitalism follows the pattern of the parasitic life forms—in which successive host organisms, nearing exhaustion, stripped of their assets, and no longer promising quick returns on investments, are abandoned—and capital resumes its search for new and as yet underexploited hosts. In the past two decades, the foci of crises moved from Argentina to Malaysia, to Yeltsin's Russia, Mexico, Iceland, Ireland, and Greece and are now shifting to Italy and Spain and threaten to expand to embrace the whole of the eurozone. No place is nowadays fully and truly insured against being targeted as the next "weakest link" in the nonsystem of world economy sustained by the nonsystem of planetary politics. The last role assigned to nation-states, those relics of the West-phalian settlement, is to deploy the state's rights and capacities for "legitimate coercion" in defending the financial markets against the unpredictable or deliberately ignored consequences of their freedom and to resuscitate their successive victims in order to render them once more amenable to another round of parasitic exploitation.

VDS: As you mentioned, Europe is a useful laboratory for us to under-stand liquidity and the interregnum. In this phase, you have written of how power and politics have been decoupled. This is nowhere more evident than in the European Union, which has tried to render as apo-litical as possible the very political process of constructing a new order. It is now struggling to find a popular consensus for a form of governing that is emblematic of the double bind that you have identified. Would it be fair to say that the European Union has been a success as a techno-cratic experiment in politics but a failure in trying to devise new ways of organizing and taming power for social purposes?

ZB: I am not sure, to be frank. I suppose that Europe is smarting under the contradictory pressures of a double bind type: it struggles for a uni-fied policy while using for that purpose an aggregate of autonomous and formally sovereign agents uniquely entitled to legitimize the successive steps on the road to unity. Just imagine modern centralized nation-states relying for their integration on the consent of provinces and parishes as they are stripped one by one of their *Rechtsgewohnenheiten* (customary rights). Imagine traffic bylaws in a modern city dependent for their obser-vation on car and truck drivers signing the Highway Code. What haunts the story of European integration is the jarring discrepancy between ends and means, between the set task and the tools chosen or available for their implementation. The borderline separating the autonomy of EU member states and prerogatives of the "technocratic politics" of Brus-sels's unelected bureaucracy (or, in bureaucratic parlance, the boundaries between centralized and "subsidiarized" functions) is hotly contested. In that struggle, amounting to an undeclared yet perpetual war, both sides use the strategy common to all bureaucracies: to untie their own hands while tying as firmly as possible the hands of the other side—to wit, to leave a lot to their own discretion while little (preferably nothing) to the decisions of the other side. The overriding strategic principle is to become the element of uncertainty in the other side's decision making while preventing its decisions from becoming elements of uncertainty in their own. Membership in the EU, being principally a give-and-take contract, means that this boils down in practice to each side attempting to regularize legally the "take" part and deregulate the "give" part.

vDS: In your book *Europe—An Unfinished Adventure* you pointed out how "social policy" Europe, inspired by the Christian and social democracy of Konrad Adenauer, Alcide de Gasperi, Paul-Henri Spaak, and Robert Schumann, augured an alternative to a European order and an international system based on power politics.[1] As you already pointed out in 2004, the European social model is, at best, under severe challenge, clinging to state-driven solutions to problems generated beyond its borders. It will probably be in tatters as the effects of the current financial crisis are felt from Greece to Ireland. The obvious solution seems to be to try to reconstruct some form of a truly "European" social state, beginning with a political union. Yet the EU seems to lack what you have called "a shared vision of collective mission." Is there not the risk, as Karl Polanyi warned, that in the interregnum of which you speak entire communities that are now exposed to market forces without the shield of a social policy Europe will seek out other solutions?

zB: Vaclav Havel, who knew the practice of political action better than most, if not any other humans, noted that "to predict the future one needs to know which songs the nation is willing to sing," but added right away that "the snag is that no one can know what sorts of songs the nation would prefer to intone next year." I fully endorse his opinion, for all I know, a decent political theory. And so my answer to your question is that, yes, there is such a risk, but each calculation of its size can be challenged as presumptuous.

IN my long life the pendulum of singing preferences has moved both ways. The need for a social state (pioneered, let's remember, by Otto von Bismarck and David Lloyd-George!) was once beyond left and right; then came the turn of the need to dismantle the social state to bid for national consensus. In both cases, the dominant opinion followed the transformations of capitalist economy reflected in the policy of states responsible for securing conditions for its regular reproduction. In the first case, that condition was the successful buying-selling meeting of capital and labor. In the second, it was (and thus far remains, at least in our part of the planet) the successful buying-selling meeting between client and commodity. No wonder that the funds deployed by the capitalist state to sustain the social state look better utilized if used to "recapitalize" banks and other credit institutions. However, one may guess that this shift tends to weaken the compact between states and their citizens—though such weakening is reflected not so much in the songs flowing from public media as in the growing mistrust in the extant political institutions and procedures as well as in the steadily spreading political apathy.

One more comment is in order here, or rather a big question never before properly posited, let alone answered: Just how far can one go in defending whatever remains of the social state with the means at the disposal of a single state or even group of states? Can't the social *state* be made truly secure and lasting only in the framework of a social *planet*? Indeed a big question, demanding no less than a thorough revision of the axiological and teleological foundations of the social state idea—and that before designing the as yet nonexistent political institutions reflecting such a revision. And demanding to do all that under conditions of shrinking instead of growing planetary resources. (See, for instance, Harald Welzer's recently published, thoroughly researched study of impending "climate wars.")[2] Well, the jury is still out, and there is little chance of its returning soon with a verdict on which they all agree.

VDS: In *Culture as Praxis* you wrote, "The 'we' made of inclusion, acceptance and confirmation is the realm of gratifying safety cut out (though seldom as securely as one would desire) from the frightening wilderness of an outside populated by 'them.' The safety would not be obtained unless the 'we' were trusted to have the power of acceptance, and the strength to protect those who have already been accepted."[3] As we try to look past the interregnum, and again using Europe as a laboratory, do you see it as necessary that a European "we" emerge so that a social Europe can be rebuilt beyond the national states?

ZB: That must be indeed the first step, though only the first—and in all probability already oriented toward a "social planet" and a Europe conscious of undertaking its "global responsibility" role as sketched ten years ago in my *Europe—An Unfinished Adventure* and in a much more elaborated fashion presented in Ulrich Beck's recent studies of and designs for "cosmopolitics."

THE emergence and entrenchment of a "European we" can hardly be achieved, however, unless in tandem with designing and putting in operation the institutions underpinning the experience of "European community": theory and practice, the "institutional logic" and the "Weltanschauung logic" can only run parallel, or rather intertwine, supporting and reinforcing each other.

VDS: You have written, drawing from Umberto Eco, about Europe's ability to communicate an "idiom" that will permit it to play a different role in a global world. If we can focus more closely on Europe's relations with its neighbors, not only to the east but also on the southern shores of the Mediterranean, some have argued that Europe, and the European Union, have acted in an "imperial" manner, initially with eastern and central European states who joined the EU and now with its "neighborhood." Would you say that Europe is a "vanishing" mediator, or does it still have an imperial reflex?

ZB: As in all cases of "stimulus diffusion" or "bringing gifts," or indeed all processes vacillating between coercion and persuasion, spreading the

"European idiom" means walking on a thin rope. There is no black and white here, but infinite shades of gray. No foolproof insurance against sliding into the "imperial reflex" and no guarantee that the model of "vanishing mediator" or of the "informal, open cooperation" recently postulated by Richard Sennett in the *Hedgehog Review* will be obeyed in full and that its practicing will be free of distortion:[4] *informal*, which means that the rules of coexistence are not designed and imposed in advance but are expected to emerge in the course of cooperation; *open*, which means that everyone is invited to learn and teach at the same time; and *cooperation* rather than mere debate, meaning that participants are not motivated by their desire to prove that they are right while all others are wrong and that there are no winners and losers because everyone emerges from cooperation wiser and richer in experience and know-how. Taking responsibility is inconceivable without simultaneous acceptance of such risks.

VDS: You have written extensively on modernity, postmodernity, and modernization. Europe has been central to almost all narratives about modernity and modernization for the past five centuries. Do you think this is still the case? Or has the emergence of new powers such as China, Brazil, and South Africa, very much infused with modern impulses, meant that there may be multiple forms of modernity emerging?

ZB: In our times of speed-space (to use Paul Virilio's term) and "information highways," the itineraries of stimuli once territorially fixed around the "limen" of empires and civilizations described in such detail by Arnold Toynbee have lost territorial continuity. Hybrids of modernization do not follow the movements of imperial troops and territorial conquests. They may and they do crop up on any part of the planet, leaping with ease between distant places and in each case unraveling the possibilities endemic to the "modernity" pattern but undisclosed or rejected elsewhere. Multiplicity of "modernities" cannot be avoided. Diversification is an inalienable effect of the leveling-up temptation and effort, just as discontinuities are inalienable from continuity of societal development. This, by the way, is a most powerful argument for acquiring, practicing, and developing the art of "informal, open cooperation" along the lines suggested by Richard Sennett.

VDS: You have described very eloquently the interregnum that defines the contemporary era and have described an almost unstoppable momentum of the processes associated with modernization. If we project forward, is it the case that the Proteus of modernization will always be a feature of social life? Can liquidity ever bring us the certainty that will end the interregnum? If it does not, or cannot, at what point do we say that we are no longer in a transition but have begun a new phase, albeit one that is ill-defined?

ZB: Your guess is as good as mine. This is, after all, a guessing game, and whose guess is right and whose mistaken can be responsibly judged only with the benefit of hindsight—retrospectively. In the state of interregnum, everything may happen, whereas nothing can be undertaken with full confidence. It's only in the aftermath of its completion that the victors rewrite its fits and bounds as "laws of history" and insert their verdicts in the school curriculum.

Perhaps our interregnum defies prediction more than similar periods of "disorganization" did in the past—and this because of the persisting hiatus between capacity to act and capacity to define the purpose of acting: the noncommensurability of means and goals. Powers float in Manuel Castells's "space of flows," while politics stays locked firmly in the "space of places."[5] No one control powers, while if left to themselves, powers are notorious for their inability to self-control and stay on course for a protracted stretch of time. Emancipation of powers from political (or any other form, for that matter) control leads to the reversal of Max Weber's logic of "rationality": means "secrete" or "exude" aims instead of serving them. As a result, everyone—notably including the political operators, however shrewd and insightful—keeps being surprised and repeatedly caught unprepared by "events."

Can this situation persist infinitely? Certainly not. There are, so to speak, natural limits to running through a minefield while doing next to nothing about disarming the mines and, if anything, adding to their numbers. The mines of the current interregnum have been assembled and continue to be fabricated by the unsustainability of our way of life, resulting in the depletion of planetary resources and the slow, yet relentless and accelerating erosion of life's conditions. Complete with the earth's population expected to reach nine billion in a matter of two or three decades, such a situation portends the advent of what a growing number of scholars, and Harald Welzer most emphatically and convincingly among them, describe as wars of redistribution of increasingly scarce resources, something that can be prevented only if a new formula is found and applied to human cohabitation, a formula alternative to that focused on "economic growth" (and thus the continuing deterioration of living conditions) as the sole medicine for all and any social ills—which is universally deployed at present and defended tooth and nail by the dominant powers of the day. If nothing is done, people will be mass-murdered, not, as their grandfathers were, for ideological reasons, but because someone somewhere needs and wishes the resources they sit on, have, and want to keep for their own survival.

VDS: Many in Europe, looking to a range of experiences such as those in Italy, Hungary, and Romania, fear that recent events are not death pangs but sudden reversals that could lurch us back to a period of instability and reverse many of the processes that we assumed had brought us past a point of no return. Is this an exaggerated fear, or does the uncertainty of transition open spaces for political and social movements whose responses to the crises exploit the lack of clarity about destination with the certainty of a rearview mirror?

ZB: The ancient biblical call "Back to your tents, o Israel!" looks increasingly prophetic when viewed from the perspective of developments you've pinpointed. Xenophobia, the desire to separate from "strangers" and keep them at a distance or get rid of them once and for all, is gaining in volume and intensity everywhere—including the most unexpected regions, where it was believed to have been cast into oblivion and hoped to stay there for the duration. This resentment—nay, hatred—focusing on immigrants and other "alien bodies" has not come from nowhere: our increasingly atomized society of consumers, inherently inhospitable to human solidarity, breeds competitiveness, rivalry, one-upmanship, and a propensity to aggression and exclusion. Condensing and focusing the resentment of others on specific groups or categories allows people to let off some steam, to unload at least partly the accumulated fears and angers—but in addition it panders to the nostalgia for lost and badly missed companionship and solidarity. From lynching the hapless foreigners (and so burning the fear and hatred of "otherness" in effigy) through marching with neo-Nazi banners and slogans and demanding that governments remove the immigrants who came and stop those who intend to come, and up to the racist manifestations, petards throwing, and fisticuffs on football stands—all in close company and support of "others like me"—it also helps to experience the longed-for warm and cozy "we-feeling": to live through a short-lived yet immensely intense "carnival of solidarity." For people smarting under the unbearable burden of seemingly incurable uncertainty and overwhelmed with fear of abandonment and loneliness as much as by shame of their own impotence and unworthiness, this, truly, is manna from heaven. A dose of "weekend solidarity" helps us bear another week of its spectacular and painful absence. Your list of countries affected will surely expand as long that "ersatz solidarity" is the only one that our society is capable of offering to those who need it.

vds: You mentioned that, unlike our ancestors, we do not have a destination or, if you will, a project that will define our purpose and through which we can gain a sense of direction by beginning to define a "global society," a "global economy," and a "global politics." Who is the "we" that can form this global society and global politics?

zb: "Global politics" (in other words, the remarriage of power and politics, but at the global level this time) is not an objective in its own right, but the means to reach objectives—all and any of them. Divining and designing the agencies of "global politics," followed by putting them in operation, is in my view a metademand or a metacondition that needs to be fulfilled for any of the ills presently haunting human cohabitation, including the fragility of the human condition, to be cured or at least durably mitigated. In other words, it is the necessary, though hardly sufficient, condition of such a cure or mitigation. Without it, we have no instruments adequate to handle the task effectively.

And that task is nothing less than a radical change in the mode of life we are currently practicing—individually and in common. Not endowed with the capacities of a prophet, I cannot, from my point in space and time, prognosticate the form that change will eventually take; neither can I predict its contents. Neither the form nor the content are in any way predetermined; both will emerge in the process of change. Most likely, however, the change will need to overturn the consumerist formula of problem solving and pursuit of happiness. It will need to entail as well the replacement of the present kind of cohabitation that acts as a social factory of competition and rivalry by another, one that functions as a social factory of solidarity and mutual trust. And it will need to reinstate the mutual responsibility of community for its members and of each individual member for the community in its rank of the guiding principle of human togetherness, as well as of the supreme measure of its humanity. This is required if the change is to bring us anywhere near the cure of the social ailments responsible for our present and prospective troubles.

VDS: Finally, the postwar consensus, founded on embedded liberalism, had a central role for the collectivization of risk in industrialized society. Can we construct a global politics that reproduces this collectivization to counter the power of global financial markets and the spreading commodification of social life?

ZB: The proof of the pudding is in the eating. Whether we can do what you ask can be proved only by trying. The only thing that can be said with any degree of certainty is that the future of humanity (indeed the question of humanity's having a future) depends on our determination in trying and the success of the trials.

12

"Create global social policy"

Photo courtesy of Bob Deacon.

BOB DEACON

in conversation with Rianne Mahon

Bob Deacon is emeritus professor of international social policy at the University of Sheffield and holds the UNESCO-UNU Chair in Regional Integration, Migration and the Free Movement of People at UNUCRIS in Bruges, Belgium. He has acted as consultant or adviser to several countries, as well as organizations such as the World Bank, UNICEF, and the UN.

In a frank conversation, Bob Deacon, a preeminent expert on global social policy, explains the history of the concept as theory, policy, and practice, focusing primarily on welfarist policies since the acceleration of globalization in the 1970s. He argues that some problems, like disease, migration, and trade, cannot be dealt with at the level of the state and require international cooperation between states, supranational organizations, and nongovernmental organizations, acting both locally and in the global arena. Calling on his own involvement in the development of such processes, he explains the difficulties of such initiatives and makes a number of concrete suggestions about how they might be implemented in the future. Throughout, Deacon elucidates how specific contexts and political pressures interact with abstract ideas in a fraught and contested policy space. He also stresses, unlike many commentators, that individual politicians and policymakers can indeed play pivotal roles in driving or derailing progressive policy. He also makes a number of challenging claims that are sure to provoke debate. Deacon advocates the concept of a global social protection floor, which would act as a sort of baseline global safety net, and is unapologetic for his universalism. Indeed he argues that it is the emergent economies that, for various reasons and perhaps paradoxically, are most likely to oppose new directions in global social policy.

RM: Is there a need for a global social policy? Isn't social policy really best left to the national level, where bonds of social solidarity are strongest?

BD: When I first started to think about global social policy, I didn't invent the idea. I might have invented the phrase, but there was already, in reality, a global social policy. Since the end of the Second World War there were already global institutions and intergovernmental organizations in effect addressing issues at a global level. You already had the International Labor Organization (ILO) going back to 1919, which was trying to articulate a set of standards for workers internationally; you already had the World Health Organization trying to address issues of health globally; and, as we'll perhaps talk about later, we already had the World Bank, which was beginning to get into the business of social policy. So nobody needed to invent the institutions—they were already in existence for decades and addressing issues of labor standards, poverty, eradication of diseases like TB, and working for universal education at a global level.

Another way to answer your question is to say that social problems do increasingly cross borders. Disease is the most obvious example, and fighting the spread of epidemics like avian flu and eradicating diseases such as polio and TB require some sort of international agreement. Moreover the more competitive trade arrangements between countries have grown, the more issues of what should be appropriate labor standards have become international. Poverty in one place has an effect elsewhere. The whole migration issue by definition requires attention at a global level and cannot be resolved entirely within the boundaries of one nation-state. So the reality is that global problems and global policies have existed for a very long time. All my work has done is to begin to think more systematically about it. But you are right, of course, in suggesting that bonds of social solidarity are strongest at a national level. This only raises the challenge to us all of how we re-create those bonds at a transnational level.

RM: So why did it become important to focus on global social policy, especially in the 1990s?

BD: Two things, I think. One is that, obviously, during the late 1970s, the 1980s, and into the 1990s, what we now know as globalization happened. There was a particular set of political decisions to reduce the barriers between countries in terms of the flows of money, ideas (which was a technological development, if you like), and to a lesser extent the flows of people. So these issues of world interconnectedness became more apparent, but also the particular nature of globalization, the fact that it took a particular form, that it took the form of the reduction of regulation, the increased role of the market, the inclination to say that a global market will solve all our problems and facilitate economic growth, all that exacerbated some of these cross-border issues that I mentioned. So it was the nature of this neoliberal globalization process that made it more urgent to look at global social policy in a more systematic way.

The other thing—and this is, I think, how a number of us stumbled upon these issues and then began to realize they needed to be addressed—was the collapse of the Berlin Wall and the communist project. Some of us were interested in the question "Now, if the world is no longer divided into the communist and capitalist blocs, the issue becomes what kind of capitalism, what kind of global capitalism will predominate?" We know there are different kinds of capitalism. There is social democratic capitalism, which taxes and spends, redistributes and regulates. And there is the other extreme, which is neoliberal capitalism, which taxes less, spends less, and relies far more heavily on the market. Choices therefore needed to be made, not least by the postcommunist states, about the future direction they would be following. And in some sense that also meant that the world needed to decide how it was going to fashion this global capitalist project. What we discovered was that the choices that were being made in the postcommunist countries were being very heavily influenced by the already existing international organizations, especially by the International Monetary Fund (IMF) and the World Bank, that were seeking to drive a policy of marketization, privatization, deregulation, reduction of state activities (in, for example, the area of pensions), and they were competing with organizations like the ILO, which was trying to say something rather different. So there was a contest of ideas about the future direction and the nature of these postcommunist regimes that made us realize that these were quite important global debates that we needed to address.

RM: There were also some major developments on the international scale, such as the World Summit for Social Development in Copenhagen in 1995, where participants concluded that people needed to be at the center of development and that this meant the elimination of poverty and social exclusion and the restoration of full employment as core development objectives.

BD: Copenhagen was, I suppose, the high point in a series of UN conferences that had been taking place in the 1980s and 1990s trying to articulate some kind of global policy. So the Copenhagen conference did set up and suggest a set of principles or policies that, if they were implemented, would address some of the worst aspects of neoliberal globalization. So that was happening. Seeing how far some of those policies could be developed became one of the things we were interested in.

RM: Did this help to inspire the Globalism and Social Policy Programme (GASPP), of which you were one of the founding members?[1]

BD: That's right. It's interesting that GASPP was funded by a Finnish governmental agency. That was a reflection of the recognition that if the world had now become a single global marketplace, then the future of the social democratic approach to all of this, which was the Nordic approach, perhaps had to be articulated at a supranational level. So the grand idea—the absurdly grand idea—was that therefore we should outline a set of ideas, a set of arguments, a set of policies that would shift us from a global neoliberalism (which reduced expenditures and increased the role of the private sector and so on) and replace that by some kind of global social democracy. There would be systems of global taxation that would enable us to address global problems; there would be systems of global regulation that would cross borders; and there would be the articulation of a global set of social rights. So we'd begin to fashion a global politics for a more socially just, more socially regulated international market. That's where GASPP came from. That was our vision, if you like. So for a few years we got together—some of the key players in the UN system and in academia—to try to work out how that might be developed more concretely in specific policy areas and in practice. I think one other thing to say here is that GASPP was therefore also addressing the issue of global social governance. As I've already mentioned, there were competing international organizations, the World Bank on the one hand and the UN system on the other, with different ideas about health policy, social security policy, and so on. We wanted to see whether it was possible to strengthen the UN and its capacity to articulate these policies at a global level.

RM: How did you go about doing that?

BD: By gathering together people who had experience in all these organizations. We ran a series of seminars between about 1997 and 2002, and each of them addressed a slightly different aspect of the issue. World trade was one, global health was another, global poverty alleviation was a third. Through these meetings, we generated a set of policy briefs, a journal (*Global Social Policy*) that would try to spread those ideas and encourage other people to research and think about them, and we took the opportunity to intervene with briefs at some of the global conferences that were taking place.[2]

RM: What's the link between the kind of things you were trying to do and the UN's Millennium Development Goals (MDGs)? Are they quite different?

BD: Yes. In a sense, the MDGs was the first global social policy because it established a set of targets and policy objectives for the whole world. The problem was that this set of policy objectives was really quite limited; it was not as ambitious as the Copenhagen Summit's declarations of 1995, and it hadn't really been discussed in any effective intergovernmental process or in a process involving civil society. The MDGs were rather dropped into the global arena very hurriedly by Kofi Annan (the UN secretary-general), the World Bank, the IMF, and the OECD (Organization for Economic Cooperation and Development). And the problem with the MDGs, from our point of view, was that they were still rather specifically targeted on limited goals such as the alleviation of the worst forms of poverty. This is important, of course, but the MDGs didn't address issues of inequality, for example. They did not address the structural causes of inequality. They were concerned with basic reproductive health rather than the development of effective health services. So their vision was very limited and fit rather neatly alongside the broader neoliberal project. It didn't in any way fundamentally challenge those policy directives. The MDGs did not really address the kinds of global social policies that would alleviate poverty and the agencies responsible. They were global targets with no global policies.

RM: When the World Bank focused on poverty in the 1990s, it championed an approach targeting the very poor and creating the resources for this by cutting universal programs that include those aimed at the middle class, which they considered able to purchase the services that they need—health, education, and so on—privately. You have argued, however, that universality remains very important. Why?

BD: You're absolutely right that one of the dominant policy approaches in the 1990s, developed by the World Bank, was to focus public expenditure on the poor and to regard the solution to the problem of poverty as being addressed by spending some money solely on the poor. The problem with that approach was—and we know from the history of welfare state building in Europe—that actually good welfare states, good systems of social policy, are built as much for the middle class as they are for the poor. To put this at its most extreme: the poor benefit indirectly as a consequence of universal social expenditures for everybody. And the trick in the whole history of welfare state building was to encourage the middle class and others to pay taxes to spend on welfare, and the way to do that was to ensure that those welfare expenditures would be for everybody. I'm talking here about high-quality universal health, education, and social security that the poor would also benefit from. And so we argued that the Bank and its approach to targeting had fundamentally not understood that history. It had got it completely wrong. The Bank was stuffed with neoliberal economists, trained in Chicago and other schools, who had no experience whatsoever either in practice or theoretically with the welfare state building project in Europe. We tried to re-inject that into the global debate.

RM: Earlier you mentioned the impact of the fall of the Berlin Wall and the "liberalization" of eastern Europe on your own thinking. Did this also contribute to any rethinking within major international organizations like the IMF?

BD: I would say there was more debate about these issues inside the World Bank rather than inside the IMF. I have yet to see any IMF documents that seriously enter into that debate. The Bank was different because some of the Nordic countries generated a trust fund for social and sustainable development. This was a set of monies available for Bank personnel to access, often in collaboration with some Nordic scholars. What happened was that you saw the importation into the Bank of some of the Europeans, so therefore you got, to simplify it, the

Europe versus USA debate going on inside the Bank, which, for a while, generated discussion. And there is evidence that the Bank's thinking shifted to some extent toward a more inclusive, universalistic approach. Some of the documents of the most recent years contain the notions of equity and of improving public expenditure as their themes. So there has been a shift in thinking inside the Bank.

RM: Why did GASPP become difficult to pursue?

BD: What became very clear was that we were rooted in a kind of European tradition; we were arguing for sets of policies that we had seen as being successful within the developed economies. But when we came to argue that within global arenas, there was resistance. There was resistance from many voices from the global South. And those voices were articulating the view that many countries in the South had already been subject to northern prescriptions for how they should run their economies. So the whole structural adjustment process undertaken by the Bank and IMF, whereby money was lent to developing countries on the condition that they develop certain sorts of targeted, prioritized policies, led to an increasing voice in the global South. Both civil society and governments were fed up with being dictated to from the North about their economic and social policies. And so even though we were trying to argue for a more progressive set of social policies, we were tarred with the same brush. This was seen as a "northern, imperialist, colonialist, protectionist" project. That was one element of resistance that became apparent.

AND we recognized that that was fundamentally important. Let me give you one concrete example. There was an attempt, not by us in the GASPP, but curiously by Gordon Brown, then U.K. chancellor of the exchequer, who echoed some of our thinking. What he said was that we needed a set of global social policy principles and that wherever the Bank or the IMF or anybody else was intervening in countries, they should respect these principles, they should ensure investments in health and education; really, he was articulating a set of policies for countries which were not dissimilar from the kind that we were also trying to articulate. But when that idea tried to get injected into the UN system, particularly in 2000 at the UN summit in Geneva, there was wholehearted resistance from the southern countries. I was at the meeting at the time when India and Bangladesh and Indonesia and other countries said, "No. These are your policies, not ours. These are your principles, not ours. Who's going to pay for them? Not you. We don't want any discussion of these things."

THAT was how this line of argument became very difficult. So we realized that two things had to happen: first, you had to bring southern voices into this debate much more clearly; second, one should think in terms of supranational policies being better articulated at a regional level. And so for a period of time we focused on regional social policies, suggesting that MERCOSUR (Mercado Comun del Sur, or Southern Common Market; its members include Argentina, Brazil, Bolivia, Paraguay, Uruguay and Venezuela), ASEAN (Association of Southeast Asian Nations), the African Union, and other regional groupings of countries might, rather like the European Union, develop cross-border policies of redistribution and regulation and rights. That was something that followed from this North-South impasse.

RM: How successful were those regional initiatives?

BD: There have been some developments of those cross-border policies in some of those regions.[3] The African Union has now developed an African social policy. There's a big gap between words and reality, but at least there is a framework. The Latin American story is one where now you really have a reconfiguration of Latin American regionalism with a set of new governments with a set of relatively progressive policies. You begin to see UNASUR (Union of South American Nations) articulating health and other policies for cooperation between those countries. So there have been some developments, but I wouldn't overstate it.

RM: You have this regional focus, but one of the major contemporary initiatives is focused on the idea of a "global" social protection floor. Where did this idea come from? How did it come about?

BD: It has been quite an interesting development. It happened only a couple of weeks ago; I was at the ILO at the time. The ILO, which has taken the lead on this, has agreed that it will recommend to all countries that they should establish a set of guarantees: that every resident in a country should be guaranteed access to health services and income sufficient for them to be able to meet their needs (whether it's children or at working age but not able to work or in old age). This initiative is quite important because the ILO historically has focused most of its efforts on workers. This is a recommendation for all residents of each country. So that's why it's very important. The global social protection floor recommendation is associated with a set of principles which say that social policies in each and every country should adopt the principle of equity, the principle of universalism, and the principle of the dignity of the beneficiaries, and it goes on to say something about progressive forms of taxation as the basis for funding.[4] So really this is, as a set of words and a set of recommendations, really very progressive.

so how did this happen, when in the year 2000, as I was just telling you, the whole idea was knocked off the agenda? I think three things probably came together. One is that in the intervening period a number of southern countries, particularly in Latin America but to some extent also in Africa, began actually to fashion their own, more progressive universal social policies. You had the conditional cash transfers in Latin America; you had universal social pensions in Africa. Therefore the southern voice could come in with a set of policies that were echoes of some of the arguments that had been articulated in the North. So, if you like, this was no longer the North trying to drive the agenda because now there was also a South-South dialogue of what were desirable social policies. That's one thing: the rediscovery of the importance of universalism within many countries in the global South.

The second thing was the global economic crisis of 2008. Something had to be done. There was a brief moment when it was recognized that this crisis had social effects that we needed to address. The UN Chief Executive Board, which exists to try to coordinate the different UN agencies, met in Paris in 2009 (fortuitously under the leadership of Juan Somavía, director-general of the ILO since 1998) to discuss what to do. And he was able to articulate a set of global policy principles, including the idea of the social protection floor, at that time.[5] So one is the southern shift, two is the global crisis, and three is the importance of individual players and individual policymakers inside the global policymaking arena, particularly within the ILO but also in the United Nations Children's Fund (UNICEF) and even later in the World Bank. In other words, there were key individuals who saw the importance of driving this policy.

RM: And the ILO has been quite crucial in that under Somavía's leadership.

BD: Somavía, if you remember, chaired the Copenhagen summit. So he came from that progressive UN conference in 1995, moved to being the director-general of the ILO, and then he clearly used his position as director-general not only to try to develop ILO policies but also as a platform for selling these to the rest of the world. For example, in 2004 the ILO initiated the World Commission on Globalization, which supported, in effect, many of the things that we had been saying in GASPP: that there should be a more socially just globalization.[6] And Somavía very skillfully persuaded other global players to see the sense of some of his arguments. As a result, the ILO was invited to be a participant in the G20, which was emerging as the global center of power, replacing the G8.

RM: Is this because the G20 includes some of the emerging nations?

BD: Exactly. Some Latin American ones and notably South Africa, China, and India. And the ILO is one of the few international organizations in addition to the IMF to be co-opted into that process, giving it another platform for arguing for these ideas. So Somavía was very important in selling this approach to other agencies in the global policymaking process. In addition, inside the ILO Michael Cichon became the head of the Social Security Department in 2005, and it was clear then, if not even before, that he had a vision of the ILO articulating recommendations on social protection not only for all citizens but also for all residents in all countries.

RM: You very carefully use the word *residents* and not *citizens.*

BD: There are some criticisms of the social protection floor recommendations—and I'll come to your point in a minute—and one is that it doesn't specify how these countries should go about ensuring these guarantees. It does not recommend, for example, that there should be universal social cash pensions. So you could say that this is a vacuous recommendation because it leaves it up to countries. I'm not as convinced by that argument as some are. I think the recommendation does have weight and the recommendation is important in political debates within countries.

RM: And we don't have a world government.

BD: Exactly. But the one weakness is that this is a recommendation for residents. On the one hand, that's much better than citizens, but it's not everybody on the planet because countries decide who their residents are, and that can exclude, for example, illegal migrants or asylum seekers. So there was a spirited move by the workers group at the International Labor Conference when that clause was discussed to argue, "At least we must have an aspiration to include all the people on the planet, even if we have to start with residents now." That was defeated. However, if you read the fine print of that particular clause, it says—it is very cleverly worded—that the recommendation should apply to "all residents and children, subject to national regulations," and that can be interpreted as all residents subject to residency regulation and all children subject only to the age at which people are regarded as children. So the progressive interpretation of that clause is that all children of the planet are included in this recommendation regardless of their status. And some see that as a very important step. Again, it's only words, and it's up to governments to do something about it, but in terms of global policy debate, it's quite significant.

RM: How important is this new global consensus on the social protection floor? Do we have a more unified, progressive, global social policy compared with the days of the ILO–World Bank contest in the 1990s?

BD: Yes, but let's see whether it works. I mean, yes, as we've said, all of these actors—the ILO, UNICEF, the UN generally, even the World Bank, the G20—have all in different ways endorsed the importance of this. There is to be created and to meet for the first time a new social protection interagency coordination board which will be jointly chaired by the ILO and the World Bank—which is a historic moment—to address this issue of advancing the idea of social protection globally.[7] There are two worries, however. One is the Bank's involvement in all of this, which on the one hand seems positive, but could always flip over, and they could then use their position inside this alliance to shift the discourse back to safety nets and targeting. There is some evidence that that may even happen, so bringing the Bank in is two-edged. We'll have to see what happens.

But the real issue is whether, despite that large shift toward an endorsement by a large number of actors of that idea, Ban Ki Moon, the secretary-general of the UN, will say "social protection floor" as often as he says "MDGs." In other words, whether it becomes *the* global discourse, where it gets written into the post-2015 future UN development policy and whether it gets written into the Rio+20 document. Now, we already have the Rio+20 document, which is a hopeless, huge document that articulates everything but says nothing, and which does have the phrase *social protection floor* as subclause N of twenty other points in one bit on the green economy, and therefore clearly is not going to shout it out loud. The post-MDG process, namely what is going to replace the Millennium Development Goals as UN policy, is at this very minute being discussed. The secretary-general is going to establish a high-level panel to have some consultations and discussions about that. We already know that one of the joint chairs of that panel is David Cameron, the British prime minister. And in David Cameron's hands, a global social protection floor is not safe. So my worry is that, despite this important shift forward in the global discourse that involves a number of agencies, the concept may still not fly.

RM: That's quite depressing. What about you? You've also stressed the importance of individuals. Somavía stepped down in September 2012 as head of the ILO. Will that make a difference?

BD: It depends partly on what he does. It's not clear whether he has, personally, a political strategy to try to still use his position somehow inside the UN system to try to argue his ideas or whether he really is going to retire. The person who replaced him as director-general is Guy Ryder, and we will have to wait and see when he picks up the reins at that job whether he regards this bit of ILO policy as important. Let's hope he does. But it does not all depend on particular individuals or on the ILO. If you like, the ILO was the vehicle to launch this social protection floor on the global agenda, but now it has to be delivered, and civil society actors both globally and nationally are clearly going to be important to push national policies in that direction.

RM: When I was reading the earlier documents, I was quite impressed by the attempt not only to get these principles established but also to establish an effective new global governance mechanism—to get the agencies working together at the global scale, at the regional scale, and in individual countries. So, say, within Chile you would have the Chilean government, Chilean NGOs, and international organizations in Chile working together around these sorts of things. Is that still on, or was that just the early dream?

BD: There are two things. The idea of the ONE-UN (that the UN should speak with one voice, with one policy, with one boss in each country with more power to discuss with governments how to implement policies) is still there. There have been pilot projects in a number of countries, and the conference that assessed the progress of those pilot countries was fairly positive, and there's a chance that they will be extended. Whether in those countries the UN chooses to focus on the social protection floor is a question that would have to be discussed, and that would largely be in the hands of the United Nations Development Program (UNDP), which is a bit of a rogue player in this, as it's never quite clear to what extent the UNDP is wedded to this idea. At the global level, as I said, there is now a board that tries to knock the heads together of a number of global agencies, which is a step forward. It's no longer the era of the Bank versus the ILO, the Bank versus the WHO (World Health Organization). There has been some attempt to get these international organizations to collaborate on a common platform. The G20 was quite important in articulating that. So it's not yet a radically reformed system of global social governance, but it's a step in the right direction. A radically reformed system of global social governance would also raise taxes globally, would fund these agencies from their own tax-raising activities, and that has not happened and is unlikely to happen.

RM: That's what I was going to get to right now: the financial side of this. Something like the Tobin Tax, wasn't that still on the agenda?[8]

BD: It is still on the agenda. I mean, none of this will work properly at the global level unless there is some sort of independent funding for international actors. There have been steps. There are specific global funds for HIV/AIDS, primary education, and so on, but not yet for social protection. Where there has been the establishment of global funds, these are dependent on countries' donations or philanthropic donations, which are not to be discounted, but there's still no capacity to raise revenues at a supranational level. The step that goes closest to that is the agreement of a large number of countries to raise a tax on airline tickets, with that revenue pulled unto UNITAID,⁹ which then goes into a global fund for malaria eradication and other global funds. So it is an important step. It is an agreement among certain countries rather than a clear policy of the UN itself. But we will see.

RM: What is your view of UNICEF? You have mentioned UNICEF as a major player, but we haven't really developed that.

BD: UNICEF historically has always been relatively progressive on these global debates. This goes back to the work of Giovanni Cornia and Richard Jolly and others.

RM: Do you mean UNICEF's efforts in the mid-1980s to push for "Adjustment with a human face"?[10]

BD: Exactly. That was a critique of neoliberal structural adjustment, and that was driven by key intellectuals in UNICEF. Today there are also key intellectuals in UNICEF. One of them is Isabel Ortiz, who has done a lot of work in articulating the case against the global austerity measures at the moment. They've just produced two or three very good books on countering global austerity and pointing out how revenues could be raised to be given to public expenditures even within poorer countries to advance the social protection floor and also invest in children and their health and education.[11] So yes, UNICEF has historically played a quite important role and continues to do that.

The other organization that we haven't discussed is the IMF. In the end, because the IMF remains powerful in terms of the conditions it lays down to countries that need to borrow money from it, the acid test would be if the IMF recognized the importance of creating fiscal space within countries to develop something like the social protection floor. UNICEF has been arguing very closely with them that they should. The ILO had a historic meeting with the IMF a couple of years ago, which came to an agreement that there should be more recognition within the IMF of the need for this kind of thing. There have been three countries—Vietnam, El Salvador, and Mozambique—about which it has been recently reported that the ILO and the IMF and other actors have sat down to work out concretely what would be the cost of improving the social protection floor in those countries.[12] The IMF has been on board as far as one can see from the reports in those discussions. Maybe that's more important than any of these other considerations. We'll see whether the IMF is prepared to acknowledge the importance of those issues.

13

"Understand that power is diffuse and change is constant"

PETER J. KATZENSTEIN

in conversation with Raffaele Marchetti

Peter J. Katzenstein is the Walter S. Carpenter Jr. Professor of International Studies at Cornell University. He was ranked by the *Economist* as the most influential scholar in international political economy.

Photo courtesy of Peter Katzenstein.

Apreeminent expert on international political economy, Peter Katzenstein offers a nuanced analysis of the current state of world power. Shying away from both misplaced optimism and economic apocalypticism, he argues that the main trend facing the modern, crisis-riddled world is a diffusion of power around the globe and among a range of actors on the international stage. Starting from such an actor-based approach, he argues that many of the woes facing the world today were not caused by concepts like "the market" or "the crisis" but rather by a set of interactions among actors. Indeed he suggests that the current crisis is endogenous to the liberal democratic system and was brought about by policies actively pursued by political and economic elites on both sides of the political spectrum in Europe and the United States. He urges a prudent approach to the complex modern political and economic system, suggesting that those already eulogizing the European project are getting ahead of themselves, as are those overstating the importance of China in shaping geopolitics. He bluntly states that predictions are nearly impossible for economists, political scientists, and politicians and that we should strive for prudent pragmatism rather than grand strategies or economic technocracy. Katzenstein ends the discussion with a call for a system of education that focuses on global history and mutual understanding that would focus on the role of identity—rather than simply security and economic interests—in shaping our social and political behavior.

RM: How would you describe the world in which we live from a political perspective?

PK: It is a world in which power is diffusing. I understand power not only in the conventional sense of being able to coerce other people to do one's bidding, but also in several other ways. Institutional power is diffusing: more institutions are active today than thirty or fifty years ago. Structural power is diffusing: the United States is no longer as prominent in structuring the international system as it was thirty or forty years ago. Because of a variety of social and technological developments, productive power—an imperfect term—has shifted to individuals, nongovernmental organizations, and social movements, bypassing political elites. Productive power, structural power, institutional power, and, last but not least, coercive power are all diffusing. This is the overarching trend in the world in which we live. It makes governing and governance more challenging, interesting, and innovative. It opens many new possibilities, and it creates many new risks.

RM: How did we end up here? What do you think generated this new context?

PK: I think some of these developments were spontaneous and unregulated. Yet even though technological change is in the end always politically determined, its effects often work only indirectly. When the U.S. Defense Department created the Internet as part of the cold war deterrence system in the 1960s, it did not really have a clue about the transformative effect this might have on world politics one or two generations later. The American military-industrial complex thus empowered millions of political actors across the world, which was not really what it had planned to do. Technological and social change often brings in its wake unintended consequences. Other changes, by way of contrast, were very much directed and driven by self-regarding elites or popular movements.

Most often change is the result of the combination of intended and unintended consequences. That, for example, was the case for the neoliberal policy of the 1980s and 1990s, which was strongly championed by the United States and Britain and converted into a legally binding policy paradigm by France and Germany, as Rawi Abdelal has shown. The globalization movement that the United States and Britain favored was basically ad hoc and bilateral. Yet eventually what evolved was rule-based financial globalization, sponsored by France and Germany. This started in 1985, when France staffed the leading positions of the IMF (International Monetary Fund), OECD (Organization for Economic Cooperation and Development), and the EU. The leaders of these international organizations were appointed by the socialist government in France and sponsored rule-based globalization. Germany, and in particular its central bank, insisted on generalized liberalization of finance among all states, through a clause called *erga omnes* attached to any international treaty.

The EU signed many treaties with many states, and within a few years financial liberalization and globalization had spread to all corners of the world. Twenty years later European leaders are paying the bill for the systemic policy of globalization which they favored and pushed successfully. They are battling financial markets, and at this stage all we can safely say is that they are not winning. Financial globalization has momentous political consequences on elites and on everyday life. It was the result of political initiatives that had intended and unintended consequences. It disempowers many states, empowers hundreds of millions of individuals by lifting them out of poverty, and benefits a handful of financial corporations, and on the historical record of the past three decades leads to a serious financial crisis at least once every decade. The financial crisis and the great recession that today continues to grip the world economy, and Europe in particular, were unintended consequences of the policies adopted by self-regarding elites.

This example should be viewed in a larger historical context. *Anglo-America* is an old-fashioned term not much used these days. It does resonate, however, with the experience of the past three centuries, in which Anglo-America ruled over world politics. Although it lost relatively small military encounters, like the Boer and Vietnam wars, Anglo-America did not lose a major war in three centuries. In the twentieth century it defeated all comers: right, left, and center. The neoliberal movement of the 1980s and 1990s insisted that privatization and deregulation were unmitigated goods, and it came knocking forcefully at European and Japanese doors. As a strong ally of the United States, Japan went along and Europe remade itself. Japan's bubble economy has yielded two lost decades of growth and deepening self-doubt. And the Japanese experience may, at least to some extent, be repeating itself now in Europe and the United States, with political consequences that are polarizing international and domestic politics. Furthermore we have not yet seen the last of the continuing financial crisis that started in 2007. I see no reason to believe that American-inflected crisis management will not provoke a larger systemic crisis that will test financial systems even more seriously than the crisis of 2008 and will put into question the reserve currency status of the dollar. Things that were inconceivable before September 2008 are no longer unthinkable.

RM: That's interesting, because the usual account of the story of globalization points to the end of the 1970s and beginning of the 1980s and at Reagan and Thatcher rather than the European socialists.

PK: I think that historical narrative is correct. The macro-Keynesian stabilization efforts of the 1970s had exhausted themselves and proved unable to deal with stagflation. And the McCracken Report, *Government and Inflation* (1976), showed that you could not stabilize the global economy at the supranational level through coordinated national fiscal policies. A new approach was needed. And that approach was articulated in the 1980s by the transnational political alliance linking Ronald Reagan with Margret Thatcher—generating a political movement with a new policy paradigm. In the area of finance, this policy paradigm was translated into systemic rules by the Europeans. The Americans would have been happy to practice self-interested power politics and to make bilateral deals. Not so the Europeans. Coping with and responding to Reaganism and Thatcherism became the foundation for the reinvention of the European movement in the 1980s in the form of the Single European Act. Later came the European Monetary Union (EMU) and the hope that it would solve simultaneously the pressing political and economic problems of the day—anchoring a united Germany in Europe and readying Europe for financial globalization.

And now we are smarter as we begin to realize that the EMU did solve some problems at the cost of creating others. This is how policy and politics evolve. We are always chasing that elusive and forever unobtainable golden calf of economics: a stable, dynamic equilibrium. I am, incidentally, less pessimistic about Europe than most people and certainly less so than bankers who make a lot of money both welcoming as profoundly stabilizing and at the same time criticizing as profoundly destructive whatever solutions political leaders come up with for the crisis of the day, week, month, or year. Traders make money selling the euro both long and short and detest leaving any money on the table. European integration has always proceeded by crisis. So why could it not proceed by a big systemic crisis? And I have an almost infinite trust in lawyers papering over chasms of policy and politics just to stop the ship from going under.

RM: There is also a third narrative, held, for instance, by Javier Solana, according to which the twenty-first century began in 1978 with the change of position toward the market by the Chinese communists.[1] Of course, the twentieth century then ends in 1989 with the fall of the Soviet Union. How would you integrate this argument into your account?

PK: I think it refers to an important development in an overly dramatic fashion. I think that China's rise is a very important fact in Asia. Will China become a global power? I do not know, but I am profoundly skeptical. I think China is well on its way to becoming one of Asia's dominant powers, and perhaps even *the* primary power in Asia. But what does this precisely mean? What is our understanding of the geography of Asia? I, for one, am not in favor of strictly materialist geopolitical approaches to regionalization. The United States is an Asian power and so is Russia. This makes the political constellation for any one state to become Asia's primary power very difficult. Does China have global aspirations? Of course, and these aspirations are already visible in Africa and Latin America.

By and large this is improving political and economic choices for African and Latin American states and hopefully living conditions for the peoples of Africa and Latin America. China is evolving innovative and admirable policies for its own development and the betterment of the living conditions of its own peoples. That these policies are now being studied and perhaps adapted in new settings is a good thing, as it broadens the repertoire of policies and practices for development and the alleviation of poverty, which for me is a very positive development. And should Chinese power be overbearing and its policies be flawed, African and Latin American states and peoples will draw the conclusion that it is not in their interest to cooperate with China and accept Chinese investment and aid. But none of this constitutes a dramatic rupture in global history. It is instead the manifestation of the diffusion of power that is defining current world politics, including politics in China. I think that people who envy or admire China excessively lack judgment. These can be very different types of people, such as conservative defense hawks in America looking for the coming war with China (just as they were looking for the coming war with Japan twenty years ago), or Chinese nationalists making up for almost two centuries of humiliation with ill-conceived and ill-considered policies dressed up in the outmoded fashions of the nineteenth century. The return of a Sinic world on either the global or regional level is not an option. Rather than *rupture* or *return* I favor the concept of *recalibration* when I think about China's rise. We are witnessing a recalibration of power along several dimensions in an era in which power is diffusing.

Chinese intellectuals and politicians are acutely aware of China's many vulnerabilities and are left cold by the breathless prose of economics journalists whose books are stocking the shelves of stores in international airports to satisfy the reading curiosity of the globe-trotting business class. Where are China's weaknesses? The most important one is demographic. China is the most rapidly aging society in the world. And Chinese elites are very aware of this and the problems that will come in its wake in a few decades' time. I recall the frustration of Japanese demographers in the 1980s when they were simply unable to attract the political and public attention, not to speak of the attention of admiring or envious Americans, to discuss a problem staring Japan in its face at the very moment when it was ready to step out on the stage of world politics. The same sequel may be repeating itself today with regard to China.

A second major weakness of China is doubts about the legitimacy of its political system. China's politicians and bureaucrats have accomplished much and have much to be proud of. Yet they lack a secure sense of self-confidence. Their political position hangs on the ability of providing the economic growth and jobs that have transformed China in the last generation. The support of the population, it is thought (and nobody knows this for sure), is dependent on continued improvements in living standards. Also important are the political costs of increasing social inequality and getting a grip on what, to outsiders like myself, at times look like rampant corruption and shocking displays of arbitrary rule, especially at the local level. Japan has lived through two decades of economic "crisis" with no question raised about the legitimacy of its often corrupt and ineffective political system. We do not know what a Chinese economic "crisis" would look like, but the widespread assumption inside and outside of China is that it would have significant political consequences. We do, however, know that after capitalism's proverbial seven fat years, there inevitably follow seven lean ones. Capitalist China has not yet experienced its lean years. Until it does, the issue of legitimacy will linger. Incidentally, I would caution those who wish those lean years to come sooner rather than later. There are too many Chinese people who remain desperately poor and who are as entitled to a better life as are the peoples in all other parts of the world. Furthermore, China is a vital engine of growth for Asia and for the world economy. When China sneezes, the rest of us will catch cold; an unstable China will destabilize global capitalism.

RM: Going back to your general description of the world in which we live, characterized by what you have identified as the diffusion of power, two questions arise: Who has taken advantage of all these changes? And who has paid the greatest price?

PK: The largest beneficiary, I think, has been about 400 million people in the Chinese countryside. World capitalism has never before produced an alleviation of poverty on this scale in so short a time. The greatest support for globalization is therefore to be found in Asia and China. Any reasonable defense of globalization must start here, at this admirable alleviation of appalling poverty. Globalization has affected, less dramatically, the middle classes in China and India. The Indian middle class, for example, now numbers well over 300 million. All this has developed within a matter of a few decades. It has been an extraordinary turnaround. There has been an undeniable improvement in the well-being of humankind that is unparalleled in history. That seems to me very clear, and yet it is often overlooked in public debate. The people in China and India, however, know this fact very well.

On the other hand, these changes are clearly hurting, in the OECD world, the established working class. It is hurting many of the young and those without requisite skills. It has brought about a growing gap in "the Western world" where the gains of a fairly small part of the population are paid for by the excess hours worked by the others. Standards of living have basically kept up because people work longer hours. Since there are many differences between the different variants of capitalism, it is hard to generalize. But, generally speaking, there is a growing gap between rich and poor, not only in formerly socialist economies like China and Russia but also in capitalist countries that used to be more or less egalitarian, such as Sweden and the United States.

How do we weigh the pros and the cons—the pros of lifting hundreds of millions of people out of poverty as opposed to the disadvantages of adversity of probably tens of millions of unskilled, underskilled, unemployed, marginalized populations that have lost their stake in the system and are generating a politics, on the right and on the left, which is both ugly and understandable? I do not know of a universal metric other than the metric of politics, which remains local or national.

RM: From this perspective, do you think that the decisions taken by Anglo-American and European leaders in the 1980s can be considered a self-defeating strategy that at the end of the day benefited other countries more than their own?

PK: Perhaps, and if so it would be another instance of the unintended consequences of change. The freeing up of capital, which now moves around the world with few restrictions and looks for productive investments, does have effects in rich countries, some of them harmful. I, for one, early on did not recognize fully the power shifts these decisions would bring about. Practical, pragmatic, and self-interested choices are motivated by short- and medium-term considerations. Rarely do we have the capacity to think strategically. We talk often about strategy, especially in the academy, but we do not really think or act that way. So there is a great disconnect between talking and doing. As the saying goes, God gave the physicists all the easy problems. I am not critical of politicians who do not preordain the consequences of their choices a few decades hence. We are all more or less blind, trying to figure out whether the trunk of the elephant is its tail. This is not to deny the obvious fact that those who deny the existence of elephants are blinder than the others. And in America, as in all other countries, we have, and always have had and will have, a lot of people denying the existence of elephants.

This lack of long-term collective intelligence is built into politics as his-toricized practice, where people have primarily one task: to grapple with the problems at hand. We all make conjectures about the future and none of us are very good at it. Some, of course, think that they are smarter than all the others. If we look at the so-called emperor of the social sciences, eco-nomics, for example, we can readily show how terrible we all are at making accurate forecasts. If economics is the emperor, it is an emperor without clothes. Recently, for a paper that I have written with a colleague of mine, Stephen Nelson, I looked up the economic forecasts of the Open Market Committee of the U.S. Federal Reserve. Getting things right meant, in this case, forecasting over a period of three to six months. The members of the committee are very knowledgeable in business and economics and can draw on the support of a very large and very well-trained group of staff economists. Their forecasts for the quarterly movement of the American economy in the 1990s, for which data are now publicly available, was cor-rect about 4 percent of the time, which is quite a bit lower than the 70 percent figure that former chairman Alan Greenspan has claimed in one of his recent papers. As in Hans Christian Andersen's wonderful story, we simply do not have enough children running around and pointing out the silliness of an emperor without clothes. Nakedness should instill a bit of humility when economists lecture the rest of us about what we must do to please the dictates of what they understand to be human rationality. When lectured to by a naked emperor people are permitted to laugh, no? Our ability to forecast and predict accurately is very limited because the system in which we live is highly complex and loosely coupled, and that makes prediction very difficult. And what is true for national economies is, of course, even more true for the global political economy.

RM: Taking into account this complexity and the difficulty it entails, still, do you see an overall trend of convergence or divergence in the context of globalization?

PK: I see contestation rather than convergence or divergence. I do not recognize overall linear trends inscribed by a master narrative onto history: the ultimate victory of this or that ideology, this or that country, this or that chosen people. All of these narratives and the models of the world they imply are based on wishful thinking. I do not believe in teleologies of history. I see conflict and contestation that work themselves out one way or the other and in the process of working themselves out create the grounds for the next round of contestation and conflict. If you think about Japan in the 1980s, it went through a decade of "internationalization," and a large number of Japanese students came to America. Most of them had a great time for a year or two making connections in American universities that would be useful in the future and learning a bit of American social science (and playing golf free of charge). And then they went back. This has now stopped. For a variety of reasons Japan has turned inward in the past decade. For Japan's internationalization always was a modernized form of nationalism. It never meant globalization. Japan today is both converging and diverging as it continues to live in its parallel word next to China, the United States, the rest of Asia, and the rest of the world.

China's experience is bound to be different. That country has gone through a linguistic revolution in mastering English, which is an extraordinary thing to watch; in sharp contrast to America, China will do just fine without Google translator. But apart from the linguistic revolution, it is the worldwide Chinese diaspora that makes China so different from Japan. China is not only a nation-state and a civilizational state; it is also a commonwealth of trading communities that has enormous strength and reach. The Sinicization of Africa now under way is carried out not only by state-owned corporations seeking long-term investment deals to secure vital raw materials. Sinicization is also a consequence of Chinese traders setting up shop and thus transforming the character of African cities without any links to the Chinese state. The Chinese diaspora has been a force in world politics for the past 150 years.

In short, it is the mixture of things, not linear trends, that define current world politics and which I find most interesting. And mixtures always engender new political conflicts and new human possibilities.

RM: So you don't agree with the kind of sociological reading of the slow diffusion of a certain kind of modernity.

PK: I can eat my hamburger (and I was raised in Hamburg, which is why I am choosing the example) at a McDonald's franchise in Ithaca or Tokyo's Roppongi. But Roppongi's teriyaki burger cannot be had in Ithaca. I am told, but cannot vouch for it personally, that the Golden Arches in Moscow are so attractive because they offer sales personnel with a smile, apparently a rarity in Moscow, and clean toilets free of charge.

Those multiple modernities, which we can find so readily in Beijing, Amsterdam, London, Rio, and Moscow, are embedded in a larger context. If you ask me what precisely is meant by that term *multiple modernities*, it means, at least for me, a dedication to the enhancement of human well-being through science and technology and human rights and human dignity. Well-being, rights, and dignity are political values that are foundational for political authority wherever it is exercised in the world. No political leader can any longer serve without acknowledging their relevance, whatever their political import may be in practice. These values are constitutive of the civilization of modernity and are no longer controlled by any political authority. They are global processes perhaps unleashed in part by the Enlightenment and in part by Anglo-America. They now have taken hold in all corners of the world, and whatever their historical lineage, they are no longer the exclusive property of any one part of the world—America, Britain, Europe, the West, or wherever. They are instead constitutive of a global world and all of humankind.

RM: I have one more point on the issue of globalization. Many would argue that the most significant trend in today's world is the slow movement away from a predominantly Western system. Do you agree with this? If so, is this a change we should be happy or worried about?

PK: My question is always "What is 'the West'?" Are we talking about the United States; North America, including Mexico; Central America, Latin America, the Americas—all different instances of an American world? Or are we talking about the European world, and if so, Europe with or without eastern Europe, Russia, Turkey, or North Africa? All of these entities are lumped together under the rubric of *the West*. The term suggests a unity that simply does not exist or exists only in the imagination of some intellectual or political entrepreneurs with particular political projects. *The West* is a highly contested political category. So let's ask if American influence is receding. Together with Benjamin Brake I have just written a paper on the Americanization of law.[2] It is true that American business law has advanced internationally in the past thirty years, in line with the innovations in American financial and business practices. But in constitutional law, the development has been the reverse. American legal influence is receding, not advancing. Intellectual constructs grounded in linear thought, here notions of the growing Americanization or "de-Americanization" of the world, are both incorrect.

And what is true of law is true, for example, of popular culture, areas in which I am currently doing some work. The United States has an important influence on the world, for example, in the case of movies; this does not mean that it remakes the world in its own image, for example, in the case of popular music. The world has an undeniable effect on the United States, yet this does not mean that somehow America will become "de-Americanized." Change reconfigures existing arrangements; it does not destroy them. We are not moving from a world that was Western to a world that is Eastern. Instead the world is reconfiguring now—as it has in the past and will in the future. The Mongolian Empire came and went, in a hurry, and left few visible footsteps. Civilizational processes like Americanization and Sinicization are evidence of continuing processes of reconfiguration on the wind-swept plains of world politics.

WHAT about Europe? It is often said, especially in the United States, that Europe is dying. Apparently it is a slow death that has lasted for decades, even centuries. Because Europe's growth rate was below the American one, it apparently suffered from terminal illness, and one country in particular, Germany, which for the past half-century has preferred a low-growth to a high-growth model, to the consternation of American economists and politicians. Now suddenly it turns out that Germany does not seem to be all that dead, and conflating Germany with Europe in the American imaginary creates intellectual problems all of its own. In fact Europeans have some reason to think that their governance model is superior to the American one: less stalemate and polarization in domestic politics; more economic aid; more peace-keeping troops; and more constitutional blueprints in foreign affairs. Europeans like to think of Europe as a good, normative power. I am less sure. European hypocrisy, measured by the distance between word and deed, is absolutely world class and easily comparable to American, Russian, and Chinese hypocrisy. (Incidentally, I believe hypocrisy is a diplomatic virtue, not a vice.) It appears to be clear, at least to me, that Europe has developed a distinctive polity based on the partial pooling of national sovereignties, which is deeply attractive in many parts of the world. "Is the West declining?" is a deceptively easy and probably some-what wrong-headed question, it turns out. But whatever its meaning, I think that the mix of European and American influences is shifting.

What about the East? In the first part of my career I studied Japan. I was not a Japan specialist, because I did not learn the language. But I did write several books on Japan. This was in the 1980s, and the prevailing view then was that Japan was going to eat America for lunch. The Japanese were buying Hollywood studios, the Rockefeller Center, all the Van Gogh paintings available at auctions, and, last but not least, many U.S. congressmen. There were apparently no limits to either Japan's resources or its appetites. This all ended up in a spectacular economic bubble that eventually burst at the end of the decade. Japan was going to be *the* technological superpower of the twenty-first century, together with the United States. Japan had a particular vision of itself as a civilian rather than military power. The Japanese Athens was going to hire the American Sparta to fight its wars. The Japanese Athens was going to define the parameters of change in all consumer capitalist societies. That was the inescapable endpoint of Japan's primacy in technology and ingenuity. Everybody would own a Sony Walkman and watch movies made by Japanese-owned studios on Japanese-built computers. Or so the conventional wisdom of the 1980s believed. Things turned out differently. Last time I looked, Sony was being run by a Scotsman and everyone is carrying around iPods, iPhones, and iPads. So, is the world becoming Eastern? I doubt it. Is it increasingly being inflected by Asia? This seems very self-evident to me. When 2.5 billion hardworking and increasingly prosperous Chinese and Indians are knocking at the doors of power and privilege, the world will of course reconfigure itself, not by a master plan but through loosely coupled processes that shift political resources and capacities to address new political contests and conflicts.

RM: But, at least in pure economic terms, many projections in GDP show that soon China will be number one and India will be number three in the world. So, in a way, we're seeing the movement of the center of economic development to the East, which has not been the case since probably the sixteenth century.

PK: This, I think, is a serious argument. It would be foolish to deny the rise of the Chinese and Indian economies. In the case of China, I do not look at this as a strictly territorial economy but also as a deterritorialized economy. In a forthcoming book, Mark Selden offers, roughly, the following data for the production of the iPad, which you buy in American stores for $499. Where do the profits accrue in the value chain of production? About $260 accrues to Apple, about $150 goes to suppliers (in Korea, Taiwan, the United States, and other countries) for major technologically sophisticated components such as flat screens. Another

$50 goes to producers of other components. This leaves about $30 for Chinese workers assembling the iPad. Put differently, a tiny proportion of the total value added does *not* end up in the pockets of multinational corporations working inside or outside of China. This characterizes China's high-tech industries more generally. The pattern of foreign investment in China differs greatly from that in South Korea and Japan, which also required foreign capital to industrialize. Unlike its two East Asian neighbors, China has been much more willing to rely on foreign corporations to own and drive its high-tech industries.

That said, it needs to be acknowledged that the term *"foreign" capital* deserves some thought in this case. China's industrialization drive relied on Chinese capital to industrialize (including from Hong Kong, Taiwan, and the overseas Chinese); between two-thirds and three-quarters of the capital that fueled China's economic rise was Chinese. The Chinese developed China with very considerable distributional consequences. China's economy is much more open to the world economy than is any other of the large economies. This fact is of enormous importance for the structure of the global economy. And in the case of high-technology industries, it has quite understandably spurred a big debate in China. Should China take heed of the Belgian development experience? In the 1950s and 1960s Belgium attracted many foreign petrochemical corporations, and when those corporations changed their strategies after the oil shock of 1973, Belgium suddenly found itself in a very difficult position, with much lower prospects of economic growth and a very restricted choice set. This is an example that Chinese policymakers and intellectuals are pondering, even if they are not thinking about the concrete case of Belgium.

The openness of the Chinese economy and the rise of China thus complement the openness of the American economy and America's rise. There is an enormously symbiotic relationship, as liberals are pointing out to the chagrin of realists. The decline of the territorial economy of the United States is one thing, bemoaned recurrently during the past half-century. But nobody is bemoaning the decline of the deterritorialized American economy, as illustrated by the Fortune 500 corporations.

American multinationals have maintained their position in global competition. They are extremely productive, highly competitive engines of growth. Apple is enormously profitable, but it does not generate jobs inside the United States. The profits are paid out on Wall Street, while the unemployed stand in line in Flint, Michigan. American corporate life is, in that sense, very much an integral part of the world as much or more than it is part of the American economy. And this too is a subject of debate in the United States. It would not surprise me if, in the coming decades, America's predicament becomes also China's, especially given the strength of its diaspora. Overseas Chinese capital plays an important role in Asia, and its global role is likely to increase with the rise of China, as is the importance of the capital controlled by state-owned and private corporations. Does this mean that the world economy will be run by the East? I don't think "East" and "West" capture adequately these crisscrossing processes. They impose metaphorical unities that have nothing to do with the realities of economic life and market processes.

RM: According to many, the current financial crisis is putting under strain the democratic form of governance we have been living in, especially in the Western world. Do you agree with this assessment?

PK: I don't think that this formulation captures the dynamics of the crisis very well. It makes the financial crisis appear like a deus ex machina, an uncaused cause, a rare event that is generated outside of the system of democratic capitalism. This is the language of bankers and politicians whose policies have brought about the crisis, and quite self-consciously so. Financial crises are endogenous to democratic capitalism. They are created by self-interested economic and political elites and the policies they have pushed and pursued for their more or less narrowly conceived self-interests. As soon as the crisis hit and became systemic in the autumn of 2008, the vast majority of the dogmatic free market advocates on Wall Street, in the business community at large, in politics, and in the academy suddenly became devout Marxists. My greatest wish, unfortunately left unfulfilled at the time, was that I could simply pack my suitcase, take a tape recorder, and go and interview some of the most prominent devotees of this suddenly celebrated form of Marxism in America. I cannot tell you how much I regretted not to be able to record the artful pirouettes that were being performed, from the celebration of the free market to the celebration of big government, and back to the celebration of the free market, all within a matter of a few months. Historical amnesia has, in this case as in many others, wiped the slate clean again, except for the pesky Tea Party, which is keeping a record on who did and did not support the bailout. For more than a century American business has profoundly distrusted the American state for the simple reason that it never had to confront a self-confident aristocracy or working class and thus could never get a sense of its real and enduring strength. Without the experience of victory in political battle, the American business class often turns paranoid about government regulation, when in other countries it remains cool-headed and shrewd.

Many of the businessmen and Republicans who are loudest to protest heavy-handed government regulations were very willing, even eager, to get government bailout funds. In late 2008 the only thing that saved American finance from collapse was the state, and specifically the Federal Reserve, which injected about $2 trillion of liquidity into the economy to prevent a total freezing of capital markets. That is one of the reasons why it is now in the cross-hairs of conservatives: it did all of this without any consultation or oversight by Congress. Central banks and democratic theory are very distant cousins.

What was at risk in 2008 was not capitalism but the financial system as it had evolved over the previous thirty years. The financial crisis is not an exogenous shock but a development of the Reagan-Thatcher revolution that became institutionalized as a conventional wisdom that everybody except the American left accepted. And that acceptance certainly includes the Democratic Party, including the Clinton administration in the 1990s, and virtually all members of Congress. Financial crises are endogenous to democratic capitalism when it decides to deregulate financial markets. In reaction to the continuing crisis, reforms have been modest and are often being rolled back in the process of implementation. The conditions for an even bigger crisis down the road thus persist as the joint outcome of democratic politics and financial deregulation. America's best and brightest, including my Cornell students, are drawn to Wall Street in large numbers. And the best and brightest will always find ways around even the smartest government regulations. An entire culture has grown up around this financial model, and short of a big crisis, bigger than 2008, I do not see that culture changing in the near future. My students listen to me with a bemused expression on their faces. With the Dow Jones at 13,000 and the bonuses flowing as freely as before, what is Professor Katzenstein talking about, they ask. And when I tell them that it is the wings of a butterfly in a far distant land that will flap one quiet morning once too often, and that this may bring down the entire edifice of the global financial system, they look at me with the certainty of a people who have never seen a black swan. But those black swans exist, and they may reappear. If they do, and in sufficient numbers, they will force policy changes on a democratic capitalism, which in the United States to date has remained impervious to the profound anger expressed on both extremes of the political spectrum.

RM: Again, even accepting your argument about the endogeneity of the crisis to the democratic system, do you think that the crisis will force us to reshape democratic life as we have experienced it so far? One might think, for instance, of the Rodrik dilemma, according to which you cannot have deep globalization, national self-determination, and democratic politics all together. In a way, this crisis seems to suggest that the kind of democracy we have built and lived in so far may be unable to withstand this kind of crisis.

PK: This question is cast in very general terms. The small open European states have lived with crisis and internationalization for the better part of a century. There was a period from the mid-1950s to the early 1970s when they did extremely well. Then some of them fell onto harder—and, in the

case of Iceland recently, disastrous—times. But on the whole, these countries have done very well. The implicit answer contained in the question
you pose denies the viability of these small, open, democratic, and prosperous states, which rank among the top fifteen political economies in
the world, along all sorts of indicators of economic and social well-being.
They have figured out how to make the global economy work to their
advantage. The question is: What can larger states learn under conditions
of acute crisis? The learning capacities of democracies will be tested and
tested severely in a big crisis. Whether these capacities will be sufficient
we will find out only should that crisis come.

The politics of small democratic states does point to a general lesson. If you do not succeed in embedding the economy politically in a
set of social relations that guarantee legitimacy, contested as that process will always be, you will encounter great difficulties. Contemporary
Icelandic politics offers a powerful example. The economic calamity of
reckless finance required, first, a conviction in a court of law of political
and financial malfeasance, symbolic as the process of truth and recon-
ciliation was, so that the political community could move on. Then it
required a set of compensatory policies that distributed the costs of the
crisis upward, not downward, sheltering marginal populations in the
interest of equity and legitimacy.

This is the politics of very hard times. It remains to be seen whether
Britain and the United States, as the models of a liberal form of capitalism, can come up not with that solution but one that delivers similar
results in a different context—should they have to confront a crisis of
similar magnitude. Southern European countries, like Greece, were rolling the dice in a system of casino capitalism and rolling it for too long.
Their lucky run came to an end. And now they have to figure a way out,
with the unwilling help of European countries whose banking systems,
primarily German and French, were pushing easy credit to support the
gamble. To think of this as the irresponsible Greeks and the responsible
Germans is a mistake. It is a transnational configuration of creditors and
debtors that has created a crisis that Europe, south and north, is now
confronting and seeking to address. The fact that the process of coping

with crisis is messy should not be a surprise to anybody, least of all to the small open European states that are far removed from models of consensual politics when it comes to distributing the costs of crisis.

THE United States suffers from a different problem, no less serious and deeply implanted in its democratic politics. We have an electorate, pandered to and misled for a generation by politicians of all persuasions, which continues to believe that you can get something for nothing: increasing benefits from the state without the payment of taxes. This is a colossal failure of the collective imagination and one brought about and reinforced by democratic politics. The capacity to dream is one of America's greatest strengths and in this case also one of its enduring nightmares. For this dream exists as a total disconnect from economic reality. For me the question is not about the learning capacity of democratic capitalism but the different learning capacities of different types of democratic capitalisms in different kinds of crises.

RM: There are two dimensions that are very much at the center of the debate about market integration and democracy. On the one hand, there is the issue of perhaps unavoidable reduction of the welfare state, especially in Europe, and on the other hand, an increase in technocratic governance of politics.

PK: I think that technocratic governance is a short-term Band-Aid because the political class, especially in southern Europe, is delegitimized. Technocracy may provide for a transition from one state of the world to another, but I do not believe that it will become a lasting form of governance in Greece, Italy, or other countries. There will be a return to democratic politics or perhaps another kind of politics. But politics will prevail over technocracy.

The welfare state is, for me, not measured statistically in terms of percentage of GDP going to specific benefit programs. It is, rather, an institution that imbues meaning to political life. And that meaning needs to be redefined. In the 1950s West German chancellor Konrad

Adenauer indexed social security to forestall the impending impover-ishment of most old people in Germany as inflation was threatening to diminish the value of their meager social security payments. Life expec-tancy meanwhile has grown substantially during the past half-century. People now live much longer and much healthier lives but still wish to retire when they are fifty-five or sixty. Something will have to give as the underlying demographic base and the financial resources available no longer correspond. Should payments be curtailed? Should people work longer? Should they develop alternative plans of saving for retire-ment? These are difficult and contentious questions, and in the course of political debate the meaning of concepts like old age, retirement, and work are likely to acquire somewhat different meanings than they had half a century ago. The concepts of volunteer and part-time work, for example, open up political possibilities that might help bridge the gap between fiscal necessities and citizen expectations.

Starting a decade or two ago, many countries in Europe in fact began to gradually extend the working life of their citizens, almost imperceptibly. This is having effects, but the effects may not be large enough to make up for the financial short-fall. I think Europe is there-fore confronting a difficult choice between multiculturalism and wel-fare. Population growth is insufficient to support the generous welfare state that European countries have built since the Second World War. Europe is not aging as rapidly as China, but since higher proportions of its population are entering retirement in the next couple of decades, it has to grapple with these issues sooner. The import of foreign work-ers would alleviate the problem. But it is not clear that European countries have a sufficiently high political tolerance for accelerating the trend toward multiculturalism. Immigration, ethnic definitions of citizenship, border controls are thus all wrapped up in the ques-tion of the welfare state. It is a tough question, illustrated by the fact that Turkish membership in the EU has been an issue for several decades now. The battle of Vienna in September 1683 remains a his-torical marker that the Austrians, in particular, have never forgotten. For Americans, this is incomprehensible, just as the Confederate flag controversy makes no sense to Europeans. Memory politics is universal, but it intersects with contemporary politics in idiosyncratic and often unpredictable ways.

RM: Beyond the current discussion on the financial crisis, there are a number of problems that are usually listed when the discourse about globalization is placed at the center of the discussion. What do you think are the most pressing problems that we face today?

PK: The environment. This is a serious problem because we don't have governance mechanisms to deal with it. And we are losing critical time. We can reverse some damage, but doing so will probably be more expensive than making smaller adjustments in good time. Who is the "we" I am invoking here? I think of this as a problem for all of humankind. It is an overarching problem. The scientific evidence, to the extent that I can understand it, looks very strong, and that evidence is backed up by real life experience in upstate New York. The cross-country ski season has been cut in half during my adult life in Ithaca during the past forty years as snow coverage has melted away. The conventional international political mechanisms are not in place because in important countries domestic political mechanisms are not geared up to address the problem. The United States, for example, is unable to come to terms with this problem in its domestic politics. By contrast, China has made enormous strides, for example, in the introduction of environmentally friendly coal technology.

But all the gains made in the cleaner production of energy are more than offset by the pollution caused by the increase in cars on the road. China (and India), it turns out, like all other polities, are unable to stop the automobile revolution, a defining characteristic of a capitalist mass-consumption society. In fact, with the exception of North Korea, no society in the twentieth century has been able to stop this revolution, and North Korea is hardly a model worth emulating. At the international level we encounter acrimony and stalemate. The pent-up demand for higher economic growth is fed by the psychological needs of societies moving out of poverty and the political needs of regimes for securing their shaky legitimacy or, in the case of America, a deeply polarized politics. Europe has evolved more of a consensus and more international action, but the issue remains contentious even there.

RM: Beyond the environment, do you see any other particularly significant global problem?

PK: Education is probably the only way of developing the sensibilities of taking the Other more seriously and the Self a little less so. That is one reason I take my teaching seriously. You have to open the eyes and hearts of undergraduate students. It is a slow process. But I simply do not believe that history is the repetition of sameness, as some realists do. History rhymes; it does not repeat. We have to understand the rhyme and reason of history. Furthermore history has a very long reach, and we have to deal with that reach in our individual and collective lives to the best of our abilities. I visited Israel in 2012. Arabs and Israelis are both peoples with very deep scars and traumas. They have traumatized each other and themselves. How do you get beyond the traumas that life has inflicted? Although some nationalist politicians and intellectuals are still invoking the traumas of the past, China, aware of its long history, for example, does not strike me as a traumatized society. The United States is not traumatized for the opposite reason; it remains blissfully ignorant of history. Fed by historical awareness of amnesia, the ability to move beyond trauma offers avenues for reinvention and thus dealing with the problems of the future. For very different reasons, China and the United States both have that capacity, and this is a source for hope.

RM: Education is crucial. However, there are many kinds of education and many different kinds of knowledge that are produced. It cannot be as simple as general education.

PK: You are certainly right on this score. The knowledge we produce often centers only on Self. That is both necessary and understandable.

It is also very human. But since there now exist more connections in the world than ever before, the costs of focusing only on Self have become greater. If in the teaching of history, for example, we could get the world to focus on developments in Europe, with its internationally and transnationally coordinated teaching of modern European history, this would be a huge advantage. Japan and South Korea have taken some halting steps in this direction. China and Japan have not, and neither have the United States and Iran or Israel and its Arab neighbors. This is a great calamity. For only a shared understanding of the past can provide a foundation for developing a shared sense of the future.

RM: If education is a major remedy or major policy in which you should invest time and energy, what kinds of actors can we rely on to develop such a remedy?

PK: In this particular instance I have been talking about high school and college teachers. But if you are looking for more general policy solutions, I would say we should look to political elites and political leaders. How are they and how should they deal with this highly interconnected world that is partly global and partly international? I would say, "With caution and as educators." Here is a widely reported story which I tell my students about Robert Rubin, former head of Goldman Sachs and President Clinton's secretary of the Treasury. Rubin ran the U.S. Treasury in the 1990s the way he had run Goldman Sachs before. At the end of the hour-long staff meeting that each morning ended at 8 a.m., he posed his final question, and it was always the same question at both Goldman Sachs and Treasury: "What do we have to do today?" And his favored answer was: "Nothing? Good!" Because he was aware that the world of finance was so much more complex than his capacity to understand that world and that any action, however well intentioned, was likely to be overwhelmed by its unintended consequences and the systemic disturbances it would create.

As a guide to how to move in a complex, loosely coupled system, this maxim of prudential realism strikes me as wise. Political caution, however, should go hand in hand with political education. Rubin did not do enough to educate others of the systemic risks he was building into his favored world of globalization, and he probably did not educate others about the necessity of extending the Self to incorporate the Other in ways that went beyond financial takeovers. Political leadership requires educating the political base, and many of our leaders could do better on that score. High school history teachers are entitled to some help. Realists and liberals shy away from questions of Self and Other, the political identities that motivate much of contemporary politics. The shortcoming is not restricted only to political leaders; it also marks several important social sciences and important strands of international relations scholarship.

RM: What do you mean by taking identity seriously?

PK: Understanding fully that people are moved in part by who they are and what they want to become and who they remember they once were. Politics is not just about material interests, which is how many liberals and realists think about the world. Incorporating an identity perspective requires a kind of political imagination not well captured by realist and liberal thought. These powerful perspectives prefer, rather, a truncated and more parsimonious vision: politics as barter. Politics is horse trading on the racetrack of power politics and in markets of opinions and goods. Actually, those horse trades and markets are embedded in broader sets of understanding. We play and trade with each other because, in some ways, we have come to trust one another. Where did that trust come from? Prudential realism and prudential liberalism need to be enriched by an awareness of the importance of identities and identity shifts in a world in which change is a constant and identities are forever up for grabs.

QUESTION THE ROLE OF DEMOCRACY

14

"People want and need solidarity and social reproduction"

CRAIG CALHOUN

in conversation with Monika Krause

Craig Calhoun is director of the London School of Economics and Political Science. He is a former president of the Social Science Research Council and Global Distinguished Visiting Professor at New York University.

Photo courtesy of the London School of Economics and Political Science.

In this unique take on the nature of modern political economy, Craig Calhoun argues that the ongoing crisis is not simply a crisis of capitalism but is instead a crisis of the modern "package" that linked politics, economics, and social relations in a specific way. Bringing a sociologist's sensibility to the issue, he claims that the most worrisome aspect of the crisis is the fact that it poses a grave threat to what he terms *social reproduction*, namely the institutions and systems that support education, health care, and other goods underpinning social welfare and solidarity. He points out that different forms of democracy and social welfare provision are contextual, so simply calling for more democracy or more social welfare is an inadequate response to the current problem. While he champions some specific solutions to obvious causes of the crisis, like controls on massive speculative financialization, he urges greater thought about how we approach our next social and political steps. Democracy, in this conception, should be judged on whether or not it brings about desired ends, not simply based on vague ideological criteria. (There are, after all, Calhoun points out, civil society actors in modern democracies who actively champion social inequality and the dysfunctional status quo.) Lasting solutions, Calhoun suggests, lie both in broader-based social solidarity and large-scale institutional implementation and in a recognition of the variety of forms in which social services are provided.

MK: In recent years we have lived with this sense of crisis—and we've been repeatedly told we are in crisis. Yet no one seems quite sure what kind of crisis it is; it is a situation that is hard to read. How would you characterize the present moment?

CC: I think that we're in a period of disorganization and destabilization. The combination of capitalism—with its intensification of economic production, its new technologies, its global expansion—with nation-states and structures of political power is in turmoil. And the relationships between the economy and politics, between legal systems and corporations and state economic policies, and structures of social solidarity and cohesion, are in flux.

My sense is that we have had a sort of package that linked these different dimensions of life relatively stably (only relatively) and organized directions of change for the past three hundred and something years. Various theories and ways of thinking about this focus on one or another of these dimensions. They say, "It's really capitalism; it's the capitalists, period." But I think it's really the package—capitalism, the nation-state, and a way of organizing social cohesion and social reproduction—that has come apart. And it's pointless to argue about whether it's really capitalism or the state that is more primary. It's the way they are connected that has shaped the conflicts of the era and the ways in which democracy has been achieved. Democracy has been achieved within nation-state frameworks with close relations to capitalism and the sort of possessive individualism that capitalism engenders. The era has seen internal patterns, to be sure, but it's shaped by this package as a whole. And it is this package that has become unstable.

It's not that there is necessarily any immanent end to capitalist expansion—that there couldn't be further expansion, that there couldn't be new technologies. There are some trends, such as the dynamism of some of the emerging powers (China and Brazil and so forth), that are consistent with a reorganization of capitalism, its continued expansion, continued intensification, continued production of new technologies, continued intensification of exploitation of labor, but with shifting hegemonic power or shifting centers of innovation. However, the way this has been linked to political power and social reproduction seems to me at issue. The era of the past 350 years—"modernity," if you want to call it that—has been shaped both by the development of a world system of nation-states and by some of the double movement that Karl Polanyi talked about, with a push for greater development and exploitation of productive capacities, and a reciprocal movement to strengthen social reproduction and the institutions that do that. This has been organized partly through firms and so-called economic organizations and corporations, and partly through states and state-level welfare systems. Part of what we see now is a real crisis in all the institutions that have organized solidarity and social reproduction and stabilized the systems of capitalism and nation-states. I think a very big area where there will need to be better policies and better follow-through is what I call *social reproduction*: education, health care, and these other arenas in which there is a deficit and upheaval and sometimes active destruction of current institutions.

MK: So it is not simply an economic crisis?

CC: This way of thinking about it reflects a distinctive, modern idea that there is economics on the one hand, and politics and social issues on the other hand. I think that's partly a way of imagining things; it's an imaginary of the world that shapes how the world gets organized. It's partly ideological and confuses us because it implies that there is a separation between the economy and politics, between market and state, which I think there never was. There is, at most, a partial autonomy of these from each other, but never a full autonomy. It's ideological to fantasize about there being a complete separation.

I do think capitalism is hugely important in this. But within capitalism, the extreme financialization exacerbated the undermining of the package. It's very important to understand that capitalism is not just markets or property; it is a particular type of institutional arrangement linking these units in a package—the same way that the nation-state is an institutional arrangement that creates a civil population of its citizens. These are inextricably interrelated, but the interrelations can become perverse rather than harmoniously reinforcing.

This has been a capitalist epoch, in which there has been a push given to social change by capital accumulation processes and by the particular forms of production and organization and distribution and so forth that have taken place in this era. And that's very powerful. But the way the organization takes place is also very much shaped by nation-states. The modern capitalist world-system is a world-system of nation-states, and the process of globalization that has been going on is one in which states have played integral roles and still play an integral role, individually and in relation to each other in various kinds of complex organizations. States have grown more and more important throughout the era, and they have grown not just as vehicles for power on their own but as organizers of support systems for economic activity (building roads, operating complex currency systems, conducting financial bailouts, all of those sorts of things) and as providers of support for the social reproduction process (creating schools, creating health care systems).

Reflecting on this package is really important because something like a corporation isn't simply a creature of markets or of capital or the capitalist economy; it's a creature of law and state power that is sustained and maintained by the institutional support, and it's among other things a welfare system for people who work within it. Issues such as who has health care benefits and who doesn't today partly depend on where people work in the system and where they are located in relatively large, relatively stable employment structures like corporations. So we shouldn't see something like the corporation as being in one of these categories, such as the economy or politics; it's in all of these, in a sense.

MK: What are the sites of this crisis in social reproduction?

CC: I think we have to ask about institutions in examining this further. What are the institutions that hold things together (or don't)? That provide for social reproduction (or don't)? That provide for relative peace and stability (or don't)? I think that we can still speak about, broadly, the capitalist world economy (in certain ways more than ever); we can still speak about there being nation-states (though with more interstate agreements and a layer of multinational organizations); and we can still speak about there being a civil society realm and social reproduction. But too easily we leave out of that picture the question of what happens to the big institutions that enable things to work on large scales in this system. The level of education, of health care, and indeed the organization of large-scale economic activity itself are all interdependent.

In the rich countries of the world, there has been a range of institutions involved in the provision of social reproduction: governments, nonprofits, corporations, social movement organizations, campaigns to deliver service directly, and so forth. All of these are cutting back what they can provide. And the capacity for autonomous social delivery is declining. It is not declining across the board, but rather it is declining in complex patterns. You have, for example, religious organizations that are major deliverers of various kinds of social reproduction services to lots of people. Some of them are declining and some of them are not.

If you look at the world of universities, on the one hand, university degrees seem very important to a lot of people, but there are also lots of graduates who are unemployed, the public funding for universities is being cut, but the attempt to harness them to various economic agendas is as intense as ever. This idea is that they should be used as research and development operations to create innovations for the economy and so forth. They are globalizing in new ways, but at the same time countries are trying to run them as a mode of international competition. There's a huge upheaval, and this extends to earlier levels of education. We see more private growth and cuts in government funding. It looks different in China. China is building new universities but suppressing certain parts of university life that we have thought important. How will that play out? Will China want to build the humanities and social sciences as much as the science and technology part? Will it encourage a level of intellectual freedom that matches creativity? These are important questions, but they are different questions from the outright de-funding of higher education that's taking place in some other countries.

The story of health care is partially similar. There's a set of cases where health care became provided directly on a national level, and the resources for that provision are being reduced, and there are increasing struggles over who's eligible. There are cases where it wasn't provided directly but there were national subsidies, often through insurance systems. And there are cases like the United States, where it was overwhelmingly provided privately. The private resources are now changing and being undercut, and there's an attempt to have a policy solution.

Education and health care are probably the two biggest versions of this, but there are a lot of other versions where the story is about the extent to which we are not organized to provide public goods and provide them in a relatively inclusive fashion. In the extreme version, this provision would be really egalitarian, but even if not egalitarian, inclusive. In my view, those are overlapping but distinct issues. Does everybody get some level of provision, and how equal is the provision? Often democratic movements in recent years have become hung up on one or the other of those without understanding the whole package. A major terrain here is that of institution building and competition around institutional forms, public and private as gross categories. But within each of those there are really different things going on.

I would point not just to schools or hospitals but also to corporations of various kinds. I would point not just to government-organized institutions and nonprofit institutions but also to for-profit corporate institutions. Business corporations still exist and are still powerful, but there are some powerful shifts; IBM, for example, gave way to Microsoft, which gives way to Apple. But this is still within the same realm of corporate organization. But fewer and fewer people have membership in that kind of organization. I think it's worth thinking about corporations not just in terms of their ownership and market capitalization but as membership structures because of the ways in which they deliver employment and welfare benefits. This matters in various different contexts, not just in the OECD (Organization for Economic Cooperation and Development) countries. The biggest factor that determines whether you can get antiretroviral treatment if you have AIDS in South Africa is whether you work for a multinational corporation, which will then basically ensure access to health care benefits. In a range of different ways in the world, institutional membership is crucial. The corporation is pivotal. As corporations have become commodities to be bought and sold themselves, there has been a reduction in their delivery of benefits.

There are paradoxes. In much of the world, public education is provided as a good for elites. It's organized for the rich kids who can succeed in competitions, and private for-profit education expands opportunities for the poor. They do not provide equally good opportunities, but they do provide opportunities because the states have neglected the poor, notably in much of Latin America, for example, in Turkey, and in a variety of other places. The European model was that the state would provide—and it used to provide—in a relatively flat, semi-egalitarian fashion, although only for a minority of the population. It's becoming less equal and providing less of the proportionate resources. The story in some other places was that the state provided a very meager education; in Argentina the state-provided education was exclusive and for elites and so forth. Privately operated educational institutions often provided a public good for a wider population, ironically. It was provided on a pay-as-you-go basis. There are problems with each of these things, and figuring out how to tackle them isn't as simple as just saying

"We should have public institutions and not private ones" or "private institutions and not public ones." It's how you run them. In the United States you get the creation of a set of rules of the game that oblige large, elitist, private institutions to admit minorities into their elite training programs. This is better than not admitting minorities, but it's not the same as being egalitarian.

A related issue is whether there can be large-scale employment. There are trends in capitalist development that do not produce jobs even where they produce wealth. Therefore the main mechanism for distributing the benefits of capitalist wealth creation is being undercut. If you get wealth without jobs, you have a new problem about how you're going to distribute it. It may have been unequal before, but at least the job market pulled people in and gave workers the settings in which they could organize effectively to get a bigger share of the pie. Which is why, for most of its history, capitalism reduced inequality. The OECD countries basically got less unequal as a long-term trend until somewhere around the 1970s, when they began to get more unequal. It's been up and down, but the long-term trend is toward less inequality. The reason for that was largely employment and struggles that were rooted in employment, like labor struggles. The trade union movement not only loses some of the struggles but gets completely undercut by the changing structure of employment and by the export of industry to other countries. But even in those other countries it's not clear whether, as China moves into higher value-added parts of capitalist production, it will be able to employ the same portions of people. And the big news right now is that China is becoming a labor importer.

New technologies essentially changed the production process to the degree that industrial production isn't a major employer. Now if that happens, you can have a service industry. But how is that organized? Are we talking about household help, or are we talking about physicians working for large-scale nonprofits? Some questions about how employment gets organized and therefore how the distribution of economic wealth gets organized need to be asked. It's a policy-related area, and it is a big, problematic area because it doesn't have as obviously conducive a path to mobilization to share benefits as industrial production. Industrial production concentrated people in occupations and places in a way that was conducive to at least trade unionism if not socialism. And that may or may not be true for household labor, for example. This is not to say you can't organize household labor, but it doesn't have some of the same advantages.

MK: What are the origins of the current crisis?

CC: Neoliberalism has brought a kind of intensified attack on institutions. But I think the source of all the problems is not that the neoliberal attack created this and everything was working just beautifully before that, but that this has been intensified and brought to a head. The contradiction between individualized appropriation, property-based systems, and the drive to capital accumulation, on the one hand, and the need for social reproduction on the other hand is a long-standing contradiction that comes to a head in a distinctive way in the neoliberal era. But we get it wrong if we say that neoliberalism just produced it or, even worse, that neoliberalism was just a voluntary set of pernicious ideas produced by followers of Friedrich Hayek, or something like that. Whatever the ideological motive of that, it's a dimension of something of much longer standing. So I think that we have a continued, recurrent process of capitalist intensification, expansion, and crisis that is indefinite in its duration, that could be regrouped, could go on, could recover in some sense.

It's not the first time there has been imbalance. There have been catastrophic world wars, there has been the Great Depression and other sorts of things, but I think we have an ever more completely globalized set of relationships, and we have to deal with the very power and fragility of previous attempted fixes. The end of the long postwar boom in the world's rich economies and the end of the phase of relatively optimistic hopes for postcolonial development and a crisis in actually existing socialism come to a head in the late 1960s and 1970s, and we get a variety of fixes that work in different ways. Inadequate fixes in state socialism led to 1989 and the crisis there, which has significant ramifications that play out elsewhere, ranging from the world being awash in weapons ever since to there being much less of the kind of regime of balance of power that was characteristic of the cold war that created a sort of unhappy stability in the system.

The dreams of development hit very hard, rocky landings in the 1970s and into the 1980s, with debt crises and other things that played out very differently in different regional arenas. And some of the responses laid the groundwork for what would be resurgent economies and new levels of growth. In the OECD countries and the rich world the fix was very largely financialization. There was a shift from industrial production to reliance on other modes of making a profit and moving industrialization out to other parts of the world. But in that story and all its problems we see a theme whereby a fix, which has resolved some problems, creates new fragilities. We now see big differences between countries like Germany, which maintained more industrial production, and other countries in Europe with less. But we also see in general the way a crisis of finance could lay the OECD economies low.

The story of the transition in a number of what in the boom years were socialist or nonaligned countries into essentially capitalist societies in China and India and so forth unfolds against this backdrop and creates its own part of it. The intensification of the petroleum economy and the new economic power of those who control parts of this that becomes so apparent in the current crisis, the boom and bust, all are part of the sources of that crisis. So there have been previous crises, but our capacity to respond is weakened by the impact of previous fixes. And the capacities for recovery from the current economic crisis and the capacities for renewal of the overall system depend upon both states and social reproduction mechanisms that are pretty fragile right now.

MK: What does this mean for the prospects for democracy?

CC: I am very interested in democracy, but my main point about democracy is that there were expectations that the spread of democracy would bring a set of institutional structures that accomplished social integration, solidarity, that accomplished inclusion of internal minorities and external migrants, that brought an orientation to the public good. Democracy has been a mixed success on that. I still think we want democracy. But I also think we need to say that part of the action in these goods is that democracy is a mechanism for helping to get them and should be judged that way. So we want peace, and we ask if democracy is helping us to achieve that. We want health care, and we should ask if democratic institutions are helping us to obtain it to some extent. A big question for the world is whether we can we find good democratic ways to deliver social reproduction and social solidarity or social integration. That would be much better than other ways, but only if it delivers. And the failure of the liberal model, which is trying to deliver democracy and economic growth without social solidarity, and sometimes in antagonism to social solidarity, is a disaster.

A lot of the struggles that we think of as the popular struggles for democratization are struggles to get the state to provide for better social reproduction. And some of them are struggles to use the state to limit the destructive capacity of capitalist production or the one-sided power relations that capitalist production entails. There has always been a kind of bundling together of what we might think of as welfare provision, an attempt to balance the terms of dealing with economic power, and democracy per se. Most of the democratic movements, like the Chartist movement in the nineteenth century and the Social Democratic Party in Germany in the early twentieth century and on into the present day, haven't been simply about getting a particular electoral system or any other particular system of democracy. They have been entwined at once in all three of these realms in trying to get some happier way of managing the balance for particular protagonists in these struggles—local communities or national parties or whoever they might be.

The issue for the future is how can we reproduce and improve the institutional structures in which we live together and work together and organize our lives together. And democracy is a piece of that. But it is not, by itself, the whole issue and not very often on its own. Take elections in a number of troubled African countries, where the elections have mainly brought more violence. They have not brought more chances for ordinary people to determine the condition of their lives. The prospects for democracy, then, hinge on the way these different institutional forms work, what they provide, and what opportunities there are for participation and for steering how they work. One version of this is very undemocratic: they work on a market basis, a for-profit basis. It's possibly open and widespread, and markets in some ways can create greater opportunities. But it's not democratic in the sense of being an independent, noneconomic organization. Another sense is democratic in the political way; that is, control is organized by the states, and people may be able to use electoral processes to control the states. And then there's another sense of democratic for those organizations in which you can get involved, in which you can have some kind of direct capacity to steer how they work.

There are different levels of government, different kinds of institutions. The relationship between small institutions, in which people can have a fairly large amount of direct engagement, and large institutions is important in all this in different parts of the world. But globalizations and the expansion of nation-states, the expansion of capital, has meant that the large institutions really matter. The question of how much or how little people can engage in steering them matters a great deal. In addition to some hollowing out of benefits, which throws the management of risk and of people's lives back on individuals, there has been a loss of capacity to steer collectively for lots of people. Not for everyone. It's not clear whether this has gone up or down in China, for example, with the transformation, but in the United States, and in Europe, there is a widespread loss of capacity to steer. In that context, social movements become very important because of their efforts to try to get a grip on steering. When routine institutional mechanisms don't work, then we have both lots of movements and a lack of big integrated movements. We have both frequent participation but short-term, ephemeral organizing, and we have quite a bit of counterattack in these new surveillance systems and efforts to reduce the extent to which there is an effective public realm for movements to exert pressure on institutions.

I'll end by saying that's the background, and in a way the focus has to get to institutions and then look at these different kinds of institutions and these different sectors of institutions and think of democracy that way and not just in terms of how many nation-states have government succession by electoral means. Though I will say that I think that, for the first time in a long time, it's not clear whether we should be optimistic about continued democratization. It may be that the trends are not good on democratization and that the best ways to get the distribution of benefits won't always be through democratic political participation.

MK: Where do you see solutions to these problems?

CC: People want and need solidarity and social reproduction, that is, the integration of society and the development of good collective relationships with each other and orientation to the public collective good. And the provision of services that are necessary to the future of the societies in which we live, including the economic future. Education as a matter of social reproduction is also a matter of the education of the labor force for the future of capitalism. We need solidarity (that which holds us together); we need the provision of support for those people in society who are not in a position to buy it for themselves out of their individual wealth; and, in some places, things for all of us, including the rich (such as clean air).

I am personally still sympathetic to broadly social democratic, socialist kinds of solutions, but there are big obstacles to this in the story that I sketched out. The existing versions that have been tried for the most part on a large scale were very closely tied with large-scale industrial capitalism and to strong nation-states. They thus don't offer good examples as to how we might look forward. They also came with pretty big problems of their own, with bureaucratic structures that made them operate less in the interest of the people and more in the interests of their own staff. It rendered them less innovative than they could have been. But I think you can't dismiss the large scale. There's going to have to be some reinvigoration of large-scale provision of services that support social reproduction; that, I think, means mainly state provision. It therefore requires reviving faith in the idea of the public. We have a situation where people turn to the private, partly out of just the sense that, since the public is not working, you have to do something for yourself and your family, but partly out of a real shift in ideas in which there used to be much more optimism about the delivery of collective goods by public mechanisms. And I think that affects not only what people vote for; it affects things like who chooses a career in the public service and whether we even have a public service ideal. The model of public service is the post office and highway construction. These don't sound like highly innovative, upwardly mobile sectors, as opposed to space explorations or curing diseases.

What we need is real institutional organization and a shift in attitudes about large-scale public provision, because there's no other way to meet the scale of the challenge. I think we need new kinds of institutions or new flourishing of old kinds of institutions. It's interesting how cooperatives have handled the current crisis so much better than any other kind of economic institution, in Spain and pretty much the world. An exploration of cooperative structures seems to me valuable and important. I don't think they are all likely to be very local models. I think there has to be this large scale. Most of the romantic aspirations that have been channeled through cooperative movements and things like local barter systems and other nontraditional exchange systems aren't going to scale up, and so we need solutions on a big scale where states are the best bet, although we can try other things. We need solutions at local levels, but we shouldn't imagine that we can automatically scale up all the things that work in community forms. We may need to tip the balance to try to make the community-level institutions work better, to do more things through community-level institutions. And this may mean tolerating diversity in institutions, which some people think is contrary to national uniformity and even democracy, when democracy is conceived only in national terms.

It may be that the majority of nations will need to tolerate community-level institutions that it wouldn't choose. Tolerating that diversity may be a virtue that is not in and of itself democratic. But it may make democracy much better and happier if we have it. I think we can't ignore reforms in corporations. Things like corporate social responsibility have become a catch-phrase that carries very little serious meaning, but whether big corporations behave responsibly toward the environment, responsibly toward their employees, responsibly toward the communities in which they operate has huge effects. To write that off is a problem. It can be a focus of external movement organizing, but it's also a question about internal operations and the extent to which those corporations are operated on very short-term, overwhelmingly financial criteria, or in other ways that may still be profit making but not short-term financial to the same degree, in which even the mode of executive remuneration, the turn toward bonuses in favor of salary, turns out to be problematic. I think that reform of the corporate sector is a priority set of policy areas, and progressive forces have been way too prone to just write all that off as irrelevant. I think that the building of other institutions in the civil society realm is really important.

The big story really has been religious institutions for a long time. These have been the overwhelmingly important civil society providers. For all of the attention that gets paid to institutions that were built by the socialist movement, they pale in size compared to those built by religious organizations. These have sometimes been very progressive, sometimes very regressive. They come with all sorts of catches. It goes back to this question of reconciling uniformity with diversity and deciding how to relate those two to democracy. Should progressive forces in the United States want the Catholic Church to be active in providing services enough that they tolerate refusal to participate in giving birth control help to people on an egalitarian basis? What we have mostly done in what passes for the left in the United States has been liberal and not anything else, because it's wanted extreme uniformity—that is, the same solution for all. This is conducive to one set of institutional arrangements but not others. How much are we going to say, "It's all right for communities to provide their own health care if they reach different conclusions about what they want to provide"? Some of them will have waiting lists for elective surgeries and some of them won't; some of them will provide birth control and some of them won't. I don't know the answer because it seems to me that it is a hard question in which we're balancing two different goods; it's not that the good is on one side and the bad is on the other side. But religion is the big arena we can look at, see something, and we see a really complicated picture of good and bad. There are other arenas for building nonstate, noncapitalist institutions to sustain social solidarity and social reproduction. There are plenty of examples, and they are almost all extremely small scale.

MK: Could you comment briefly on what might be in the way of the kinds of solutions that you sketched?

CC: The very anxieties that the instability produces lead people to grasp at problematic, partial solutions. So people might say "The world's going to hell in a handbasket, and all I need is for my place in the world to have a strong defense against the rest of the world and not let anybody in," or a response of that kind.

I think we're seeing a resurgence of nationalism and anxiety-driven, problematic wings of nationalism. This is happening in lots of places. I think the anxieties are themselves problematic. I think that there's a problem for people in being able to relate direct experience and relatively local conditions to these large-scale phenomena that are going on. And it's not just hard. There are some particularly problematic ways of doing it that are afoot. Thinking that capitalism is just markets and the free use of property leaves you unable to figure out what's going on or why it's happening, and it often leads people to make choices that are contrary to their own interests because they have a poor analysis of the larger system. The belief that national integration is just a matter of pre-existing cultural similarity makes it extremely hard to choose policies that achieve integration and offer freedom and diversity. Thinking that social integration is a matter of being friends with everybody or being nice to those people you are friends with and neglecting the extent to which it is about how we relate to strangers is a block, because most of the problems are not about how we relate to friends, family, and neighbors; they're about how we relate to strangers and, specifically, strangers who are outside the very large scale of social organization in which we live.

There are, though, real interests in this. The intensification of inequality has created interests in maintaining inequality and in promoting ways of thinking that ensures its perpetuation. This is partly elites justifying their privilege to themselves, but it's also their promoting ways of thinking among the larger population to make them conducive to the maintenance of elite privilege, both inside countries and on a global scale. But mainly I'm thinking inside countries and the ways in which the ideas of freedom are used to block public-oriented and collective-oriented solutions to problems, even when the only possible solutions are collective-oriented ones. The threat of unemployment and the fear of unemployment, which is partly just that and is partly the fear of not being able to provide for your family, the fear of not being able to eat, is used to legitimate even bad employment and policies that produce more of that. So, you know, "You workers don't really want a minimum wage, do you? That would mean fewer jobs." This kind of model of ideological thinking is promoted in a broad way, and it's promoted in part by civil society actors. A good example are the Koch brothers, at the head of the second-largest privately owned industrial holding in the United States, who are known for funding conservative, free-market, and libertarian movements. There are well-funded organizations that promote these ideologies as well as much more diffuse, broad processes. The anxiety encourages militarization and arms and raises the threat of violence. I think there are big issues at the level of social imaginaries, in the ways people understand how the world works. This interacts with and affects the ways influential policymakers work. So an issue for Europe, for example, has been the extent to which those who, for a variety of reasons, were in favor of the integration of Europe sold the integration of Europe as made necessary by international competition and thus encouraged an image of the problematic outer world in relation to the "good Europe." That makes it harder to deal with some of the issues inside Europe now.

I think there are other issues that make solutions challenging at the moment. One that is commonly neglected is demography. I have mentioned it in relation to things like the age structure of the workforce and political activism and the proportion of the young, but it's also the proportion of the old. How does Japan find solutions to some of its issues, when its most politically empowered group is a growing elderly population hostile to many of the things or afraid of many of the things that will make life better in the future for younger generations? The aging of some parts of the world's population while others are still relatively young is a big block to gaining a grip on what's going on as we keep comparing things that aren't really comparable to each other. We keep imagining, for example, in European countries that the future of the country is entirely the children born in that country, and not the flow of immigrants and the children born elsewhere who will come—healthy or less healthy, bright or less bright—partly because the population of the elderly will demand others to occupy productive positions in the economy to take care of them.

I think that a problem in achieving policy solutions is that we have in most of the world's rich countries a superabundance of relatively narrow, relatively ephemeral interest group organizations and a relative weakness in getting these connected to each other and sorting out common programs. The function that used to be performed by political parties has, I think, declined, and the political parties are relatively weak and don't do this very well, but nothing else really does. There used to be newspapers associated with big, programmatic visions and certain sets of values, but they are now creatures of money for the most part. So there is a fragmenting and dissipating of popular energies. And it's a very big obstacle that we don't have an effective way of organizing the political party system, and I don't think that the solution is going to be found through political parties. Something else is going to have to be developed to replace it. It undermines the quality of political debate, which is very weak; it undermines the stability of politics; it undermines the extent to which people can think about the necessary trade-offs that are involved, since almost every effective policy is a matter of trade-offs. You get lots of single-issue resistance to any of the possible packages that would make for a decent trade-off and very suboptimal solutions as a result. The extent to which there is a structure of movement of careers in all these organizations actually encourages this, ironically.

It is another case where a better version of democracy would be great, but in and of itself the word *democracy* doesn't tell you enough to point you to a solution. If one kind of democratic peril is the pseudo-inclusion of mass populism, another is the fragmentation into a whole range of special interest organizations and groups. Conversely, in many of the less rich, less developed countries of the world, there are places where states for the most part are still able to block insurgencies. But it's hard to know when and how collective agency gets organized on a scale potentially adequate to address the issues. Too often people do not know what it is like for "their guys" to win, and instead they live permanently in fear of other people winning.

15

"It is increasingly difficult to anticipate the future of democracy by looking back at its past"

Photo courtesy of Ivan Krastev.

IVAN KRASTEV

in conversation with Richard Sakwa

Ivan Krastev is chairman of the Centre for Liberal Strategies, Sofia, and permanent fellow at the Institute for Human Sciences in Vienna. He is a founding board member of the European Council on Foreign Relations, a member of the advisory board of the ERSTE Foundation, a member of the global advisory board of Open Society Foundations, New York, and a member of the advisory council of the Center for European Policy Analysis (CEPA).

In a conversation with Richard Sakwa, Ivan Krastev paints a picture of not only a shifting global social and political landscape but of a new iteration of modernity itself. He argues that the modern crisis is unique in that public trust in both the market and political elites has been shaken simultaneously, leaving us to contend with a politics without real alternatives and with weak democracies. He traces five "revolutions" that distinguish the current modernity and suggests that, after the fall of the Soviet Union, we have arrived not at Francis Fukuyama's "end of history" but rather at the "end of the future," in other words, at the end of longing for and fighting for a utopian better tomorrow. Engaging with examples from the current geopolitical landscape, Krastev makes the challenging assertion that Russia, rather than being a failed modernization experiment, might show us a vision of our future as a market-based state with a hollow authoritarian regime. Conversely, he criticizes the EU's failed vision of being a cosmopolitan, universal model for governance, but he suggests many countries, and especially emerging economies, can learn from Europe's turmoil. From his perspective, hope for democracy, if there is to be any, will come from unexpected places, including political elites, the rekindling of reformism and curiosity, and an engagement with the here and now rather than utopian fantasy or dystopian nihilism.

RS: Let's talk about the vision of a postdemocratic capitalism which is beginning to emerge as one the major challenges facing democratic (or any) politics today. Why have the major institutions of modernity, which used to institutionalize democracy—political parties, structured ideologies, programs for the future—all lost their centrality? What's happened to them all?

IK: The paradox today is that while democracy is universally accepted as the most desired form of government, and that the will of the people expressed in free elections is the only legitimate source of power, at the same time there is a growing frustration with democratic politics as we know it.

The opening of José Saramago's novel *Seeing* best illustrates this new reality. On a rainy election day in a small country, by 4 o'clock in the afternoon almost nobody has shown up to vote. And then, as in a horror movie, all the voters come at once, but when the returns are counted it turns out that three-quarters voted with blank ballots.

The establishment, combining the government and the opposition, was shocked and paralyzed. They feared protest, but what they encountered was a puzzle. They feared revolution, but what they got was a political pathology—an epidemic of blank ballots; protest without ideology or leaders. The government did not know what to do because it could not figure out what the citizens wanted. There was nobody with whom to negotiate. After a week of government consternation the elections were held again, and this time 83 percent of the people voted with blank ballots. This is a fantastic parable that most realistically captures the spirit of modern democracy, at least in many European states. It powerfully captures the emergence of a world without alternatives. Twenty-first-century capitalism is a society wherein the consumer is forced to make a thousand choices a day, but the same person as citizen does not have much of a choice at all.

What voters in countries like Italy and Greece are starting to realize is that they can overthrow the government that they dislike, but they cannot change policies that they oppose. Equally, voters in Germany have the feeling that their own well-being is becoming dependent on how Greece and Italy vote. There is an increasing perception that the only voter that matters is the market, but the market is starting to look as capricious as a predemocratic monarch whom we can please but we cannot influence.

Political scientists have for a long time been alarmed by the fact that, in the past thirty years in the developed countries of the West, fewer people are turning out to vote and that the people least willing to vote are the most disadvantaged members of our societies (the poor and unemployed). In short, those who should be most interested in change are least convinced that democracy can produce change. Democracy is the only game in town, but is it a game worth playing?

So what went wrong? How did it happen that we live in societies that are freer than at any other moment of history—our rights are better protected, we have access to more information, we can travel freely—but at the same time people are losing trust in democratic institutions. It is not at all clear whether the drive for openness and transparency can restore trust in these institutions.

When it comes to asking what went wrong and what went right, I want to refer to five great revolutions that deepened our democratic experience while eroding our trust in democratic institutions. The first of the five great revolutions that I want to discuss is the social revolution of the 1960s that succeeded in destroying the repressive structures of the authoritarian family and put individuals and their rights at the center of politics, but at the same time led to the decline of a shared sense of purpose, ridiculing traditional totems such as the nation, class, and God.

The second revolution that remade the world of modern politics is the market revolution of the 1980s. It strongly asserted the value of choice and it opened up much space for innovation, but it also delegitimized the very idea of a public interest. Capitalism did a lot to increase the choice of the people and created freedom for consumers and citizens. But an accompanying idea was that you don't need to bother anymore about what's happening in your society, you don't need the civic-minded citizen anymore; it's enough to pursue your individual interest in the framework of the law, and the public interest is meant somehow to emerge automatically. I think this is very important because all these people spending their time in political parties, reading newspapers, and trying to get informed were very much guided by the idea of a public interest that has now been denigrated by the market revolution. If you want to make a difference, entrepreneurship rather than politics is your natural choice.

Third, you have 1989 and the "end of history," and with this comes the idea that you don't need any big ideological projects anymore. It was not so much the end of history, but it was the end of the future. In the way that secularization basically deprived us of the idea of the transcendental, 1989 as an end of the competition between capitalism and socialism put an end to the idea that the future is what really matters. In the days of the cold war the critical question was to whom the future belonged. Now that dimension has disappeared.

The fourth revolution that I find crucial is the revolution in communication, especially the Internet. On one level the Internet makes us much freer than previously because we have access to information we never had before with much greater ease, and we can spread our ideas much more effectively. We can easily connect with other people, but at the same time the Internet revolution also created "echo chambers" where like-minded people constantly talk to each other, and, as Cass Sunstein has observed, as a result of these conversations they radicalize their views. The idea of public space has been radically transformed. We no longer share common experiences as much as before, and as a result this new type of freedom discovered on the Internet makes it very difficult for any type of a mediating structure like political parties or trade unions to function. You don't need them anymore. There is a totally different idea of egalitarianism emerging—no longer connected with the notion of income equality but associated much more with an egalitarian utopia, based on the fact that on the Internet we are all free and the opinion of one person is equal to the opinion of anyone else. This is accompanied by the idea of direct democracy, very much based on how the Internet functions. The digital experience is at the very heart of the modern rebellion against meritocracy and the rule of the experts.

One of the many paradoxes of globalization is that we are living in a much more interconnected but at the same time much more fragmented and even segregated world. Democracy, the market, and the Internet: all three empower us to do what we like, and as a result we end up populating worlds and enjoying opinions very similar to our own.

The fifth revolution was born from important discoveries in the neurosciences, which strengthen the belief that most important political decisions are not made on the rational level. Political consultants, who are (some) of the major consumers of these new discoveries, have redefined the political game very much as the management of emotions rather than the competition of ideas. As a result of this, we're ending up with a political space in which consistent political programs or political ideologies don't much matter any longer.

I believe that all five revolutions in a paradoxical way have deepened our democratic experience at the level of society, but they have made it very difficult for democratic institutions to survive.

RS: This opens up a huge accountability gap, an associative gap—a whole series of vacancies. It's not clear what type of new political subjectivity your five revolutions will produce. Yes, a new type of individualism is emerging, but the civic persona—the individual-as-citizen—is also, as you are suggesting, becoming less important than the individual-as-consumer. So it's a new active-passive role, with a constant tension between consumer activism and political passivity, all under the banner of increased choice, but choices now channeled into forms of activity that are decreasingly civic, and commonly less civil, than in the period of high modernity. This all suggests that we're talking about a confluence of changes in individual subjectivity and political forms, which suggests perhaps a larger transformation taking place whose nature we're only just beginning to grasp.

IK: For the moment we are behaving as if we can simply restore trust in institutions. The promise is that transparency will restore trust in institutions as they are. In reality, it is a very unlikely scenario. Democracy is undergoing a dramatic transformation. Thirty years ago, when talking about democracy we were talking about voters, workers, soldiers. The citizen-voter was important because you also had the citizen-worker and the citizen-soldier and the citizen-taxpayer. All three are marginal figures in modern democracies. The American political philosopher Stephen Holmes has noted that most "workers" do not vote because they are illegal migrants. The worker, as a result of this new level of de-industrialization and mobility, has been very much disappearing in most parts of the developed world. It is not by accident that trade unions are starting to lose their power.

When you look to the citizen-soldier, you see a proliferation of professional armies, drones, and out-sourced agencies. You are no longer being asked to die for your fatherland. You should simply pay for others to do the killing and the dying. The army as one of the major institutions of socialization and an instrument for creating civic identity has disappeared. The school system, equally, has also very much been subverted as an instrument for creating social cohesion. And when it comes to the taxpayer—never mind that people and especially politicians try to talk about the taxpayer, the figure that really matters when we talk about economic policy is much more the investor than the taxpayer. The reader, the worker, the soldier, the taxpayer are vanishing figures; what matters today are the drones, the consumers, the investors, and the tourists. As a state, you are much more engaged in trying to shape your tax system so that your country remains hospitable to investors than being interested in taxpayers and redistribution. So, from this perspective, I really agree with you: we're talking about an important transformation of democracy on the level of practices and on the level of institutions. It is increasingly difficult to anticipate the future of democracy by looking back at its past.

Popular discussion about transparency and accountability is the best manifestation of this transformation. Let's give one example. It is common knowledge that in most of the developed countries trust in elected politicians has reached historically low levels. It is very difficult to convince a young and intelligent person that becoming a politician is a noble vocation. As the old story goes, it is easier to tell your mother that you are a pianist in a brothel than that you are a member of Parliament. In order to make politicians more accountable, Google has devised a software program that can track any statement made by a politician on a certain issue, so when politicians decide to change their opinion to please their constituents or a specific group of voters, they can easily be exposed for inconsistency. For example, it is difficult to go Detroit and oppose the bailout of the auto industry, but in other parts of the country such "subsidies" are treated with contempt. The attentive politician is always aware of context, changing priorities and needs, and this is natural. This new program makes it much more difficult for politicians to flip-flop, but it also makes it more difficult for politicians to change their view when the situation has changed or when they have learned things that they did not know before. The real heroes of democratic politics are politicians and voters able to change their opinions as a result of a rational argument. Normally, in classical democratic theory, a politician who is not ready to change his or her opinion is not perceived to be a strong democratic politician. Now accountability is designed—by this software—to reward consistency in repeating one and the same position, at the expense of flexibility and development. We are entering a strange world in which, for example, an American presidential candidate will say something outrageous during the primary campaign to win the vote of the most extreme of his supporters, and he will be expected to maintain this position to the end because what really matters is not whether it is right or wrong but whether it is consistent with what was said earlier. Consistency rather than understanding becomes the new measure of a successful politician. A democracy in which politicians are not rewarded for changing their views when faced with a strong argument—this is a different idea of democracy from anything we have encountered before.

RS: The citizen has changed, but so has the political elite, or at least the way the political elite can conduct themselves. How should a politician behave in these circumstances? And how can we characterize the political topography of the new era?

IK: The crisis of 2008 was a very important catalyst that made visible some of the trends that we had been sensing before. Let's start with the bigger picture. A major crisis emerged, and of course people compared it to the crisis of the 1930s and that of the 1970s. But in my view there was one major difference. In the 1930s society at large, but also the political class, lost its trust in the market as the best way to allocate resources and to develop the economy, and in response to the crisis a new paradigm emerged. Trust in the market was lost but was compensated for by increased trust in government as an economic manager. Confidence in the capacity of government to overcome the destructive nature of the market was a shared belief in Roosevelt's America, Stalin's Russia, and Nazi Germany. In a similar way, in the 1970s in the West societies lost trust in the government as an economic actor, but at the same time there was a regained trust in what the market can deliver.

One of the major characteristics of the current crisis is that basically we have at the same time lost trust in the market and the state, in business elites and political elites. As a result, we talk a lot today about populism and the rise of populist actors. If you look at the numerous political surveys trying to grasp what is behind the new populist moments you will see that one of the major distinguishing features of supporters of extreme populist parties (for example, the National Front in France) is that what drives their anger is not rising income inequality but increased cultural insecurity. Supporters of extremist parties in Europe as a rule are not poorer or less educated than mainstream voters, but they have less confidence that democratic institutions can resolve the problems facing societies or that established politicians can be honest about the issues confronting the "common people." So this loss of trust in the institutions of both the market and the democratic state is in my view an important consequence of this crisis.

This also helps explain why some of the earlier expectations about the impact of the crisis turned to be wrong. When the crisis started, two questions were constantly asked: Is the crisis going to result in a major drift to the left? Who will be destroyed by the crisis? The new authoritarians, such as Russia and China, the newly established democracies in eastern Europe, and even the mature democracies in the West were considered vulnerable. These questions were very much rooted in our past experience. The crisis of the 1930s buried most of the democracies in Europe, while the Great Depression provoked the only "red decade" in American history. This time things are different. We cannot see right now that the left or the center-left is gaining significantly from the crisis. In fact both the center-left and the center-right are in crisis, while political space is invaded by new and more extreme parties that in most cases transcend the classical left-right divide. The question of whether democracy or authoritarianism benefits from the crisis remains largely unanswered.

In this brave new postcrisis world the polarity between democracy and authoritarianism no longer works. It is replaced by competition between two different forms of "there is no alternative" politics. In

Europe, this takes the form of "there is no policy alternative." European leaders see themselves forced to make economic decisions outside of democratic politics. They agreed constitutionally to limit budget deficits and public debts. European voters can change governments, but they cannot change economic policies. In China and Russia the nuance is rather different and instead focuses on "there is no political alternative"; this means that governments are less dogmatic when it comes to preferred policies, but what remains unchangeable are the people in power.

The rise of "no alternatives" politics is accompanied by the "death of the future." "Goodbye, Future" is a slogan equally popular on the streets of Moscow and on the streets of Paris and Madrid. The future has lost its power to justify or valorize policies. The idea of the future is no longer the source of legitimacy of governmental action. The fact that communism is no longer on the agenda is not a problem for the legitimacy of the Chinese Communist Party. This is the final stage of the secularization of politics. What is common between "democratic Europe" and "authoritarian Russia" is that both regimes lack normative legitimacy, based in an earlier era on the aspiration to create a good and just society. Governments do what they do because this is the only thing to be done. Globalization has made a joke of the idea of ideological choices. Fukuyama's "end of history" turned out to be the "end of the future."

A peculiar feature of the austerity state is that at the policy level it looks very much like the neoliberal state. But if you examine how this austerity state is justified, it's clearly not a neoliberal state. The neoliberal state is a normative idea. Its advocates are people who believe that small government is better, that the state should be kept as far away as possible from the life of individuals. The austerity state is something different: its justification comes from the idea that in our new global world no other politics and no other policies are possible. So, instead of a return of ideology, the crisis brought about the real end of ideology. But unlike in 1950s, "the end of ideology" today means not the end of utopian politics but politics without real choices.

RS: In discussing the evolution and emergence of this new order, maybe we could step back a bit and you could speak about how 1989 turned out to be so paradoxical. At the time, the fall of the communist systems appeared to represent the triumph of Western capitalist democracy, but in the end it may prove to be the undoing of all three. The anticommunist revolutions repudiated the former grand projects of modernity and visions of the future but opened the door to the dissolution of the institutions and, as you note, the practices of Western modernity.

IK: The year 1989 was a real turning point. It was not the end of history, but it marked the end of the West's domination in world history. The cold war was a clash between two ideologies born out of the European Enlightenment: the question was whether communism or capitalism was the legitimate child of the Enlightenment. You had two systems that were in total competition with each other—but this competitive dynamic forced both to improve to retain the edge over the other. To maintain the border between the communist and the democratic worlds, the West was, for example, forced to reduce the gulf between social classes in its own societies. The birth of the democratic welfare state is a direct response to the rise of the totalitarian threat. Keynes was not in the business of destroying liberal capitalism; he was in the business of saving it. Now what we see is that since the collapse of the Berlin Wall the barriers between social classes have started to build up again. The rise of social inequality in the past forty years is among the most debated issues in the contemporary social sciences. No less alarming is that social mobility has declined not only in the United States but also in the traditionally social-democratic countries of western Europe. If you are born poor today, the probability that you will die poor is higher now than it was thirty years ago in most of the Western world. The whole social contract typical of cold war democracy was very much predicated on the cold war and the clash not so much between two superpowers as between two ideologies. And the future from this point of view was extremely important, since the whole legitimacy of the Soviet project was based on a particular concept of moving toward the future, however much the horizon of communism may have receded. In an important way, the major Soviet claim was not that the Soviet Union was really better than the contemporary West but that the future belonged to communism and that it would *become* a better and more just society in due course. The tangible social achievements of the Soviet system were no more than augurs of what was to come, but when the people in the communist world demanded the future today, then the system was doomed. From this perspective, 1989 was not really the end of history, but the future lost its very important role as a kind of horizon against which you try to compare your achievements, to resolve your problems. And the future lost its importance not merely on the level of narratives and discourses; it disappeared on a much more practical level as a result of this future orientation.

RS: Where does Russia fit into all of this?

IK: Russia can be treated as geopolitically marginal, but, in a more profound sense, today's Russia is a magnifying glass in which we can see our future. The twenty-first century was predicted to be the "new American century," the "Chinese century," the "Asian century," and even, as Mark Leonard argued, a world that would be run by the EU. Nobody predicted that it would be a Russian century. What makes Russia so unfashionable?

Russia's relationship to the future is a complex one. Russia is the successor of the Soviet Union, and the Soviet Union was the future. In the 1930s Western intellectuals visited Soviet Russia not in the way that you visit a different place but in the way that you visit a different time. It was less a spatial than a temporal experience. Already, after visiting Moscow in March 1919, the American radical Lincoln Steffens wrote, "I have seen the future, and it works." Return from the Soviet Union was a return from the future. The communist experience was the dictatorship of the future over the present. The economy of deficit was the most radical way of forcing people to save, since you had to save when there was nothing to buy. The younger cohorts were ontologically better than their parents' generation, since it was easier to envisage an improved future based on their achievements than to describe the present. In this sense post-Soviet Russia is "after the future." The time dimension has disappeared from Russian political discourse. Classical communist discourse was organized on the axis between "before" and "after," whereas contemporary Russian political discourse is lost in time and is space-centered—organized around the axis "here" compared to "there," hence the extraordinary revival of Slavophile-Westernizer discourses.

The consensus is that Russia is a remnant from a future that never came to be realized. Russia's political developments are explained either in terms of its historical legacies—communist and tsarist—or in terms of what Russia lacks compared to societies elsewhere: the rule of law, a competitive market, a vibrant civil society, and pluralist politics. But it could be that Putin's Russia, no less than the EU, is our best chance to glimpse the world to come. Could it be that many of the problems that Russia faces today come not from the past but from the future?

If the contemporary crisis-ridden EU signifies the voiding of democratic institutions and the hollowing of authority, Russia signifies the emptying of authoritarianism. Power is the capacity to project your problems onto others; now both projects have turned in on themselves. The contradictions become increasingly manifest and cannot be externalized without a substantive breakdown of the systems themselves. Thus Russia is the best demonstration that today's political world cannot be explained in terms of a simple bipolarity between democracy and authoritarianism.

Russia, unlike the Soviet Union, is a political regime with open borders and no ideology. Russia's experience breaks the traditional link between authoritarianism and the notion of a closed society. Putin's nondemocratic regime cannot survive if it decides to close itself off from the global market or if it bans its citizens from travel. But equally, in conditions of openness it cannot survive either.

Russia demonstrates the most important political trend in the globalized world: the interplay between interconnectedness and segregation. It is a perverse treatment of the idea of government as the servant of the people. The government really treats the people in the way a waiter treats his customer: do his bidding and take his money, preferably with a 20 percent tip. The notion of a power vertical is useless to understand how the power system really works in contemporary Russia, but it is a useful insight into the emergence of society that is only horizontally integrated: there are the flying classes and the walking classes, and seldom do they meet. Unlike the twentieth-century nation-state, which was obsessed with social cohesion, in the new global conditions social cohesion is no longer an elite objective.

Putin's regime can be explained neither in terms of repression nor in terms of exploitation. The elites are integrated in the global market, and they make their wealth through the exploitation of nature, not people. The task of the state is to neutralize the population. This is the "politics" of de-politicization.

Politics without alternatives is a strange world where the future is already consumed (notably, through public debt and budget deficits), the past is irrelevant, people do not demand democracy, and elites do not enjoy the dubious pleasures of authoritarianism.

RS: The Arab Spring in 2011 brought out all the contradictions between attempts to combine political modernity and social conservatism. A new dynamic of social interaction is emerging, where there is an increased emphasis on the past as a way of validating the present: the past is the new future. We already see this in the concept of postsecularism, which forces a fundamental rethinking of the view that secularism is an essential feature of modernization. Instead some of the most advanced societies are also the most religious (one need only look at the United States). In other words, the transformative ideas of modernization and modernity seem to have exhausted themselves, and therefore the only option, the only way forward, is backward.

IK: First, you're right that the return of religion is something that would have greatly surprised the modernization theorists of the 1950s and 1960s, who basically believed that secularization was part of the modernization package and that religion cannot survive in a world dominated by the market, science, rationalism, and democracy. Modernization theorists on this account turned out to be wrong. But what we see today, at least in my view, is not so much retraditionalization but the return of communitarianism, a return empowered by the emergence of the Internet. You can see that although we're talking about markets, about multiculturalism and all other forms of distancing from a particular community, recent data demonstrate that self-segregation is a fundamental part of our global experience. It is interesting to think about a simple fact. I am a Bulgarian who now lives in Vienna. If this had happened some thirty years ago, it would have been natural that I would get most of my information from Austrian media, but today I can change places all the time without changing my sources of information.

Studies conducted in the United States show that in the 1970s almost 50 percent of Americans lived in counties where it was possible for one or the other party to win elections. Now more than 70 percent of Americans live in counties where one of the parties wins a landslide victory; in other words, the majority lives in one-party counties. So while the nation-state and basically the state as we know it was a very important factor in the de-segregation of society on different levels—notably on grounds of race or income—and the idea of social cohesion was clearly important, I believe that at the moment we have a new demand precisely for segregation. This segregation can be around religious lines or other lines, but strangely enough, the more globalization we get, the more we come back to strong communitarian identities. People find it more rather than less difficult to align with the type of identity that modernity fosters.

RS: Following the Second World War, the EU offered a new model of community: it was supranational without abandoning the nation-state; it was social without being socialist; and it seemed to offer an original and viable approach to the establishment of a new type of political community. The enlargement to include the former socialist countries seemed to be a huge achievement, as finally the larger part of the European continent was united with a common purpose. But paradoxically, the moment of its greatest extension has turned out to be the moment in which its founding principles seem to have been, if not repudiated, then certainly weakened.

IK: I very much agree, and I believe one of the paradoxes is that ten years ago the Europeans tended to view the European project as the model of the future to come. We basically believed that the European postmodern state, the complex world of overlapping institutions and multiple identities, was what the future was going to offer. Now we're looking around and starting to realize that we Europeans are not simply not the future, but that what we believed was universal in the EU experience is becoming very much exceptional. The "others" are not becoming like us. Even more, we are not as postnational as we used to think. When the crisis came, we can see that in Europe we still have a very strong institutionalized solidarity, but when it comes to emotional citizenship, when it comes to people's readiness to share with others, solidarity does not easily cross national borders. Crudely put, the Germans are not ready to do for the Greeks what the West Germans did for their East German confrères twenty years ago.

What we see is that although the crisis is a common experience for the EU, we don't even have a common debate or a common position. There is not even a common conspiracy theory. All of these things happen at the national level. It's very easy during a crisis to see how people descend or retrench into the French position or the German position, and this is not only true of politicians. We had this new kind of institutional model that was forged out of the European experience during the Second World War and the cold war, and even in the postcommunist era, but this type of European identity that everyone was talking about looks to be much more problematic today than we believed it to be even ten years ago. Strangely enough, this is not accompanied by the rise of any kind of strong anti-European alternative. You cannot say that the parties who oppose the status quo offer anything to capture the imagination of the people.

BUT what you have in Europe, and I find this very disturbing, is that the democratic imagination that was on display in 1989—when West Europeans believed that it was Europe's hour and this was a chance to transform the world around Europe and basically make others like us—is replaced by a demographic imagination. Now there is this fear that we are melting down, we are aging and vanishing, and others are going to change us—there is a fear of immigration, a cultural insecurity, and it's not by accident that if you look at the major issues shaping the identities of the voters of the extreme parties, it's not the economy but cultural insecurity and immigration. So we've reached a moment when it's not simply that the EU does not believe that we are the future anymore; we've started to fear the future.

RS: How does one act as a political being today? In what way can citizenship be expressed? And what possible forms of the "good society" can one work toward?

IK: I still believe that Europe has one major advantage, and this is its rich political experience. For the past five hundred years, Europe was the major political laboratory in the world. Most of the major ideas, some of the major experiments have been here. And I do believe that one of the basic things Europe can offer is really trying carefully to reread its history, but to reread the history not with the idea of what to save but with the view of how to innovate. One of the features that I find very interesting in the rise of democracy is the following: I believe Fukuyama was right that basically the future belongs to democracy, but probably he got the "why" wrong. I think the reason why democracy is becoming so popular is that demand for democracy very often comes not from the people but from the elites. Because only in a democratic framework can government enjoy being weak.

I think an interesting story today is the extent to which governments benefit from the perception that they are weak rather than strong. The austerity state is becoming adept at telling people what it cannot do. In my view, the definition of what it means to be powerful is changing these days, and from this point of view, comparing the current crisis in the United States and the current crisis in the EU is highly suggestive. Many European countries and the United States have major debt problems, but while the Americans are managing to refinance their debt on very attractive interest rates, this is not the case for European member states like Spain, Italy, or Greece. And the problem is that today power is much more the capacity to unload your problem onto others, to position yourself within a global system in such a way that your problems are other people's problems. While saying this, I do believe that while the European Union is no longer the center of the world, it now faces the problems others are going to face in ten, twenty, or thirty years. Let's start with demography: we're an aging society, but in twenty years China is also going to be an aging society. And politics in aging societies, of course, are going to be very different. One of the major obsessions of modernity has been with youth. Youth was the most important social group in political terms. Youth is not going to be as important in aging societies, and this will change politics and our view of what is a just society.

I believe that in the next fifteen or twenty years, there is going to be a major change in the way we conceptualize the problem of justice. A century ago the problem of justice was about the relations between capital and labor, about workers' salaries and capitalist profits, so it was very much about income inequality. Fifty years ago, this was very much a social-democratic concern, focusing on education, opportunities, and social mobility. I believe that in the next fifteen or twenty years one of the major stories about justice is going to be equality and inequality in dying and being old. Tension between the rich and the poor is going to be less about how people live and consume than about how they die. This allows the EU to start to reflect on itself, having the advantage of getting there first. It will need to find solutions to problems that are going to be universal for everybody—not universal in the sense that others are simply going to repeat our experience but in asking questions about how to deal with a society in which youth is going to be a small group.

THE other major problem is the dismantling of the welfare state, which we see now is a major trend. How is it going to work? One of the suggestions I heard is that it will be most difficult to dismantle welfare states in countries in which women are politically powerful because it's not this or some other class that is affected, but women who are going to be the major victims of the dismantling of the welfare state. When there is not enough housing for old people, this is going to change the life of the modern woman. And I do believe that these types of questions and these types of problems should be where European politics should be more innovative. For sure, the Internet is changing the way that we relate to each other, and we are going to have this major impact of technology on the way political participation takes place. (Look at even Russia these days: during the protests in December 2011, who was going to speak at rallies was decided by voting on the Internet.) This new source of legitimacy, this wisdom of the crowd, is going to be very popular. Nevertheless I believe that it will be counterproductive. In short, Europe is on the verge of experimenting and adjusting to some of the major changes that others are going to face later. So Europe's biggest challenge is that we are forced to be social innovators while our instincts are nostalgic and conservative, and our mood is pessimistic.

RS: You seem to be saying that there are opportunities that new technology, shifting social trends, the empowerment of women, a new respect for the aged, and much more can be exploited—not to return Europe to its former preeminence but to find for it a new role as a pilot for a different type of future. In this context, it would be a mistake to talk about the death of Western modernity; rather we could say that modernity is now actually becoming more mature, in some ways more inclusive, less future-oriented and more focused on the real challenges of the present.

IK: At different moments of world history, major social, political, or technological changes have been experienced as the end of the world. Industrialization, with the major disruptions that it brought, was thought to be one form of the end times. Or remember how people talked about television and what television was going to do to society or politics? But at none of these periods did the end really come. Just the opposite: the major disruptions have also been the moments of real leaps forward. And it's important from this point of view to find a new form of a global reformism.

16

*"Genuine dialogue requires not only talking but a great deal
of listening"*

FRED DALLMAYR

in conversation with Ghoncheh Tazmini

Fred Dallmayr is Packey J. Dee Professor in
the Departments of Philosophy and Political
Science at the University of Notre Dame. He
is the past president of the Society for Asian
and Comparative Philosophy and is presently
a cochair of the World Public Forum "Dialogue
of Civilizations."

Fred Dallmayr has written and lectured extensively about the need
to respect plurality and foster dialogue among cultures, civilizations, and religions. In a thought-provoking conversation with Ghoncheh Tazmini, he expands upon many of the major themes of his life's
work in the context of continuing political crises. Challenging the
prevalent either/or approaches used in mainstream accounts of current
political events, he offers a more nuanced approach to philosophy and
politics that gets at the context and meaning of events. In light of the
Arab Spring and persistent American antagonism with Iran, he argues
that Islam and democracy are not inherently inimical and that the

contentious politics of the Middle East can actually be more deliberative and contested than those in often ambivalent liberal democracies. On the other hand, he cautions that popular revolt may not bring about the sort of modernization or liberalization many Western commentators envision but suggests that local developments may create constructive local modernities that need not be threatening to or opposed to the West. He advocates a broad-based approach to study and critique, referencing thinkers from across the political and geographic spectrum, which is rooted in listening, respecting others' thoughts and contexts, and finding deep understanding before engaging in criticism or action.

GT: In the Arab world, we have seen upheaval, protest, changes of leadership, and, in the case of Libya, international armed intervention. There is a battle for democratic pluralism and universal rights, but where is the Arab Spring really going? Do you think that the western European model of a liberal, secular, capitalist modernity is a feasible ideal in the Arab world?

FD: I do not much believe in historical inevitability or the operation of some mechanical "laws" of historical evolution. However, if one looks at the development of societies around the world in the past two hundred years, it is hard not to give credence to Alexis de Tocqueville's feeling that there seems to be something nearly "providential" about the advance of democracy in the world. Actually, I think this move toward democratization is stronger than the move toward a "secular age" (as Charles Taylor assumes); secularism, for me, is only a by-product, and only in some cases. People everywhere simply have a desire for freedom, not to be oppressed by autocratic (including clerical) elites. When David Pryce-Jones ascribes the idea that "Arabs want freedom and democracy" to a "Eurocentric fantasy" or inability to grasp "how other societies operate," he seems to be himself succumbing to Eurocentrism: the notion that only Europeans or people in the West are mature enough to aspire to freedom and self-rule.[1] The facts on the ground prove him wrong. Of course, it is an entirely different question whether aspiring to freedom and democracy means simply an "adaptation to Western norms and standards." If this were the case, it would surely be a "failed adaptation" (as you say).

Your question whether "the Western European model of a liberal, secular, capitalist modernity" is a "feasible ideal in the Arab world" cannot be answered directly because it buries too many other questions: What is the meaning of each term (*liberal, secular, capitalist, democracy*)? All these terms have multiple meanings. *Liberalism* can refer to libertarianism, laissez-faire neoliberalism, but also to a Hegelian notion of freedom; *democracy* can mean procedural democracy, deliberative democracy, social democracy, people's democracy; and there are different forms of capitalism and secularism in all modern Western societies. Arabs and/or Muslims will have to sort out these meanings and see which one best fits their own circumstances. You call it a "home-grown modernity." As you can see, I am neither an abstract universalist nor a narrow particularist (or relativist). I believe that all human beings have certain common traits or aspirations: the desire for food and shelter and the yearning for freedom and justice. But they pursue these yearnings in very different forms depending on culture, tradition, religion, and the like.

GT: In your book *Dialogue among Civilizations*, you speak of intercivilizational dialogue being fraught with many difficulties and possible derailments.[2] In particular you refer to memories of colonialism and imperialism, coupled with the traumas of conquest and violence. Many observers are wary of Europe and have a tendency to depreciate or debunk European or Western culture as being synonymous with cultural arrogance. In the Arab context, where, clearly, memory is tainted, would it not be safe to assume that there are broad sectors of society that resist this battle for a modernity that has a Western governing center—not only because the slogans chanted are "Western-inspired" but because the popular movements are supported by the West (even militarily, as we saw in Libya)? What is the challenge that lies ahead in reconciling diverse sectors of society with the objective of building a shared vision of a modernity that will suit diverse interests and ideologies?

FD: Now, it is true that these "derailments"—such as conquest, imperialism, and colonialism—have mostly been perpetrated by European
or Western countries, and to this extent it is also true that, in many
parts of the world, European and Western culture has become "a
synonym for cultural arrogance." Specifically in Arab and Muslim
countries, there is indeed often a resistance to "modernity" and all its
implications because there is a sense that they are "Western-inspired."
Some time ago I became familiar with the Iranian notion of *gharbza-
degi* (Westoxification). Such a complete rejection of the West can lead
to a retreat into a radical traditionalism or religious fundamentalism,
which is not helpful because it stifles social innovation and the desire
for freedom. In my writings, my recommendation is to avoid both a
stifling antimodernism or anti-Westernism and an uncritical "modernism," that is, to preserve the good things from one's own tradition
(minus the obsolete and oppressive features) and to accept the good
features of the West (minus the corrupting, destructive, and arrogant
imperialist features). Thus, for instance, in China one may wish to
preserve the good teachings of classical Confucianism, while discard-
ing the aspects of feudalism and autocracy. This, in a way, means to
steer clear of both Orientalism and its reverse, mirror image of Occidentalism. I share your opinion that the challenge ahead lies in "reconciling diverse sectors of society" (traditionalists, modernizers, and
everything in between) with the aim of "building a shared vision" of a
livable modern society. This brings us back to the notion of a "home-
grown modernity" embracing a model that is indigenous but also sub-
scribes to Western standards. This is an extremely difficult task and
requires a lot of good political sense and a willingness to experiment
with what works and what does not work (in John Dewey's sense). In
any case, ossified ideological formulas are never helpful in political
life.

GT: In your book *Beyond Orientalism*, you expressly argue against
global uniformity and the tendency toward homogenization of the
world as the consequence of the ongoing process of globalization and

the emergence a global village or "cosmopolis."[3] The Eurocentric view of the past, you argue, has been replaced or at least challenged by the rise of a global arena in which non-Western cultures and societies are increasingly active participants in shaping the future of the world (for example, China, Russia, and Iran). Was Samuel Huntington right, then? Are these diverse civilizations clashing in this cosmopolis?

FD: There is indeed a powerful tendency of this kind in our world today, fueled by the forces of economic, technological, and Internet globalization. I do not oppose globalism per se in all its forms, but for political reasons, because I suspect many of these forms do serve as a smokescreen for neocolonial forms of domination. I do not oppose cosmopolitanism either, but only such forms that, again, serve as a smokescreen or are in other ways wrongheaded. In my forthcoming book on cosmopolitanism, I argue that any future cosmopolis has to respect its status "after Babel," that is, after the dispersal of humankind into a great variety of cultures, languages, and traditions. This means that a future cosmopolis has to accept diversity and the fact (as you say) that non-Western cultures are indeed "increasingly active participants in shaping the future of the world." The question is: How will they participate? Will they engage in a peaceful way, or in a conflictual way, with wars and "clashes of civilizations" (à la Huntington) being prevalent? The past decade—which has been a decade of incessant warfare—seems to prove Huntington right. But are such clashes inevitable, or are there alternatives to warfare and global mayhem?

I have tried to accentuate the possibility of more peaceful relations. I have never claimed that the road is easy; the obstacles are immense: prejudices, ingrained hatreds, and the lust for conquest. So the effort has to be commensurate, to be carried on through education, cross-cultural engagements, international organizations and meetings. In my forthcoming book on cosmopolitanism I point this out. I criticize what Ulrich Beck has aptly called a "banal cosmopolitanism," which merely consists of globe-trotting and jet-setting, and instead emphasize normative principles or rules of the game, and especially ethical engagements and interactions across boundaries leading to genuine learning experiences.

In all these matters I have learned a great deal from the work of Hans-Georg Gadamer, the prominent European philosopher of dialogue who passed away in 2002. His emphasis on cross-cultural learning has helped me to cross the boundary between the European culture (where I grew up) and the cultures of India, Japan, China, and Iran (among many others). Following these boundary crossings, I have also learned, of course, from different mentors, for example, from the Indian *Bhagavad Gita*, with its emphasis on *lokasamgraha* (world maintenance); from the Indian Spanish thinker Raimon Panikkar, with his elaboration of the "cosmotheandric" perspective; from the American Chinese philosopher Tu Weiming, with his renewal of Confucian insights; from the Moroccan thinker al-Jabri and his rethinking of the classical Islamic tradition of philosophy; and others. A basic condition for the avoidance of "clashes" is overturning the Hobbesian conception that the "natural" human condition is one of "war of all against all." This conception was renewed and sharpened in the past century by the lawyer and theorist Carl Schmitt and his definition of politics as the "friend-enemy distinction."

In my *Integral Pluralism*, I have tried to show that this conception is basically untenable.[4] (I have also tried to dismantle Schmitt's notion of "political theology" in the same book.) Against the Schmittian definition, I have marshaled the much older definition that politics is the search for the common good or the "good life." By using the Aristotelian formula, I do not pretend that we have already an agreed-upon and shared sense of the meaning of the "good life." Rather it is precisely the task of democratic politics to engage in a continuous search through interaction, dialogue, mutual questioning, and communication.

GT: You have highlighted the fact that the non-Western world did not experience the Renaissance, Reformation, and Enlightenment, and thus modernity cannot possibly mean the same thing in non-Western societies and cultures. Many societies do not embrace a secular, hyperrationalistic view of modernity. Would the world be a safer and more peaceful place—a true global village—if only the dominant North Atlantic and Western European states accepted the fact that modernity has multiple trajectories? For example, if the West had accepted the fact that Iran became an Islamic republic or a sort of democratic theocracy all the way back in 1979, do you not think that today Iran and the United States would have had better relations (instead of talk of crippling sanctions, threats of military intervention, cyber warfare, regime change, and covert actions to destabilize the government under the guise of democracy)? Threats of regime change or destabilization can radicalize even the most moderate elements of society, which can be very dangerous and can actually stunt any form of democratic development. If Iran had been left to follow its own developmental path based on its historical, revolutionary, cultural, and religious experience, and its own civic and national identity, free from outside interference or pressure or sabotage, relations with the West would have been different. Do you not agree that there would have been a natural convergence rather than such polarization?

FD: In various places I have described myself as a friend of Iran, that is, a friend of Iran's cultural heritage and aspirations. I have visited Iran several times, traveling from Tehran to Isfahan and Shiraz. I have also visited Qom and talked with some of the Ayatollahs. I have found contemporary Iran to be an intellectually very vibrant and multidimensional place: all the major social, political, and religious issues are debated with great intensity and intelligence. (This compares favorably with some of the lethargy and conformism in some Western academic centers where all questions seem to be already settled.)

More than a decade ago, I was drawn to President Mohammad Khatami's proposal for a "dialogue of civilizations." I am friends with many Iranian intellectuals, some of them expatriates, like Abdolkarim Soroush and Ramin Jahanbegloo. So I think I have made a good faith effort to understand Iran. I fully agree with your point that the world would be a safer and more peaceful place "if dominant North Atlantic and Western

European states accepted the fact that modernity has multiple trajectories," which means that they would grant to Iran her own trajectory.

Of course, not all outside influences can be avoided. Some of these influences happen almost by osmosis: through the Internet, the media, films, music, and travels. This can hardly be excluded (unless one wants to resort to draconian measures of censorship). A totally different matter is forceful—especially military—intervention in the affairs of other countries. This is prohibited by international law and by the Charter of the United Nations, to which all the Western powers are signatories. There are some extremely hard cases; Kosovo is usually mentioned as an example. But even in these cases, outside military intervention has to be sanctioned by a decision of the United Nations Security Council. This was not done in the case of Libya, and this is why the Libyan intervention was entirely illegal. The intervention also set a bad example, as it can be used to bolster pressure for intervention elsewhere (for instance, in Syria).

Nowhere in the Charter is there any warrant for an outside regime change. In an age when most countries are at least nominally committed to democracy, it is clear that regime change can only happen democratically through the people in the country. And in that case, the change should preferably come nonviolently. As Hannah Arendt famously stated in *On Violence,* "Violence does indeed change the world—into a more violent world." How can one be sure that people who are ready to kill and butcher members or supporters of an existing regime will not also, when they come to power, kill and butcher opponents and minorities? Basically, as Mahatma Gandhi insisted, means and ends here have to be consistent; that is, democracy can only be established democratically. This does not mean that there is a moratorium on change. In fact societies and especially democracies need to be constantly reformed. But the best change comes through peaceful struggle (what Gandhi called *satyagraha*), relying on domestic people and domestic cultural and intellectual resources. All this does not mean that outsiders cannot make suggestions for change—if it is done in a friendly, nonaggressive, and noninterventionist manner.

GT: You have spoken about democratic possibilities in Islamic societies, particularly Iran. You made what you call a "modest proposal": you suggested that the theocratic element in the Iranian Constitution be transferred to an upper legislative chamber with either legislative powers equal with the lower chamber or a delaying or advisory role. The reason I bring this up is not to assess your proposal, but to suggest that Iran, and indeed other non-Western societies, may have modest proposals of their own in relation to Western governing systems and European social and cultural norms. In a perfect world, this would take the form of a prescriptive, normative dialogue wherein both parties would exchange views of how to ameliorate their systems and standards by sharing experiences and knowledge—without the desire to impose, coerce, convert, or assimilate. There is so much suspicion about motives that exchanges are stymied because of deeply entrenched prejudgments. How can we move away from this unilateral logic toward a genuine cross-cultural encounter and dialogue?

FD: I made my "modest proposal" explicitly as a friend, not an enemy; moreover it is clear to everybody that I have absolutely no power whatever to implement it. The reason I made the proposal is that there is what I consider to be an internal conflict or contradiction in the present Iranian Constitution: two regimes are juxtaposed to each other, a popular, elected regime (Majlis and president) and a nonelected Guardian Council and supreme leader. Sooner or later this conflict is bound to lead to trouble, to the great delight of Iran's detractors. In order to make for a smooth evolution, I suggested transforming the nonelected part of the Constitution into an Upper Chamber (after the British system or some other conceivable model). This would also lead to a fuller flourishing of the country. In my view, the so-called green movement is supported by some extremely bright and talented people, and it is not optimal for the country if such bright people are sidelined.

I have so far not mentioned, of course, one of the most serious reasons for the present tension or conflict between Western hegemonic countries and Iran: the issue of nuclear weapons. I do not believe or know that there is any evidence that Iran is presently developing such nuclear weapons. (Like all other countries, of course, Iran is entitled to develop nuclear power for peaceful purposes.) This question of nuclear weapons, however, leads into an apocalyptic abyss. After Hiroshima and Nagasaki, who would want to have nuclear weapons? Who or which country would be willing to use them? Such weapons are simply totally unusable; hence they should be abandoned. As Ayatollah Khamenei correctly stated, nuclear weapons are *haram*, that is, ungodly, inhuman, forbidden by the laws of God and humanity. Hence all our efforts in this area should be directed toward nuclear disarmament, especially toward the establishment of nuclear-free zones in the most tension-ridden parts of the world.

GT: You have examined the compatibility of political Islam and democracy and suggested that we need a "third way" or a middle ground where religion is located neither completely inside nor completely outside the world. What do civil society, the rule of law, or popular sovereignty look like in an Islamic republic? What institutional form would pluralism take in an Islamic republic? Do these concepts mean what they signify in secular, liberal Western societies? On a global level, we should foster universal recognition of the heterogeneity of the experiences of modernity.

FD: I translate the relation between "political Islam and democracy" into the broader question of the relation between religion and politics or religion and democracy. I have warned against two dangers or derailments: the "politicization" of religion and the "privatization" of religion. In the case of politicization, a religious faith—say, Islam or Judaism or Catholicism—arrogates to itself the role of a political regime or government; in the second case, religious faith is exiled from social life and completely confined to the inner or private domain. Against both derailments, the First Amendment of the U.S. Constitution offers a shield by stating that there cannot be an "established religion" (or state religion) but also that there must be room for the "free exercise of religion." (Similar formulas exist in many other constitutional documents; I select the U.S. version because it is short and clear.) So religion is not a political regime (with the power to coerce), nor is it a purely inward sentiment; it flourishes in a third dimension, or what you call a "middle ground." In modern political philosophy we call this "civil society." Only on this level can religion be truly uplifting and inspiring. If religion is politicized, it becomes merely another worldly power; if it is privatized, it becomes unworldly. In both cases it loses what scripture calls (and Paul Ricoeur adopts the biblical language) the capacity to be "the salt of the earth."

These comments apply especially to modern democracy and the relation between religion and democracy. Modern democracies tend to be pluralistic and thus have a great variety of religious believers and also nonbelievers. If one religion establishes itself as the government, it becomes necessarily oppressive and part and parcel of worldly power plays, thus losing its "transcending" or "salvific" capacity. This does not mean that religion cannot play a role in society; it can do this on the level of educational, philanthropic, and social service institutions. Not being the government, religion has to respect the pluralism of society, that is, respect the freedom of other religions and of nonbelievers. Religion has to respect the principle of religious freedom; otherwise it undermines itself.

This leads me back to my modest proposal regarding Iran. My proposal was designed to protect not only democracy but also the integrity and purity of Islamic faith. As the Qur'an states, "No coercion in matters of faith" ("la Ikrah fid-din"). But a religious government necessarily is coercive and hence leads to irreligion because of the involvement in worldly power struggles. During the European Middle Ages, the Vatican, a Catholic state, was involved in endless power struggles with other countries. This involvement was to the detriment of sound politics (as Machiavelli pointed out) and the even greater detriment of religious faith (as the Reformation pointed out).

Being respectful of religious freedom, religion in a democracy also has to show respect for the freedom to interpret scriptures (or hermeneutical freedom). In my forthcoming book *Being in the World*, there is a chapter dealing with the Egyptian philosopher Nasr Abu Zayd.[5] He was a fine scholar who was also a learned practitioner of hermeneutics; hence he proceeded to offer some new interpretations of Qur'anic passages. Religious authorities in Cairo excommunicated him from Islam, and even divorced him from his wife (who could no longer be married, they claimed, to an infidel). As long as religious authorities act in this way, there cannot be compatibility between Islam and democracy (since the latter requires freedom). Fortunately there are other Muslim societies where such abuse does not happen (like Morocco, Turkey, and Indonesia), supporting the hope that Islam and democracy are, after all, quite compatible.

Pluralism prevails both on the local or domestic and the global or intercultural levels. On both levels, we need creative interpretations and goodwill, mutual engagements and interactions. These things do not just happen by themselves but need to be fostered and cultivated in daily practice. It is an uphill struggle, but also a worthwhile struggle.

GT: You argue that the task is really to steer a course between "Euro-centrism" and "Euro-denial," in other words, to find a balance. We live in a global village, and it is important to also embrace the institutional benefits of the Western world. Under President Putin, Russia had to adopt Western-inspired liberal initiatives in order to attract foreign investment and technology. This translated into greater pluralism and deeper institutionalization of constitutional processes. At the same time, Putin subscribed to more "traditional" objectives, including resto-ration of a strong centralized state, a more significant relationship with the Russian Orthodox Church, a more controlled media, and revival of past symbols and imagery. Putin's method is integrative in that it retains some of the old structures and practices that are authoritarian and arbitrary, but also adaptive in the sense that the leadership is not ideologically opposed to modifying certain practices for the sake of the country's political survival. Russia seems to be following a non-model. Does this balance between autonomy and adaptation constitute what you consider the "balance" between Eurocentrism and Euro-denial? Could this balance that you speak of translate into an integrative and adaptive modernity in practical terms?

FD: Regarding Russia, we have to look not only at Putin but at what preceded Putin. After the collapse of the Soviet Union in 1991, Russia entered into a kind of social, political, and economic free fall, into a somewhat chaotic situation, with many factions competing for advantage. In order to attract foreign investment and technology, Russia had to adopt "Western-inspired liberal initiatives" (as you say). But not only general liberal initiatives were involved but a very specific type of policy, namely, neoliberal polices of absolute market freedom, that is, a completely unregulated type of capitalism (which was preferred by leading Western economists and foisted by them on the rest of the world). This led in Russia to wild economic activities and speculations. Now, this type of predatory capitalism suffered shipwreck in the West in 2007–8. I am referring to the financial fiasco, the extreme forms of subprime lending that led to the collapse of the housing market and the foreclosures pushing millions of people into poverty. This kind of rapacious capitalism is not the only way for markets to function, as several Nobel laureates in economics (like Joseph Stiglitz and Paul Krugman) have pointed out. Some kind of public market regulation is necessary, and, in effect, most European societies adhere to a form of "social market" economics. Putin obviously realized that following the unregulated market model would drive Russia into bankruptcy and financial meltdown. Hence he instituted again greater state controls of the market. The question is whether he perhaps went overboard and conjured up the old ghosts of communist collectivism. I am not sure; this would have to be watched.

In any case, as it seems to me, the only viable economic path in our time is something between total market freedom and collectivist state control—that is, something between Chicago-style neoliberalism and Soviet-style collectivism. Maybe Putin is groping for this. As you suggest, Putin's method is "not ideologically opposed to modifying certain

practices for the sake of the country's political survival." Such an exper-
imental approach is indeed required in our time, not only in Russia
but also in Europe and America. You say that, in this sense, "Russia
seems to be following a non-model," or simply the model of experimentation. You also find in this non-model a "balance between autonomy
and adaptation," which also means a balance between economic freedom and social solidarity. This latter formula I would certainly want
to endorse. You link the balance with another kind of balance: that
between Eurocentrism and Euro-denial. The two balances are not identical: the former is more economical, the second cultural. But I agree
that they are related. If Europe stands for Enlightenment and individual
freedom, and non-Europe stands for some kind of communalism or
collectivism, then the connection is clear. But we know, of course, that
the situation is not so simple. There are pockets of communalism and
collectivism in "Old Europe," and there are spaces of critical reason
and individualism in places outside Europe. Nevertheless if we use the
terms in a somewhat undifferentiated way, then we indeed need a balance between Eurocentrism and Euro-denial.

Coming back to Russia, I agree with you that Russia's approach (provided it is pursued in a tolerant and nonoppressive way) could serve
as a non-model for other countries that have been caught in the tension between modernity and antimodernity, between Eurocentrism and
Euro-denial, between Orientalism and Occidentalism. This statement
applies both to the economic context and the cultural-religious context.
In an acute manner, the tension between alternatives applies today also
to mainland China, where we find a fierce struggle between defenders
of a liberal capitalist market and defenders of state control, between
defenders of traditional culture (especially Confucianism) and devotees
of modern liberal practices.

GT: The United States portrays Russia as an authoritarian state with
expansionist instincts, not as a "normal" state or one abiding by acceptable rules of international behavior. Russia is accused of attempting to
revive the lost empire, backpedaling on democracy and challenging the

West's vital interests in the world. As a result, Western nations abstain from engaging Russia as an equal contributor to shaping the global system. I feel that these theories of authoritarian expansionism suffer from biases of essentialism and cultural ethnocentrism. They have provided a pretext for the West to expand NATO to Russia's borders and to launch an antimissile defense shield in Russia's backyard, threatening Russia's sphere of geopolitical (and security) interests. Do we face the danger of entering a new Western-instigated cold war because of these ethnocentric positions?

FD: My comments so far, I am afraid, may seem to be too naïve or optimistic and not to look the "realities" squarely in the face. My response to this charge is, first of all, that we do not face realities directly but always "interpreted" realities (hence the crucial importance of interpretation and hermeneutics, including the "hermeneutics of suspicion," which is particularly suspicious of the role of power in everything). But even when interpreting realities, I cannot help but admit that there are enormous dangers looming on the horizon, especially the danger of a new cold war, and even of a hot war (possibly a world war). When reading or listening to Western media today, one often gets the impression that we are already in the midst of a new cold war. The chief enemy in this setting is, of course, Iran, but closely behind Iran there are Russia and China. I agree with you when you say that Russia tends to be portrayed as an "authoritarian state with expansionist instincts" (as if Western powers did not have expansionist instincts) and as a country seeking "to revive a lost empire, backpedaling on democracy, and challenging the West's vital interests" (one of these interests, of course, being to have Russia completely submissive). Russia's behavior with regard to Syria has, of course, greatly stoked Western animosity (while truly "authoritarian" countries like Saudi Arabia and Qatar, which support antiregime forces in Syria with arms and money, are exempted from such animosity).

The attitude toward Russia finds a parallel in the extensive "China bashing," which is a favorite pastime of Western media today. The enormous accomplishments of China during recent decades are completely ignored while some "dissidents" are lionized (in sharp contrast to the treatment of dissidents in the United States). My intention here is not to shield China or Russia from criticism wherever there are instances of oppression or corruption. The point is one of balance. Just as there is imbalance in Euro-denial, there is imbalance and unfairness in China bashing or Russia bashing. In any case, such bashing is incompatible with the desire to have a genuine "dialogue among civilizations." There is an enormous number of lessons that the West can learn from China and Chinese traditions, and also from Russia and Russian traditions. But such learning is completely foiled by an attitude of hegemonic arrogance and self-contentment.

As has rightly been said, genuine dialogue requires not only talking but a great deal of listening, in fact the "great art of deep listening." Before talking, one needs first of all to cultivate listening, to be open to new voices, new learning experiences, and then allow the experiences to settle, to be sedimented in ways that can be deeply transformative. There is no room left for thoughtless bashing. Maybe students of politics, especially international politics, should be instructed not only about geopolitics but about attentiveness and listening.

RESPOND TO THE ECONOMIC CRISIS

17

"People who want to change things must keep pushing for change"

MANUEL F. MONTES

in conversation with Adrian Pabst

Manuel F. Montes is senior adviser for finance and development at the South Centre in Geneva, Switzerland. Previously he served as chief of development strategies and policy analysis at the United Nations.

Photo courtesy of Manuel F. Montes.

Manuel F. Montes brings a wealth of academic knowledge and a long list of credentials at various international and intergovernmental organizations to bear on the current economic crisis in this discussion with Adrian Pabst. He argues that the Asian crisis of 1997 was in many ways a "dress rehearsal" for the current global crisis and was barely confined to the developing world. In the case of both crises, he suggests, the problem was both a massive deferral on matters political and economic to the financial sector and the foisting of excessively large loans on creditors by rapacious financiers. The current model has de facto led to the public sector's bearing the costs for private sector missteps and the risks of investment being socialized while, paradoxically, the financial sector remains central to economic recovery. He concedes, however, that change will be difficult to enact and that we should avoid seeking easy answers in old economic models; he suggests provocatively that the talk of the so-called Asian model is overblown and we should not necessarily look to Asia, despite its successes, for lessons. Montes advocates more stringent regulation of the financial sector that would not so much curtail the total of its activities as decrease the emphasis on financial products while aligning finance with real economic productivity and addressing social concerns.

AP: Manuel, your work has included academia, think tanks, foundations, and intergovernmental organizations and has taken you around the world. What do you think this experience has taught you about the state of the world in the past twenty to thirty years?

MM: I guess the best place to start is to say that change is very difficult to make happen, even though the situation is always changing. Change for a more stable, more development-friendly world is not happening, and there have been setbacks. What has really struck me is that the politics of change is quite important. People who want to change things must keep on pushing for change. They cannot predict when change will happen or how it will happen, and therefore it is a very difficult process.

AP: How would you characterize the current crisis?

MM: My sense—and I am an economist—is that the world is going through the most severe slowdown since the Great Depression. This is not a new observation. But it is not clear whether we are going to have a long-term period of malaise and stagnation because the kind of changes that are needed in order to face up to the real issues involved is not addressed by the political systems that we have right now. In many cases the responses to the economic crisis have exacerbated the situation and reduced the possibility of recovery and the prospect for overcoming the crisis. In a sense it's the same observation that the political arrangements are such that—and I know this is controversial—the proper way to address the problem makes it impossible to implement the right policies. Some of these are technical solutions; some of them have a more political character. But what has really struck me is that the technical solutions do not command any political support. For example, temporarily nationalizing failing financial companies has proven to be the quickest way to restore the financial sector and avoid a catastrophic collapse of the payments system. But this approach could not be considered, except in the most academic terms, in the United States, the United Kingdom, and Germany.

AP: From your perspective as an economist, what do you think is different about the current crisis—the one that started in 2008 and is still unfolding—from previous crises, such as the Asian crisis of 1997, on which you worked extensively?

MM: What I can say is that the Asian crisis was a dress rehearsal for this one. What is different is that the current crisis struck at the very heart of the global economic system, whereas the Asian crisis of 1997 was supposed to be a local crisis. But even then, that crisis was eventually interpreted by everybody concerned as having endangered the rest of the system. So why was it a rehearsal? It was a crisis in which there was an overexpansion of liquidity and lending to countries that were considered to be "safe," good credit risks. The amount of credit that was almost forced on countries that were supposed to be creditworthy became unsustainable. Eventually the overlending stopped and collecting on previous lending began. When it stopped it created a crisis in the countries that had borrowed money. The crisis then rebounded to the places where the credit started. Many Asians like me now say that because policymakers in the developed countries and Wall Street did not face up to the real causes of the crisis then, it has now come back to bite the people that used to interpret the crisis as a matter of "bad governance." The favored interpretation of Wall Street and the U.S. Treasury was that it was all bad governance on the part of the Asian countries, that it was due to family-crony capitalism, and that it had nothing to do with overexpansion of credit that periodically happens in the global capitalist system. The response to the crisis was that there had to be better corporate governance. The Asian countries went through a treadmill of corporate governance reforms. There are still projects like that continuing in my region. People—including academics—made money out of this interpretation, but it had nothing to do with the crisis.

The crisis happened because—and here the people who were actually involved can tell you the reason—bankers came to Asia, let's say to Bangkok; they would talk to local bankers and ask, "How much money do you need?" The answer would be "Five million dollars." But the foreign bankers would say, "But you can actually get fifteen, and we want you to take fifteen." The local bankers would take the fifteen, and then they had to figure out a way to relend it. The quickest way to do that was to relend it to real estate property projects. (This is the same kind of thing, by the way, that's happened to Spain, Ireland, and Portugal.) The crisis eventually happens because you have overexpansion; you have all of these facilities that have been created that don't pay back, and therefore the loans were not good. Then, when the crisis strikes, the blame falls on the borrower and not on the lender. Spain, Ireland, Iceland, and Portugal had very small public deficits, the same way Thailand, Malaysia, and Indonesia had small public deficits. It was the private sector that was running these deficits.

But at that time, there was a theory invented in Britain that was used as a justification. It's called the Lawson Doctrine. Nigel Lawson was the chancellor of the exchequer from 1983 to 1989. He said that as long as the private sector is willing to lend, there should be no problem with private deficits. I had a paper published a year before the Asian crisis that was titled "Private Deficits and Public Responsibilities" in which I made the argument that these deficits, even if they are private, eventually become a public responsibility.[1] The current crisis in Spain is like that: the Spanish public sector had low debt and a low deficit; the private sector borrowed a lot of money from France and Germany; and when the loans could not be repaid because of the economic slowdown, they had to take money out of the public sector to pay back the external debt. Now Spain has external debts and has to borrow again from the same private sector to continue financing this debt. I like the way this has been described in the *Financial Times* as something like a "death embrace" between the public sector and the private sector. In order to rescue the private sector, the public sector has to have a deficit, but then it has to borrow from the private sector, which must be paid back if the private sector is to survive, and the spiral goes on.

AP: Based on this analysis, would you say that the idea of "privatized Keynesianism" that Colin Crouch conceptualized a few years ago is quite a useful description?[2] It underscores the way that, during the 1990s in America but also in Europe and elsewhere, the public sector in some sense shifted the debt burden onto the private sector by keeping wages stagnant (real wages in fact often fell) and essentially saying to workers, "Well, if you want to consume more, do it by borrowing, taking out mortgages, and so on." Does that capture an important part of what happened in the 1990s?

MM: Yes, it does. Yesterday I read an article in the *Cambridge Journal of Economics* about how, in the case of the United States, because wages have been kept down, the only way to maintain effective demand—which is a Keynesian concept—is to allow consumers to borrow money in order to maintain demand and sustain consumption. The objection that people like me would have is to the use of Keynes's name in vain. Keynes was a very sophisticated observer of the financial system. He was the first to argue, in *The Economic Consequences of the Peace* of 1919, that the reparations that were imposed on Germany at the end of the First World War would be unsustainable and would actually cause both a social and an economic crisis, which is the same kind of thing as the debt spiral that Spain and others are going through now.[3]

At an analytical level, Keynesians, the present-day descendents of Keynes, accuse the neo-Keynesians, people like Paul Krugman, of not understanding Keynes. But Keynes worried about the income distribution, even though it was not a very important part of what he discussed, as a way in which demand could be sustained. Let's use the term *vulgar Keynesianism*, about which many of my Keynesian friends would accuse Krugman, which was only about public spending to make up for the problem of insufficient private investment. I think Keynes would say that capitalist systems tend to have a persistent problem of insufficient demand because either the private sector does not invest enough, or, if it did, just as in the recent episode that led to the crisis, it invests in very reckless ways, through piling up, almost like a Ponzi scheme, of credit expansion. If it were living up to the tenets of capitalist morality, the private sector would tend to underinvest. And because it was underinvesting there would always be a need to maintain consumer demand or state demand. In my own view, Keynes always thought that the state had a crucial role in a capitalist economy. It has a crucial role in a crisis and it has a crucial role in ensuring that both consumption and investment demand are sufficient in normal times. But I don't think Keynes would have advocated the kind of reckless credit expansion that led to this crisis.

AP: If the expansion of credit really lies at the heart of these successive financial crises, does that raise more fundamental questions about the relationship between finance and the real economy? Is that one way of saying "We need to rethink the balance between the financial services sector on the one hand and the rest of the economy on the other"?

MM: When Keynes was writing, the financial sector was not as sophisticated as it is now. But he did understand it. He used to do the investing for King's College, Cambridge, and he made a lot of money for them. So he did understand the stock markets and all that stuff. But he also understood that there was a problematic relationship between the real sector and the financial sector. Therefore there is a need to rebalance that. This is where I think politics and political structures are almost impossible to overcome. This crisis happened in the developed countries. But in these dominant capitalist countries—and this is one key difference between this and the Asian crisis—the financial sector has almost captured the political system. This capture of the political system was probably behind the way the Asian crisis was addressed. Because that was a localized system, somehow the money could be paid back, but, of course, in the end that crisis just metamorphosed and moved to other places, like Russia and Brazil. Even then, the IMF (International Monetary Fund) tried to face up to the problem by suggesting that there should be a new mechanism globally, called the sovereign debt restructuring mechanism. At that time there was the use of the very polite term *burden sharing*.

Anne Krueger, who is well known in economic circles as a free market advocate, said that this has to be the case with the private sector, that the private sector should be part of the solution to the problem; they should recognize the losses as a result of their overlending and therefore should bear part of the cost. But now so far in, for example, the European crisis, the owners of the banking conglomerates that have lent to Spain and Portugal—except those that have lent to Greece—have not borne any of the losses. All of the losses have been passed on to the public sector. Perhaps this is a new version of vulgar Keynesianism whereby private needs are again passed on to the state sector. This is one reason why I think this solution will not work. As long as the public sector is servicing its mostly new debt to the private sector, and as long as the private sector channels these debt payments toward its capitalization instead of lending to employment- and income-creating projects, the economy will stagnate. Because the economy is stagnating, public sector deficits will continue to increase, requiring more borrowing from the private sector. And so on.

AP: Would you then agree with the characterization that the system that has emerged in the past thirty years and has been dominant is a system that privatizes profit, nationalizes losses, and socializes risk?

MM: That's a very good formulation. I come from the Philippines. We always thought that that was the formulation about the debt crises of developing countries. The first debt crisis I was involved with was the 1982 debt crisis following Mexico's default. The reason I was involved was that the Philippines was the only Asian country that became part of a crisis that affected mostly Latin America and a few countries in Africa. The debts had been built up before 1982, after the oil crises in the 1970s. There was the idea that was supposed to have been an admirable maneuver out of the oil crisis of the 1970s but ended with the oil-importing countries having to finance deficits. The Saudis would create deposits in the private sector in New York, and the private banks in New York would turn around and lend money to the developing countries, which would then use the money to finance their deficit on oil imports but also to invest. But when the crisis struck—because many investments didn't work—the costs were socialized and the risk was imposed on the developing countries. So this formulation is very good because you end up rescuing the people who are supposed to have done this admirable maneuver either through using IMF money (at the time they called it "the new money") to pay back the banks in New York, and the rest of the cost was imposed on the borrowing countries.

This is one of the things that I find very interesting about the Europeans. They have now turned the IMF into a highly leveraged institution. Ninety percent of IMF lending is to Europe, and this is how they have socialized the risk and imposed the risk on the IMF. What is scandalous about that to someone from a developing country like me is that the IMF's resources are not just those of the United States and Europe; there are resources coming from developing countries too. How can these rich countries socialize the risk and impose the cost on the developing countries through the IMF? We know that the Europeans can print their own money, while developing countries cannot because our money is not acceptable around the world, while theirs is. I don't know why they have to go through the IMF to be rescued and impose their costs onto poor people.

AP: This raises very important questions about the whole global system as it has unfolded. I'd like to ask you two questions. The first one is about the end of managed exchange rates and the changes in 1971 to the Bretton Woods system of capital controls. The other question is about the system of global governance and the institutions where the power lies. But let's start with the wider origins of the crisis in the 1990s and more recently, which is this system post-1971. What are your thoughts on these events and how they have shaped subsequent developments?

MM: The Bretton Woods system was decided upon in June 1944. The reason I like to cite that date is because the Normandy landings took place in that month. So the war had not yet been won. But they set up a system because they knew the previous systems were not working. They had this conference in New Hampshire to set up a system that they thought would face up to the problems that had been caused by the interwar system of floating exchange rates. Under the new system there would be controls on exchange rates; there would be one currency (the U.S. dollar) to which all currencies would be pegged, but that itself would be disciplined by its peg to gold. This all fell apart in 1971 because—as an economist from Yale named Robert Triffin said, right after this was put in place—this is a deeply flawed system because in the end, to provide liquidity for the rest of the world for its trade and financial flows, the United States would have to continue to run deficits, and then the United States would run out of gold. The United States de-linked in August 1971 because it was running out of the gold against which the value of the dollar had been pegged.

Keynes himself wanted a different kind of system. He wanted a system in which there would be something almost like fiat money at the global level and people would have to deposit into the IMF, which could then be assigned back and forth among countries. There was degree of self-interest on the part of Britain in this, since it had borrowed large sums of money from the United States. Nevertheless most people would think that this system was better technically because it was not pegged to gold and it was not dependent on the political requirements of a single currency (which are dependent on the domestic politics of that country) and could respond to deficits in a more technically correct manner.

Now we have a system like that of the interwar period, where there are a few dominant currencies and there are swap arrangements between large countries to solve liquidity problems. This is a very dangerous kind of system. Its biggest flaw is the danger coming from the ability of private capital to move very large amounts very quickly across borders. One day you see that Spanish borrowing costs are very low, and the next they are 7 percent. If Spain is borrowing at 7 percent and its growth is not above 7 percent, its debt is unsustainable. This is swamping the ability of the system to maintain exchange rates and interest rates that are consistent with economic growth.

AP: We'll come to possible solutions toward the end of this conversation, but I just want to ask you a second, related question: Does the current system of global governance with institutions like the IMF and the World Bank skew the system in favor of Western countries? Does this system privilege a certain form of finance capitalism that is at the expense of investment in productive activities and human development? Why do you think that system is so resilient to change and transformation? Already in the 1990s there was discussion about changing structural adjustments and bringing in other ideas. But why is that system so resilient, and what can be done to shift it away from this path that hasn't worked out for the world?

MM: One way to interpret the system that was set up at that time was that it was a system based on the way the votes were assigned to countries—the European countries—that were not large players in the global economy. That was very user-oriented because when it was set up, it was expected that the Europeans would be the biggest users. If they had just followed the normal GDP levels, it would have been the United States having 85 percent of the vote and the Europeans 15 percent, or something like that, because the postwar European economies were tiny compared to that of the United States. But they set it up and gave the Europeans a lot of votes in ways that aligned with post–Second World War anticommunist politics, accompanied by the expectation that Europeans would be the biggest users. Even the World Bank was set up basically to reconstruct Europe. So one way you could interpret this system is that it was one that responded to what the users needed.

In effect, from the 1970s, or perhaps a little earlier, when the IMF and World Bank began to be big lenders to developing countries, the voting distribution should have been changed to one that would have been oriented to what the users wanted, just as Europe had been given a large number of votes that was not justified on the basis of the size of their economies. If you ask me the reason why it has not changed, it's because the Europeans don't want to give up their dominance. One way to approach this is to blame the Europeans very clearly for being unwilling to give up their votes. To a Belgian or a Dane, the highest point of one's diplomatic career would be to sit as an executive director in the IMF, and thus they have more votes than many of these other countries. The United States officially has been quite public about trying to get the Europeans to reduce their voting weight and give more votes to the developing countries. But the United States has other concerns at this time, focused in particular on the future role of emerging economies and the need to contain them. The United States finds it congenial that the Europeans remain significant players. They find the confluence of their interests with those of the Europeans such that they don't want to or cannot force the issue. That's why it hasn't changed.

At the 2006 Singapore annual meeting of the IMF a reform of the voting structure was planned, but in the end they redistributed the votes among developing countries. I think, at a very basic level, it's a matter of not undermining the interests of Wall Street, which had previously succeeded in preventing the setting up of a sovereign debt restructuring mechanism. The U.S. government is very heavily beholden to Wall Street and the financial system. Because that is so, the financial sector would like both the Europeans and the Americans to continue to dominate the IMF and World Bank, which are the main gateways to finance, the main ways in which finance flows globally to the developing countries. It is clear that the IMF itself does not have enough influence over the European and American authorities for basically the same reason: the IMF does not have enough power to force the United States to reduce its deficits. The United States and World Bank have sufficient power over the developing countries, but insufficient power over Europe and the United States. This is the kind of configuration that is consistent with finance capital.

AP: So, paradoxically, global finance capitalism in some ways uses national governments to influence supranational institutions in order to secure its interests. There's an interesting interaction of the global and national levels at all times.

MM: In a sense, the way you described it is how it works. Of course, what is happening now is that there are other parties that are coming to be dominant in finance, like China, so the question is: What will this metamorphose into?

AP: It's interesting because you mention new, emerging powers. Of course, we've heard a lot about emerging markets in the past ten years or so, especially since the BRICS concept was coined by Jim O'Neill in 2001. In addition to these great powers from the past that are once again rising, like India and China, we also seeing other actors—the so-called middle powers, such as Indonesia, the Philippines, and others—and new structures like sovereign wealth funds that are beginning to play a greater role. How do all of these fit into the global system that we've been talking about?

MM: First, I want to say, and I really want to emphasize this, the supposed emergence of these countries is oversold. One reason is that part of their emergence has entailed their opening up their markets to, and their increased dependence on, international trade. The other thing is that many of these are still very small economies. China is certainly still not 10 percent of the global economy. In the 1500s Asia was probably half of the global economy. India's per capita income would qualify it as a Less Developed Country. It's also still a very hierarchical, caste-driven

society. I know the successes in fields like engineering have been celebrated, but that's still a very small part of their economy. These countries also have quite weak internal polities, which will make it difficult
for them to be important global players. I'm an economist, but I think
their ability to influence the global economy is actually quite limited. So
"emergence" is still far away.

In one word, including the new opportunities linked to sovereign wealth funds, the prospects of the global economy still depend
on the ability of the rich countries to get their political and economic
act together. Otherwise the system will stagnate for ten or more years,
which could be a good enough outcome if you're a capitalist, because
then you can rise again in ten years with the same rules in place. Or else
it will collapse into a system in which there will be autarchy—that's a
bad outcome—with individual countries trying to go on their own, and
the kind of commerce we have seen thus far will shrink.

AP: This leads us to the next part of this conversation, which is about
some of the main areas that you've worked in over the past thirty years:
growth and trade, globalization, development. So let's start with trade.
There are many around the world calling for greater trade liberalization
in order to get the world economy going again in the hope of boost-
ing growth through more trade. What are the prospects for significant changes in global trade? Is it really the case that trade is a major
engine of the sort of growth that is now needed? In other words, not
just growth in financial services but growth in productive activities is
required?

MM: In the immediate period, if this stagnation happens, trade is not
going to be a reliable source of positive impact as in the past twenty
years. Trade has been directed at exporting (from the developing countries' point of view) to the developed countries. But the developed countries cannot be expected to recover strongly based on their current policies, so I'm not sure that the developing countries can count on trade for
the kind of growth and development that they have been able to achieve

in the past thirty years. Volume-wise the kind of trade growth in the developed countries of the recent past is not going to be there.

Second, we know that, at least in the previous decade or so, this stupendous growth in trade was based on unsustainable, artificial conditions, dependent on the liquidity that the United States was pumping into the global economy. Any move toward a more stable financial system would require a rate of growth in trade much slower than in the years immediately before the crisis. It would also mean in many cases lower commodity prices, because part of finance-driven growth supported high commodity prices, which was good for Africa and many countries in Latin America. If commodity prices do not stay high, the high growth rates in Africa and Latin America in the years before the crisis cannot be restored. If finance can be reregulated in much the same way that it had been in the first era of the Bretton Woods system, countries would then have to grow more based on their internal dynamics instead of being overly export-dependent. Investment would have to be done in a more pragmatic and more realistic—and less speculative—manner.

AP: How do you see the impact of financialization, which has been growing for the past three decades, on development in general, and perhaps more specifically, on human development?

MM: Since 2007 the impact on human development has not been as dire as had been expected. Part of this is because of the very specific way the developed countries have reacted to the crisis. They have responded by quantitative easing, which means they have gone back to the pumping of liquidity globally, and thus finance continued to be available to the developing countries in very dangerous forms. This was the same kind of finance that came to the Asian countries before. It is dangerous because it has forced many of these countries to let their currencies appreciate, undermining their export industries and their import-competing ones.

Second, many of the developing countries have built up reserves as a result of what they learned from the Asian crisis. Because of these reserves they, particularly China, were able to undertake countercyclical policies. China undertook a lot of investments after the 2008 crisis, and these investments once again boosted commodity prices. Chinese investment was in building airports and so on, very commodity-dependent in terms of demand for metals, and it helped prop up the developing countries. But the Chinese pattern of growth after 2008 is probably unsustainable because this pattern itself creates a domestic financial bubble. This sort of reprieve is unsustainable because it is based on quantitative easing. In the coming years, depending on how the European crisis and the American crisis are sorted out, there will be much lower growth and much less possibility of depending on trade.

I do not anticipate that commodity prices will be as high as before. One reason I am not sure is that China has overinvested in steel mills and it has empty airports and other spare capacity. The Chinese authorities are aware that they cannot continue this; they need to boost domestic demand. But this is one of the most complicated maneuvers that you can think about: How do you increase consumption demand of your consumers in a significant way in a very short time? And you don't want to do it in the American way, whereby you allow consumers to finance their spending on credit. It's a very dangerous time that we live in.

AP: What's interesting about what you're saying is that, on the one hand, the impact of the global crisis has been cushioned by quantitative easing but, on the other hand, we are setting up problems for the future. So in a sense we have deferred dealing with the underlying issue, which is the relation between credit and the rest of the economy.

MM: Right, so the politics have not been aligned properly. Deferring might be a polite way to say it, but we are probably setting up a bigger crisis. In the case of the Europeans, what they need to do is to figure out a way to convince the financial sector to accept the losses incurred in the period of overlending. Then they can grow again. What the European governments have been doing is giving money to the banks so that they can pay back their creditors without imposing the condition that they must begin lending for new projects to the private sector.

This would be necessary if economic recovery were to happen in the advanced countries. This is the extent of the financial sector's control over the political system.

The way that this is normally done in many countries, when done properly, as in Sweden in 1994 and Malaysia in the 1997 crisis, is to nationalize failing banks. With the government now owning all of the bank assets, it can collect on the good loans and write off the bad ones. After all the bad assets are removed, the banks can be privatized once again. Nationalization is one way of forcing banks to start lending again to the private sector. But because of the dominant political position that the financial sector has, you can't even do this temporarily.

AP: I would like to take the last part of this interview to talk about some potential solutions that have both scholarly credibility and policy relevance. This is very much drawing on your academic research but also your vast experience in international organizations. We can perhaps start with the central point you have made about credit and overexpansion, which has led to all these bubbles that have burst. You have also suggested that we have set ourselves up for perhaps an even greater crisis in the future by engaging in quantitative easing. What would be some of the credit and monetary reforms that you would propose that could begin to deal with this unfolding global crisis?

MM: Well, basically to regulate—reregulate—the financial system in such a way that it does not become the arbiter of what kind of economic activities are undertaken. For example, you can take over a company by buying its shares—in effect, as if it had nothing to do with what the company actually does and what it employs people to do—and you can restructure it based primarily on financial principles. That kind of operation is supposed to be efficiency-oriented, but what it means is that finance's role in an economy has almost nothing to do with what the economy does—with employment, with income, with the kind of products that are produced and what is actually consumed. It's very important to regulate the system so that investment banking provides a way in which it is oriented toward new production and new risk-taking, but not in terms of only buying and selling ownership and restructuring companies. That's one important thing.

The second thing is that governments should have greater power to set the rates of return on capital—interest rates and so on. The "big bang" deregulation had been prompted by the intention to eliminate what was then called "financial repression," which set maximum interest rates on lending. This used to be considered inefficient. The idea was that by removing all of those caps on interest rates, it might be possible to finance more risky projects. But in the end we know from our experience that this opened the door to speculative lending to feed on itself. There should be regulation on the kinds of financial products that are produced and the kinds of margins and leverage that the financial sector can undertake. If you want to take a risk on a project, you should have your own skin in the project, even if you are just a financier. By removing leverage limits, companies have very little stake in it, undermining market accountability on the part of the financial system. Because they have so little invested, losses as highly levered lenders will be very small if a project fails. Thus financiers have managed to exempt themselves from market accountability. Basically I don't consider these to be earth-shaking suggestions.

AP: Now, on questions of investment and human development, where do you see the debate going? What needs to be done now that we've had, in some ways, a shift from structural adjustment toward human development, but still underpinned by neoliberal policy? What, for you, would be the next step in taking this debate in a non-neoliberal direction?

MM: One way to interpret this move toward human development is that it did not contain within it the kinds of policies that would provide more productive jobs and more diversified economies. The UN's Millennium Development Goals (MDGs) were one way to justify neoliberal policies and in a sense to pick up the wounded from these policies, to take care of the victims through social programs meant to achieve the antipoverty goals of the MDGs. What the MDGs did was to make countries responsible for the poverty in their own countries. The long-term way to do this, for an economist like me, is for government to have the possibility of intervening in its domestic economy so that it can diversify, add value to exports, and create productive jobs.

But the neoliberal structure was shrinking the policy space of these governments while giving them responsibility for poverty alleviation. Without domestic policy tools, the only way to achieve the MDGs was through resources from official development assistance, which was completely voluntary on the part of developed countries (and completely political). To be serious about eliminating the problems of structural adjustment is to return the policy space to developing country governments, to allow them to make their own policies, make their own mistakes, and make them accountable to their domestic populations. This would restore democratic accountability on the part of developing countries and their governments, which cannot then blame external conditions imposed by lenders for their policies.

AP: As you say, these principles of democratic accountability are principles not just for politics but also for the economy in the sense that we need to strengthen more participative economic decision making. How can we strengthen participation in the economy? Of course, one thing is to change global governance structures and strengthen democracy around the world, but what about corporations themselves? How can we rethink the way businesses work and strengthen the role of workers, not just for reasons of making them more democratic but perhaps also to increase innovation and productivity (so, if you like, for both ethical and economic purposes)?

MM: First of all, I would differentiate two things. One is the situation of developed countries, and other is the situation of developing countries. In the developed countries, I would say that innovation and accountability on the part of firms is mostly done through regulation, and I think regulation is important, mostly starting with the financial sector. But in developing countries, where firms are just starting up, the state needs to undertake not only regulation but investment through development banking. A large part of this is setting up state enterprises. In the United States, for example, the Tennessee Valley Authority, which allowed the South to rise again, was state-owned.[4] One way to allow the private sector to reemerge in developing countries is to give the state much more capability to tax the rich, to invest, to lend money to private businesses, and to run its own enterprises.

Recently the *Economist* discovered something: that many of the recently successful countries like China and Singapore have a lot of state-owned enterprises. Now is the time to debate their accountability and associated issues, but during their heyday they provided the innovation and the new kinds of jobs that wouldn't have been possible if you didn't have these large pools of capital, which the private sector in many developing countries cannot put together (at least not without state participation).

AP: Is perhaps one way of making that argument also to say that we can shield state enterprises from certain vested interests by, for instance, strengthening community involvement? Examples include models such as cooperatives and community interest companies which actually have the responsibility to work efficiently as a business, but their profit is reinvested in the business rather than going to shareholders or to the national treasury.

AM: I agree with that. A lot of the failures have to do with corruption, but past corruption should not be an excuse for not trying. If you don't have a private sector, how can you develop? Let us debate how to make them more accountable and less wasteful of public resources, but let us try. There are many ways such enterprises can be made accountable. What you would need is an increasing capability for the public sector and the public in general to monitor them and also the ability of the community to provide inputs and maybe to sit on the board.

THIS is definitely a viable possibility. If the state has some equity stake, it can decide whom to appoint to the board. It doesn't have to be some politician who will get an honorarium and not do anything. I think alternative structures are very possible, especially in places where civil society is well organized. This is not the case throughout the Third World, but there are countries where there are reliable political structures.

AP: You've mentioned at various points in this conversation the diverse Asian experience, notably in the Philippines, your own country. Would you say there are insights from the Asian experiences, in all their plurality and diversity, that are important for either developed countries or developing countries elsewhere in the world?

MM: My reaction to that, and I hate to disappoint you, is that I am not sure Asia can teach other countries much except in the details. In the first place, there is very little intellectual work and debate in Asia about whether there is something special about Asia's strategies. Most of the debate on Asian economic strategies is happening elsewhere, not in Asia. In the second place, a lot of the Asian success rode on a very specific sector: the electronics industry. Asian authorities following the time-tested state policies of industrialized countries and not believing in the myths of neoliberalism, deployed the state to engage with this industry that emerged at that very specific time. Other countries could have done the same. Perhaps the cold war accommodation to Asian exports by the United States played some role in making Asia's entry into electronics easier.

While the state plays a major role in successful Asian countries, even between China and Korea there's a very big difference. Korea insisted on building its own private sector from the very start. China did not, except in a very implicit way, because officially state-owned enterprises were meant to be the dominant structure of its economic system. Korea has pursued a much more standard path to becoming an industrialized country. In the case of China, will it be possible to create enterprises rapidly enough to provide international competitiveness?

AP: So it's not about the size of the state or its relative power, but about how smart and effective it is at promoting the right sorts of policies?

MM: Right. It is about states and international mechanisms being accountable to the parties that are most adversely affected by their actions. This, however, will require states being able to be less beholden to money politics—both nationally and internationally. Countries whose elites and officials have become dependent on money politics have been unable to undertake reforms and policies that ensure stable economic growth and development.

18

"Capitalism as a mode of power"

**SHIMSHON BICHLER
AND JONATHAN NITZAN**
in conversation with Piotr Dutkiewicz

Shimshon Bichler teaches political economy at colleges and universities in Israel. Jonathan Nitzan teaches political economy at York University, Toronto.

Photo courtesy of Shimshon Bichler and Jonathan Nitzan.

In a unique two-pronged dovetailing discussion, frequent collaborators and coauthors Jonathan Nitzan and Shimshon Bichler discuss the nature of contemporary capitalism. Their central argument is that the dominant approaches to studying the market—liberalism and Marxism—are as flawed as the market itself. Offering a historically rich and analytically incisive critique of the recent history of capitalism and crisis, they suggest that instead of studying the relations of capital to power we must conceptualize capital *as* power if we are to understand the dynamics of the market system. This approach allows us to examine the seemingly paradoxical workings of the capitalist mechanism, whereby profit and capitalization are divorced from productivity and machines in the so-called real economy. Indeed Nitzan and Bichler paint a picture of a strained system whose component parts exist in an antagonistic relationship. In their opinion, the current crisis is a systemic one afflicting a fatally flawed system. However, it is not one that seems to be giving birth to a unified opposition movement or to a new mode of thinking. The two political economists call for nothing short of a new mode of imagining the market, our political system, and our very world.

PD: Let's start from a fairly general big picture of the economic system. Please look around and tell me what you see as the key features of the current market system.

SB: Although it may not seem so at first sight, your question is highly loaded. For me to describe the current economic system and market system is to accept these terms as objective entities, or at least as useful concepts. But are they?

PD: So what terms would you use? Is there an alternative approach?

SB: Yes, there is an alternative approach, but before getting to that approach, we need to identify the problem with the conventional one. In my view, terms such as economic system and market system are misnomers. They are irrelevant and misleading. Nowadays they are employed more as ideological slogans rather than as scientific concepts. Those who use them often end up concealing rather than revealing the capitalist reality.

Of course, this wasn't always the case. In the seventeenth and eighteenth centuries, when capitalism was just taking hold, there was nothing apologetic about the market. On the contrary, the market was seen as the harbinger of progress: a powerful institution that heralded liberty, equality, and tolerance. "Go to the London Exchange," wrote Voltaire. "A place more dignified than many a royal court. There you will find representatives of every nation quietly assembled to promote human welfare. There the Jew, the Mahometan and the Christian deal with each other as though they were all of the same religion. They call no man Infidel unless he be bankrupt."[1]

The market has had a dramatic impact on European history, partly because it emerged in a seemingly unlikely setting. After the nomadic invasions and the fall of the imperial civilization of the first millennium AD, Europe developed a highly fractured social regime we now call feudalism. This regime was based on self-sufficient rural estates, cultivated by peasant-serfs, and ruled by a violent aristocracy. Technical know-how during that period was limited, the agricultural yield meager, and trade almost nonexistent. Power relations were legitimized by the sanctified notion of a "triangular society," comprising prayers, warriors, and tillers (or, in a more political lingo, priests, nobles, and peasants). Merchants and financiers had no place in that scheme.

But not for long. The feudal order began to disintegrate during the first half of the second millennium AD, and this decline was accompanied—and to some extent accelerated—by the revival of trade and the growth of merchant cities such as Bruges, Venice, and Florence. These developments signaled the beginning of a totally new social order: an urban civilization that gave rise to a new ruling class known as the "bourgeoisie," an unprecedented civilian-scientific revolution, and a novel culture we now call "liberal."

Because of the specifically European features of this process, the market came to symbolize the negation of the ancien régime; in contrast to the feudal order, which was seen as collective, stagnant, austere, ignorant, and violent, the market promised individualism, growth, well-being, enlightenment, and peace. And it was this early conflict between the rule of feudalism and the aspirations of capitalism that later galvanized into what most people today take as a self-evident duality: the contrast between the state, or "politics," and the market, or the "economy."

According to this conventional bifurcation, the economy and politics are orthogonal realms, one horizontal and the other vertical. The economy is the site of independence, productivity, and well-being. It is the clearinghouse for individual wants and desires, the voluntary arena where autonomous agents engage in production and exchange in order to better their lives and augment their utility. By contrast, the political system of state organizations and institutions is the locus of control and power. Unlike the flat structure of the free economy, politics is hierarchical. It is concerned with coercion and oppression and driven by command and obedience.

In this scheme, the economy—or more precisely, the "market economy"—is considered productive (generating wealth), efficient (minimizing cost), and harmonious (tending toward equilibrium). It is competitive (and therefore free). It seeks to increase well-being (by maximizing utility). And if left to its own devices (laissez-faire), it augments the welfare of society (by sustaining economic growth and increasing the wealth of nations). The political system, by contrast, is wasteful and parasitical. Its purpose is not production but redistribution. Its members—the politicians, state officials, and bureaucrats—seek power and prestige. They eagerly "intervene" in and "monopolize" the economy. They tax, borrow, and spend and in the process stifle the economy and "distort" its efficiency. Sometimes "externalities" and other forms of "market failure" make state intervention necessary. But such intervention, the argument goes, should be minimal, transitory, and subjugated to the overarching logic of the economy.

PD: So the "market" serves the role of a new ideology for the bourgeoisie?

SB: Exactly. The portrayal I've just painted owes much to Adam Smith, the eighteenth-century Scotsman who turned the idea of "the market" into the key political institution of capitalism. Smith's invention helped the bourgeoisie undermine and eventually topple the royal-princely state, and that was just for starters. Soon enough, the market became the chief ideology of the triumphant capitalist regime. It helped spread capitalism around the world, and it assisted in the fight against competing regimes, such as fascism and communism. In the Soviet Union, where production was beset by chaotic planning and accompanied by tyrannical rule, organized violence, open corruption, and restricted consumption, the market symbolized the "other life." It was the alternative world of freedom and abundance. And this perception is still hammered home by the ideologues of capitalism. In the final analysis, we are told, there are only two options: the market or Gosplan (the Soviet state planning ministry). If we don't choose egocentrism and liberty, we end up with planning and tyranny. And that is it. There is no other alternative, or so goes the dogma.

The ideological basis of these arguments was bolstered in the late nineteenth century by the official split of classical political economy into two distinct academic disciplines: political science and economics. The term *economics* was invented by Alfred Marshall, the Cambridge University don who coined it to denote the new "marginalist," or *neo*-classical, doctrine of political economy. Marshall, who wanted economics to be a real science, gave it the same suffix as that of phy*sics* and mathema*tics*. He also wrote the first economics textbook (the definitive edition of which was issued in 1890), wherein he set the rigid boundaries of the discipline, elaborated its deductive format, and articulated many of the examples that are still being used today.

Despite its aspirations, economics never became a real science, and for a simple reason: it couldn't. Science is skeptical. Unlike organized religion, which is infinitely confident, science thrives on doubt. It relies not on static ritual and unchanging dogma but on seeking novel explanations for ever-expanding horizons. It tries to understand, not to justify. Now none of this can be said about economics. If anything, we can assert the opposite: the inherent role of economics was not to explain capitalism but to justify it. When economics first emerged in the late nineteenth century, capitalism was already victorious. But it was also highly turbulent and increasingly contested by critiques and revolutionaries, so it had to be defended, and the ideological part of that defense was delegated to the new priests of liberalism: the economists. In order to perform their role, the economists have elaborated an intricate system of mathematical models. This system, they claim, proves that a free, totally unregulated economy—if we could ever have one—would yield the best of all possible worlds, by definition.

The conventional counterclaim, marshaled by many heterodox critiques, is that neoclassical models may be elegant, but they have little or nothing to do with the actual world we live in. And there is certainly much truth in this observation. But the "science of economics" is besieged by a far deeper problem that rarely if ever gets mentioned: it relies on *fictitious quantities*.

Every science rests on one or more fundamental quantities in which all other magnitudes are denominated. Physics, for example, has five fundamental quantities—length, time, mass, electrical charge, and heat—and every other measure is derived from those quantities. For instance, velocity is length divided by time; acceleration is the time derivative of velocity; and gravity is mass multiplied by acceleration. Now, as a science, economics too has to have fundamental quantities— and the economists claim it does. The fundamental quantity of the neoclassical universe is the unit of hedonic pleasure, or "util."

PD: Can you explain this idea in more detail? How does the util form the basis of the neoclassical economic universe?

SB: The answer begins with the conventional bifurcation of the economy itself into two quantitative spheres: "real" and "nominal." According to the economists, the key is the real sphere. This is the material engine of society, the realm of tangible assets and technical know-how, the locus of production and consumption, the fount of well-being. The nominal side of the economy is secondary. This is the sphere of money, prices, and finance, of inflation and deflation, of speculative bubbles and stock market crashes. Although highly dynamic, the nominal sphere doesn't have a life of its own. Its money magnitudes are merely reflections— sometimes accurate, sometimes inaccurate—of what happens in the real sphere. And the reflection is *quantitative*: the price quantities of the nominal spheres mirror the substantive quantities of the real sphere.

In the final analysis, *all economic quantities are reducible to utils*. The util is the elementary particle of economic science. It is the fundamental quantity, the basic building block out of which everything economic is made. The utils themselves, like Greek atoms, are identical everywhere, but their combination yields infinitely complex forms that economists call "goods and services." Every composite of the so-called real economy—from the aggregate quantities of production, consumption, and investment to the size of GDP, the magnitude of military spending, and the scale of technology—is the sum total of the utils it generates. And the price magnitudes of the nominal economy—for instance, the dollar prices of an industrial robot (say, $5 million) and a trendy iPhone ($500)—merely represent and reflect the util-denominated quantities of their respective real quantities (whose ratio, assuming the reflection is accurate, is 10,000:1).

And here we come to the crux of the matter: this util—this basic quantum that everything economic is supposedly derived from—is *immeasurable* and in fact *unknowable*!

Nobody has been able to identify the quantum of a util, and I very much doubt that anyone ever will. It is a pure fiction. And since all so-called real economic quantities are denominated in this fictitious unit, it follows that their own quantities are fictitious as well. To measure "real GDP" or the "standard of living" without utils is like measuring velocity without time, or gravity without mass. (I should note here that a similar critique can be leveled against classical Marxism. The elementary particle of the Marxist universe is socially necessary abstract labor. This is the fundamental quantity that all real magnitudes are made of and which the nominal spheres [should] reflect. And yet no Marxist has ever measured it.)

So, just as in Hans Christian Andersen's "The Emperor's New Clothes," everyone pretends. The students, dazed by the endless drill of "practical" assignments, do not even suspect that their "computations" are practically meaningless. Most professors, having graduated from the meat grinder of neoclassical training, have had all traces of the problem safely erased from their memory (assuming they were aware of it in the first place). And the statisticians, whose job is to measure the economy, have no choice but to concoct numbers based on arbitrary assumptions that nobody can either validate or refute. The entire edifice hangs in thin air, and everyone keeps quiet, lest it collapse.

PD: What you are saying is that one of the very few supposedly solid foundations of our life—the notion that something economic is measurable and thus "objective"—is a fiction?

SB: Yes. And this, mind you, is the dominant ideology that rules the world.

EVERY cog in the corporate-government-military megamachine—from business managers and state planners, through army officers and central bankers, to financial analysts, accountants, and tax experts—is hardwired to the conventions and rituals of this doctrine. They are all conditioned by the same never-to-be-questioned mantras of the capitalist matrix: that the economy is productive and politics parasitic; that the market is equilibrating and the state destabilizing; and, of course, that we constantly need to check the excesses of government, deregulate the economy, and increase competition.

So we come back to your original question, I cannot characterize contemporary reality in terms of its "economy" and the "market system." These are misleading categories to begin with. They force us into a rigid neoclassical template, block our vision, and stifle our imagination. They make creative thinking all but impossible. If we want to transcend these barriers and think openly, the first thing we need to do is dispense with these categories altogether.

And this is the time to do so. We live in a deep crisis, and deep crises can sometime lead to an intellectual renaissance. They tend to foster critical thinking, generate novel methods of inquiry, and help us devise alternative forms of action. The Great Depression of the 1930s triggered such a revival. That crisis transformed the way we understand and critique society: it gave birth to liberal "macro" economics and anticyclical government policy; it rejuvenated Marxist and other streams of radical thinking in areas ranging from political economy to philosophy to literature; and, by shattering many of the prevailing dogmas, it allowed the mutual insemination of ideologically opposing approaches.

PD: Some say that the 2007–9 crisis was indeed a trigger for such a reevaluation, but are we actually seeing any real change in the way the economy is perceived?

SB: I don't think so. One would have expected a revival similar to that which followed the Great Depression in the current crisis, but so far the signs of such a revival are nowhere to be seen. A small chorus of mainstream economists, such as Paul Krugman, Nouriel Roubini, and Joseph Stiglitz have criticized their discipline. But besides moral indignation and contrarian predictions, their critiques offer nothing that is fundamentally new. The real disappointment, though, is the theoretical weakness of the left. During the 1930s, radical movements and organizations were energized by novel theories of capitalism and detailed platforms for its replacement. That isn't the case today. The antiglobalization, ecology, and Occupy movements lack this source of energy. They don't have a new theoretical foundation to build on, and without such a foundation, they find it hard to develop an effective critique of capitalism, let alone a clear alternative that would come in its stead.

This weakness creates a vacuum that is increasingly filled by religious and radical right movements. And with the global crisis continuing and the ruling class teetering on the verge of panic, there is a real possibility of a massive shift to the right, not unlike that of the 1930s. I think that such a shift will be difficult to prevent, let alone counteract and reverse, without a totally new theoretical alternative.

PD: In light of Shimshon Bichler's insights into the ideological role of economic theory, is it still relevant to talk about capital, capitalism, and capitalist culture? It sounds as if we are back in the nineteenth century.

JN: I think these terms remain relevant. Our world, of course, is rather different from that of the nineteenth century, but it is still very much capitalistic. In fact it is more capitalistic that it ever was. When we were growing up in the 1950s, we rarely heard words such as *capitalist, capitalism*, and *capitalist regime*. They sounded like anachronistic remnants of a bygone era. They might have been relevant to the cruel reality of Victorian England that Marx experienced and analyzed, or to old communist propaganda banners, but not to the middle of the twentieth century. By the 1950s Victorian England was a very distant memory, and communist parties seemed to be losing their proletarian appeal to the tide of rising wages. The terminology of classical political economy, having become useless, sank into oblivion.

This was the heyday of the cold war, and the dominant ideology emphasized the wonders of "modernization." The old colonial system was disintegrating, the Western welfare-warfare state was expanding, and many workers no longer lived at subsistence levels. Instead of the "class struggle," pundits started talking about an "affluent society." There was no longer any need, they argued, for the dialectics of Marx's historical materialism. The positivist path of Auguste Comte offered a much more efficient and just method of managing industrial society.

It was therefore surprising to witness the recent revival of *capital* and *capitalism*. The terms first reappeared in mainstream lingo after the collapse of communism in the late 1980s, and within less than a decade they were already commonplace in academic writings and popular discourse. This time around, though, they were used not as ideologically contestable concepts but as part of the natural order of things. As Michel Houellebecq observes in *The Possibility of an Island*, for most of those born into the neoliberal order, protesting layoffs or economic policy, let alone the regime itself, seems as absurd as protesting weather changes or locust infestations. The contemporary global natives can imagine no meaningful alternative to the capitalist order, and the rulers know it. Their oppressive tolerance has helped assimilate the critique of capitalism into its own mass culture, as Herbert Marcuse so eloquently anticipated in his *One-Dimensional Man*.

PD: So does that mean that *capitalism* has somehow become a misleading slogan?

JN: Not at all. The term still represents the world we live in. When Marx invented the notion of the "capitalist regime," he referred not to the narrow economic domain or even to liberal ideology more broadly. For him, the capitalist regime denoted a new *totalizing logic*, a material-ideal system that dominates society and governs its historical trajectory. Individuals in this scheme, whether they are workers or capitalists, are secondary. Regardless of where they are situated in society, they all obey the same supreme subject: capital itself. The logic of capital affects everything. It dictates the nature of ownership, power, and authority; it influences the technological process; and it shapes human consciousness. It seems to me that this broad description of the rule of capital, a condition that Marx was the first to identify and describe, is more valid today than it ever was.

PD: So is capitalism a constant, making evolution a frivolous concept? In the dynamic picture of European politico-social systems you have written about with Bichler, is capitalism the only "unchangeable element"?

JN: What has changed, I think, and dramatically so, is the *specific nature* of capitalism. Marx's science and the bourgeois political economy he criticized were creatures of their time. Both were informed by the apparent separation of the sweatshops, factories, and "civil society" of merchants and industrialists on the one hand from the ancient statist-political regime on the other. Both were impressed by the atomistic nature of capitalism, its anarchic competition, the disciplinary role of technology, and the apparent automaticity of the system's cyclical gyrations and long-term tendencies. And both were marked by the scientific revolution from which they emerged: the demand and supply of the liberals reproduced Newton's forces of attraction and repulsion, while Marx's historical laws of motion paralleled the new cosmology of the heavenly bodies; their equilibrium and disequilibrium tendencies replicated Newton's duality of inertia and force, and their analytical methods employed the new techniques of calculus, probability, and statistics.

However, by the late nineteenth and early twentieth centuries, the classical portrayal and analysis of capitalism no longer seemed valid. There were several reasons for this growing mismatch. First, the rise and expansion of large organizational units—from big business to big government to big unions—made it difficult to speak of an atomistic society, let alone of its automatic regulation. Second, there emerged a whole slew of new processes—from total war and the permanent war economy, through large-scale government policies, to the growth of a "labor aristocracy" and leisure time, corporate management, inflation, and large-scale financial intermediation—developments with which the classical political economists were completely unfamiliar and which their old theoretical schemes could not accommodate. Third, with the rise of fascism and Nazism, the primacy of class and production was challenged by a new emphasis on masses, power, state, bureaucracy, elites, and systems. And fourth, the objective and mechanical cosmology of the first political-scientific revolution was undermined by uncertainty, relativity, and the entanglement of subject and object. Science, including the science of society, was increasingly challenged by antiscientific vitalism and "postism" of various stripes.

These developments resulted in a deep rupture: while capitalism has become increasingly universal, the unified theory that once explained it has disintegrated. Bourgeois political economy has been divided and subdivided. Instead of a single study of capitalism, we now have a multitude of distinct disciplines—economics, politics, sociology, psychology, anthropology, international relations, management, finance, culture, gender, communication, and whatnot—all trying to barricade their own turf and protect their proprietary categories. The same has happened with classical Marxism: what once stood as a totalizing critique of capitalism has been fractured into a tripod of neo-Marxian economics, a neo-Marxian critique of culture, and neo-Marxian theories of the state. And if this wasn't bad enough, in between all the cracks emerged the rapidly multiplying antiscience dogmas of postmodernity that deny the possibility of a universal logic altogether.

PD: What would your solution be to these fragmented approaches toward something that governs the very way we live, earn, spend, and accumulate?

JN: I think we can no longer rely on the prevailing theories and dogmas. They are fractured and exhausted. If we wish to change society, we ought to embark on a totally new path. And the first step in that path is to revolutionize the way we understand capitalism. The grip of capital is *universalizing*, and so should be our attempt to comprehend and counteract it. We need theories and research methods that are not disjoined and fractured but encompassing and totalizing. And in devising these theories and methods, we should focus not on the world of yesterday but on the capitalist reality of today and, indeed, tomorrow.

PD: Even neoliberals agree that we need to reinvent or reinforce political economy, as we have lost a vital link between politics and the market. So what should be the centerpiece of today's political economy?

SB: The centerpiece is still capital, but we have to think about it in a totally new way. Capital is not a means of production that generates hedonic pleasure, as the liberals argue, and it is not a quantum of abstract labor, as the Marxists claim. Rather capital is power, and only power.

Note the emphasis on the word *is*. Capital, Nitzan and I claim, should be understood not in *relation* to or in *association* with power, but *as* power. This figurative identity is very different from the conventional creed. Marxist and mainstream analysts often connect capital with power. They say that capital "affects" power or that it is "influenced" by power, that power can help "augment" capital or that capital can "increase" power. But these are all *external* relations between *distinct* entities. They speak of capital *and* power, whereas we talk about capital *as* power.

Further, and more broadly, we argue that capitalism is best viewed not as a mode of production or consumption but as a *mode of power*. Machines, production, and consumption are part of capitalism, of course, and they certainly feature heavily in accumulation. But the role of these entities in the process of accumulation, whatever it may be, is significant only insofar as it bears on power.

To explain our argument, let me start with two basic entities: prices and capitalization. Capitalism—as both liberals and Marxists recognize—is organized as a numerical commodity system denominated in prices. The capitalist regime is particularly conducive to numerical organization because it is based on private ownership, and anything that can be privately owned can be priced. This basic feature means that, as private ownership spreads spatially and socially, price becomes the universal numerical unit with which the capitalist order is organized.

Now, the actual pattern of this numerical order is created through capitalization. Capitalization, to paraphrase the physicist David Bohm, is the "generative order" of capitalism. It is the flexible, all-inclusive algorithm that continuously *creorders*—or creates the order of—capitalism.

PD: What exactly is capitalization?

SB: Considered most broadly, capitalization is a symbolic financial entity; it is the ritual that capitalists use to discount risk-adjusted expected future earnings to their present value. This ritual has a very long history. It was first invented in the proto-capitalist burgs of Europe during the fourteenth century, if not earlier. It overcame religious opposition to usury in the seventeenth century to become conventional practice among bankers. Its mathematical formulae were first articulated by German foresters in the mid-nineteenth century. Its ideological and theoretical foundations were laid out at the turn of the twentieth century. It started to appear in textbooks around the 1950s, giving rise to a process that contemporary experts refer to as "financialization." And by the early twenty-first century, it has grown into the most powerful faith of all, with more followers than all the world's religions combined.

Nowadays capitalists—as well as everyone else—are conditioned to think of capital as capitalization, and nothing but capitalization. The ultimate question here is not the particular entity that the capitalist owns but the universal worth of this entity defined as a capitalized asset.

PD: And how does this mechanism of capitalization actually work?

SB: Take the example of a capitalist who considers buying (or selling) an Exxon share with annual earnings of $100. If the discount rate is 10 percent, or 0.1, the capitalist will capitalize the asset at $1,000 (expected earnings of $100 on a $1,000 investment represent an expected return of 10 percent, or 0.1). The expected earnings themselves are partly objective, partly subjective. The objective part is the actual earnings that will become known in the future, say, $50. But the capitalist in our example expects $100, meaning that he or she is overly optimistic. We call this overoptimism "hype," and this hype has a quantity—in this case, 2 (= $100/$50). If the capitalist were overly pessimistic, with a hype of say ½, the expected earnings would be only $25. The discount rate also comprises two components: the normal rate of return—say, the yield on relatively safe Swiss government bonds—and a risk assessment. In our case, the normal rate of return may be 5 percent, but if Exxon is assessed to be twice as risky as Swiss government bonds, the discount rate will be twice as high, at 10 percent (= 2 x 5 percent).

Neoclassicists and Marxists recognize the existence of capitalization—but given their view that capital is a real economic entity, they don't quite know what to do with its symbolic appearance. The neoclassicists bypass the impasse by saying that, in principle, capitalization is merely the mirror image of real capital—although, in practice, this image gets distorted by unfortunate market imperfections. The Marxists approach the problem from the opposite direction. They begin by assuming that capitalization is entirely fictitious—and therefore unrelated to the actual, or real capital. But then, in order to sustain their labor theory of value, they also insist that, occasionally, this fiction must either inflate or crash into equality with real capital.

It seems to me that these attempts to make capitalization fit the box of real capital are an exercise in futility. First, as I already noted, real capital lacks an objective quantity. Second, the very separation of economics from politics—a separation that is necessary to make such objectivity possible in the first place—has become defunct. Indeed capitalization is hardly limited to the so-called economic sphere.

Every stream of expected income is a candidate for capitalization. And since income streams are generated by social entities, processes, organizations, and institutions, we end up with capitalization discounting not the so-called sphere of economics but potentially every aspect of society. Human life, including its social habits and its genetic code, is routinely capitalized. Institutions—from education and entertainment to religion and the law—are habitually capitalized. Voluntary social networks, urban violence, civil war, and international conflict are regularly capitalized. Even the environmental future of humanity is capitalized. Nothing escapes the eyes of the discounters. If it generates expected future income, it can be capitalized, and whatever can be capitalized sooner or later *is* capitalized.

The all-encompassing nature of capitalization calls for an encompassing theory, and the unifying basis for such a theory is power. The primacy of power is built right into the definition of private ownership. Note that the English word *private* comes from the Latin *privatus*, which means "restricted." In this sense, private ownership is wholly and only an institution of *exclusion*, and institutionalized exclusion is a matter of organized power.

Of course, exclusion does not have to be exercised. What matters here are the right to exclude and the ability to exact pecuniary terms for not exercising that right. This right and ability are the foundations of accumulation. Capital, then, is nothing other than organized power. This power has two sides: one qualitative, the other quantitative. The qualitative side comprises the institutions, processes, and conflicts through which capitalists constantly *creorder* society, shaping and restricting its trajectory in order to achieve their redistributive ends. The quantitative side is the process that integrates, reduces, and distills these numerous qualitative processes down to the universal magnitude of capitalization.

PD: Let me raise a very broad question: What is power? Can power be an economic force? What is the link between power and capital? We are used to thinking about capital as an exclusively economic category, but you seem to understand it differently. How exactly do you understand it? What are the more practical consequences of your approach to understanding current economic-cum-political systems?

JN: As Hegel tells us in *The Phenomenology of Mind* and elsewhere, and as Max Jammer shows in his *Concepts of Force*, power is not a thing in itself.[2] It is a relationship between things. Consequently power cannot be observed as such. We know it only indirectly, through its effects. In religion, the power of the gods is revealed through their alleged deeds and miracles, while in science power is revealed through its measureable consequences. We know of gravity not by observing it directly but by measuring the quantitative relationship between mass and acceleration. Similarly with capital as power: we know the power of owners indirectly, by the numerical magnitude of their capitalization and the way it *creorders* society.

PD: And how does capitalist power *creorder* society?

JN: To answer this question, we first need to make a distinction between the creative and productive potential of society—the sphere that the American political economist Thorstein Veblen called "industry"—and the realm of power that, in the capitalist epoch, increasingly takes the form of business. This distinction is crucial not least because it runs counter to the conventional creed; in common parlance, industry and business are synonyms, whereas for Veblen they were antonyms.

Using as a metaphor a concept invented by the physicist Denis Gabor, we can think of the social process as a giant hologram, a space criss-crossed with incidental waves. Each social action, whether of industry or of business, is an event, an occurrence that generates vibrations throughout the social space. However, there is a fundamental difference between the vibrations of industry and the vibrations of business. Industry, understood as the collective knowledge and creative effort of humanity, is inherently cooperative, integrated, and synchronized. It operates best when its various events resonate with each other. Business, in contrast, isn't collective; it's private. Its goals are achieved through the threat and exercise of systemic prevention and restriction—that is, through what Veblen called "strategic sabotage." The key object of this sabotage is the resonating pulses of industry—a resonance that business constantly upsets through built-in dissonance.

Business sabotage affects both the direction and pace of industry. The impact on the direction of industry is so prevalent that we often don't see it. The most obvious effect is the progressive subjugation of billions of minds and bodies to the single-minded Moloch of profit-making and the consequent stifling of individual and societal creativity. And that is just the beginning. Consider the following examples: the systematic destruction of public transportation in the United States and elsewhere in favor of the ecologically disastrous private automobile; the development by pharmaceutical companies of expensive remedies for concocted "medical conditions" instead of drugs to cure real diseases that mostly afflict those who are too poor to pay for treatment; the promotion by global conglomerates of junk food in lieu of a healthy diet; the imposition of intellectual property rights on societal knowledge instead of the free diffusion of such knowledge; the invention by high-tech companies of weapon technologies instead of alternative clean and renewable energies; the development by chemical and biotechnology corporations of one-size-fits-all genetically modified plants and animals instead of biodiversified ones; the forced expansion by governments and realtors of socially fractured suburban sprawl instead of participatory and sustainable urbanization; the development by television networks of lowest-common-denominator programming that sedates the mind rather than stimulates its critical faculties. The list goes on.

These and similar diversions permeate the entire structure of capitalism. They can be seen everywhere, that is, provided we are willing take off our neoclassical blinkers. And if we accounted for them all, we would have to conclude that a significant proportion of business-driven "growth" is wasteful, not to say destructive, and that the sabotage that underlies this waste and destruction is exactly what makes it so profitable.

The other form of business sabotage is the impact it has on the pace of industry. Conventional political economy, both neoclassical and Marxist, postulates a positive relationship between production and profit. Capitalists, the argument suggests, benefit from industrial activity, and therefore, the more fully employed their equipment and workers, the greater their profit. But if we think of capital as power, exercised through the strategic sabotage of industry by business, the relationship should be nonlinear: positive under certain circumstances, negative under others.

And that is exactly what the historical data tell us. In the United States, Great Britain, and Canada, for example, the share of capitalists in national income (measured by profit plus interest) has tended to rise as growth accelerated and the rate of unemployment declined—but only up to a point. After that point, rising growth and declining unemployment—in other words, less sabotage—have tended not to increase but to *reduce* the income share of capitalists!

The case of the United States is illustrative. In the 1930s, when the sabotage of industry by business was extreme and official unemployment hovered around 25 percent, the share of capitalists in national income stood at around 11 percent. Then came the Second World War; employment and production soared, and the income share of capitalists rose to nearly 16 percent. But that was the peak. As the war effort continued, business sabotage of industry was almost eliminated and unemployment fell to less than 2 percent. However, the share of capital in national income, instead of rising as conventional political economy would have predicted, dropped sharply, reaching a low of 12 percent, barely above its depression level. This situation was obviously unacceptable to capitalists; so after the war, sabotage was reinstated, unemployment rose to between 5 and 7 percent, and capitalists' share in national income soared to an all-time high of nearly 19 percent. It seems that "business as usual" (high capitalist income) and the "natural rate of unemployment" (the strategic level of industrial sabotage) are two sides of the same capitalist coin. Perhaps this combination is what economists have in mind when they speak about equilibrium.

PD: Can you further concretize the notion of capital as power? How is this concept related to what economists call "profit maximization"?

What does it tell us that standard economics and other social sciences do not?

JN: Power is never absolute; it's always relative. For this reason, Bichler and I argue, both the quantitative and qualitative aspects of capital accumulation have to be assessed differentially, relative to other capitals. Contrary to the claims of conventional economics, capitalists are driven not to maximize profit but to "beat the average" and "exceed the normal rate of return." Their entire existence is conditioned by the need to outperform, by the imperative to achieve not absolute accumulation but *differential accumulation*. And this differential drive is crucial; to beat the average means to accumulate faster than others, and since the relative magnitude of capital represents power, capitalists who accumulate differentially increase their power—that is, their broad strategic capacity to inflict sabotage.

The centrality of differential accumulation, we claim, means that in analyzing accumulation we should focus not only on capital in general but also—and perhaps more so—on *dominant capital* in particular, that is, on the leading corporate-governmental alliances whose differential accumulation has gradually been placed at the center of the political economy. The importance of this process can be illustrated by the recent history of the United States. Over the past half-century or so, differential accumulation by U.S. dominant capital has advanced in leaps and bounds. In 1950 the average net profit per firm among the top one hundred U.S.-incorporated companies was roughly 1,600 times larger than the average net profit per firm in the U.S. business sector as a whole; by 2010 this multiple was fourteen-fold larger, at over 23,000!

This massive increase in differential accumulation quantifies the growing power of U.S. dominant capital; the other side of this trend is the qualitative power processes that differential accumulation quantifies and distills into a single magnitude. Much of our work over the past three decades has been devoted to examining this quantitative-qualitative underpinning of power, in the United States and elsewhere.

PD: Let's turn to the economic downturn of 2008–9. We used to hear that it is natural, after the boom like the one we had in the past twenty years, to have a downturn. Given the supposedly cyclical nature of the market system, we should theoretically not worry. But from consumers to bankers, we are all worried. So what is different now?

SB: In light of what was said so far, I think that what we are experiencing now is not an economic downturn, or even an economic crisis, but a *systemic* crisis, a crisis that threatens the very existence of the capitalist mode of power. This crisis has been lingering for more than a decade. It started not in 2008, as most observers argue, but in 2000, and it shows no sign of abating.

PD: Can you further clarify what you mean by "systemic crisis"?

SB: Let me take, for a moment, the viewpoint of the capitalists. As they see it, the key barometer of success and failure is not the growth of production or the level of employment but the movements of the stock market. The stock market capitalizes their expected future earnings—and by so doing distills and reduces their collective view on the future of capitalism down to a single number.

Now, if we examine the history of the U.S. stock market, measured by Standard & Poor's 500 stock index, we see that, over the past century or so, capitalists endured four "major bear markets." Each of these major bear markets was characterized by a massive drop in prices, ranging between 50 and 70 percent in "constant dollars." Note, however, that these declines, although roughly similar in quantity, were very different in quality. Each of them signaled a major—and unique—*creordering* of capitalist power:

> The crisis of 1906–20 (–70 percent) marked the closing of the American frontier, the shift from robber-baron capitalism to large-scale business enterprise and the beginning of synchronized finance.

The crisis of 1929–48 (–56 percent) signaled the end of "unregulated" capitalism and the emergence of large governments and the welfare-warfare state.

The crisis of 1969–81 (–55 percent) marked the closing of the Keynesian era, the resumption of worldwide capital flows, and the onset of neoliberal globalization.

And the current crisis—which, as I noted, began not in 2008 but in 2000, and is still continuing (–50 percent from 2000 to 2009)—seems to mark yet another shift toward a different form of capitalist power, or perhaps a shift away from capitalist power altogether.

The current crisis is marked by *systemic fear*. Capitalists today are not just uncertain or worried; they are scared. Their apprehension is not about this or that aspect of capitalism but about capitalism's very existence. Many of them now fear that the capitalist order itself may not survive, at least not in its current form.

PD: What indication do we have that capitalists suffer from "systemic fear"?

SB: A key gauge of this systemic fear is the way capitalists price their equities. The capitalization ritual is unambiguous: it instructs capitalists to discount not the current level of profit but its estimated *long-term* trajectory. So, under normal circumstances, changes in stock prices should show little or no direct correlation with changes in current profit—and indeed they usually don't. But periods of systemic fear are anything *but* normal. During such periods, capitalists doubt the survival of their system, and that doubt makes them lose sight of its future; with the capitalist future having become opaque, the "long-term profit trend" loses its meaning, and with no estimates of long-term profits, capitalists are left with nothing to discount.

In a capitalized world, the inability to capitalize is a mortal threat. So capitalists, desperate for something to hang on to, abandon their sanctified reliance on the expected future and latch on to the present.

Numbed by systemic fear, they discount not the eternal long-term trend of profit but its day-to-day variations. And that is exactly what we observe in the current crisis: since 2000, equity prices, instead of moving independently of current profits, have tracked those profits remarkably closely.

This type of panic-driven breakdown is not unprecedented, though. It also happened in the 1930s. Much like today, capitalists in the 1930s were struck by systemic fear, and much like today, they abandoned the capitalization ritual. Moreover, and crucially, the reason for the breakdown was pretty much the same: in both periods, capitalist power had become so great that capitalists lost confidence that they could retain that power, let alone increase it.

PD: This claim seems counterintuitive: shouldn't capitalists be more confident the more powerful they become?

SB: Only up to a point. Capitalist power is distributional, measured by relative capitalization, so a capitalist group with $300 billion in net assets is three times as powerful as a group with only $100 billion. Now, in beating the average and exceeding the normal rate of return, dominant capital accumulates differentially. And since capital is distributional power, differential accumulation is the augmentation of distributional power.

Distributional power, though, is clearly bounded. No group of capitalists, no matter how sophisticated and ruthless, can ever own more than everything there is to own in society. Moreover, in practice, capitalist power is likely to stall long before it reaches this upper limit.

The reason is rooted in the conflictual dynamics of power. Capitalists cannot stop seeking more power; since capital *is* power, the drive to accumulate is a drive for more power, by definition. But that very quest for power generates its own barriers. Power hinges on the use of force and sabotage, so the closer capitalist power gets to its limit, the greater the resistance this force and sabotage elicit; the greater that resistance, the more difficult it is for those who hold power to increase it further;

the more difficult it is to increase power, the greater the need for even more force and sabotage; and the more force and sabotage, the higher the likelihood of a serious backlash, followed by a decline or even disintegration of power.

It is at this last point, when power approaches its societal "asymptotes," that capitalists are likely to be struck by systemic fear—the fear that the power structure, having become top-heavy, is about to cave in. And it is at this critical moment, when capitalists fear for the very survival of their system, that their forward-looking capitalization is most prone to collapse.

PD: What comes next for power, capital, and the market?

JN: To answer this question, we need a new—and very different—research institute. To *re*-search means to search again, and that is exactly what the current theoretical-ideological impasse calls for. As we have reiterated throughout this interview, the existing approaches to capitalism, liberal and Marxist, have run their course. They rely on the wrong assumptions; they use fictitious building blocks; they employ misleading categories, concepts, and research methods; and most important, they often ask the wrong questions. They lead us to a dead end.

Capitalism is not a mode of production and consumption; it is a mode of power. And in order for us to transcend this mode of power, we first need to properly understand its structure, development, and crises. In short, we need a cosmology of capitalist power. Such a cosmology, though, cannot be concocted out of thin air. A new cosmology emerges not from the self-organization of Platonic ideas but from the relentless *empirical* inquiries of flesh-and-blood researchers. The detailed empirical investigations of these researchers yield new evidence and novel regularities; the new evidence and regularities undermine and eventually shatter the old dogma; and with the old dogma having been debunked, the door is open for a new system of assumptions, concepts, questions, and theories.

This is how modern science was born in the sixteenth century. It emerged not from re-idealizing religion or revamping moral theory but from empirical research. It was the celestial observations of Nicolaus Copernicus, Tyco Brahe, Johannes Kepler, and Galileo Galilei, the hands-on surgical procedures of Andreas Vesalius, the discovery of systemic circulation by William Harvey, the chemical experiments of Richard Boyle, and the detailed analysis of magnetism by William Gilbert, among others, that helped undermine the old dogma. And it was this empirical research that eventually gave birth to a novel method of inquiry we now call *science*. "There is no empirical method without speculative concepts and systems," says Albert Einstein, but also, "there is no speculative thinking whose concepts do not reveal, on closer investigation, the empirical methods from which they stem."[3]

PD: Can you illustrate this theoretical-empirical duality in the study of political economy?

JN: Certainly. Take the Keynesian revolution of the late 1930s. Although Keynes and his followers retained the Newtonian determinism of neoclassical economics (utility-maximizing agents, individual rationality, perfect competition, and so on), their framework nonetheless undermined basic tenets of bourgeois orthodoxy. It separated the macro sphere of government and state from the micro world of consumers and producers; it offered different ethics for private and public management; and it allowed, and indeed called for, stabilizing fiscal and monetary policies by governments.

However, even this limited bourgeois revolution would have been impossible, indeed inconceivable, without a prior empirical-statistical basis, in this case, the prior development of systematic national accounting. The first steps in that direction were taken at the end of the nineteenth century in Europe, the United States, and other countries, and they culminated in the foundation in 1920 of the U.S. National Bureau of Economic Research and the official publication of the country's first national accounts in 1934. Without this emergent empirical picture of national aggregates, it is doubtful that Keynes could have imagined a distinct macro perspective, let alone a theory that related its underlying flows and stocks.

PD: What does that mean for radical students of society in general and for the study of the capitalist mode of power in particular?

JN: In order for us to develop—and negate—the cosmology of capitalist power, we too need an empirical infrastructure, and that infrastructure is yet to be created. The importance of such infrastructure for radical undertakings can be gleaned from the evolution of twentieth-century Marxism. When Lenin wrote *Imperialism: The Highest Stage of Capitalism* in 1917, the data on which he based his argument were meager and fractured. There were no organized statistics, no time series, and no aggregate facts to speak of. Much of his evidence was drawn from works published twenty years earlier by the left-liberal political economist John Hobson. The situation was quite different half a century later. In 1966, when the American Marxists Paul A. Baran and Paul M. Sweezy published *Monopoly Capital*, systems of national accounts had already been implemented, primarily in the developed countries, and aggregate data analysis had become increasingly commonplace.[4] This new infrastructure enabled Baran and Sweezy to enlist the help of Joseph D. Phillips, a statistical expert who subjected their thesis to systematic empirical examination. The result, published in the famous appendix to their book, was an empirical feat that Lenin could not have fathomed. And yet even Baran and Sweezy had to restrict their analysis to the United States, and particularly to its macro economy: national accounting was still far less developed in the rest of the world; organized statistics for corporations and financial intermediation were still in their infancy; and global databases were not yet on the radar screen. It was only in the 1980s, with the transnationalization of capital and the advent of cheap computing, that a global statistical picture, however imperfect, became a practical possibility.

These new data and the relative ease with which they can be accessed through the Internet offer research opportunities that earlier critical thinkers could only dream of. However, I think we need to bear in mind that these databases have been conceived and developed to serve the capitalist mode of power, not to undermine it. They are geared toward the interests of accumulation, and, as such, they reflect the assumptions, categories, methods, and theories of neoclassical economics—the ruling ideology of the accumulators. This fact serves to explain why Marxists have found it increasingly difficult to distance their empirical analyses from those of their class enemy. Having failed to develop their own statistical methods and corresponding data, they have gradually been forced to use those of the neoclassicists. And by using these methods and data, they ended up, often without noticing that they were doing so, validating the very approach they seek to reject.

We need to get rid of all this baggage. To be radical means to go to the root, to start from scratch. We need to develop new questions, new method, new categories, new data, and, finally, an entirely new mode of accounting. We need to *re*draw the capitalist map in a manner that will uncover and depict the logic and reality of capitalist power. We need to measure the aggregate and differential manifestations of this power in different regions, countries, and sectors and at different levels of analysis. We need to identify the specific strengths and weaknesses of that power so that we can know how to resist and overturn it. And to do all of that, we need to revolutionize the way we think, interrogate, and investigate.

This kind of revolution demands an organizational Ctrl-Alt-Del. It requires a *new, autonomous research institute,* a nonacademic scientific organization that will be independent of neoclassicism, Marxism, and postism. The purpose of this research formation will be to lay the empirical-theoretical groundwork for a new cosmology of the capitalist mode of power, as well as a countercosmology to help us *creorder* a humane alternative.

MAKE DEVELOPMENT POSSIBLE

19

"The best approach to economic development is pragmatism"

Photo courtesy of Jomo Kwame
Sundaram.

JOMO KWAME SUNDARAM
in conversation with Vladimir Popov

Jomo Kwame Sundaram is a former United
Nations assistant secretary-general for eco-
nomic development in the Department of
Economic and Social Affairs. He also served
as the honorary research coordinator for the
G24 Intergovernmental Group on International
Monetary Affairs and Development.

Few people understand as well as Jomo Kwame Sundaram the economics of development and the field of development economics and
have his range of analytical experience in the field. In this historically
rooted and policy-oriented interview, he delves into the characteristics
of development and growth. He argues that in examining development
we should look to difference, context, and history rather than to economic formulas or one-size-fits-all policies. He outlines the challenges
and opportunities facing many developing countries, including their
relationship to developed countries, existing power structures, and
global financial and monetary mechanisms. Within this context, he
suggests that commonly held notions of inequality must be contextual-
ized, showing that the current convergence of living standards between
developed and developing nations may, in some instances, only be the

reversal of previous negative trends rather than a real step forward, and that decreased international inequality may be distracting us from growing intranational inequality. Given these kinds of trends, he suggests new directions for the study and practice of development. Finally, the discussion turns to his thoughts on the current crisis, about which he suggests that early efforts for international solidarity have been replaced by a fragmented politics that risks making the world even more beholden to financial institutions and that threaten growth and development for the global North and South alike.

vp: During the Great Recession, developing countries did better than developed countries. What are the reasons for this differing performance? Is it a short-term trend or a long-term one?

jks: Something similar happened in the mid- and late 1970s, when the Western world experienced stagflation. Japan and most developing countries did well, at least until the 1978–79 second oil price spike, which hit Africa especially hard and helped send it into a quarter-century of near stagnation. This time developing countries did well during the middle of the past decade before the collapse of demand in developed countries and commodity prices slowed growth in the South. Also, not all countries have thrived. It is often suggested that at least all large developing economies did well, but even this is not quite true. Natural resource exporters have done well as mineral prices have risen much more than agricultural prices. But price volatility reminds us of how vulnerable this recent spurt was, and already we are seeing even the faster-growing developing economies slow down. We should be careful not to make broad generalizations in these circumstances, even about the so-called economies in transition, which you know much better than I do.

vp: According to the late Angus Maddison, before 1500 all countries had roughly the same GDP per capita (about $500 in 1985 prices), but by 1900 the gap between the groups of countries that are now called developed and developing increased to 6:1.¹ In 2000 it was roughly at the same level. But in the second half of the twentieth century, while sub-Saharan Africa, Eastern Europe and the former Soviet Union, and Latin America continued to fall behind and failed to reduce the gap with the West, several developing countries (Japan, South Korea, Taiwan, Singapore, and Hong Kong) managed to join the "rich club," while others (Southeast Asia, China, and, more recently, India) succeeded in considerably bridging the gap with rich countries. Are we seeing the reversal of the five-hundred-year trend, with convergence replacing divergence, or a temporary deviation from the trend?

JKS: I see convergence and divergence as epiphenomena. The key question then is: What are the underlying phenomena? The way you have framed the question suggests that you are interested in comparing average output. But it is not clear that consumption is directly related to production, especially given global economic integration. Very few would disagree that differential investment rates are the major determinant of productive capacities. And in the decade before the current crisis, Greece had the highest rates of investment and productivity increases in the OECD (Organization for Economic Cooperation and Development), notwithstanding the currently convenient myths of Greek laziness. Apparently Greek workers' productivity and wage levels did not deter private investors from investing for at least a decade. Of course, increased productivity makes higher wage remuneration possible, but there is no automatic guarantee that wages will rise with productivity.

IT is also important to consider the sources and sustainability of growth as well as related resource and demographic constraints. Investments due to domestic resource mobilization will have different implications compared to foreign direct investments. Investment decisions of foreign investors will tend to consider the relative medium-term profitability of investments. While domestic investors may also enjoy similar options, there is considerable historical evidence of the importance of the nationality of investments. Public investments are also more likely to be national in orientation compared to private investments. All these factors shape and sustain the accumulation process and hence the likelihood of sustained productivity increases.

The sustainability of growth is also influenced by whether it is dependent on the extraction and depletion of exhaustible, nonrenewable natural resources, especially mineral resources. Despite considerable condemnation of the resource curse, much recent growth in developing countries, as well as a few developed countries, has benefited from such resource extraction and may be difficult to sustain. The currently favored framework of converting natural capital into fiscal capital may also be problematic, elucidating as much as it obscures. Different demographic transitions have many ramifications that may bear on the sustainability of growth. In short, it is a complicated process.

The continuing economic crisis appears to have slowed economic growth very considerably, especially in the developed economies. While growth in developing countries took a big hit in 2009, it has recovered in many countries since then, only to decline once again. Strong, sustained, and inclusive economic recovery does not seem to be around the corner, and it is possible that the economic stagnation of the North may drag down the remaining economic growth in the South. This type of convergence of growth rates is certainly not going to achieve the kind of economic convergence you were implying. During the 1950s and 1960s some convergence took place as much of the developed world recovered from the devastation of war, while postcolonial economies were able to grow rapidly as they implemented policies more conducive to development. The 1970s were a mixed decade, but after that, much of Latin America and Africa saw slow growth. Japan has not experienced much growth since the 1990s, while the growth records of Southeast Asian nations have been rather mixed since the 1997–98 Asian crisis. For convergence to take place, sustained and rapid per capita growth in developing countries is necessary. It is not clear that the recent growth in East Asia will be sustained throughout the region.

It seems possible that a number of economies will be able to achieve sustained growth, and this will, of course, reduce the degree of inequality among nations at a time when many of those nations themselves are experiencing greater national-level inequalities. Insofar as international inequalities account for much more of overall global inequality than intranational inequalities, convergence as it occurs may mainly refer to international inequalities only, while there may not be clear trends in terms of overall global inequality. In other words, much depends on how we define and understand convergence itself. Moreover many factors influence living standards. There is little evidence that productivity increases necessarily raise the incomes of producers. For instance, significant increases in agricultural productivity have often translated into lower commodity prices rather than higher incomes for producers. Over the course of the twentieth century, primary commodity prices declined relative to the prices for manufactured goods. Similarly the prices of tropical agricultural products declined compared to those for temperate agriculture over the same period. More recently the prices of manufactured goods from developing countries have declined compared to those from developed countries.

If the producers are wage earners, much will depend on the nature of wage determination and wage contracts. The West Indian economist and Nobel laureate Arthur Lewis suggested that there are different types of labor markets. Where unemployment is high, workers are willing to accept wages close to subsistence. But where labor is organized and collective bargaining as well as working conditions are regulated, wages are more likely to rise with productivity increases. For instance, for several decades living standards in China did not rise as fast as productivity, but in recent years living standards have risen as employers experience labor shortages and expect greater skill requirements from their workers. With greater social protection and provisioning (public health, education, housing), the social wage may increase much more than is suggested by the money or real wages that workers receive.

In recent decades, however, we have seen a general decline in social provisioning in many societies. This is true not only of many so-called welfare states but also of postcolonial societies featuring some tax-financed social provisioning. In China, Russia, and many other so-called economies in transition, such social provisioning has also declined. As a consequence, the welfare of individuals and families depends much more on what they can afford based on their market incomes. Similarly the recent period has seen greater income inequality in most, though not all, societies. The era of economic liberalization has witnessed not only increasing income inequality at the national level but also growing concentration of wealth assets at the world level.

VP: But prices for some important commodities, like oil, actually increased in the twentieth century and are now at a very high level. You suggested previously that resource abundance may in fact be a blessing, not a curse. Oil exporters of West Asia (Saudi Arabia, the Gulf states) are the second large region of the South (after East Asia) that is catching up with the West, but its economic model is very different. Unlike in East Asia, productivity in these countries did not increase much, but the terms of trade did improve considerably, so consumption and living standards were growing faster than productivity. Insofar as the oil rents are used not only for consumption but also for investment in human resources and infrastructure, high resource prices may result in real catch-up development. Would you agree?

JKS: What one does with the economic surplus, whether profits or rents, determines the sustainability of growth. Look at how Norway and Holland used their oil rents to diversify and to enhance other productive capacities. And contrast this with most other oil-producing countries. In Libya and other countries living standards rose, and they did well on some human development indicators, but it is not clear that the new economic capacities and capabilities could sustain growth without resource rents. The Malaysian national oil company, Petronas, was seen as well-managed, but it is not clear that Malaysian oil wealth has been well invested, either abroad, where most investments are still shrouded in secrecy, or domestically, where the evidence is hardly inspiring. For other economies, you have wealthy elites with considerable wealth, much of it held overseas. So even if you have income flows from such assets, it is not clear that they will be deployed developmentally to raise living standards in the short and long term.

Let us be clear about where growth comes from, more generally. It comes from investments, which in turn come from economic surplus and, of course, innovation. Under capitalism, this surplus is often identified with profit. Classical economics posits perfect competition in which many small producers produce the same product consumed by many different consumers. In the real world, this is the exception, not the rule. In the real world, I would suggest, the surplus includes not just what mainstream economics calls profits but also rents, typically associated with what is termed *imperfect competition*. In this case, we are talking about resource rents. There are many kinds of resource rents, and income from resource rents can be deployed for any purpose, for consumption of different types or for investment of different types, current or delayed. Norway, for instance, has done many innovative things with its oil revenues. Libya utilized its oil rents to become the top scorer in terms of the Human Development Index in Africa and the Arab world. But this speaks of economic welfare or consumption levels that may rise thanks to oil rents income. Whether oil rents are successfully used for developmental purposes can be a distinct question involving how they are invested for productive purposes rather than to enhance welfare or consumption.

VP: Do you believe that the collapse of the Soviet Union proves that centrally planned economies and socialism are not internationally competitive?

JKS: Again, the question has to be deconstructed. We have certainly not seen the end of centrally planned economies. Consider a large conglomerate. Almost by definition, it is diverse, variegated. Yet at some level, there is a degree of centralized planning for the conglomerate as a whole. The main difference probably is that when things go wrong and this is reflected in the corporation's performance, action is likely to be taken to address mistakes and inadequacies. Although centrally planned national economies were not monolithic and unchanging, the impression is that they were slow to change and correct themselves. It is not clear why this was the case, but surely this must give pause to proponents of centrally planned economies.

As for socialism, as you well know, there are many different understandings of what this term means. For the right, anything associated with the public sector is socialist. By this definition, Singapore, Israel, and some of the oil welfare states would be the most socialist in the world owing to the size of the public sector in those economies, even after the modest privatizations that have taken place in recent decades. For others, however, government intervention is what defines an economy as socialist. Crudely put, the greater the degree of regulation and government intervention, the more socialist the economy is. By this definition, most European economies would be considered quite socialist owing to the pervasive role of the state. Of course, there are many other understandings of socialism. Soon after the collapse of the Soviet Union, for example, the Nobel laureate Joseph Stiglitz argued in favor of the continued relevance of his version of the socialist project.

The recent crisis has contributed to the revival of interest in Keynesian economics, triggering a strong response from the right, which would depict Keynesianism as socialistic because of the envisaged countercyclical role of state intervention. Similarly much of the recent interest in the potential of public-private partnerships envisages a much more nuanced understanding of the functioning of the economy. Public provisioning of public goods, including infrastructure, is increasingly deemed necessary, not only for sustainable development but also for advancing the public interest. While there may be very limited interest in a return to the Soviet status quo ante outside of Russia, the current crisis, as well as greater recognition of the growth of inequality and other social problems, has revived public interest in economic alternatives, including those sometimes deemed, broadly speaking, socialist.

And, as you know, the collapse of the Soviet Union was not economically determined. On the contrary, the economic collapse of Russia and most other Soviet republics did not precede but rather followed the collapse of the Soviet Union. In fact, as you have shown in your own work, only over two decades later, in 2012, has the Russian economy reached its output level of 1989, the last year before the collapse.[2] Nevertheless one has to concede that most people are not aware of the facts and actual sequencing, wrongly believing that the economic collapse of Soviet-style socialism could not be prevented by Mikhail Gorbachev. Hence they wrongly believe that Boris Yeltsin saved Russia from economic collapse caused either by Gorbachev or those who sought to oust him.

VP: You mentioned that the current crisis has provoked the return of more socialist, or at least Keynesian, thinking. What is so special about the recent economic crisis, the so-called Great Recession? Does it mark, as some argue, a turning point in the development of the capitalist system, or it is just a cyclical downturn?

JKS: The recent economic crisis has many specific characteristics that distinguish it from earlier crises. On one level, it reflects not only the hegemony of finance in recent decades but also the specificities of uneven financial liberalization and globalization due to political settlements, institutional reforms, and corporate responses. Hence while the circumstances of a particular conjuncture shape developments, one cannot reasonably claim that the full consequences of letting Lehman Brothers collapse and saving AIG were all predetermined. Similarly it has also been affected by many subsequent developments all over the world, which have shaped the subsequent course of events. Very importantly, for example, there was strong support for fiscal and other stimuli to overcome the economic downturn in late 2008, but by the end of the following year, proponents of fiscal austerity were successfully invoking financial market responses to the sudden increase of sovereign debt to bail out financial institutions in order to reverse these policies.

The appetite for international cooperation for a strong, sustained, and inclusive recovery has been the other victim, and the specific challenges of saving the eurozone have further constrained such efforts.

Insofar as financial fragility is an inevitable consequence of financial and economic expansion following recovery, there are key cyclical features to what has happened. But it is misleading to think solely in terms of business cycles, not only because history never completely repeats itself but also because conjunctural features are extremely important as well, especially in understanding what has been going on over the past half-decade. However, this does not necessarily mean that we are going to witness a profound transformation of capitalism. Undoubtedly the Great Depression of the 1930s resulted in a significant transformation of capitalism, with the New Deal, Keynesianism, the Bretton Woods institutions, and the Marshall Plan.

For example, it is not even clear that finance will be much more effectively regulated following this crisis, not only internationally but even within most national economies. Needless to say, there is very little attention being given to prioritizing the interests of the real economy in relation to those of finance. Despite growing recognition of the great increase in inequality in recent decades, there are no major proposals to reverse this trend. And perhaps most important for our shared future, there has been little serious effort to ensure continued economic development, social progress, and environmental sustainability.

VP: On behalf of the United Nations, you have argued at the G20 and elsewhere that economic policies in response to the crisis have not been expansionary enough, causing the recession to become deeper. What should have been the appropriate policies? What are the lessons we should learn from this recession? And most important, could it happen again on a greater scale?

JKS: Although the United Nations has a very limited mandate on financial matters, together with the Bank of International Settlements we were trying to focus attention long before the crisis on the unsustainability of macrofinancial trends. With the outbreak of the crisis, international organizations, including the IMF (International Monetary Fund), were briefly on the same page as us, agreeing on the need for international cooperation as well as a strong, robust countercyclical response to the crisis. Unfortunately the consensus was short-lived, lasting only through 2009.

Heavy borrowing to save the financial system greatly increased sovereign debt. This was then invoked to cut government spending, especially on fiscal stimuli, to preserve credit ratings and to placate bond markets. In the eurozone and other economies in similar situations, governments could not borrow by printing money. In these and other ways, policy tools previously available to sovereign governments were no longer available. Instead governments had to rely on, and have become hostage to, private financial markets.

The United Nations has consistently urged countercyclical macroeconomic policies, not only to accelerate and sustain economic recovery but also to prevent booms from generating bubbles, and ensuring fiscal balance over the business cycle rather than in any particular year. We have been very much in favor of sustained fiscal stimulus efforts; we believe that priority should be given to ensuring social protection for all as well as meeting infrastructural priorities for the future. We have also advocated inclusive multilateralism to sustain international macrofinancial cooperation to ensure a strong, sustained, and inclusive economic recovery for all, but also to ensure an inclusive financial system supportive of the aspirations of sustainable development, including economic development, social progress, and environmental—including resource—sustainability.

As you know, several developed economies, especially in the eurozone, are already in recession once again. Prospects for economic growth in developing economies are being revised downward after being unexpectedly resilient during the early years of the downturn. But perhaps more important, there are very few prospects of a strong, sustained, and inclusive recovery in sight anywhere on the horizon. We are living in an era when the prospects for protracted stagnation do not seem to bother most mainstream politicians in the developed world. There is no Roosevelt for our times and no cold war to inspire or encourage initiatives such as the Marshall Plan.

vp: Are you saying that we are facing the possibility of something like another Great Depression? Without a new, true Great Depression, can we even think about having a Roosevelt for our times emerge?

jks: The collapse in 2009 was sharp, but there were some green shoots of recovery too, but subsequent fiscal austerity and other developments have resulted in stagnation in most if not all OECD economies. But the levels of unemployment are not comparable to the situation during the Depression, and living conditions are certainly better than they were eight decades ago, partly helped by the emergence of the welfare state and "automatic stabilizers," as diminished as they have become in recent decades. Even if you have a Great Depression, there is no guarantee of the emergence of a Roosevelt for our times. Sadly, the international community has simply not been able to act together to fill this void.

vp: Imagine a debate happening between two scholars in 1960 about where the future economic miracle would happen: one is betting on a more free, democratic, and entrepreneurial India and Latin America, whereas the other is predicting the success of authoritarian (even sometimes communist), centralized, and heavy-handedly interventionist East Asia. Today we know the right answer. But there is no consensus on what predetermined such an outcome. Why did not a single country in Latin America become an economic miracle? Where—and why—shall we see future economic miracles?

jks: Frankly, I am skeptical of any kind of cultural or even institutional determinism. For example, between 1930 and 1980, for a variety of reasons, Brazil was the fastest-growing economy in the world on average but also one of the most unequal societies, and not only because it was the last country to abolish slavery. Before that, in the late nineteenth and early twentieth century, Argentina grew rapidly, principally as a raw materials producer but also with some related industrial activity. There is a great deal to learn from American history and prewar

American economic thinking. After all, the USA was the first country in the modern period to successfully wage a war of national liberation. And it was Alexander Hamilton, an immigrant from the British Caribbean, who was responsible for conceptualizing and designing the major economic institutions for an independent nation.

Hence 1776 was symbolically very important, not only as the beginning of the Industrial Revolution and the year of publication of Adam Smith's *Wealth of Nations* but also, of course, as the year the American Revolution began. But as we also know, the United States did not take off industrially until after the Civil War. If the Southern Confederacy had won and slavery had been preserved, the United States would have remained much more agricultural, like Australia. Instead it rejected free trade and promoted manufacturing through governance and other institutional measures that would make mainstream economists today cringe. My point is simply that history and facts can be differently invoked to tell various stories, to support the advocacy of alternative policies and institutional reforms.

And of course, the first half-century of Soviet development was very impressive for many different reasons, and we should not forget that most of this was achieved in the face of great hostility. But we also need to admit that the Thatcher-Reagan counterrevolution was successful in its own right on a global scale. Right now capitalism is the only show in town, and the debate is among varieties of capitalism rather than between capitalism and some systemic alternative. Also, I do not believe that all dirigisme or state intervention is developmental. It could just as easily be self-serving for the leaders or decision makers concerned. And when they do not expect to survive in power for long, there is even less incentive to think in the long term or to be developmental. Hence the political and, hence, policy short-termism of electoral systems may not be conducive to development.

The ideology of economic liberalization and private property in recent decades has undoubtedly greatly exaggerated its virtues and understated its problems. Nevertheless this does not mean that everything associated with the public sector is better than the private sector.

More balanced and comprehensive analysis enables us to understand when property rights may provide incentives conducive to development. For example, the medium- to long-term land-lease rights introduced during the 1980s in China provided the incentives to significantly raise agricultural investments and output. Greater agricultural incomes increased investments in township and village enterprises that became the main source of manufacturing growth until the mid-1990s. The Chinese approach of cautious experimentation, "crossing the stream by feeling the stones," contrasts with the one-size-fits-all' shock therapy of the Russian and other less successful, if not disastrous transitions.

AS in Korea, Singapore, and elsewhere, state-owned enterprises have done well in China, contrary to the claims made by the advocates of privatization and property rights. We also know that privatization has been successful in cases as diverse as small retail enterprises in Hungary and the employee-share-ownership takeover of National Freight in the United Kingdom. The success of cooperatives in various different circumstances also points to the viability of other property arrangements and principal-agent relations.

It is important to recognize that the best approach to development, considering the wide variety of circumstances that different developing countries face, is pragmatism. A national development strategy must begin by considering available options as well as constraints. The main task is to overcome the major bottlenecks to achieving development. Clearly economies with greater resources are more likely to be able to overcome the constraints they face. And of course, domestic constraints may be easier to overcome than international constraints, which are generally more likely to be beyond the scope of government influence. Not surprisingly, therefore, much of the contemporary discussion of limits to policy space focuses on international constraints, even if these are mediated by domestic institutions, including markets.

VP: What particular international constraints limiting policy space for developing countries are most important?

JKS: I would identify two types. First, the legal commitments made by governments to rule-making and enforcing multilateral organizations, such as the World Trade Organization; international treaties, whether bilateral or plurilateral; and policy conditionalities associated with loan and other such agreements. Second, governments often conform to the constraining expectations of others. This can be for many reasons. For example, the education and training of economists, lawyers, and others often serves to define what is considered appropriate professional behavior. The international media can also serve to discipline the behavior of decision makers such as central bank or finance ministry or trade ministry officials. Policies or decisions can be applauded or disapproved of. Challenging the "conventional wisdom" can be very difficult. For example, when Malaysia imposed capital controls in early 1998, the international financial media promised nothing but gloom and doom. Although I believe the controls were too late, they certainly did not have the consequences predicted, but the media response shows how governments and decision makers can be effectively disciplined by the masters of the media, the interests they represent, and their ideological and policy preferences.

VP: Capital, most economists believe, should flow from rich countries, where it is in abundance, to poor countries, where it is scarce. But in several recent decades, many developing countries, China in particular, are maintaining current account surpluses (saving more than they invest) and using their savings to finance Western investment. Why is capital flowing uphill? Why do countries that export capital appear to grow faster than capital importers? And what is the best way to deal with these global imbalances?

JKS: In recent decades capital account liberalization has been promoted as part of overall financial liberalization by the most powerful economies in the world, including the OECD. Under Article 6, Section 3 of the IMF's Articles of Agreement, all national authorities have the sovereign right to manage their capital accounts. Emerging market economies, especially in East Asia, particularly after the 1997–98 Asian crisis, have felt compelled to accumulate reserves for self-protection (not "self-insurance," as there is no insurance element involved). However, it would be wrong to presume that all reserve accumulation is for self-protection purposes. For example, export-oriented growth has been promoted by various international development agencies over the past few decades. One policy option for this purpose is an undervalued exchange rate, which not only encourages exports but also deters imports. Hence rapid growth results in rapid reserve accumulation that generally involves capital exports.

Furthermore the U.S. dollar was officially designated the international currency after the Second World War by fixing the price of gold at $35 per ounce. Although the fixed exchange rate system came to an end in the early 1970s, the greenback continues to be the currency of choice internationally, while the currencies of other major economies—such as the euro, yen, and pound sterling—continue to remain the convertible international currencies of choice. Not surprisingly, this has involved "capital flowing uphill," from the fast-growing emerging market economies to developed economies enjoying seigniorage from the issue of currencies used by foreigners, especially those with low savings rates unable adequately to finance investment rates. Hence emerging market economies have been running current account surpluses, with which they have accumulated considerable foreign exchange reserves, mostly held in the major convertible international currencies, especially the U.S. dollar. The United States and, to a lesser extent, the United Kingdom have been quite happy to sell Treasury bonds to foreign bondholders. This has been less true of eurozone countries, while almost all Japanese sovereign debt, which proportionately greatly exceeds the sovereign debt of all other countries, is held by Japanese bondholders.

Hence the medium- to long-term solution to major persistent current account imbalances requires rebuilding productive and export capacities of the persistent deficit economies. In the short to medium term, exchange rate adjustments may help, but supposed market determination of exchange rates may actually worsen the problem, as financial asset holders may seek security by acquiring low-yield assets in currencies perceived as more stable.

VP: One could say, then, that China made the United States an offer that was too good to refuse: "We'll underprice our exchange rate to promote export-oriented development, but in return, we'll provide you with credit by investing our current account surpluses in your Treasury bonds, so that you'll have a chance to consume more than you produce and to invest at the expense of our Chinese savings (because American domestic savings are so low)." Is this the right way to describe the logic of events?

JKS: You do not need such a deal for all that to happen. With the ascendance of Deng Xiaoping in China in the 1980s, the United States was only too happy to woo China to isolate the Soviet Union. With the end of the cold war in the 1990s, the United States was quite happy to lower production costs and consumer prices by sourcing increasingly from abroad. But with its huge population, there was a fallacy of composition issue, as China was not just another East Asian export-oriented producer. With its huge supplies of labor, wages did not rise with productivity gains; instead consumers, increasingly abroad, enjoyed the consumer surplus from increased productivity, not only in terms of quantity but also quality.

During the first two decades, state-owned enterprises were important, and contrary to the impression in the West, most did well, especially with critical support from the state. But the agrarian surplus from greater farm production also accelerated the development of so-called township and village enterprises. Meanwhile, FDI (foreign direct investment) has grown in importance, not because China needs foreign capital but rather for access to foreign markets, technology, and expertise. The business arrangements involved are varied and quite innovative, accelerating the tendency to think in terms of global value chains and related issues. If you look at the trends, the large Chinese current account surplus is relatively recent, perhaps less than a decade old, mainly because of its imports of raw materials and intermediate manufactures from the South. Certainly the huge surplus with the United States dates only to the middle of the past decade. And the preference for U.S. Treasury bonds and other financial assets has to do with availability, the nature of the international financial system, and the perceived need for greater self-protection, especially after the 1997–98 Asian financial crisis.

VP: You have been known as an advocate of imposing controls over capital flows even before the Asian currency crisis of 1997–98. Opponents of capital controls would argue that the free flow of goods, services, people, and technology is best for our world. Isn't that (still) the case? What is the rationale for allowing the free movement of goods (and labor) and prohibiting the free movement of capital?

JKS: As I mentioned earlier, the IMF's Articles of Agreement clearly guarantee the sovereign right of national authorities to manage their capital accounts while promoting the liberalization of the international trade in goods and services. In the past two decades or so before the recent crisis, the OECD, IMF, and others actively promoted capital account liberalization, arguing that it would promote growth, stability, and foreign investments in poor countries. Even before the Asian crisis over a decade and a half ago, it was clear that average growth had declined while volatility and instability had greatly increased.

And while cross-border flows of funds have greatly increased, green-field foreign direct investments have declined proportionately, besides becoming more concentrated in fewer countries. Capital account management can easily encourage desirable green-field FDI while limiting other types of undesirable or problematic cross-border flows of capital. As we also know, obstacles to the free flow of people across borders have actually grown in recent decades, while xenophobia and racism toward migrants have become much worse with economic stagnation and growing unemployment. It is also misleading to believe that the strengthening of intellectual property rights in recent decades has enhanced cross-border flows of technology. Such flows have become much more expensive and difficult, especially with the decline of publicly funded research and technology promotion and extension.

vp: You have written extensively on industrial policy in East Asia.[3] Many countries tried industrial policy as a tool of catch-up development, but in Latin America, Africa, and the former Soviet Union import substitution was not successful: it led to the creation of "industrial dinosaurs" that could exist only with state support and behind protectionist walls but went bankrupt once such protection was withdrawn. They say in East Asia they know the secret of industrial policies that really works. What is it?

jks: EPconEP is our abbreviation for "effective protection conditional on export promotion." Basically it recognizes that for industrial latecomers, import substitution is often necessary for industrial promotion. However, it is very easy for protected industries to become heavily dependent on and protective of trade protection as well as other privileges provided by governments to encourage import substitution in particular sectors or industries. This is the common criticism of rent seeking, which can easily become entrenched and a long-term burden for the rest of the economy.

Hence such supported industries must be encouraged, if not forced, to become internationally competitive within a reasonable timeframe. Exports discipline industries, both quantitatively and qualitatively, in that products have to be considered acceptable in terms of quality and have to be price competitive, especially to break into new markets. It is also important to ensure that the ministries or agencies are effectively able to supervise and promote such industries.

vp: Development theories in the postwar period went through a full circle—from Big Push and import substitution industrialization to neoliberal Washington consensus to the understanding that neither the former nor the latter really works in engineering successful catch-up development. Meanwhile economic miracles were manufactured in East Asia without much reliance on theoretical development thinking, but rather through experimentation by strong politicians.

JKS: I am not sure the trajectory described is best summed up as a full circle. I tend to take a more dialectical view of how ideas evolve in response to realities, perceptions, and criticisms. History almost never repeats itself, and cycles are never quite circles.

VP: It was Hegel who argued that history repeats itself twice, whereas Marx added, "the first time as tragedy, the second time as farce."

JKS: Well, it is true, as you suggest, that sustained rapid economic growth and transformation in East Asia has never been profoundly influenced by grand economic development theories, orthodox or heterodox. Instead one sees a deep pragmatism, a willingness to reconsider received ideas, whether domestic or foreign in origin. Cautious experimentation is another expression of such pragmatism. But I would also insist that pragmatism has meant a focus on constraints and bottlenecks, and especially a willingness to address and overcome them.

However, one has to be cautious with the idea of strong politicians making the difference. This can easily become an apologia for developmental despotism, and ultimately despotism in the name of development. In my view, what has made the difference is a long-term perspective as well as a long-term commitment to development, perhaps for reasons of national pride, or even if only to preserve the regime by means other than repression alone. Most electoral systems tend to encourage policy short-termism, as rapid results are needed to ensure reelection, or worse still, to maximize rent capture while the political means are available. And so the institutional reform challenge is to strengthen the incentives for developmental governance. This is precisely how the good governance debate should be respecified and reoriented.

VP: Where does development economics stand today, and what are the most promising ideas for the future?

JKS: The emergence of a distinct branch of economics known as "development economics" has had very mixed consequences. For many mainstream economists, development economics is ersatz economics. For many, it has flirted with the other social and historical sciences in ways that are said to corrupt and compromise the supposed superiority of economic abstraction. The emergence of development economics soon after the rise of Keynesian economics has also been problematic, not least because of the alleged dirigisme of both. The counterrevolution against Keynesianism from the late 1970s was soon followed, if not accompanied, by a counterrevolution against development economics. Beginning in the 1980s, many deemed it unwise, if not unnecessary, to teach or study development economics. All that needed to be done, it was claimed, was to apply the immutable laws of economics to so-called developing economies.

And of course, the counterrevolution against Keynesian economics implied a rejection of parts of Samuelson's "neoclassical synthesis" with "bastard Keynesianism." So the result was not a return to Milton Friedman's monetarism, which had also been deemed irrelevant, but instead it turned into a hodgepodge of new economic fads favoring economic liberalization, deregulation, the end of planning, and the strengthening of private property rights, including so-called intellectual property rights (IPRs). Thus, in the name of promoting competition and eliminating economic rents, its oligopolistic antithesis has become the very basis for rentier accumulation. Hence, for instance, financial rents have become far more significant than when Keynes railed against them, while IPRs have become the most important basis for allegedly Schumpeterian rent acquisition in the real economy.

So while it is quite right to reconsider the microeconomic foundations of macroeconomic life, much of this is in a world of make-believe. Similarly macroeconomic dynamics in the developing world need to be better understood, even if as caricatures of what is happening in the developed world. After all, abstraction in economic analysis involves caricature, focusing on the most salient aspects of otherwise indistinguishable economic relations and dynamics. The most promising future for development economics, I believe, lies in critical interaction with both orthodox and heterodox economics. This implies a necessary renewal of development economics but also greater humility on the part of economists more generally, especially in understanding and informing contemporary challenges of economic development in oligopolistic market economies at both national and global levels.

20

*"Developing countries can bring in advanced technology
and actively catch up with developed countries"*

KEMAL DERVIŞ

in conversation with Kemal Kirişci

Kemal Derviş is vice president for global economics and development at the Brookings
Institution.

Photo courtesy of the Brookings
Institution and Kemal Derviş.

An expert on economic trends, poverty, and governance, Kemal
Derviş focuses in his discussion with Kemal Kirişci on a number
of such issues. One of his primary concerns is the paradoxical parallel
reduction of the per capita income gap between developed and developing states and the increase in the income gap within states. The very same
trends driving growth in general are, he argues, responsible for allowing developing countries to catch up and reduce global poverty, while
allowing for a dangerous concentration of wealth among a small group
of elites. While he champions the power of the market and sound pro-
trade policies to drive development, Derviş also supports development
aid—especially when it is highly targeted and well governed—to address

specific social and economic problems. Turning his attention to Europe, Derviş defends the European model of "social" democracy, which he claims is taken for granted and perhaps underappreciated. Arguing for greater integration in the face of the euro crisis, he also calls for deeper pan-European politics and economic policies. At the heart of his broader argument is a belief in the need for increased global governance to address the many issues—from the financial sector through global warming and migration—that, due to the forces of globalization, truly affect us all.

KK: Can you give me an assessment of the state in which the world finds itself from your perspective?

KD: My area of specialization is macroeconomics, growth, and world economic trends. I think one can distinguish several important trends when we look at the world economy. The first really important trend is that, after many decades, I would say a century and a half, of divergence in terms of average per capita income across countries, we've seen over roughly the past two decades a new phenomenon which we could call convergence, whereby the per capita income of the emerging market economies in particular, but lately even of less developed countries taken as a whole, has started to grow much faster than in the advanced countries.

In that sense, we've entered a new era because, since the Industrial Revolution of the early 1800s roughly to the post–Second World War decades, there had essentially been divergence. The advanced countries were growing richer, and the gap between them and the rest of the world was becoming larger. This was true, of course, during the colonial era, and it lasted until about the late 1950s. Then the phenomenon of divergence slowed, and per capita income, in aggregate, grew at roughly the same rate in the advanced countries and in the rest of the world. Then convergence really started in the late 1980s and early 1990s. Now we have per capita income in developing countries—in aggregate, again—growing at roughly two to three times the per capita income in developed economies, which changes completely the structure of growth in the world economy. Whether that will continue in the future is a big question. But I think that globalization, the ease with which technology travels across frontiers, the institutions that many of the emerging and developed countries have built—and which are stronger than they were twenty or thirty years ago—and the lessons that have been learned from policy mistakes of the past, all mean that developing countries can bring in advanced technology and actively catch up with developed countries.

KK: Would you be able to give a few examples of such policy lessons that have been learned or of instances of the successful import of technology?

KD: In terms of policies, most developing countries have opened to the world markets, facilitating foreign direct investment, importation of technology, learning, exchange of students, and much more. Of course, the Internet and the information revolution have made it even easier for information to flow. So today, in terms of knowledge and information, the world is far more connected than it has ever been. Instead of trying to build economies behind closed borders, countries, both developed and developing, are interacting with and using global markets. China is the largest success story here. This acceleration of growth is, of course, good news; if you take China, per capita income has in recent years grown at an annual rate of about 9 percent. India, which was a slow-growing economy until the mid-1980s, has also picked up, which means another 1.2 billion people benefiting from growth. Of course, I am talking here about averages, not everybody. I will come back to that because the issue of income distribution within these countries is a very important one.

Developing countries have also become increasingly dependent on trade and on international financial markets, and they've become increasingly interdependent among each other. However, while the average growth rates in developing countries are growing rapidly, that does not mean that cyclical problems do not transmit themselves across borders. We're seeing today, for instance, that the eurozone crisis is having an important effect on the whole world economy, and especially on China, which is a major exporter to Europe. Also, of course, financial markets transmit the worries of investors across international borders. There is simply more interdependence now, and it goes both ways. If there were a major crisis in China, for instance, it would now affect the whole world economy.

Another trend accompanying this restructuring of the world economy is a tendency in many countries for the income distribution to become more unequal. This is not true everywhere. It is quite clear that in many countries—very much so in the United States, the United Kingdom, China, and many others—the Gini coefficient, which is an overall measure of inequality, has increased. There are also OECD (Organization for Economic Cooperation and Development) studies that document this phenomenon.[1] Within that overall increase in inequality in many countries there is a rather dramatic phenomenon, which is the great concentration of income in the top 1 percent of the population. In the USA, which is the most accentuated example of this, the share of the top 1 percent in the late 1970s was about 8 percent of GDP; at the end of the past decade, depending on which measure you take, it was close to 20 percent. This kind of concentration at the top has not been seen since the 1920s. Things seem to be going in the same direction in many countries, but with differing speeds and at different levels. Continental Europe, for instance, has less concentration at the top, but this is changing. So this phenomenon is global and is affecting countries that until now have been more equal in their income distribution.

There is a lot of debate about the major causes of this. One factor certainly is technology. Labor-saving technology has, at least in the short term, reduced the need for labor while creating a skill premium in the workforce. Very skilled participants have a far more dramatic advantage than they did twenty or thirty years ago. The other causal phenomenon is what is called "winner-take-all" markets. As the size of markets has increased, top performers have a market or an audience of hundreds of millions and earn benefits thanks to scale effects that were not possible in the past. This includes those in management. There is a debate on how to measure the quality of management, but managers who have a reputation for being the best have salaries, bonuses, and benefits that have gone up in an unprecedented fashion. A related factor here is the growing importance of the financial sector. Its size has increased, and the scale at which it operates has multiplied. A large proportion of the top 1 percent or top 0.1 percent earners are in the financial sector. So a certain financialization of capitalism is a contributing factor to this increase in inequality.

Finally, there are political factors linked to globalization, to the fact that capital is very mobile, while labor, and particularly unskilled labor, is far less mobile. And this has led to a weakening of labor unions and of the bargaining power of labor, which no doubt has also contributed to increasing inequality. All these factors are at work, but they operate in different ways in different countries; one cannot make huge, sweeping, global generalizations. But I think one can say that there is a tendency within countries toward inequality, and that in particular there is a tendency toward income concentration at the very top of the income distribution. We have a new situation in which differences in average income across countries are becoming smaller, and if we exclude a small group of very poor countries (often conflict-ridden), the large majority of emerging countries are closing the gap with advanced countries. But when we look at the internal income distribution we find that it is becoming more unequal. These income-related developments have major geopolitical and governance implications.

KK: Address precisely what is happening with this growing inequality. One area on which you worked extensively while at the United Nations Development Program and at the World Bank is poverty and the reduction thereof. The president of the World Bank, Robert Zoellick, has said that great strides have been taken in poverty reduction. Would you agree with this assessment? And where do we fit this development into the overall picture?

KD: First, yes, I do agree with that, and I think it is very much linked to the factor I emphasized earlier, namely the very substantial acceleration of growth in a large number of developing markets. Forty years ago China was a terribly poor country; India's poverty then was even worse. Both these giant economies have been growing rapidly. Hundreds of millions of people there are close to becoming middle class. The same can be said for many Latin American countries and some African countries. So in that sense, in terms of income growth, the past few decades have seen more people moving out of poverty than perhaps in the entirety of world history.

That does not mean, of course, that poverty has disappeared. There are two reasons for persistent poverty. One is that not all countries are participating in the global convergence, often due to conflict and breakdown in governance. In a country like the Democratic Republic of Congo (DRC), for instance, we have evidence that the real income of the poorest part of the population is probably not better today than it was fifty or a hundred years ago. So there are these pockets of poverty that remain, and when you add them up they remain very important. And to these numbers you have to add all those who remain at the bottom of the income distribution in all the rapidly growing economies. India, for example, with a growth rate that has been averaging around 7 percent, still has hundreds of millions of people living below basic subsistence (the World Bank's $1.25 a day standard).[2] So yes, great strides have been made, but the fight against poverty is far from finished. And depending on what measures you take, anywhere between 700 million and two billion people can still be characterized as very poor. One important factor here is that countries where there is civil war, civil conflict, and breakdowns in governance are those that probably right now are totally unable to participate in world growth. So conflict, especially internal conflict, is one of the most important causes of persistent extreme poverty.

KK: That brings us to the issue of governance. What is your reflection on the way international institutions and organizations are addressing this problem of global governance, such as civil wars? What improvements or reforms can be made to these organizations?

KD: Progress in the most vulnerable and poorest countries is, of course, always something that depends a lot on what happens internally. But the regional and global contexts are also, of course, very important. For example, extreme fluctuations in energy or food prices, which are a minor annoyance for advanced countries, are sometimes catastrophic for countries that might depend on only one or two exports. Or, with conflicts, you might have a whole generation of children who remain outside the education system and therefore are likely forever to be unable to acquire the skills needed for a modern economy. You have whole generations that are "lost" this way. So there is much to be done by the international community, both politically and on the economic front.

Politically the United Nations remains the legitimate and overall framework for trying to prevent and reduce conflict. Even if the record of the UN is a mixed one, it does have some success stories. For example, the former secretary-general, Kofi Annan, was able to play a constructive role during the postelection crisis in Kenya in late 2007 and early 2008. Thanks to the UN's preventative diplomacy, Kenya was spared an internal conflict of the kind that other countries have seen. Sometimes the work of the UN is not visible precisely because it is preventative work no one hears about it. But there are also times when prevention fails and conflicts escalate, becoming very bloody. Such conflicts can even reach genocidal proportions, as was the case in Rwanda in 1994.

On the economic side, one area where a lot of progress has been achieved is health, particularly with respect to vaccination campaigns. Vaccination of children and the eradication of some diseases such as smallpox can be a fantastic engine for improving the health status of a population. I think if we look at the catastrophe of AIDS, which is still a major burden on humankind, the actions of the international community have been effective in terms of prevention and helping make available medicines that allow people who are affected to continue to live their lives. So in the medical sector, where you can have very focused and concentrated intervention, we have had some important successes. I think in education it is less so. There has been progress, but often the progress is quantitative rather than qualitative. We see a great increase globally in the number of children in school, but when you measure the extent of learning and capacity, you often find that many international investments have been ineffective. And of course, education and skill formation remain basic tools for pulling the poorest populations out of poverty. So I think that broadly, on the education side, international institutions have not been as successful.

And then, of course, there is general development aid, general aid to the economy. There is a big debate here. Some people claim this is not useful; some even say this is counterproductive because it generates dependence. Others say it can be useful in increasing investment, in financing infrastructure, and in jump-starting growth processes in various sectors. Appropriate measurement is very important here. For example, if you try to look just at aid, where it goes and what results it generates, it's a little bit like looking at medicine and measuring the population that takes, let's say antibiotics, and then you say that those who take antibiotics are sicker than those who don't. So you have mixed up cause and effect. Very often aid is given to those places where development is most difficult, where there is the greatest amount of poverty and the weakest governance. And if you compare those countries to others with better governance or better growth dynamics but who receive less aid, you will easily find, using the previous logic, that aid has not been effective in the former. But if you are more careful with your measurement, I think it is still fair to say that aid which is well-directed and carefully administered and protected against corrupt practices does have a significant positive effect on poverty reduction.

KK: Could you give some examples of cases where aid has been successful and where it has been a disaster in terms of poverty reduction?

KD: If you look at countries like Mozambique, Ghana, and Tanzania—these are countries that received quite a lot of aid and where development has accelerated, where governance is reasonably good, and where I think one can see positive effects of aid flows. On the other hand, if you look at all the money that was spent on the DRC, the results are nowhere to be seen. This was the case when the former dictator, Sese Seko Mobutu, as president of then-Zaire, was simply stashing away the aid he was receiving into his own accounts. You have examples of this sort also in Latin America in the past, where dictators of small countries, like Anastasio Somoza in Nicaragua, amassed great wealth for themselves and their families by diverting aid. So you have both types of examples that can be shown to have existed.

KK: How do you reconcile the nation-state with globalization? And, especially, how do you reconcile democracy (as a facet of the nation-state) with globalization in a world where, precisely due to globalization, the nation-state is quickly losing its capacity to exercise its sovereignty?

KD: I have read with great interest and admiration Dani Rodrik's latest book on the paradox of globalization and the impossible trilemma between the nation-state, democracy, and economic progress linked to globalization.[3] Now I think this is a major challenge in the sense that markets really have become global; global linkages are very strong. We saw this clearly when then-prime minister of Greece George Papandreou proposed in November 2011 a referendum to accept or reject the policy package agreed with the EU, the European Central Bank, and the IMF. Markets went crazy for twenty-four hours, and the proposed referendum was killed, both by markets and by European leaders. So you have basically global financial markets that work in minutes and days, whereas democracy is a process that needs time for discussion and interaction. And, particularly in a crisis situation, to reconcile democracy with the markets is extremely difficult. I think this is the biggest challenge for the twenty-first century.

In the twentieth century a good part of the world found a way to embed markets in democratic political institutions. This is Ruggie's "embedded liberalism," building on the fundamental concepts developed by Polanyi.[4] A balance was constructed between the state and democratically determined economic and social policies, and the quite free markets that operated to generate profits and returns for investors but also allocated resources fairly efficiently. The state acted as both a regulator and a redistributor of resources, particularly in Europe. I think this model is now under great stress, and this is part of what Rodrik's argument is all about.

Now, as markets have become global, if capital is unhappy about, for instance, taxation in a particular country, it can go to another country. Labor cannot do this, at least not unskilled labor, and migration is associated with many difficulties. This has greatly strengthened the bargaining power of capital and is one of the reasons for the deteriorating income distribution within countries that I mentioned before. So how do we get out of this dilemma? Rodrik comes to the conclusion that we have to slow down globalization in order for democratic institutions and nation-states to regain greater control over economic and distribution processes. He is no doubt right that globalization has proceeded at a pace whereby many nation-states have lost their ability to regulate and to redistribute. On the other hand, I tend to think (while I fully agree with Rodrik's diagnosis) that the forces of globalization and the political strength of global capital are so strong that it would be very difficult to attempt to slow down globalization. It would also have costs. Globalization is an engine of growth, and foreign direct investment is a carrier of technological know-how, so slowing down globalization is not cost-free.

That is why I think we now are entering an age when stronger global governance mechanisms are needed to embed the global market in a democratic human society. We see this whole dilemma being played out in Europe in a most dramatic way. In a way it's like a laboratory for the rest of the world on how to reconcile market-driven forces with social and political mechanisms that reflect democratic aspirations and legitimacy. We're in the middle of this crisis in Europe, and I don't know how it will end, but many people believe that either Europe will fall apart and go back to nation-states, or it will have to integrate much more strongly, and integrating more strongly, of course, means building supranational institutions and supranational legitimacy.

You cannot generalize from Europe to the rest of the world, but I think that, in an essential way, this same dilemma exists for the whole world. Either there will be global financial regulation that is harmonized and coordinated across borders, or the financial sector will again create major problems for the world economy. Similarly either there will be cooperation globally on limiting climate change and effective institutions that oversee and regulate the emission of greenhouse gases, or we face a truly threatening long-term trend of global warming, which in a few decades could already have very costly effects on humanity. By giving these two examples, I am trying to underline the need for global economic governance and global political cooperation and the need to somehow build a political space in the world where citizens can relate to these global mechanisms and not just view them as an intrusion, as a constraint, as an illegitimate technocratic diktat coming from some unelected officials somewhere in an international bureaucracy. This is the big challenge.

KK: We do not seem to be moving in that direction, when you look at elections in Europe, for example. What meaning do you attribute to this rise of the right in Europe?

KD: Europe is a laboratory, and the debate about what will happen in Europe is open. But it is clear that if Europe wants to come out of this crisis, it either has to go back to a system of nation-states, losing a lot of the advantages provided by the European Union, or it has to integrate much more. The problem is that politics remains very local, whereas many of the problems we are talking about are regional or global. That's the main challenge now: how to build a bridge between local politics that determine election outcomes and the perception of global problems and possible solutions to global problems. I can't say that I have a clear answer. Language here is also a major problem. I once met a Greek EU politician who said that the fundamental reason why we cannot build a more integrated Europe is that a Greek politician cannot go to Berlin and address a German audience in German and a German politician cannot go to Portugal and make a political speech in Portuguese. The elite can communicate among themselves, but when it comes to political campaigning, to really linking up with the majority of citizens, the language barrier is an important one, and it's not clear how you might have a pan-European political party without having pan-European politicians, and these politicians would need to be attractive in several countries. There have been very few such figures. I think of Joschka Fischer as a pan-European politician, but it's hard to come up with examples or models.

KK: How do you project that to the rest of the world?

KD: That becomes an even greater challenge. But there are some interesting examples. In principle the secretary-general of the UN can, and often does, have a global appeal that is quite strong. President Obama was received like a rock star when he toured Europe as a candidate in 2008.

KK: You have long been an advocate of social democracy. Do you see it making a comeback in Europe? And how might it address the unemployment situation as the continent goes through a fiscal crisis? Can social-democratic means stimulate growth?

KD: First, I'd like to stress that when one looks at the past fifty years or so, social democracy in Europe has been very successful. It has generated societies where there is a great deal of social security, where there is universal health coverage, where education is strong, and it was able to combine this with strong market economies, good export performance, and fairly decent growth. In fact it is that social-liberal synthesis that social democracy produced which, I think, in the end made it obvious that it was a superior form of social organization to what existed in Eastern Europe and contributed a lot to the final downfall of the centralized communist model. Many things that social democracy achieved are now taken for granted in Europe. And there is something else that is taken for granted and that is that there is peace on a continent which for many centuries not only tore itself apart but also exported its wars.

Having said that, I believe that social democracy now faces a huge challenge because the emergence of very competitive economies in the developing world, globalization, and scale effects all mean that European countries need to adjust to this new world. They also have to adjust to an important demographic transition, which increases very significantly the cost of retirement and health care in old age. This is, of course, shared by some other countries, such as Japan. I don't think that the fundamental model that European social democracy developed, namely the combination of flexible markets with a redistributive state, is invalid. I think it is a model that remains viable and, as shown in some countries, like the Scandinavian countries, whether or not they are now governed by social democratic parties, a very generous social system can be retained while having a well-performing economy. But the model needs major renovations and major additions. First, Europe has to keep climbing the technological ladder, and it has to make sure that as developing countries take larger market shares in many traditional capital goods and manufacturing activities, Europe must remain focused on new technologies—perhaps on clean and green technologies that are going to be an important part of the next decades' industrial transformation in the world. Instead of trying to keep uncompetitive industries alive, I think Europe has to move forward in restructuring itself and basing its growth on the most advanced technologies and most skill-intensive technologies. In general, that's true for the more advanced countries as a whole.

I also think that when it comes to this whole issue of retirement and managing demographic change, one has to be very innovative and creative. There is no way that a society in which the average life span reaches ninety or ninety-five can have a situation where people retire at sixty and then for thirty or thirty-five years are supported by the rest of society. When people lived to sixty-five or seventy, it was a different situation. Now that does not mean that people who worked forty to forty-five years should not have an easier time later in their life, and I think retirement has to be flexible. The work week might be shortened gradually, and in many professions it might be quite possible to work for three days a week rather than five. Older people have a wealth of experience to share with younger workers. All this has to be, I think, flexible, with a lot of choice, and based on partnerships between the public and the private sectors. There is a huge area of reform there that relates to people working in their sixties which is needed in Europe and where I think social democracy can invent new ways of doing things. Actually I believe that if people can have part-time productive work, this will contribute to the happiness of sixty- and sixty-five-year-olds rather than subtract from their happiness. But you also cannot ask people who have worked for forty or forty-five years to continue working for another five or ten years at the same rate and in the same way as they worked before. That kind of compromise is one of the keys for social-democratic success in Europe.

Finally, integration. I think the current financial crisis confronts Europe—and particularly the eurozone—with a very stark choice. The common currency cannot be managed without a common fiscal policy, a common financial sector with deposit insurance at the European level, and with a central bank that is ready to intervene when needed to provide liquidity (rather like the Federal Reserve does in America). You cannot deprive a country of a central bank. Every area with a common currency needs a central bank that stands behind that currency and the regions of that common currency area. I'm talking about a framework, of course. I'm not saying a central bank needs to provide inflationary finance or bail out large government deficits. But it has to be there to backstop the currency and backstop the economy, as it does in America. And I think this reality means that Europe needs to be much more integrated.

This probably is—or should be—the number one priority for European social democrats: finding a way to define the European model for the twenty-first century based on solidarity, markets being regulated by the state to provide dynamism but at the same time being moderated by a democratic process, figuring out how to do this in a globalized world, how to do it as Europe rather than as Italy, Spain, or Germany alone, and how to explain to citizens that the success of Europe depends on that kind of integration with that kind of model. I think if the European social democrats get together and adopt that as their platform and fully commit themselves to this, they could have another wave of success. Indeed they could save Europe. Why not, for example, get in the habit of having social democrats from other countries on the executive committees of various states' social democratic parties? It might be difficult to introduce them into parliaments, but maybe you could have national lists on which a contingent is given to sisters and brothers from neighboring countries.

KK: Is there something the globe could learn from a European model of social democracy that is reforming and restructuring itself?

KD: I think achieving the kind of political space I'm talking about globally would be very difficult. The secretary-general of the UN is the kind of position that could have a strong global appeal. But I think for the kind of political cooperation that I mentioned we first have to develop some regional examples of this. Europe is a good example, and Europe should be able to do this. But Latin America as well may be an example where this is feasible. The Arab countries hopefully might be able to achieve it. And in Asia there are cooperation structures that could evolve in that direction. I don't think these cooperative structures should be seen as an alternative to universal structures such as the UN, IMF, World Bank, or World Trade Organization. These are all needed. But I think the political energy for supranational dimensions of politics has to come first from the regional level. And Europe here again, because it has achieved quite a lot despite its problems, could be a leader.

WHAT is needed are regulations and rules and norms that are regional and then become global. It is very hard for 192 countries at the UN to negotiate. It might be easier for the United States, Europe, an Asian economic community, a Latin American economic community, and an African community (and Africa needs this kind of integration very much) to work together in a more practical way. There has to be harmonization of financial regulation; there has to be an approach to taxation that doesn't allow capital to always move away as soon as taxes rise or to restructure itself in such a way as to minimize tax payments despite large profits. There have to be ways in which the international community jointly manages migration. Migration is a positive thing, but it has to be managed. The adjustment costs, the political problems that it can generate have to be foreseen and managed together. So there are many ways in which I think international cooperation can be strengthened, but as I said, it is easier to try these things out at the regional level first. This is not to say it will not be difficult, but I wouldn't give up on it. I think the twenty-first century may well see this kind of politics finally emerging from the old-style, purely nation-state-focused model.

KK: To move from Europe to the Middle East, what do you make of the Arab Spring and this "Arab struggle"? To what extent is there a relationship between these movements and the globalization that we've been talking about in a region of the world that seems to have been left behind in terms of globalization?

KD: It is true that in some ways the Arab region has followed global trends more slowly, although in many ways, through financial markets and through oil, it is a region that is very integrated. I believe that certain basic human rights and certain basic democratic aspirations, including economic aspirations to a decent life, are really universal, and the communications revolution and the Internet make it much harder to isolate one part of the world from other parts. If a regime is authoritarian and produces very good economic and social results, then I think it can last for a long time, and we have some examples of this, for instance in Singapore. But most of the "Arab regimes" were authoritarian without producing decent results for the majority of their people. I think this just cannot go on.

There is, of course, also the issue in many Arab countries of borders that were created by imperial, post–Second World War powers which don't necessarily reflect the social, national, religious, and ethnic structures that exist (which is obviously true of Africa as well). Finally, when you speak of the Arab world, there is an amazing dichotomy between the oil exporters, who have extreme wealth and are benefiting hugely from the global economy, and countries that are not oil exporters that are much poorer and have the greatest frustrations in terms of their economic aspirations. If there was more cooperation among the Arab states, where money could be invested on a larger scale, especially from oil-rich states into poorer ones, progress would be much faster and easier. But, of course, to achieve this you need governance and investor and social confidence. Greater integration has a lot of potential in the Arab world, but it can be realized only if there is more political cooperation.

The Arab Spring has shown us that there is such as a thing as "the Arab world." It is not just a group of countries. Of course, they are very different countries, but it is not by accident that these political movements are occurring almost simultaneously throughout the Arab world. I believe that, in the medium term, we will see greater integration in the Arab world, and that is actually a very important thing for better economic performance.

21

"Because the Chinese growth model became so successful in ensuring catch-up development it has become extremely appealing in the developing world"

VLADIMIR POPOV

in conversation with Piotr Dutkiewicz

Vladimir Popov is an interregional adviser in the United Nations Department of Economic and Social Affairs and professor emeritus at the New Economic School in Moscow.

Photo courtesy of Vladimir Popov.

Vladimir Popov brings decades of policymaking and analytical experience to bear on the current state of the global economy. He argues that while the global economy is highly unstable, capitalism itself is not in crisis. In fact he suggests that there have been periods in recent history when socioeconomic instability has been greater than today. On the other hand, he points to the dramatic decrease in the power of labor and growing social inequality in developed and developing world, as well as the continuing underregulation of finance, as worrisome aspects of the contemporary state of Western capitalism. Looking to the developing world, Popov sees a number of rising powers, not only emerging economies but potential challengers to the international political world order. Chief among these is China, which Popov suggests may well begin to act as not only an economic but a social and governance model for a number of developing states. He is, however, less optimistic about Russia, which he feels has lost both domestic developmental momentum and international clout. He predicts that future economic miracles are going to emerge in East and South Asia and in the Middle East and North Africa (Turkey, Egypt, Iran), not in Latin America and sub-Saharan Africa. Popov's is a measured assessment of the current state of the world: not undergoing a systemic crisis even though approaching one.

PD: The global economic situation is visibly unstable. At the same time, the ideas guiding our economic and social policies are focused on the world of yesterday, not of tomorrow, regardless of the continuing systemic instability. There are also the same taboos and "no go" areas (most glaringly, continuing opposition to serious international regulation of derivatives and speculative investment). Can you explain this?

VP: The world is unstable, of course, but not to the point that there is a crisis of global capitalism. It will come eventually and it is pretty inevitable, because there is a beginning and an end to every social system, but for capitalism this may be not tomorrow. The inability to agree about the regulations of the financial markets may be a mistake, but it may be an optimal strategy, at least from the point of view of large corporations and governments. Even in most democratic countries, the best interests of the voters are not necessarily always reflected in governments' policies; it is the interests of large capital that have greater weight in the priorities of national governments. Financial capital apparently considers the opportunity to profit from "bubbles" and speculation a greater benefit than the costs associated with the risk of social unrest due to instability and social injustice.

PD: But what is financially beneficial in the short term, as you are saying, can in the long term be quite damaging to capital itself. My question, then, is whether you really think that capital is such a short-term-perspective player?

VP: I think it really is. It was proven more than once that capital has a short-term planning horizon. Class conflicts of the nineteenth and twentieth century leading to revolutions and the two world wars that took so many lives had the potential of eliminating capitalism (if not the whole civilization) completely. But the politicians were taking these risks. The story of the recent recession and, in fact, of each and every financial bubble since the Tulip Mania of 1637, is quite similar. There were and are relatively simple measures to prevent the formation of bubbles (government regulations of the financial sector inside countries and control over capital flows between countries), but after the strengthening of regulations following crises (say, the enactment of the Glass-Steagall Act of 1933 after the Great Depression) they were relaxed and then abolished under pressure by interested lobbies—in this case, the financial sector. In a similar vein, fifty years from now researchers will write PhDs on what prevented governments in the early twenty-first century from agreeing on measures to cut emissions of greenhouse gasses and to prevent global warming.

PD: Maybe, then, social inequalities trigger greater social and political instability?

VP: In recent years, instability and social inequalities have been growing, but it is important to put the issue into historical perspective. In 1982, for instance, things looked much worse for global capitalism than they do today, even worse than they did during the Global Recession of 2008–9. In terms of average per capita income, the world is at the highest point ever: world average income per capita in 2012 exceeded the all-time high level before 2008–9. Profit margins and the rate of profit in the United States in 2012 exceeded the level of the past fifty years—they were higher only in the early 1960s—and they keep growing. The unemployment rate in the United States reached a peak for the postwar period in 1982 at 9.7 percent, while in 2013 it fell below 8 percent. Even in 2009 it only approached, but did not exceed, the level of 1982. It is true that real wages in the United States are still below their level of the early 1970s, but this is exactly the reason why profits are so high: what is bad for the workers is good for capital.

Income inequalities within countries, measured by the share of the richest 1 percent (or 5 percent or 10 percent) of the population in total income or by Gini coefficient of income distribution have been growing for over thirty years, but in most countries are still below the levels that existed before the Second World War (which led to the emergence of the world socialist system and to the dramatic decline in the inequalities within countries). To give one example, in the United States the share of the nation's total income held by the top (richest) 10 percent of the population was 40 to 45 percent in the 1920s–30s, fell to 30 to 35 percent in the 1940s–80s, and started to increase again since the early 1980s, reaching 45 percent in 2005.

In the 1970s and early 1980s there was high, double-digit inflation in major Western countries that followed two oil price shocks—that of 1973 and 1979—in addition to slow growth, so-called stagflation. The first oil price shock followed the Arab-Israeli War of 1973, the second one—the Iranian Revolution, both events associated with the strengthening of anti-Western sentiments in developing countries. Plus there was the Portuguese Revolution of Red Carnations of 1974 and the subsequent collapse of the last colonial empire, and a humiliating defeat of the United States in Vietnam in 1975.

PD: Is there a middle ground between capital and labor, or does the logic of capital preclude that?

VP: I think there is a middle ground, if there are proper checks and balances that preclude capital from extorting too much profit at the expense of social stability. If there are no checks and balances, capital can easily undermine its own foundations. As Marx says in *Capital*, (quoting a contemporary British author) "With adequate profit, capital is very bold. A certain 10% (profit) will ensure its employment anywhere; 20% certain will produce eagerness; 50%, positive audacity; 100% will make it ready to trample on all human laws; 300%, and there is not a crime at which it will scruple, nor a risk it will not run, even to the chance of its owner being hanged."[1] Checks and balances in different periods came in the form of the workers movement, two destructive world wars, the Russian socialist revolution of 1917, the Great Depression of the 1930s, the expansion of the socialist system after the Second World War, the Chinese Liberation of 1949, and the collapse of the colonial system in the 1960s. Income inequalities were rather low before 1500 but increased since then, until the twentieth century, and started to decline thereafter.[2] The share of the top 10 percent of households in total income in twenty-two countries, mostly Western, in 1870–1917 was normally 40 to 50 percent, but it decreased to 31 percent in 1945 and to 27 percent in 1981. Since the socialist countries stopped catching up with the West (this happened in the 1970s), the gap between the rich and the poor within Western countries themselves started to increase. And it keeps growing and probably will continue to grow until some kind of dramatic event plays the role of checks and balances and reverses the trend.

PD: What kind of big picture of capital-labor relation is emerging from your analysis?

VP: The big picture is this: in the early 1980s the relative strength of capital versus labor in Western countries and the strength of Western countries themselves versus Second and Third World (socialist and developing) countries were at their lowest levels in the twentieth century. This produced a counterreaction in the form of the conservative wave in Western countries in the 1980s. After Thatcher and Reagan (early 1980s) and especially after the collapse of the Berlin Wall (1989) and the USSR (1991), world capital started to increase its share in national income at the expense of labor; there was high unemployment and no growth of wages despite constant increases in productivity. Income inequalities were on the rise. Such trends are good for profits, and profits are good for capital accumulation, but they also lead to increased social tension and the risk of unrest.

PD: WHAT about the advancement of East Asian countries? They were quite successful in their catch-up development in the 1950s and 1960s, and some of them even joined "the rich countries club."

VP: True, whereas inside countries income inequalities have increased since the 1980s, between countries there was a convergence going on. Since 1950 the ratio of income per capita in developing countries is getting higher compared to developed countries. This is a reversal of a divergence trend of 1500–1950, when the income gap between the North and the South kept growing. So far, only five countries or regions that were previously developing managed to join the rich country club: Japan, South Korea, Taiwan, Hong Kong, Singapore. But in coming decades, many more developing countries, especially in East Asia, will probably do the same. After the collapse of the USSR, the position of the South versus the North deteriorated, and the cause of a new world economic order conducive to the catch-up development of the South experienced a setback. But not for long. The rise of China, India, and other developing countries strengthened the bargaining power of the South, filling the gap that emerged after the breakdown of the Soviet Union.

PD: What are the implications of the rise of China for the world?

VP: Usually these implications are seen in forthcoming geopolitical shifts, in the emerging shortage of resources leading to the new increase in raw material prices, and so on. But there may be less expected and more far-reaching consequences as well.

First, the rise of China, if it continues, would become the turning point for the world economy because for the first time in history a successful economic development on a major scale would be based on an indigenous (not Western-type) economic model. Because the Chinese

growth model became so successful in ensuring catch-up development, there is no surprise that it has become extremely appealing in
the developing world. The attractiveness of the Chinese model of economic growth today could be compared with the popularity of the
Soviet model of catch-up development in the Third World in the 1960s.
Even though the Soviet model collapsed, the Chinese model became the
logical and natural heir of the Soviet model; it is no longer a centrally
planned economy, but it is by no means the model of a liberalized market economy that is recommended by the advocates of the Washington
and even post-Washington consensus.

Second, the rise of China can lead to the profound reform of the
world economic order and international relations. Trade protectionism,
industrial policy, undervaluation of the exchange rate via accumulation of foreign exchange reserves (also, as argued, a variety of export-
oriented industrial policy), and control over international capital flows
can become legitimate tools of catch-up development. There may be a
new regime of protection of intellectual property rights and technology transfers, new regulations for international trade in energy and
resources, new rules for international migration, new agreements about
cutting emissions of pollutants (reconsideration of the Kyoto Protocol),
and much more.[3]

Besides, the principles of international relations can change radically as well. The "Beijing consensus" may not yet be a rigorous term,
but it is clear that the Chinese approach to international politics (no
interference into domestic affairs, no military interventions, no trade
embargoes) provides the developing world with a real alternative for
building relations with other countries.[4] China rejects the use of force,
embargoes, and sanctions in international politics nearly as a matter of
principle. Even in its relations with Taiwan, China was always pushing
for wider economic and cultural exchanges, whereas Taiwan's authorities resisted. The new rules of international relations may (1) explicitly
limit the use of force only to cases of severe violations of nonpolitical
rights (i.e., mass repressions, hunger, ethnic violence, and so on) and
prohibit the use of force against liberal authoritarian regimes (just for

the sake of "establishing democracy") and (2) prohibit unilateral military interventions (without the consent of the UN).

These less expected consequences of China's rise could create favorable conditions for the catch-up development of the South. Now, in the twenty-first century, the rise of China would make the dirigisme-based model of development not only attractive but also legitimate, and will create a new international economic climate favoring such a catch-up. We may well witness "the triumphal march" of the Chinese model in the South. Not all developing countries have the same institutional capacity as China—the necessary component of the successful non-Western growth model—but many do, and those who do not would eventually be compelled to move in the direction of limiting inequality and strengthening institutional capacity, even though in China itself high income inequalities threaten to undermine its strong institutional capacity.

PD: Moving westward with our conversation, we have the huge economies of Russia and the EU. Let's start with Russia. There are very contradictory messages coming from Russia watchers about the state of the economy and the state of the state. Can you share your thoughts on this issue?

VP: The USSR ambitiously compared itself to the United States and was proud of its status as the second superpower (aspiring to become the first superpower). Time changed the yardsticks for comparison. We live in an age of diminished expectations. Russia today has to compare itself to *other developing countries*. Russia is richer than sub-Saharan Africa and South Asia and is roughly at par in terms of per capita income with Latin America, the Middle East and North Africa, and East Asian countries. Life expectancy in Russia is lower than in Latin America, the Middle East and North Africa, and East Asian countries, and distribution of income is often worse (except for Latin American countries), but levels of education are still higher, and recently institutional capacity has increased to virtually late-Soviet levels (higher than in Latin

America and Africa, although not as high as in East Asia and the Middle East and North Africa).

PD: The time comparison may be less flattering for Russia. Which is or would be the most successful of the past three centuries for Russia?

VP: According to one journalist, nineteenth-century Russia can definitely be proud of great Russian literature and arts, Pushkin and Dostoyevsky, Repin and Tchaikovsky. There were also things Russia should be ashamed of in that century: serfdom and the tsarist regime, the Pale of Settlement for the Jews, and poverty of the peasantry. What could Russia have been proud of in the twentieth century? The attempt to build a just society: the first state of the workers and peasants in the world, free education and health care, elimination of illiteracy, avant-garde arts, the defeat of fascism, the achievements in space exploration, Nobel Prize winners and ballet. What should Russia of the twentieth century be ashamed of: Stalin's purges and labor camps, the mass famine of 1932–33, authoritarianism, and oppression of dissidents.

What should Russia be ashamed of in the twenty-first century: corruption and bribery of state officials, oligarchic capitalism, deindustrialization of the economy and decline in R&D, income inequalities, deterioration of health and education, increase in mortality, the clericalization of the society, and cultural degradation. What can Russia be proud of in the twenty-first century: nothing. It is a second-rate, normal developing country. In no area is it number one. It is behind this or that nation in each and every field. And it lacks the ambition to become number one. This is an extreme view, of course, but there is truth in it.

PD: This expression "normal developing country" is from the article by Shleifer and Treisman? You seem to agree with their analysis?

VP: In 2004-5 Andrew Shleifer and Daniel Treisman published an article titled "A Normal Country: Russia after Communism."[5] They compared Russia to Brazil, China, India, Turkey, and other developing countries and argued that in terms of crime, income inequalities, corruption, macroeconomic instability, and other typical curses of the Third World, Russia is by far not the worst—somewhere in the middle of the list, better than Nigeria, worse than China. In short, a *normal* developing country. They were right in the sense that Russia really degraded to the status of a normal developing country during the 1990s.

PD: What is a "developing country," then? Can you compare Ghana and Russia, Somalia and Russia without being frivolous?

VP: For the purposes of our conversation, let us define a developing country as one with per capita income below, say, 50 percent of the average OECD (Organization for Economic Cooperation and Development) level (roughly 30 percent of the U.S. level). These countries are "developing," that is, catching up with the developed countries. There are oil-rich countries, such as the Persian Gulf States and Equatorial Guinea, that should be considered developed according to this criteria, and they are starting to resemble developed countries according to other criteria as well: education levels, life expectancy, productivity levels in nonresource industries, and technological sophistication.

PD: So what about the USSR?

VP: The USSR was an *abnormal* developing country. The Soviet Union put the first man into space, had about twenty Nobel Prize winners in science and literature. Out of about forty living laureates of the Fields Medal (awarded since 1936 and recognized as the "Nobel Prize in mathematics"), eight come from the former Soviet Union (which had about 5 percent of the world population). The USSR had universal free health care and education (the best among developing countries), low income inequalities, and relatively low crime and corruption. By 1965 Soviet life expectancy increased to seventy years, only two years less than in the United States even though per capita income was only 20–25 percent of the U.S. level.[6]

THE market reforms of the early 1990s caused an unprecedented reduction of output and living standards. From 1989 to 1998 Russia experienced a transformational recession: GDP fell to 55 percent of the pre-recession 1989 level. In 1999–2008 the Russian economy was recovering at a rate of about 7 percent a year and nearly reached the pre-recession peak of 1989. But in 2009, due to the collapse of oil prices and the outflow of capital caused by the world recession, Russian GDP fell again by 8 percent. Now the pre-recession (1989) level of GDP was surpassed only in 2012. For over two decades there was no improvement in living standards for most Russians.

The transition to the market economy in the 1990s brought about the dismantling of the state. The provision of all public goods, from health care to law and order, fell dramatically. The shadow economy, which the most generous estimates place at 10 to 15 percent of the GDP under Leonid Brezhnev, grew to 50 percent of the GDP by the mid-1990s. In 1980–85 the Soviet Union was placed in the middle of a list of fifty-four countries rated according to their level of corruption, with a bureaucracy cleaner than that of Italy, Greece, Portugal, South Korea, and practically all the developing countries. In 1996, after the establishment of a market economy and the victory of democracy, Russia came in forty-eighth in the same list of fifty-four countries, between India and Venezuela.

Russia became a typical "petrostate." Few specialists would call the USSR a resource-based economy, but the Russian industrial structure changed a lot after the transition to the market. Basically the 1990s were a period of rapid deindustrialization and "resourcialization" of the Russian economy, and the growth of world energy prices since 1999 seems to have reinforced this trend. The share of output of major resource industries (fuel, energy, metals) in total industrial output increased from about 25 percent to over 50 percent by the mid-1990s and stayed at this high level thereafter. This was partly the result of changing price ratios (greater price increases in resource industries), but also the real growth rates of output were lower in the nonresource sector.

The share of mineral products, metals, and diamonds in Russian exports increased from 52 percent in 1990 (USSR) to 67 percent in 1995 and to 81 percent in 2007, whereas the share of machinery and equipment in exports fell from 18 percent in 1990 (USSR) to 10 percent in 1995 and to below 6 percent in 2007. The share of R&D spending in GDP was 3.5 percent in the late 1980s in the USSR but fell to about 1 percent in Russia today. (By comparison, China sits at 1.3 percent; the United States, Korea, and Japan at 2 to 3 percent; Finland at 4 percent; and Israel at 5 percent.) So from this angle as well Russia really looks like a normal resource-abundant developing country.

PD: Russia has one of the most sophisticated arms industries. This requires high levels of coordination and sophistication in several industrial areas simultaneously, from machinery to manufacturing to software, and so on. No other developing country has a similar capacity.

VP: That statement would be true with respect to the USSR: no other developing country had such a capacity to produce sophisticated weapons, so the USSR was an abnormal developing country. But we can hardly say this today about Russia, which cannot even produce its own drones, the staple equipment for future conflicts. In most areas China is at least as technologically advanced as Russia; it produces nuclear weapons and space rockets, has its own Beidou Navigation System (an analogue of America's GPS, Russia's GLONASS, and Europe's Galileo) that will become global soon. A plant in Shenyang previously was assembling and now produces Russian SU-27 fighter jets. In some areas, such as electronics and information technology, including supercomputers, China is apparently more advanced than Russia. In other areas, such as wind energy, ultra-high-voltage power transmission, and clean coal technology, China is not only ahead of Russia, but is the *world* leader. And, of course, in international students' mathematics and science competition, China comes first most often, whereas Russia is not even among the top ten.

PD: What about society? Russia is hardly comparable with Nigeria or Sudan along the main social indicators.

VP: Maybe not with Nigeria and Sudan, but the comparison with other developing countries in terms of, say, life expectancy is not flattering for Russia: sixty-seven to sixty-eight years in 2010–12 against seventy-five to eighty years in Albania, Argentina, Bahrain, Barbados, Belize, Brunei, Chile, Costa Rica, Cuba, Ecuador, Jordan, Mexico, Oman, Qatar, and Uruguay. The deterioration in the social area was truly unprecedented; many authors wrote about this, including you and me.[7] Income inequalities increased greatly: the Gini coefficient increased from 0.26 in 1986 to 0.4 in 2000 and 0.42 in 2007 (where it remained in 2011). But the inequalities at the very top increased much faster: in 1995 there was no person in Russia worth over $1 billion; in 2007, according to *Forbes*, Russia had fifty-three billionaires (third place after the United States and Germany), and in 2011 the number of billionaires in Russia increased to 101—more than in Germany but less than in China, where the number increased from twenty in 2007 to 116 in 2011 (plus thirty-six in Hong Kong and twenty-five in Taiwan). Russian billionaires, however, had more wealth than Chinese—about $500 billion, or one-third of annual GDP.

Worst of all, the criminalization of Russian society grew dramatically in the 1990s. Crime rose gradually in the Soviet Union since the mid-1960s, but after the collapse of the USSR there was an unprecedented surge. In just several years in the early 1990s, crime and murder rates doubled and reached one of the highest levels in the world. By the mid-1990s the murder rate stood at over 30 per 100,000 inhabitants (against one to two persons in Western and Eastern Europe, Canada, China, Japan, Mauritius, and Israel). Only two countries in the world (not counting some war-torn collapsed states in developing countries, where there are no reliable statistics anyway) had higher murder rates: South Africa and Colombia. And in Brazil and Mexico the rate was two times lower. Even the U.S. murder rate, the highest in the developed world—6 to 7 per 100,000 inhabitants—paled in comparison with the Russian rate.

The Russian rate of deaths from external causes (accidents, murders, and suicides) by the beginning of the twenty-first century had sky-rocketed to 245 per 100,000 inhabitants. This was higher than in any of the 187 countries covered by World Health Organization estimates in 2002. To be sure, in the 1980s murder, suicide, and accidental death rates were quite high in Russia, Ukraine, Belarus, Latvia, Estonia, Moldova, and Kazakhstan; they were several times higher than in other former Soviet republics and in Eastern European countries. However, they were roughly comparable to those of other countries with the same level of development. In the 1990s these rates rapidly increased, far outstripping those in the rest of the world. The mortality rate grew from 10 per 1,000 in 1990 to 16 in 1994, and stayed at a level of 14 to 16 per 1,000 until 2011. This was a true mortality crisis, a unique case in history, when mortality rates increased by 60 percent in just five years without wars, epidemics, or eruptions of volcanoes. Never in the postwar era had Russia experienced such a high mortality rate as in the 1990s. Even in 1950–53, during the last years of Stalin's regime, with a high death rate in the labor camps and the consequences of wartime malnutrition and wounds, the mortality rate was only 9 to 10 per 1,000.

To understand Russia today one has to evaluate the record of the past twenty-five years. In the late 1980s, during Gorbachev's perestroika, the Soviet Union was aspiring to join the club of rich democratic nations but instead degraded in the next decade to the position of a *normal* developing country that is considered neither democratic nor capable of engineering a growth miracle. For some outsiders a normal developing country may look better than the ominous superpower posing a threat to Western values. The insiders, however, feel differently. Most Russians want to find a way to modernize the country to make it prosperous and democratic. But they also feel that something went very wrong during the transition; the policies and political leaders of the 1990s are totally discredited. And that is why Putin-Medvedev's policy received over 50 percent approval ratings, even in the midst of economic recession.

PD: So there are no reasons for optimism? Can we try to find some?

VP: There are some. By 2012 the economy finally surpassed the pre-recession level of 1989. Personal consumption on average was nearly 50 percent higher than in the late 1980s, but government consumption of goods and services was about the same, whereas investment was only 50 percent of the level of the late 1980s. Unemployment dropped from 13 percent in 1999 to 6 percent in 2007, and after an increase during the 2008–9 recession (to 8.4 percent) dropped again to 6 percent in 2012. Inflation declined from over 2,500 percent in 1992 and 84 percent in 1998 to single digits in 2009–12. (In fact monetary policy in recent years is excessively restrictive and is damaging economic growth.) The budget deficit turned into a surplus in 2000–2008, and government revenues and expenditures as a percentage of GDP began, ever so slowly, to rise; foreign debt as a percentage of GDP decreased, capital flight decelerated, and currency reserves expanded. During and after the recession of 2008–9 the consolidated government budget, as could have been expected, went into the red, but it returned to balance in 2011; foreign exchange reserves fell from nearly $600 billion in 2008 to $380 billion in mid-2009, but later recovered to about $500 billion and stayed at this level well into 2013.

But the most important result of the past twelve years is probably this: the growth of the economy and the stability of leadership have finally led to increased order and an improvement in the social climate. The number of murders, having hit a sky-high peak in 2002, dropped back down by over 50 percent since then; the number of suicides has also been on the decline; the birth rate, which struck a fifty-year minimum in 1999, has begun to rise, as has the number of registered marriages (although this is partly a result of the demographic wave of the 1970s); the divorce rate, having reached a maximum after many years, is now on the down slope. The Russian population, which fell from 148.5 million in 1993 to 141.9 million in 2009, started to grow in 2010 for the first time in nearly twenty years. In effect, this means that Russia is gradually stepping away from the edge of the abyss of anarchy and chaos, into which it systematically descended in the 1990s. Income inequalities have not grown since 2007.

These improvements in the social sector in the past few years are most encouraging. Economic growth and low inflation alone cannot prevent the disintegration of the country if social inequality and crime increase. Building the vertical of power and intensifying centralization may not be able to stop the collapse of the state, if they don't bring about stronger law and order and limit the shadow economy. In fact Putin has been criticized precisely for taking all power into his own hands without greater order resulting. Well, now it seems that the first signs have appeared of a real, rather than an ephemeral, stabilization: the crime and suicide rates are falling, the mortality rate has leveled out, the number of marriages and the birth rate are rising, and the divorce rate is down.

PD: What are the most important economic policy mistakes in Russia today? Is there a chance that the Russian bear will become an Asian tiger in terms of economic growth?

VP: The current real exchange rate of the ruble (the ratio of domestic to world prices) is too high. Therefore a drop in world energy prices could easily provoke a new currency crisis and interrupt economic recovery, despite what would seem to be the major contribution to stability provided by the large currency reserves. Domestic fuel and energy prices remain several-fold lower than world levels, creating incentives for inefficient energy consumption and the highest energy intensity in the world. Unlike in eastern European countries and many of the former Soviet republics, where the price of fuel and energy is already approaching world levels, the restructuring of the Russian economy is still far from complete.

What Russia should have done in past years was slowly devalue the exchange rate of the ruble, accumulating reserves even faster or spending these reserves on imports of machinery and equipment, and at the same time increasing domestic prices for oil, gas, and electricity, while compensating the producers for losses from the rising cost of energy with the benefits of stronger competitiveness resulting from the depreciating ruble rate. This could have increased the savings and investment rate, especially if supplemented by the expansion of budgetary financed investment into infrastructure. However, such a policy is not even on the drawing board for the moment. Besides, macroeconomic policy is too restrictive. Russia brought inflation down to single digits during the economic recession of 2008–9 and subsequent recovery. This policy is hindering economic growth.[8]

When in 2000 Putin became president for the first time, I wrote a policy memo entitled "Why the Russian Economy Is Unlikely to Become a New 'Asian Tiger.'" In particular, I argued that there was a need to increase government investment into infrastructure (to trigger the increase in private investment) and to maintain the low exchange rate of the ruble in order to promote export-oriented development. I wrote:

> At the moment there are no indications that the new Russian government has the courage required to break this vicious circle of populist policies, and to embark on a new export oriented growth strategy. Quick progress in adopting the outlined measures does not seem to be politically feasible, but some steps in this direction are more or less inevitable, especially in the longer term. One can be fairly certain, however, that rapid economic growth without major progress in most, if not in all of the above-mentioned policy areas is extremely unlikely.[9]

Today this diagnosis and these policy proposals are still relevant.

PD: So what is the conclusion: Which development path is more advantageous for less developed countries, and how do they get onto and stay on this path? Where is fate, and where is choice?

VP: There are two groups of developing countries that emerged out of the era of colonialism. The first one—Latin America, the Russian Empire, and sub-Saharan Africa—tried to replicate the Western exit from the Malthusian trap by destroying traditional institutions (agricultural community). This group of countries experienced an immediate increase in income differentiation, a rise in savings and investment, and in the growth of productivity, but at the price of rising social inequality, deterioration of institutional capacities, and worsening of starting positions for catch-up development.[10]

Other developing countries (in East Asia, South Asia, and the Middle East and North Africa) were less affected by colonialism and managed to retain their traditional institutions. This delayed the transition to modern economic growth until the mid-twentieth century but preserved good starting positions for economic growth: low inequality and strong institutions. Eventually slow technical progress allowed them to find another (and less painful) exit from the Malthusian trap. Increased income permitted the share of investment in GDP to rise without a major increase in income inequality, worsening of institutional capacity, and decrease in life expectancy.

China and Russia are examples of countries that have taken these different development paths. The roots of the impressive long-term performance of China lie in the exceptional continuity of the Chinese civilization, the oldest in the world that managed to preserve its uniqueness and traditions without major interruptions. I am arguing that institutional continuity is more conducive to growth than attempts to replace existing institutions by allegedly more advanced institutions imported from abroad. Like Russia in 1917, China reestablished collectivist institutions in 1949 as a response to the failure of Westernization. Unlike Russia after 1991, China in 1979–2012 managed to preserve "Asian values" institutions that are based on the priority of community interests over the interests of the individual. However, the rapid increase in income inequality since 1985 could be a factor leading to weakening of collectivist institutions, which is the single most important threat to the continuation of fast economic growth in China.

PD: Are you saying that everything depends on objective circumstances that no policymaker can change and that policies that can be consciously chosen do not matter?

VP: Whether we try to explain differences in Chinese and Russian economic performance recently, since the start of market reforms in China (1979) and Russia (1989), or to explain differences in economic performance under central planning (China in 1949–79 and Russia in 1917/29–91), variations in trajectories of institutional development turn out to be a crucial factor. This is not to say that these trajectories totally predetermine all economic outcomes; other factors, including good and bad policies, certainly do play a role. But, as the saying goes, there is nothing more endogenous than government policy; it is not easy to have good policies with bad institutions. In practice there are only so many historical junctions where there is a chance to change policies and to move to a different trajectory of institutional development.

Institutional capacity of the state, according to a narrow definition, is the ability of the government to enforce laws and regulations. While there are many subjective indices (corruption, rule of law, government effectiveness, and so on) that are supposed to measure the state institutional capacity, many researchers do not think they help to explain economic performance and consider them biased. The natural objective measures of state institutional capacity are the murder rate (noncompliance with the state's monopoly on violence) and the shadow economy (noncompliance with the economic regulations). China is unique on both counts: it has the lowest indicators in the developing world comparable to developed countries.

Most other countries in Asia and North Africa have similarly low indicators, unlike Latin America, sub-Saharan Africa, and Russia. And, of course, strong institutions are needed for mobilization of domestic savings and for their efficient transformation into investment—this is *sine qua non* of rapid economic growth. Although at early stages of development countries with high income inequalities managed to increase their savings rate, eventually it never rose as much as in countries of the second group three hundred years later, which exited the Malthusian trap without allowing an increase in inequality.

PD: Is this why you are predicting that future growth miracles will occur in East, South, and West Asia and in North Africa, whereas sub-Saharan Africa, Latin America, and Russia will fall behind?

VP: Exactly. The litmus test for the interpretation of economic history is a question on which economists sharply disagree: Where will the next economic miracles occur, if at all? If the suggested interpretation is correct, the next large regions of successful catch-up development will be the Middle East and North African Islamic countries (Turkey, Iran, Egypt), South Asia (India), and East Asia (where these miracles are unfolding as we speak), whereas Latin America, sub-Saharan Africa, and Russia will fall behind. The conventional wisdom, however, seems to point to democratic countries that encourage individual freedoms and entrepreneurship, such as Mexico and Brazil, Turkey and India, as future growth miracles, whereas rapidly growing, currently authoritarian regimes, such as China and Vietnam or Iran and Egypt, are thought to be doomed to experience a growth slowdown, if not a recession, in the future. The proponents of these views say that without free entrepreneurship and democracy, technical progress will always suffer.

But the history of economic forecasting is quite telling. Imagine, for a moment, that the debate about future economic miracles is happening in 1960: some are betting on more free, democratic, and entrepreneurial India and Latin America, whereas others predict the success of authoritarian (even sometimes communist), centralized, and heavy-handed government interventionist East Asia.

What is unknown, however, is whether the gradually weakening capacity of the Chinese state in the reform period will continue to weaken further, which will convert China into a normal developing country. In this case Chinese rapid growth will come to an end and there will no longer be a question of what is so special about the Chinese economic model. At the end of the day, eventually all countries and regions, including Russia, sub-Saharan Africa, and Latin America, will grow strong institutions and will catch up with the rich club, but this will take more time and will be associated with more costs.

22

"Developing countries are in an unprecedentedly strong position in the world economy"

Photo courtesy of Jiemian Yang.

JIEMIAN YANG

in conversation with Li Xin

Jiemian Yang is a senior fellow and the president of the Shanghai Institutes for International Studies and a member of the Shanghai Committee of the People's Political Consultative Conference.

The rise of China is, for the most part, either overhyped or downplayed, depending on the context and the economic and political opinions of the commentator. Yet fairly infrequently are Chinese experts actually consulted. In this detailed interview, Jiemian Yang delves into the importance of China and other emerging developing economies in the contemporary global context. This is an assessment of China as a major global player, inexorably linked to developed states yet one that needs to modify its existing policies to become a true global player. Professor Yang also makes the bold claim that the current global crisis, rather than undermining globalization, is in fact proving globalization's importance and in many cases strengthening global governance structures. While acknowledging the severity of the crisis, Yang sees many global political and economic factors—ranging from fiscal interconnectedness to the proliferation of interstate agreements to demographics—that give rise to hope for stability and growth in both the developed and the developing world.

LX: How would you evaluate world economic developments in the past decades since the end of the cold war?

JY: In the first decade of the twenty-first century, the world economy has witnessed the biggest change since the industrial revolution. Much different from modern history, a group of developing countries rather than just a few have emerged, including not only big ones such as China, Russia, India, and Brazil (BRIC) but also medium-size economies like Vietnam, Indonesia, Nigeria, Turkey, and others. This represents significant progress in the world economy.

Along with the very fast growth of the emerging economies, the developed Western countries also experienced a quite strong growth period generally since the end of the cold war until 2007; there were some benefits coming from integrating Soviet Bloc countries into the international economic order, but the system remained dominated by the Western countries. The huge new input of relatively cheap labor into the global production chains from China, India, and other developing countries effectively lowered the cost of global manufacturing, allowing predominantly Western consumers to maintain their way of life and access to cheap commodities. The other important contribution of the newly integrated developing economies to the Western market system is their relatively high savings rate, especially in China, with their great pool of foreign exchange reserves to be invested in the developed countries' bond and capital markets. Such evident money "surplus" effectively lowered the borrowing cost of capital in the developed countries themselves, thus allowing them to finance their own business. Although some people would later accuse the emerging countries of providing too much low-cost lending to the developed countries, and they think this is the main reason for the great financial crisis, I think they are totally wrong and misleading, as the cause of the financial bubble is located entirely in the developed countries.

LX: But the speed of growth was not the same?

JY: You are right. Emerging economies developed much faster than the Western countries. In the globalization context and with the emerging countries reforming their own economic institutions, economic factors like people, goods, money, and technology could move more freely than before. Their economic management level has improved substantially, with more stable macroeconomic policy, transparency, continuity, and stability and improved company governance according to market principles. All these have greatly promoted productivity in the emerging countries. With their huge resources and populations as the multiplier, their economic output has grown in an unprecedented way.

As a result, the balance of economic power between the developing and developed countries became more equal than before. The financial and economic crisis since 2008 has accelerated the process. So, in general, the developing countries are in an unprecedentedly strong position in the world economy.

LX: As you said, the world economy has developed very strongly over the past two decades, and in particular the emerging economies grew impressively. But since the eruption of the subprime debt crisis in the United States, the world economy has been very fragile. With this background, how do you foresee the world economy in the next decade?

JY: It's true that the world economy is facing the biggest challenge since the end of the cold war. All the major economies need to deal with the challenges cautiously and prudently. For example, in order to regain momentum, the major economies need to restructure their internal and external imbalance, render the distribution of wealth more equally, and so on. If all these preconditions are met, in general we can remain optimistic about the world economy in the next decade for several fundamental reasons. First, the number of middle-income countries has increased quite significantly, which has led to the expansion of the global middle class. As the middle-income population of the world rises in the emerging and developing countries, so will consumer demand commensurately rise. The newly added consumption will offset the weak demand in the developed countries, to become a new engine of the world economy. Second, most of the developing countries and emerging economies are still at the starting period of the process of technological modernization, and their level of urbanization has barely achieved 50 percent. This means that developing countries have a very big potential to tap in terms of utilizing technology diffusion from the developed countries and using infrastructure investment as an important economic development driver. Third, according to a UN forecast, the world population will reach 7.6 billion by 2020 and the share of the active labor force will remain at a stable level. The continuous supply of labor population will provide the world economy with the demographic dividend for another ten years at least. Fourth, because of the huge pressure of resource and energy demand, the innovation activity in the sectors of new energy, new materials, and the biotech industry might accelerate. In purchasing power parity (PPP) terms, in the 1980s, 1990s, and 2000s, the world economy has developed with an annual growth rate of 3.2 percent, 3.1 percent, and 3.5 percent, respectively. However, the rate in the next decade could surpass 4 percent based on the factors mentioned above.

LX: What do you think about the different economic roles of developed countries and developing countries in the next decade within the world system?

JY: The next decade could be a very interesting period to observe the changes in the world economy. In general, the world economy will maintain a three-speed growth scenario, with the developed countries growing at a slow pace, the BRICS (Brazil, Russia, India, China, and South Africa) growing more robustly, and the other emerging economies growing at an accelerated speed. The developed countries are still struggling with many challenges, including fiscal difficulties, social reform, aging populations, and falling competitiveness. Though they might be able to recover from the crisis in several years, their growth rate cannot be as high as in the past decade and their share of the world economy growth will decrease to 25 percent. The BRICS have contributed around half of world economic growth in the past decade, but in the next decade, their share will decrease a little, to 40 percent. However, China will still contribute around 30 percent of economic growth to the world every year in the next decade. The so-called Next-11 (N-11) countries' annual growth rate might rise from 4.3 percent of last decade to 5.4 percent in the next.[1] If this happens, the landscape of the world economy will witness its biggest power transition since the industrial revolution. In PPP terms, the economic shares of the South and the North have already evolved from 3:7 to 5:5 in the past twenty years. But in next decade this ratio might be further adjusted to 6:4, which suggests that the developing countries as a whole will surpass the developed countries in economic growth by a substantial margin for the first time in modern history.[2] This landscape may be more important than anything else in both international economic and political senses.

LX: What are your predictions about developments in international trade and monetary systems in the next ten years?

JY: My general observation is that the dynamics of multipolarization will further deepen from trade and production to currency and investment. In the previous two decades the weight of world trade and production activities has shifted from the North to the East and South. In the next ten years South-South trade led by the BRICS will further expand. Meanwhile the role of emerging and developing countries in international direct investment and the portfolio market will experience a significant rise in the coming years, including their mutual investment. This will greatly weaken the status of Western transnational corporations in monopolizing and dominating international investment and production.

LX: What about the monetary system?

JY: I expect that big changes will occur in the structure of the international monetary system. With the power shift from West to East, the dominant status of the U.S. dollar is expected to continue declining. The role of the Japanese yen and the British pound will also experience a further fall. The euro will probably survive this crisis and sustain its previous status. The status of the renminbi will see a steady and obvious rise in the world economy. This is based on two assumptions. The first is that China will be able to sustain the momentum in its economic performance in the next ten years. The second is on the policy side; China is determined to liberalize its capital accounts regulation and let its currency go out to the world in a progressive way.

China is accelerating its financial sector reform and opening-up process, despite the fact that the leadership change in 2012 meant that the priority for the government was to maintain stability. In future decades China is set to transform from an exporter of merchandise to an exporter of capital. When the world is still stuck in financial and debt crisis, Chinese capital flow is no doubt a stabilizing force for the world economy. Chinese outward FDI (foreign direct investment), which was over $60 billion in 2011, is expected to equal its inward FDI, which was over $110 billion in 2011, in the next five years. This is partly due to its increasing demand for overseas energy and raw materials.

LX: How do you see the trends of global economic governance and the role of emerging economies in it in the next ten years?

JY: The world is in and will continue to endure a period of fragmentation. As a result of the global power diffusion, global economic governance is expected to become more fragmented. Old structures like the G8 will try to maintain their presence, while new ones will emerge. The

U.S. National Intelligence Unit projected that the multispeed development of the world economy will lead to a shortage of political willingness to solve mass global issues. For future global governance structures, fragmentation is the most likely scenario, while harmonization and disintegration at the two extremes are either very difficult or too costly.

LX: So what is in store for us in the area of global governance?

JY: Facing emerging common opportunities and new challenges, both developed and developing countries will establish new functional institutions based on different issues, interests, and positions, so as to increase flexibility and effectiveness in cooperation. Global governance, including on economics, is going to be like the "variable geometry" suggested by George Yeo, the foreign minister of Singapore, which means the participants will choose to cooperate more on specific interests and topics rather than on ideological principles.

DUE to the low efficiency and effectiveness of global trade and financial initiatives, major countries will have stronger incentives to promote regional or cross-regional integration as substitutes. Competition between traditional and emerging economies will further increase surrounding the regional integration process and institutional frameworks in Asia-Pacific, Africa, and Latin America. Trans-Pacific partnership is an abstract idea, but it is deployed as a strategic initiative to assert the U.S. presence in Asia. This will increase the options for countries but also raise the cost of transactions in international cooperation. My hope is that strategic competition in Asia will make the system better rather than worse in the next ten years.

LX: Are you joining those who say that globalization is over?

JY: No, in fact globalism and multilateralism are not doomed or dead. First, the global economic institutions, especially the IMF (International

Monetary Fund) and the World Bank, have been revived and strengthened in this crisis. This indicates increasing demand for global governance and is the major driving force to sustain global multilateralism, though countries become inward-looking and tend to favor regional supply. Second, the rise of emerging economies is also beneficial to global institutions to some extent. One example is that U.S. pressure will encourage China to support multilateralism. As a response to the deadlock of the Doha Round and the U.S. and European demands for more concessions from emerging economies, the BRICS will call for a more important role to be played by the UN Conference on Trade and Development.

FURTHERMORE global economic governance will be further "greened" by the rise of environmental and climate change issues. The value of environmental sustainability and inclusiveness should be more streamlined into the Bretton Woods system. Knowledge and consciousness is irreversible; the role of nonstate actors will continue rising. Their participation is more active in global development and trade systems; for example, environmental NGOs have got formal representation in the decision-making structure of some climate finance mechanisms.

LX: What are the main factors that prevent globalization from collapsing?

JY: In short, the continuing crisis. We have seen a more balanced and equitable representation between developed and developing countries in global economic governance structures since this financial crisis. Formally, emerging economies have received more quota and voting rights in the IMF and the World Bank; however, more important at the informal level was the upgrading of the G20 to summit level, signaling an enlarged global leadership. The BRICS as a group are expected to get a veto in IMF and the Bank in the next ten years. A small step today and tomorrow will entail a big step forward in the longer term. But the transition will not be easy to achieve, as we have seen with IMF quota reform.

LX: What do you think are the major risks for world economic development in the next ten years?

JY: World economic development faces great uncertainties and risks, which call for more strategic management and international coordination. First and foremost, increasing strategic competition and political conflicts, if not well managed and controlled, pose the greatest threat to the world economy. One of the key conditions for the world economy to enjoy rapid development in the past two decades was the relative stability of great power relations. There is uncertainty whether this will continue, since the relative decline of Western countries in economic strength has fueled their suspicion and distrust toward emerging powers.

Second, external and internal development imbalances also need to be seriously dealt with. Globally developed countries need to control their sovereign debts and adjust their consumption models, while some other countries need to increase domestic consumption and reduce dependence on investment. With the rise of emerging and middle-income economies, the income gap at the global level is narrowing, while domestic inequality is expanding. Domestic imbalances could produce severer and more destructive political conflicts. Therefore the ability of the developed countries to successfully transform their economic structures will be vital for the sustainable development of the world economy.

Third, we need to be cautious about systemic financial risk. Worldwide fiscal stimulation and monetary relaxation in countering the 2008 global financial crisis could provoke worldwide inflation. The European debt crisis must find an exit, if there is one, through spending more instead of less, as it involves such a high political cost. The European Central Bank is giving up its stability orientation and getting more Fed-like and expansionary. Emerging economies like the BRICS are also following the global trends of relaxation to maintain the momentum of their economies.

Fourth, protectionism is a chronic disease that is difficult to overcome. The world of today is different from that of the Great Depression in that we now have a more complex set of global trade rules. The World

Trade Organization has played a very important role in containing protectionist measures, but its role is limited. Countries are designing more
complicated or hidden measures, such as controversial technical standards, to close their markets.

Fifth, the limit of resources and the threat of climate change will
bring enormous challenges for the world economy. Resource competition in the global market will grow between emerging and developing
countries as global power structures shift to the South. Global energy
and resource governance need to adapt to this change. Meanwhile the
threat of global climate change makes the substitution of fossil fuel a
necessity sooner or later. A global top-down push is indispensable for
this grand global transformation. Fortunately the global community is
still sparing no effort in carrying forward global climate negotiations.

LX: How will China adapt itself in the next decade to strengthen its
competitiveness and to make a greater contribution to the world
economy?

JY: Thanks to the historic opportunity of a benign external political
and economic environment and the prudent policies of the leaders of
our country, China's economy has achieved a miracle in modern world
economic history. But we know that the world economic situation has
changed, and we need to make some changes in response.

I would like to stress the changes in several aspects. First, we will start
our change internally. In the past, we mainly depended on investment
and export to drive our economy, with our consumption restrained for a
long time. However, I want to clarify one point: although our consumption has not grown as fast as our investment and export, it still grew at
quite a fast rate compared to the rate of other countries. The only problem is that consumption growth is lagging behind general GDP growth.
The fundamental reason for that is the increasing income gap. Due to
many complex factors, mainly the incomplete market economic system,
the benefits of economic growth in China have not been evenly distributed in society. As the economies in the West are still weak, our export

also faces great challenges. Our own environment and social conditions do not allow us to continue the past growth model any longer either. So our government has determined to transform our economic growth model and improve our income distribution condition in the following years, which is fully reflected in our twelfth Five-Year Program. If these domestic reform measures can be implemented, I believe China will have improved economic fundamentals.

Second, I think we need to restructure our foreign economic strategy, to pay more attention to cooperation with the emerging and developing countries while maintaining our cooperation with the Western countries. As mentioned earlier, the emerging and developing countries now play much bigger roles in the world economy than they did in the past, and they have huge potential to cooperate in many areas. China now has the advantage in capital, construction capacity, manufacturing capability, and some technologies, while many other emerging and developing countries have the advantage in resources, labor, and some industrial sectors. South-South cooperation is facing a historical moment, and we should make every effort to grasp this opportunity and construct win-win results for both sides. For sure, the Western countries will still be our important economic partners. Their markets will remain important for us. Above all, their technology and innovation will stay ahead of us for many years. We still have great complementarities to tap.

Third, China will cooperate with our international partners and friends to cope with the challenges. We need to prevent protectionism from impeding international economic activities; we need to maintain a stable international financial condition in order to ensure the confidence of the markets and guard against other serious financial shocks; we need to further reform the world economic governance system so that it can reflect the changed world economic map and be more relevant and effective. I have quite strong confidence in China's economy. And I believe our economy will remain open to any economies in the world. Through cooperation with others, we will not only make ourselves better but will also make a greater contribution to the world economy.

Conclusion
Richard Sakwa

If there is a single central feature of the Great Recession as outlined in these conversations, it is that the contemporary crisis is one of the reproduction of social forms and ideas, if not of the social and environmental bases for the sustainable development of humanity itself. This comes out explicitly in the conversation between Craig Calhoun and Ivan Krause but is evident throughout the others. This brief conclusion will draw out some of the key elements of this multiple crisis of reproduction.

The first is a crisis of the reproduction of the future. As Ivan Krastev notes, time horizons in the postcommunist era are shortened, since the end of communist utopianism was accompanied by the denigration of all progressive visions of the future. It is quite understandable why this has occurred, since the communist revolutions everywhere were accompanied by the sacrifice of the present on the altar of the future, with whole peoples destroyed in the cause of the implementation of future-oriented projects. The burden of expectation fell on the future, thus apparently absolving the ruling elites of ethical responsibility today. However, the rejection of this classically Leninist trope has not been accompanied by the assumption of greater weight by the present. What Milan Kundera called "the unbearable lightness of being" in communist Czechoslovakia has been perpetuated in new ways. This is captured in part by Zygmunt Bauman's idea of living in an "interregnum," where the rules and conventions of one social order no longer apply to the next, and instead permanent and accelerated change, what he calls "liquid modernity," becomes characteristic of the age.

Although the nature of historical time has changed and we now live in an apparently postideological age, in practice contemporary historical time shares many qualities with the previous era. Instead of aspirations being projected on the future, today there is greater emphasis on the past, accompanied by a greater horizontal burden of expectation on spatial visions of the future. The slogan "Back to Europe" after the fall of the Berlin Wall in 1989 itself became a political project, later reinforced by aspirations (mostly successful) to join the European Union and NATO. Such a spatialized vision could have no place in most of the post-Soviet world. Where it was pursued, as in Georgia, it provoked in 2008 the most dangerous of all conflicts in the post–cold war era. Struggles over energy resources are also taking spatialized forms, as conflicts over various islands in East Asia demonstrate. The end of the future has been accompanied by the restoration of geography as a political project, resulting in the accentuation of geopolitical conflicts.

The second crisis focuses on problems associated with the reproduction of capitalism itself. Given the importance of the topic, we devote a large part of the book to discussion of the contours of the economic crisis, as well as the crisis of economics and of the social forms associated with the present economic order. Several leading economists and political economists have provided us with in-depth analysis of this in various conversations in this book, so here I will limit myself to just a few comments. It is clear from the conversations that the key feature of the Great Recession is the failure of the regulatory regime of what used to be called "late capitalism." In other words, the collapse of the organized communist alternative in 1989–91 had been prefigured by a long decline in belief in the efficacy of state action. There was plenty of evidence to suggest that nationalized industries and heavy-handed government interventionism could lead to deleterious consequences (above all, expansive bureaucracies and irresponsible laborism), accompanied in some states by the creation of a whole service class parasitic on the regulatory regime itself. However, exponents of unbridled neoliberalism fell into an equally naïve trap: the belief that markets, freed from state fetters, would be able to generate self-sustaining and self-correcting mechanisms. The Great Recession is a vivid reminder that there can be market failure just as much as state failure.

In fact the rise of "finance capital" over the past thirty years dwarfs anything envisaged by the great theorists of imperialism in the early twentieth century, Rudolf Hilferding, J. H. Hobson, and, not least, Vladimir Lenin. If the "real" part of the world economy amounts to some $60 billion, the annual flood of derivatives, credit default swaps, and other forms of financialization is several orders of magnitude greater, amounting to no less than $60 trillion. It is out of this enormous imbalance that the current recession was born. From the phenomenon of "banks too big to fail" to the development of a "bonus culture" in which executives and financial players are awarded wages of ever-increasing multiples of the average wage, monstrously unequal societies are born. To make up for declining real wages, the great mass of the middle class in developed societies, above all in the United States, resorted to loans and credits, as did governments themselves. Richard Duncan goes so far as to argue that capitalism, in the old meaning of applying capital for productive investments, giving rise to profits which in turn are reinvested, has given way to a new system that he classifies as "creditism." In his book *The Dollar Crisis* he describes how "globalization was not going to work. The U.S. would have a bigger and bigger trade deficit, and the American economy would continue to be hollowed out. . . . Global imbalances were blowing bubbles in the trade-surplus economies. . . . The unlimited credit expansion enabled by the post-gold, post–Bretton Woods international monetary system was where it all began."[1]

It is not clear what will be the political consequences of the relative decline of Western economic power. We do not need to indulge in exaggerated fantasies of American "declinism" to note that the undisputed status of the United States as the world's no. 1 military, political, and economic superpower will come to an end in the not too distant future, and probably sooner than it thinks. As Kishore Mahbubani demonstrates, "In 1980 the American share of the global economy was 25 per cent in purchasing power parity terms, while China's was 2.2 per cent. By 2016 the U.S. share will have declined to 17.6 per cent and China's will have risen to 18 per cent."[2] Such a global shift in economic weight will undoubtedly be accompanied by demands for power redistribution at the global level as those countries that had formerly been in the "periphery" insist on advancing their concerns. The old Anglo-American hegemony will be challenged as never before, as conventional interpretations of the leadership of "the West" and its associated ideological superstructure, which today takes the form of neoliberalism, will no longer be able to take its preeminence for granted. Capitalism, as Shimshon Bichler and Jonathan Nitzan note, is a form of power; only if there can be some fresh thinking, they argue, on the relationship between the market and the state can the strains of the present system be overcome.

For Immanuel Wallerstein, this has been a long-term process with profound ideological consequences. In the latest volume of his magisterial sequence analyzing the capitalist world-system, Wallerstein argues that "centrist liberalism" was able to absorb its rivals spawned in the traumas of the industrial and French revolutions, notably conservatism and radicalism, to become the sprawling great "political meta-strategy" of our times. Over the past two centuries liberalism has fended off challenges from the left and the right, while working constantly to find ways to reconcile capitalism with the modern state. Centrist liberalism has become the universal legitimating "geoculture" of our epoch, reflected in the triumphal "end of history" ideas at communism's fall, to enjoy an almost unchallenged hegemony today.[3] The state has certainly become hospitable to capitalism, but it now seems to deal only with the residual tasks—training the workforce and dealing with welfare issues—while the economic system gets on with creating wealth and is to be meddled with only at the risk of dire consequences. Several of our contributors stress the need to rethink the role of the state in conditions of contemporary capitalism; others note that this eviscerated representation of modern society, in which humans are reduced to workers and consumers (if the population is required at all), is hardly a viable basis to create a dynamic community. Implicit in much of this argument is that a return to metaphysics, the concerns of the spirit, is essential to balance the hypereconomization of contemporary social being.

This brings us to the third dimension, the reproduction of society itself. Several of the conversations bring up problems associated with the nature and role of the welfare state, of education, health care, and other mechanisms whereby a modern society seeks to reproduce itself in a healthy and competitive manner. The Great Recession is beginning to prove a defining turning point, with a retreat from state provision under the pressure of the perceived and in some cases the actual need for budget cuts. This can be seen at its most extreme in Greece, but the phenomenon in developed countries is more widespread. The means of reproduction are in crisis as well as the forms. In response, in developing societies there is a new awareness of the need to focus on "human development" as the corollary of entering the international division of labor. China is now devoting more resources to consumption, but at the same time its educational system is adapting to the challenges of an internationally competitive system. This is happening when the developed world is beginning to dismantle some of its achievements. State-supported welfare, education, and health care systems have delivered enormous public goods, but they have not delivered profits to the private sector, and it is for this reason that they are now being opened up to for-profit providers, even though there is no sustained evidence that the quality of universal provision will be enhanced. If we are to believe the argument advanced by Naomi Klein, corporations are seizing the opportunity created by the Great Recession to open up whole new swaths of social life to the market principle.[4]

A fourth dimension of the conversations was the debate over how the institutions of global governance need to adapt to the new challenges. Although there have been fundamental changes in the world economy and polity, the institutions of global governance remain frozen in the mid-twentieth century. The Bretton Woods system remains in operation (notably in the form of the World Bank and the International

Monetary Fund), and there is a clear demand for a shift in voting rights and leadership selection to reflect the growing power and responsibility of the global South. Clearly the existing convention that the head of the World Bank should be an American and the head of the IMF a European has outlived its purpose. There is also a greater demand for these institutions, in one way or another, to limit the world of offshore tax havens.[5] The siphoning of revenues offshore and the commensurate tax minimization starve public services of resources. The United Nations system remains at the heart of global governance, yet the status of the five permanent members (China, France, Russia, the United Kingdom, and the United States) is clearly no longer congruent with the real balance of power in the world today. Most reform ideas focus on the idea of a single European Union seat and perhaps an enlargement of the permanent members with the inclusion of countries such as Brazil, India, Nigeria, and South Africa. Clearly the old format of the G8 can offer little substance to the resolution of global problems, hence the creation of the G20 in the wake of the onset of the Great Recession in 2008.

Whatever shape reform of the international governance system may take, it is clear that the strategic issue is to find some way to give voice to rising economic and political actors. This will necessarily lead to the diminution of the voice of the old imperial powers; after their clear abuse of the system in the 2000s (notably over the invasion of Iraq), few can doubt that reform is greatly overdue. Clearly the notion of global *government* is far-fetched at the present stage of planetary development. The 192 states represented in the United Nations are not likely soon to give up their sovereignty for some supranational commission on a global scale. This only places yet more pressure on devising more effective institutions of global *governance*, in a system that can encompass the enhanced needs of the rising powers of the South while preventing the introduction of the tyranny of the majority. Ultimately all this must be directed at preventing a return to the great power conflicts that bedeviled Europe up to the "great catharsis" of 1939–45.

Fifth, several conversations either explicitly or implicitly discussed the "end of the future," and with that the crisis in the reproduction of alternatives. This could be designated a crisis of solutions. We seem to lack a language, let alone the institutions, to resist the encroachments of the private sector in spheres that in the past had operated according to a different logic, above all based on ideas of service, duty, and the public good. The old "solidarity" institutions, such as trade unions and even political parties, are in clear decline; in their place inchoate forms of social activism, often using new forms of social communication (Twitter, Facebook), have only partially been able to compensate. The Occupy movement has evolved from its early manifestations as Occupy Wall Street and has engaged in new forms of mutual aid, notably in Occupy Sandy to help those who suffered the effects of the hurricane in 2012. Occupy Our Homes has taken on a rather more radical edge, challenging the systemic failures leading to bank foreclosures, homelessness, and bank-owned empty houses. In Britain, U.K. Uncut has pursued tax dodgers and looks to find alternatives to austerity policies. These policies, as suggested earlier, are being used to change the very basis of the traditional welfare social contract, to foster marketization and profiteering.

Restless change is a characteristic of modernity, and while some populist and traditionalist movements seek to restore some golden age, the challenge for radical movements of critique and engagement is to build new forms of solidarity that respond to the current needs of society. It is no good reproducing old social forms just for the sake of doing so; instead only new social movements that engage with the real challenges of the present and forge a convincing vision of the future will be able to shape remedies for us all. The fundamental challenge is to find new ways of institutionalizing altruism. Already millions devote their time to philanthropic and charitable work, but at the local and indeed national level this lacks the ability to challenge the existing hierarchy of power.

There are plenty of critiques of neoliberalism, or, to use Wallerstein's rather broader term, "centrist liberalism," but rather fewer alternatives. In the French presidential elections in 2012 Jean-Luc Mélenchon fought a surprisingly strong campaign not on the basis of old-fashioned leftist slogans but on the cry that "neoliberalism has failed"; ultimately, however, it was not clear what was offered as an alternative. In South Korea the reforms since the 1997 economic crisis resulted in the opening up of the stock market to foreign investors, with international shareholders demanding short-term profits to boost their yields, leading to the British disease of short-termism. Labor laws were also relaxed, but even that has not prevented a sharp fall in growth rates. Fear of falling behind has provoked an extraordinary focus on educational achievement as the path of individual advancement. None of this provides an ideal recipe for "happiness," increasingly the new currency of social achievement.

There are numerous other facets of the contemporary crisis of reproduction of existing social forms. One of the most significant is the possible failure of the European Union to sustain itself other than as a free market area. The challenges facing the EU are well known, notably the lack of solidarity in evidence between northern and southern members of the eurozone. Its old model of social welfarism was already transformed by the Lisbon agenda to create more flexible and competitive labor markets. Its original core purpose as a peace project was challenged as it became little more than a different form of expression of the Western hegemonic system, and has thus been unable to extend the zone of peace farther east, beyond the old Soviet borders. Its peacemaking impetus is certainly far from exhausted, and in the Balkans the continued accession agenda means that its transformative power remains undiminished. This may be the natural limit of the Union, and dreams of encompassing Turkey, some post-Soviet states, and even countries in the South have been placed on indefinite hold. Nevertheless, for Bauman and many others, the EU remains the source of inspiration, leaving open the possibility of re-creating a social state and zone of solidarity.

We envisaged these conversations as a way of elucidating the dimensions of the current crisis, but we were also intent on their offering ideas about remedies. Plenty of general ideas have emerged, accompanied by some very specific proposals. What is remarkable is the unanimity that only evolutionary and inclusive approaches can work to counter the exclusive logic of contemporary capitalism and the wild-eyed revolutionism of earlier years. Notably Ha-Joon Chang insists that only a pragmatic gradualism can create the foundations for a more sustainable economic system. The sentiment is echoed by Peter Katzenstein, who also tempers exaggerated predictions about China's rise and the beneficial effects of the European Union. He rejects rather too solidified notions of "crisis" or the "market" and instead posits a series of complex interactions between actors. Mike Davis insists that solutions have a spatial dimension, above all the "humanizing" of urban spaces. A persistent theme is the way that poverty and inequality, in incomes but also in access to opportunities for personal development, exacerbate existing divisions and act as brakes on economic development. Evolutionary approaches can be radical, but for that they need to be based on sustained critique of the present order.

One of the major challenges facing even traditionally homogeneous societies is increasing national diversity. One of the key responses since the 1960s, certainly in the Anglo-Saxon world, has been multiculturalism. It is important to stress that multiculturalism is not a single policy response but more of a general approach based on accommodation and flexible adaptation to changing needs. Undoubtedly there have been failings, above all in permitting a degree of ethnic ghettoization, as in some northern British cities. For this reason the idea has come under severe criticism in recent years, above all for its putative deleterious effect on social coherence. The right perceives multiculturalism as destructive to the rights of the dominant culture; the left perceives it as undermining other forms of solidarity, above all based on class. Will Kymlicka argues that the recognition of cultural diversity does not entail essentializing group characteristics but instead allows the dynamic development of new communities based on a range of national experiences. His stress on mutual understanding rather than what can be a condescending tolerance helps us out of the impasse that many societies have driven themselves into in dealing with rapidly diversifying agendas, based not only on rights but also on obligations to broader communities.

One of the themes that comes out clearly in these conversations is the emergence of what can be called multiculturalism on the global scale.

The era of colonialism is now long gone, and with increasing confidence the two hundred–strong world community of nations each wishes to make its contribution to global politics and development. Jiemian Yang certainly makes this point in regard to China, but so too does the great Kazakh writer and social activist Olzhas Suleimenov. A veteran of the international peace movement in the late Soviet years, he remains committed to the cause of international peace. This can be achieved only through genuine dialogue, and the philosophical grounds for such a discourse are outlined by Fred Dallmayr. The argument is taken further by Vladimir Yakunin, who emphasizes the need to invert the old pyramid, in which socioeconomic factors took priority; instead a new hierarchy needs to be instated in which humanity's spiritual needs are given due weight. Only on that basis can a genuine dialogue between nations and civilizations take place.

Thus this book has not provided any easy ready-made remedies, but if it has pointed out how we can begin to contribute to the dialogue and understanding without which any remedy is meaningless, then it will have succeeded in its task.

Notes

Note to Chapter 2

1. Christopher R. Duncan, *Civilizing the Margins: Southeast Asian Government Policies for the Development of Minorities* (Ithaca, NY: Cornell University Press, 2004).

Notes to Chapter 3

1. Representative agent models assume that the economy behaves as if there were only one agent in the economy, who maximizes his or her expected utility. This assumption is made because it is much simpler to model the behavior of one person, given his or her preferences and constraints, than to model the behavior of a group of heterogeneous people interacting in quite complex ways.

2. Joseph E. Stiglitz and Bruce Greenwald, *Towards a New Paradigm in Monetary Economics*, Raffaele Mattioli Lectures (Cambridge: Cambridge University Press, 2003).

3. The Commission was created by President Nicolas Sarkozy of France; it was chaired by Professor Joseph E. Stiglitz; Professor Amartya Sen was chair adviser; and Professor Jean-Paul Fitoussi was its coordinator.

4. Joseph E. Stiglitz, *The Price of Inequality: How Today's Divided Society Endangers our Future* (New York: Norton, 2013).

5. In this model agents live a finite length of time, long enough to overlap at least one period of another agent's life. The competitive equilibrium is not necessarily efficient, and the economy may exhibit complex dynamics.

6. Janet Currie, "Inequality at Birth: Some Causes and Consequences," *American Economic Review* 101 (May 3, 2011).

7. The Gini coefficient is a statistical measure of income dispersion on a scale of 0 to 1, where 0 corresponds to perfect equality, and 1 corresponds to perfect inequality where one person owns everything.

8. The balanced budget multiplier implies that the government simultaneously raises taxes and spending, by the same amount, which should stimulate the economy and create jobs by raising demand without increasing the deficit.

9. Jessica Silver-Greenberg and Peter Eavis, "JPMorgan Discloses $2 Billion in Trading Losses," *DealBook*, May 10, 2012, http://dealbook.nytimes.com/2012/05/10/jpmorgan-discloses-significant-losses-in-trading-group/.

10. Joseph E. Stiglitz, José Antonio Ocampo, Shari Spiegel, Deepak Nayyar, and Ricardo Ffrench-Davis, *Stability with Growth: Macroeconomics, Liberalization and Development* (New York: Oxford University Press, 2006); Joseph E. Stiglitz, José Antonio Ocampo, and Shari Spiegel, "Capital Market Liberalization and Development," in José Antonio Ocampo and Joseph E. Stiglitz, eds., *Capital Market Liberalization and Development* (New York: Oxford University Press, 2007).

Notes to Chapter 4

1. Richard A Posner, "How I Became a Keynesian: Second Thoughts in the Middle of a Crisis," *New Republic*, September 23, 2009, http://www.tnr.com/article/how-i-became-keynesian.

2. Ha-Joon Chang, *23 Things They Don't Tell You about Capitalism* (London: Penguin, 2011).

3. Purchasing power parity (PPP) income figures account for the fact that market exchange rates are basically determined by international trade, while overall living standards are also determined by nontraded goods and services, especially costs of personal services, like wages for taxi drivers or waitresses. PPP income figures tend to make the incomes of poorer (richer) countries higher (lower) than their market exchange rate income figures, as personal services in those countries tend to be cheap (expensive).

Notes to Chapter 5

1. Monterrey Consensus of the International Conference on Financing for Development, final text of agreements and commitments adopted at the International Conference on Financing for Development, Monterrey, Mexico, March 18–22, 2002, United Nations, 2003, http://www.un.org/esa/ffd/monterrey/MonterreyConsensus.pdf.

2. The Commission of Experts of the President of the UN General Assembly on Reforms of the International Monetary and Financial System, UN General Assembly, September 21, 2009; Joseph E. Stiglitz, *The Price of Inequality: How Today's Divided Society Endangers Our Future* (New York: Norton, 2013).

3. Vladimir Popov, "What Makes the Current Crisis Unique? Is It Overextension of Financial Instruments?," *Transition*, April 21, 2009.

4. Bilge Erten and José Antonio Ocampo, "Building a Stable and Equitable Global Monetary System," in José Antonio Alonso, Giovanni Andrea Cornia, and Rob Vos,

NOTES ♦♦♦ 437

eds., *Alternative Development Strategies for the Post-2015 Era* (London: Bloomsbury
Academic, forthcoming); J. A. Ocampo, *Reserve Reform*, Project Syndicate, April
22, 2009; J. A. Ocampo, *What Should Bretton Woods II Look Like?*, Project Syndicate, November 4, 2008.

5. Stephany Griffith-Jones, José Antonio Ocampo, and Joseph E. Stiglitz, *Time for a Visible Hand: Lessons from the 2008 World Financial Crisis* (New York: Oxford University Press, 2010).

6. The Commission of Experts of the President of the UN General Assembly on Reforms of the International Monetary and Financial System.

7. Ricardo Hausmann, Dani Rodrik, and Andrés Velasco, "Growth Diagnostics," revised March 2005, http://www.hks.harvard.edu/fs/drodrik/Research%20papers/barcelonafinalmarch2005.pdf.

8. Luis Bértola and José Antonio Ocampo, *The Economic Development of Latin America since Independence* (New York: Oxford University Press, 2012).

Notes to Chapter 7

1. For example, Peter Calthorpe and William Fulton, *The Regional City: Planning for the End of Sprawl* (Washington, DC: Island Press, 2001).

2. Yochai Benkler, *The Wealth of Networks: How Social Production Transforms Markets and Freedom* (New Haven, CT: Yale University Press, 2006).

3. Michael Hardt and Antonio Negri, *Multitude: War and Democracy in the Age of Empire* (London: Penguin, 2005).

4. Mike Davis, *Ecology of Fear: Los Angeles and the Imagination of Disaster* (New York: Vintage Books, 1999).

5. Mike Davis, *Planet of Slums* (London: Verso, 2007).

Note to Chapter 9

1. This is a reference to Lev Gumilev's concept of "passionarity."

Notes to Chapter 10

1. Immanuel Wallerstein, *The Decline of American Power* (New York: New Press, 2003), 50.

2. Ibid., 56.

3. Immanuel Wallerstein, *World-Systems Analysis: An Introduction* (Durham, NC: Duke University Press, 2004).

4. Immanuel Wallerstein, "Globalization or the Age of Transition? A Long-Term View of the Trajectory of the World-System," *International Sociology* 15, no. 2 (2000): 249–65.

5. Immanuel Wallerstein, "World-Systems Analysis: The Second Phase," *Review (Fernand Braudel Center)* 13, no. 2 (1990): 287–93.

6. Immanuel Wallerstein with Giovanni Arrighi and Terence K. Hopkins, "1989, the Continuation of 1968," *Review (Fernand Braudel Center)* 15, no. 2 (1992): 221–42.

Notes to Chapter 11

1. Zygmunt Bauman, *Europe—An Unfinished Adventure* (Cambridge, UK: Polity Press, 2004).
2. Harald Welzer, *Climate Wars: What People Will Be Killed for in the 21st Century* (Cambridge, UK: Polity Press, 2012).
3. Zygmunt Bauman, *Culture as Praxis* (London: Sage, 1999), xxxi.
4. Richard Sennett, "Humanism," *Hedgehog Review* 13, no. 2 (2011), http://www.iasc-culture.org/THR/THR_article_2011_Summer_Sennett.php.
5. Manuel Castells, *The Informational City: Information Technology, Economic Restructuring, and the Urban Regional Process* (Oxford: Blackwell, 1989).

Notes to Chapter 12

1. GASPP was a joint research initiative of the University of Sheffield's Department of Sociological Studies and STAKES, the National Research and Development Center for Welfare and Health, Helsinki, Finland.
2. A regular update on global social policy issues is now published on www.gsp-observatory.org. For an elaboration of some of these ideas, see Bob Deacon, *Global Social Policy and Governance* (London: Sage, 2007).
3. See Bob Deacon et al., *World Regional Social Policy and Global Governance* (London: Routledge, 2010).
4. ILO, "Recommendation Concerning National Floors of Social Protection (Social Protection Floors Recommendation)," No. 202, International Labour Conference (Geneva: ILO, 2012).
5. More on this can be found in Bob Deacon, "Shifting Global Social Policy Discourses and Governance in Times of Crisis," in P. Utting et al., eds., *The Global Crisis and Transformative Social Change* (Basingstoke, UK: Palgrave Macmillan, 2012).
6. ILO, *A Fair Globalization: Creating Opportunities for All*, report of the World Commission on the Social Dimension of Globalization (Geneva: ILO, 2004).
7. See http://www.socialprotection.org/?q=inter-agency-board. The Social Protection Inter-Agency Cooperation Board came into being as a "a light, lean and agile interagency coordination mechanism—composed of representatives of international organizations and bilateral institutions—to enhance global coordination and advocacy on social protection issues and to coordinate international cooperation in country demand-driven actions" (http://www.social-protection.org/gimi/gess/ShowProjectPage.do?pid=1625). The first Social Protection Inter-Agency Cooperation Board meeting took place on July 2 and 3, 2012, in New York at the UN

headquarters and was chaired jointly by the ILO and the World Bank. Although international nongovernmental organizations were formally present as observers, they took an active part.

8. The Tobin tax, named after the economist James Tobin, is a proposal to tax foreign exchange transactions designed to cushion exchange rate fluctuations, which would also raise revenue to fund global public goods.

9. UNITAID is a global health initiative launched in 2006 that is partially funded by a levy on airline tickets.

10. G. Cornia, R. Jolly and F. Stewart, *Adjustment with a Human Face* (Oxford: Clarendon, 1987).

11. I. Ortiz, J. Chai, and M. Cummins, *Identifying Fiscal Space: Options for Social and Economic Development for Children and Poor Households in 182 Countries*, UNICEF, Social and Economic Working Papers, 2011; I. Ortiz, J. Chai, and M. Cummins, *Austerity Measures Threaten Children and Poor Households: Recent Evidence in Public Expenditures from 128 Developing Countries*, UNICEF, Social and Economic Working Papers, 2011; I. Ortiz and M. Cummins, eds., *A Recovery for All: Rethinking Socio-Economic Policies for Children and Poor Households* (New York: UNICEF, Division of Policy and Practice, 2012).

12. "Towards Effective and Fiscally Sustainable Social Protection Floors," preliminary draft, May 10, 2012, preliminary report prepared for the meeting of the G20 Labor and Employment Ministers in Guadalajara, Mexico, May 17–18, 2012, on the state of ILO-IMF collaboration in exploring the fiscal feasibility of national social protection floors in selected countries (Geneva: International Labor Office, International Monetary Fund, May 2012),t http://www.social-protection.org/gimi/gess/Ress ShowRessource.do?ressourceId=30810.

Notes to Chapter 13

1. Javier Solana, speech at the International Political Science Association annual conference, Madrid, June 2012.

2. Peter J. Katzenstein and Benjamin Brake, "Lost in Translation? Non-State Actors and the Transnational Movement of Procedural Law," *International Organization* 67, no. 4 (2013).

Notes to Chapter 16

1. David Pryce-Jones, "In the Phony 'Spring,' Arab Politics Stay the Same," *National Review Online*, April 15, 2011 http://www.nationalreview.com/david-pryce-jones/264861/phony-spring-arab-politics-stay-same (retrieved June 15, 2012).

2. Fred Dallmayr, *Dialogue among Civilizations: Some Exemplary Voices* (New York: Palgrave/St. Martin's Press, 2002).

3. Fred Dallmayr, *Beyond Orientalism: Essays on Cross-Cultural Encounter* (Albany, NY: State University of NY Press, 1996).

4. Fred Dallmayr, *Integral Pluralism: Beyond Culture Wars* (Lexington, KY: University of Kentucky Press, 2010).

5. Fred Dallmayr, *Being in the World: Dialogue and Cosmopolis* (Lexington, KY: University of Kentucky Press, 2013).

Notes to Chapter 17

1. Manuel F. Montes, "Private Deficits and Public Responsibilities: Philippine Responses to Capital Inflows," in *Papers and Proceedings of the International Symposium on Macroeconomic Interdependence in the Asia-Pacific Region* (Tokyo: Economic Research Institute, Economic Planning Agency, Government of Japan, March 1997), 409–60.

2. Colin Crouch, "Privatised Keynesianism: An Unacknowledged Policy Regime," *British Journal of Politics and International Relations* 11, no. 3 (2009): 382–99.

3. John Maynard Keynes, *The Economic Consequences of the Peace*, reprint (New Brunswick, NJ: Transaction, 2003).

4. See Bruce J. Schulman, *From Cotton Belt to Sunbelt: Federal Policy, Economic Development, and the Transformation of the South, 1938–1980* (Durham, NC: Duke University Press, 1994).

Notes to Chapter 18

1. Quoted in Amos Elon, *Founder: A Portrait of the First Rothschild and His Time* (New York: Penguin, 1996), 109.

2. Max Jammer, *Concepts of Force*. Dover Books on Physics (London: Dover, 2003).

3. Albert Einstein, foreword to Galileo Galilei, *Dialogue Concerning the Two Chief World Systems: Ptolemaic and Copernican* (1632), translated by S. Drake, 2nd ed. (Berkeley: University of California Press, 1953), xxviii.

4. Paul A. Baran and Paul M. Sweezy, *Monopoly Capital: An Essay on the American Economic and Social Order* (New York: Monthly Review Press, 1966).

Notes to Chapter 19

1. A. Maddison, *Statistics on World Population, GDP and Per Capita GDP, 1–2008 ad*, OECD, http://www.ggdc.net/MADDISON/oriindex.htm.

2. Vladimir Popov, "Russia: Austerity and Deficit Reduction in Historical and Comparative Perspective," *Cambridge Journal of Economics* 36 (January 2012): 313–34.

3. Jomo Kwame Sundaram et al., *Southeast Asia's Misunderstood Miracle: Industrial Policy and Economic Development in Thailand, Malaysia and Indonesia* (Boulder, CO: Westview, 1997); Jomo Kwame Sundaram and Michael Rock, *Economic Diversification and Primary Commodity Processing in the Second-tier Southeast Asian Newly Industrializing Countries*, UNCTAD Discussion Paper No. 136 (Geneva: UNCTAD, June 1998); Jomo Kwame Sundaram, ed., *Southeast Asia's*

Industrialization: Industrial Policy, Capabilities and Sustainability (Basingstoke, UK: Palgrave, 2001); Jomo Kwame Sundaram, ed., *Competitiveness in Asia: How Internationally Competitive National Firms and Industries Developed in East Asia* (London: Routledge Curzon, 2003).

Notes to Chapter 20

1. *Growing Income Inequality in OECD Countries: What Drives It and How Can Policy Tackle It?* (Paris: OECD, May 2012).
2. See, for example, Andy Sumner, *Global Poverty and the New Bottom Billion: What If Three-Quarters of the World's Poor Live in Middle Income Countries?*, IDS Working Paper (Brighton, UK: Institute of Development Studies, September 2010).
3. Dani Rodrik, *The Globalization Paradox: Democracy and the Future of the World Economy* (New York: Norton, 2011).
4. John Gerard Ruggie, "International Regimes, Transactions, and Change: Embedded Liberalism in the Postwar Economic Order," *International Organization* 36, no. 2 (1982); Karl Polanyi, *The Great Transformation: The Political and Economic Origins of Our Time* (Boston: Beacon Press, 2001).

Notes to Chapter 21

1. Karl Marx, *Capital*, vol. 1, chapter 31, "Genesis of the Industrial Capitalist," various editions.
2. Branko Milanovic, Peter H. Lindert, and Jeffrey G. Williamson, "Pre-Industrial Inequality: An Early Conjectural Map," mimeo, August 23, 2007, http://www.economics.harvard.edu/faculty/williamson/files/Pre-industrial_inequality.pdf; Vladimir Popov, *Why the West Became Rich before China and Why China Has Been Catching Up with the West since 1949: Another Explanation of the "Great Divergence" and "Great Convergence" Stories*, NES/CEFIR Working Paper No. 132 (Moscow: Center for Economic and Financial Research, New Economic School, October 2009).
3. M. Montes and V. Popov, "Bridging the Gap: A New Economic Order for Development," in Craig Calhoun and Georgi Derluguian, eds., *Aftermath: New Global Economic Order* (New York: New York University Press, 2011).
4. Joshua Ramo, *The Beijing Consensus* (London: Foreign Policy Centre, May 2004).
5. Andrei Shleifer and Daniel Treisman, "A Normal Country," *Foreign Affairs* 83, no. 2 (2004).
6. Vladimir Popov, *The Long Road to Normalcy: Where Russia Now Stands*, UNU WIDER Working Paper No. 2010/13 (Helsinki: United Nations University, World Institute for Development Economics Research, 2010).
7. Piotr Dutkiewicz and Vladimir Popov, "Ahead or Behind: Lessons from Russia's Postcommunist Transformation," in A. Kuklinksi and B. Skuza, eds., *Turning Points in the Transformation of the Global Scene* (Warsaw: Polish Association of the Club of Rome, 2006).

8.　Vladimir Popov, "Russia: Austerity and Deficit Reduction in Historical and Comparative Perspective," *Cambridge Journal of Economics* 36 (January 2012): 313–34.

9.　Vladimir Popov, "Why the Russian Economy Is Unlikely to Become a New 'Asian Tiger,'" PONARS Policy Memo 129 (2000).

10.　A detailed explanation of the theory and the statistical evidence is in Popov, *Why the West Became Rich before China and Why China Has Been Catching Up with the West since 1949*, CEFIR/NES Working Paper no. 132, October 2009 note 2.

Notes to Chapter 22

1.　N-11 refers to the next eleven emerging economies—Bangladesh, Egypt, Indonesia, Iran, Mexico, Nigeria, Pakistan, Philippines, Turkey, South Korea, and Vietnam—identified by Goldman Sachs investment bank and economist Jim O'Neill as having a high potential of becoming, along with the BRICS, the world's largest economies in the twenty-first century. CEFIR/NES Working Paper 132 (October 2009).

2.　IMF, World Economic Outlook Database, April 2012.

Notes to Conclusion

1.　Richard Duncan interview, "A New Global Depression?," *New Left Review*, no. 77 (September–October 2010): 6; Richard Duncan, *The Dollar Crisis: Causes, Consequences, Cures* (London: Wiley, 2005).

2.　Kishore Mahbubani, "Keeping the Ship on Course," *World Today* 68, no. 7 (2012): 7.

3.　Immanuel Wallerstein, *The Modern World-System IV: Centrist Liberalism Triumphant, 1789–1914* (Berkeley: University of California Press, 2011); see also the review by Jennifer Pitts, "A Liberal Geoculture?," *New Left Review*, no. 77 (September–October 2010), 136–44.

4.　Naomi Klein, *The Shock Doctrine: The Rise of Disaster Capitalism* (London: Penguin, 2008).

5.　See Nicholas Shaxson, *Treasure Islands: Tax Havens and the Men Who Stole the World* (London: Vintage, 2012).

Contributors

ZYGMUNT BAUMAN is emeritus professor of sociology at the University of Leeds. Bauman has become best known for his analyses of the links between modernity and the Holocaust and of postmodern consumerism. He was awarded the European Amalfi Prize for Sociology and Social Sciences in 1992 and the Theodor W. Adorno Award of the city of Frankfurt in 1998. In 2010 he and Alain Touraine were awarded the Príncipe de Asturias Prize for Communication and the Humanities.

SHIMSHON BICHLER AND JONATHAN NITZAN are political economists. Shimshon Bichler teaches political economy at colleges and universities in Israel. Jonathan Nitzan teaches political economy at York University, Toronto. Their books include *The Global Political Economy of Israel* (2002) and *Capital as Power: A Study of Order and Creorder* (2009). All of their publications are available for free from the *The Bichler & Nitzan Archives* (http://bnarchives.yorku.ca).

CRAIG CALHOUN has been the director of the London School of Economics since September 2012. He was president of the Social Science Research Council in the United States from 1999 to 2012 and a university professor of the social sciences at New York University from 1996 to 2012. Calhoun received his doctorate in sociology and history from Oxford University and a master's degree in social anthropology from Manchester University. He has edited several books, including most recently *The Roots of Radicalism* (2006), *Knowledge Matters: The Public Mission of the Research University* (with Diana Rhoten, 2011), and *Nations Matter: Culture, History, and the Cosmopolitan Dream* (2007). He cofounded, with Richard Sennett, professor of sociology at LSE, the NYLON program, which brings together graduate students from New York and London for cooperative research programs.

HA-JOON CHANG teaches at the Faculty of Economics and the Centre of Development Studies, University of Cambridge. His books include *The Political Economy of Industrial Policy* (1994), *Kicking Away the Ladder* (2002), *Bad Samaritans* (2007), and *23 Things That They Don't Tell You about Capitalism* (2011). Chang has worked as a consultant for numerous international organizations (including various UN agencies and the World Bank), governments, private sector firms, and NGOs. He is the winner of the 2003 Gunnar Myrdal Prize and the 2005 Wassily Leontief Prize (jointly with Richard Nelson).

FRED DALLMAYR is Packey J. Dee Professor in the Departments of Philosophy and Political Science at the University of Notre Dame. He is past president of the Society for Asian and Comparative Philosophy and is presently a cochair of the World Public Forum "Dialogue of Civilizations." He has published more than thirty books and is also the editor of a twenty-volume series on Global Encounters. Among his recent publications are *Integral Pluralism* (2010), *The Promise of Democracy* (2010), *Return to Nature?* (2011), and *Being in the World: Dialogue and Cosmopolis* (2013).

MIKE DAVIS is a distinguished professor in the Department of Creative Writing at the University of California, Riverside, and an editor of the *New Left Review*. Davis taught urban theory at the Southern California Institute of Architecture before he secured a position at University of California, Irvine's History Department. He also contributes to the British monthly *Socialist Review*, the organ of the Socialist Workers Party of Great Britain. As a journalist and essayist, Davis has written frequently for, among others, *The Nation* and the United Kingdom's *New Statesman*. He was a 1996–97 Getty Scholar at the Getty Research Institute and received a MacArthur Fellowship Award in 1998. He won the Lannan Literary Award for Nonfiction in 2007. His publications include *City of Quartz: Excavating the Future in Los Angeles* (1990) *and Planet of Slums: Urban Involution and the Informal Working Class* (2006).

JOE DAY is a design principal of Deegan-Day Design and serves on the faculty for architectural design and critical studies at the Southern California Institute of Architecture. Residential and institutional projects by Deegan-Day Design have been featured in *Praxis*, *Architect*, *Dwell*, and *Metropolis*. In 2012 Day was a Louis I. Kahn Visiting Assistant Professor at the Yale School of Architecture and recently contributed a new foreword to Reyner Banham's seminal *Los Angeles: Architecture of the Four Ecologies* (2009). His forthcoming *Corrections and Collections: Architectures for Art and Crime* examines an intersection of museum and prison design since Minimalism.

BOB DEACON is emeritus professor of international social policy at the University of Sheffield and holds the UNESCO-UNU Chair in Regional Integration, Migration and the Free Movement of People at UNUCRIS in Bruges, Belgium. His most recent books are *Global Social Policy and Governance* (2007), *World Regional Social Policy and Global Governance* (2009), and *Social Policy and International Interventions in South-East Europe* (with Paul Stubbs, 2007). He is a founding editor of the journals *Critical Social Policy* and *Global Social Policy*. He is currently writing *Global Social Policy in the Making: Foundations of the Social Protection Floor*, to be published by Policy Press. He has acted as a consultant or adviser to the World Bank, ILO, UNICEF, UNDP, UNDESA, European Union, Council of Europe, ICSW, and several countries.

VINCENT DELLA SALA is an associate professor at the School of International Studies and Faculty of Sociology at the University of Trento, Italy, and an adjunct professor of European studies at the Johns Hopkins School of Advanced International Study in Bologna, Italy.

KEMAL DERVIŞ is vice president for global economics and development at the Brookings Institution. He is also a member of the Executive Committee of the Istanbul Policy Center at Sabanci University and chairman of the International Advisory Board of Akbank. He was executive head of the UNDP, a member of the Turkish Parliament, and minister for economic affairs and the Treasury of the Republic of Turkey, responsible for Turkey's recovery program after the devastating financial crisis that hit the country in February 2001. His works include *Inequality in America: Facts, Trends, and International Perspectives* (cowritten with Uri Dadush, Sarah Puritz Milsom, and Bennett Stancil, 2012) and *A Better Globalization: Legitimacy, Governance and Reform* (with Ceren Özer, 2005).

JAN DUTKIEWICZ is a PhD candidate in the Department of Politics at the New School for Social Research. His research focuses on the interaction between humans and nonhuman animals, environments, and artifacts, as well as on the rationalities, behaviors, and discourses engendered by different forms of employment, governance, and political engagement. His work has been published in journals, including the *Journal of Organizational Change Management.* He currently lectures on liberal democratic political thought at Clark University.

PIOTR DUTKIEWICZ is a professor of political science and the director of the Center for Governance and Public Policy at Carleton University in Ottawa. He was editor in chief of a twenty-one-volume series on Local and Regional Development in Poland and Eastern Europe (1986–89) and editor (or coeditor) of twelve other books, the most recent of which is *Democracy versus Modernization: A Dilemma for Russia and for the World* (coedited with Vladislav Inozemtsev, 2012) and *Russia: The Challenges of Transformation* (coedited with Dmitri Trenin, 2011). He has received an honorary doctorate from the People's Friendship University, Moscow (2006) and the Russian Academy of Public Administration (2007) for his contribution to the development of Canada-Russia relations and academic achievement.

KEVAN HARRIS is a sociologist and postdoctoral research associate at Princeton University's Department of Near Eastern Studies. He has written on the political economy of the Middle East, development in the global South, and the politics of welfare and labor movements worldwide.

PETER J. KATZENSTEIN is the Walter S. Carpenter Jr. Professor of International Studies at Cornell University. Recently Katzenstein was ranked by *The Economist* as the most influential scholar in international political economy. He served as president of the American Political Science Association (2008–9). He was elected to the American Academy of Arts and Science in 1987 and the American Philosophical Society in 2009. Since 1982 Katzenstein has served as the editor of over one hundred books that Cornell University Press has published under the imprint of the Cornell Studies in Political Economy. Katzenstein's best-known work, *A World of Regions: Asia and Europe in the American Imperium,* was published in 2005.

KEMAL KIRIŞCI is the TUSIAD Senior Fellow at the Foreign Policy Program of the Brookings Institution in Washington, D.C. Kirişci served as a professor in the Department of Political Science and International Relations at Boğaziçi University, Istanbul until January 2013. His areas of research interest include European integration, asylum and immigration issues in the European Union, EU-Turkish relations, Turkish foreign policy, ethnic conflicts, and refugee movements. He has previously taught at universities in Britain, Canada, Switzerland, and the United States. His recent books include *Land of Diverse Migrations: Challenges of Emigration and Immigration in Turkey* (coedited with A. İçduygu, 2009), *Turkish Immigrants in the European Union: Determinants of Immigration and Integration* (coedited with R. Erzan, 2007), and *Turkey and Its Neighborhood* (2012). Kirişci is also the coeditor of the special issue of *New Perspectives on Turkey* (2009) on the transformation of Turkish foreign policy.

IVAN KRASTEV is chairman of the Centre for Liberal Strategies, Sofia, and permanent fellow at the Institute for Human Sciences in Vienna. He is a founding board member of the European Council on Foreign Relations, a member of the advisory board of the ERSTE Foundation, and a member of the global advisory board of Open Society Foundations, New York. He is also an associate editor of *Europe's World* and a member of the editorial board of *the Journal of Democracy and Transit—Europäische Revue*. His latest books in English are *In Mistrust We Trust: Can Democracy Survive When We Don't Trust Our Leaders?* (2013), *The Anti-American Century* (coedited with Alan McPherson, (2007), and *Shifting Obsessions: Three Essays on the Politics of Anticorruption* (2004). He is a coauthor with Stephen Holmes of a forthcoming book on Russian politics.

MONIKA KRAUSE is a lecturer in sociology at Goldsmiths, University of London. She is a Poiesis Fellow at the Institute for Public Knowledge at New York University and a member of the Junior Fellows' network at the Centre for Interdisciplinary Research at the University of Bielefeld.

VLADIMIR KULIKOV graduated from the Institute of Asian and African Countries at Moscow State University in 1977. From 1977 to 1991 he worked as a researcher in the Institute for Oriental Studies (Russian Academy of Sciences) and from 1991 to 1995 served as its deputy chairman. Currently he is a member of the Executive Committee of the World Public Forum "Dialogue of Civilizations."

WILL KYMLICKA is the Canada Research Chair in Political Philosophy at Queen's University in Kingston, Canada, and a visiting professor in the Nationalism Studies Program at the Central European University. His work, translated into thirty-four languages, has focused on how democratic countries address issues of ethnic, racial, and religious diversity, with a special focus on the theory and practice of multicultural citizenship. He is the author of seven books published by Oxford University Press, including *Multicultural Citizenship* (1995) and *Multicultural Odysseys: Navigating the New International Politics of Diversity* (2007). With Keith Banting, he is codirector of the Multiculturalism Policy Index project.

LI XIN is a professor at the Institute for World Economics Studies and director of the Center for Russia and Central Asia Studies of Shanghai Institutes for International Studies. He is the standing director of the National Council of China Society of Russian, East European and Central Asian Studies and the National Research Centre for Shanghai Cooperation Organization, as well as vice president of the Shanghai Association of Russian, East European & Central Asian Studies. His recent books include *Marxism's History of Economic Thought* (2006), *The Comparative Institutional Analysis of Transition Economies* (2009), and *Reform of the Social Security System* (2010).

RIANNE MAHON holds a CIGI chair in comparative social policy at the Balsillie School of International Affairs and is a professor in the Department of Political Science at Wilfrid Laurier University in Waterloo, Ontario. Her earlier work focused on the role of the state in industrial restructuring and the shaping of post-Fordist labor markets in Canada and Sweden from a gender and class perspective. Over the past decade she has coedited several books—*The OECD and Transnational Governance* (with S. McBride, 2007), *Leviathan Undone?* (with R. Keil, 2010), and *Feminist Ethics and Social Politics* (with F. Robinson, 2011)—and written numerous articles and book chapters on the politics of child care, seen as part of a broader, gendered process of redesigning welfare regimes. Her current work focuses on the role of international organizations in disseminating social policy discourses and the (contested) translation of such traveling ideas.

RAFFAELE MARCHETTI is an assistant professor in International Relations at LUISS, where he also holds a Jean Monnet European Module on EU's Engagement with Civil Society. His research interest concerns global politics and governance, transnational civil society, and democracy. Among his publications are *La politica della globalizzazione* (2013), *Global Democracy: Normative and Empirical Perspectives* (2011),

Civil Society, Ethnic Conflicts, and the Politicization of Human Rights (2011), and *Conflict Society and Peacebuilding* (2011).

MANUEL F. MONTES is a senior adviser for Finance and Development at the South Centre in Geneva, Switzerland. He had been chief of development strategies and policy analysis at the UN, where he led the writing team in its annual flagship report on global development, the World Economic and Social Survey. He has held visiting scholar positions in Helsinki, Tokyo, and Singapore. He holds a PhD in economics from Stanford University and held the Central Bank Money and Banking Chair at the University of the Philippines from 1984 to 1991. His book publications in the field of economic development include *Short-Term Capital Flows and Economic Crises* (2001), *Poverty, Income Distribution and Well-Being in Asia During the Transition* (2001), and *Realizing the Development Potential of Diasporas* (2011).

JOSÉ ANTONIO OCAMPO is a professor and the director of the Economic and Political Development Concentration in the School of International and Public Affairs, a fellow of the Committee on Global Thought, and co-president of the Initiative for Policy Dialogue at Columbia University. He has occupied numerous positions at the United Nations and his native Colombia, including UN undersecretary-general for economic and social affairs, executive secretary of the UN Economic Commission for Latin America and the Caribbean, and minister of finance of Colombia. His most recent books include *The Economic Development of Latin America since Independence* (with Luis Bértola, 2012), *Development Cooperation in Times of Crisis* (edited with José Antonio Alonso, 2012), and the *Oxford Handbook of Latin American Economics* (edited with Jaime Ros, 2011).

ADRIAN PABST is a senior lecturer in politics at the University of Kent. His research and teaching are at the interface of political thought, political economy, ethics, and religion. He is the author of *Metaphysics: The Creation of Hierarchy* (2012) and the editor of *The Crisis of Global Capitalism: Pope Benedict XVI's Social Encyclical and the Future of Political Economy* (2011) and has written numerous articles in leading international journals.

VLADIMIR POPOV is currently an interregional adviser in DESA, UN, and professor emeritus at the New Economic School in Moscow. He has written extensively on various issues of economics of development and transition. He is the author and editor of eleven books and numerous articles in the *Journal of Comparative Economics, Comparative Economic Studies, World Development, Post Communist Economies, New Left Review*, and others academic journals, as well as essays in the media.

RICHARD SAKWA is a professor of Russian and European politics at the University of Kent and an associate fellow of the Russia and Eurasia Programme at the Royal Institute of International Affairs, Chatham House. He has published widely on Soviet, Russian, and postcommunist affairs. Recent books include *The Quality of Freedom: Khodorkovsky, Putin and the Yukos Affair* (2009) and *The Crisis of Russian Democracy: The Dual State, Factionalism, and the Medvedev Succession* (2011).

SHARI SPIEGEL is a senior economic affairs officer for the UN's World Economic and Social Survey Team. She is the coauthor and coeditor of several of books and articles on capital and financial markets, debt, and macroeconomics. Spiegel served as executive director of the Initiative for Policy Dialogue, a think tank presided over by Joseph Stiglitz at Columbia University. She has extensive experience in the private sector, most recently as a principal at New Holland Capital and as head of fixed-income emerging markets at Lazard Asset Management. She also served as an adviser to the Hungarian Central Bank in the early 1990s.

JOSEPH STIGLITZ is a recipient of the Nobel Memorial Prize in Economic Sciences (2001) and the John Bates Clark Medal (1979). He is also the former senior vice president and chief economist of the World Bank. He is a University Professor at Columbia University and also chairs the University of Manchester's Brooks World Poverty Institute. He is the author of *The Price of Inequality: How Today's Divided Society Endangers Our Future* (2013), *Freefall: America, Free Markets, and the Sinking of the World Economy* (2010), and *Globalization and Its Discontents* (2003).

OLZHAS SULEIMENOV holds the title of People's Writer of Kazakhstan, "Man of the Twentieth Century" (awarded in 2000 to ten outstanding figures of Kazakhstan). The author of many poetry books, essays, linguistic studies, and journal articles, he was the head of the Union of Writers and the Union of Cinematographers of Kazakhstan, as well as a deputy member of the Supreme Soviet of the USSR from 1984 to 1991. He is the founder and director of the international antinuclear movement Nevada-Semipalatinsk that stopped nuclear testing in the USSR (1989 until today). He has been on diplomatic service since 1995 as an ambassador extraordinary and plenipotentiary of the Republic of Kazakhstan in Italy, Greece, and Malta. From January 2011 to the present he has served as an ambassador of the Permanent Delegate of Kazakhstan to UNESCO.

JOMO KWAME SUNDARAM has been the assistant director-general of the Economic and Social Development Department in the Food and Agriculture Organization of the United Nations since August 2012. He was assistant secretary-general for economic development in the UN Department of Economic and Social Affairs from 2005 until mid-2012 and (honorary) research coordinator for the G24 Intergovernmental Group on International Monetary Affairs and Development from 2006 until 2012. In 2007 he was awarded the Wassily Leontief Prize for Advancing the Frontiers of Economic Thought. He has authored and edited over a hundred books and translated twelve volumes besides writing many academic papers and articles for the media.

GHONCHEH TAZMINI is a research fellow at the Instituto de Estudos Estratégicos e Internacionais in Lisbon. She received a doctorate in international relations at the University of Kent at Canterbury. She is the author of *Khatami's Iran: The Islamic Republic and the Turbulent Path to Reform* (2009) and *Revolution and Reform in Russia and Iran* (2012), as well as numerous articles and opinion pieces. She has collaborated with research centers and think tanks in Iran.

IMMANUEL WALLERSTEIN is a senior research scholar at Yale University. He is the author of *The Modern World-System* (4 vols., reprinted 2011), *Utopistics, or Historical Choices of the Twenty-first Century* (1998), *Decline of American Power: The U.S. in a Chaotic World* (2003), and *European Universalism: The Rhetoric of Power* (2006). He was the founder and director of the Fernand Braudel Center (1976–2005) and president of the International Sociological Association (1994–98). He is the recipient of fifteen honorary degrees from thirteen countries and the Distinguished Career in Sociology Award of the American Sociological Association and is a Fellow of the American Academy of Arts and Sciences.

PAUL WATSON is an international conservationist and environmental activist. A cofounder and former member of Greenpeace, Watson has, since 1977, run the Sea Shepherd Conservation Society, a direct action group focused on marine conservation.

The group is now the subject of an American television reality show, *Whale Wars*. His publications include *Where War Lives: A Journey into the Heart of War* (2008) and *Ocean Warrior: My Battle to End the Illegal Slaughter on the High Seas* (1996). In 2000 *Time* magazine named him one of the twentieth century's environmental heroes.

VLADIMIR YAKUNIN is head of the Department of State Politics of the Faculty of Political Science at Lomonosov Moscow State University, founding president of the World Public Forum "Dialogue of Civilizations," and president of Russian Railways Joint Stock Company. He is the author of several books, the most recent of which is *Some Global Rays of Hope: Voices from Rhodes 2011* (coedited with Fred Dallmayr, 2012). Yakunin is a regular contributing author to the media, both in Russia and abroad.

JIEMIAN YANG is senior fellow and president at the Shanghai Institutes for International Studies and a member of the Shanghai Committee of People's Political Consultative Conference. He is on the boards of the China National Association for International Studies, the Chinese People's Institute of Foreign Affairs, the National Association of China-U.S. Friendship, the National Association of American Studies, Shanghai Association of International Relations, Shanghai Institute for International Strategic Studies, Shanghai Association of Taiwan Studies, and many other organizations. His honors include national special awards, the Shanghai Outstanding Talent Award, and several Shanghai Awards in Social Sciences. Yang has published many papers and books on international relations and U.S. foreign policy. His most recent books include *Sino-U.S. Relations in Post–Cold War Era: Elaboration and Exploration* (1997), *Sino-U.S. Relations in Post–Cold War Era: Comparative Studies on Foreign Policies* (2000), and *The Taiwan Issue and the World Configuration of Powers: Changes and Challenges* (coauthored, 2002).

MUHAMMAD YUNUS is a Nobel Prize winner (2006) for combating poverty via the microcredit system that he developed in Bangladesh and spread to other countries in Asia. He previously was a professor of economics, where he developed the concepts of microcredit and microfinance. These loans are given to entrepreneurs too poor to qualify for traditional bank loans. Presently he is a chancellor at Glasgow Caledonian University. Yunus also serves on the board of directors of the United Nations Foundation, a public charity created in 1998 with the entrepreneur and philanthropist Ted Turner's historic $1 billion gift to support UN causes. The UN Foundation builds and implements public-private partnerships to address the world's most pressing problems and broadens support for the UN. Yunus is the author of *Creating a World without Poverty: Social Business and the Future of Capitalism* (2009) and *Banker to the Poor: Micro-Lending and the Battle against World Poverty* (2003).

RUSTEM ZHANGOZHA is a professor and chief research fellow at the Institute of World Economy and International Relations of the National Academy of Sciences of Ukraine. He is a member of the World Association of Writers (PEN Club) and the author of more than seven hundred publications, including five monographs, on the geopolitics of modern civilization, culture, literature, and art.

Index